Mediated Democracy

To the late James L. Baughman, and the still-living Wisconsin Idea:

The notion that university research should be applied to solve problems and improve health, quality of life, the environment, and agriculture for all citizens of our state, nation, and world.

Mediated Democracy

Politics, the News, and Citizenship in the 21st Century

Michael W. Wagner
University of Wisconsin–Madison

Mallory R. Perryman
Virginia Commonwealth University

FOR INFORMATION:

CQ Press
An imprint of SAGE Publications, Inc.
2455 Teller Road
Thousand Oaks, California 91320
E-mail: order@sagepub.com

SAGE Publications Ltd.
1 Oliver's Yard
55 City Road
London, EC1Y 1SP
United Kingdom

SAGE Publications India Pvt. Ltd.
B 1/I 1 Mohan Cooperative Industrial Area
Mathura Road, New Delhi 110 044
India

SAGE Publications Asia-Pacific Pte. Ltd.
18 Cross Street #10-10/11/12
China Square Central
Singapore 048423

Printed in Canada

Library of Congress Cataloging-in-Publication Data

Names: Wagner, Michael W. author. | Perryman, Mallory K. author.

Title: Mediated democracy : politics, the news, and citizenship in the 21st century / Michael W. Wagner, Mallory K. Perryman.

Description: Thousand Oaks, California : CQ Press, 2021. | Includes bibliographical references.

Identifiers: LCCN 2020021035 | ISBN 978-1-5443-7915-9 (paperback) | ISBN 978-1-5443-7914-2 (epub) | ISBN 978-1-5443-7913-5 (epub) | ISBN 978-1-5443-7912-8 (ebook)

Subjects: LCSH: Communication in politics—United States. | Press and politics—United States. | Mass media—Political aspects—United States. | Democracy—Social aspects—United States.

Classification: LCC JA85.2.U6 W34 2021 | DDC 320.97301/4—dc23

LC record available at https://lccn.loc.gov/2020021035

This book is printed on acid-free paper.

Acquisitions Editor: Scott Greenan
Editorial Assistant: Sam Rosenberg
Production Editor: Rebecca Lee
Copy Editor: Tammy Giesmann
Typesetter: Hurix Digital
Proofreader: Sally Jaskold
Indexer: Integra
Cover Designer: Ginkhan Siam
Marketing Manager: Erica DeLuca

20 21 22 23 24 10 9 8 7 6 5 4 3 2 1

Contents

Tables and Figures

Tables

Figures

About the Authors

Michael W. Wagner, PhD (Indiana University, 2006), is professor of journalism and mass communication at the University of Wisconsin-Madison. He is also the founding director of the Center for Communication and Civic Renewal at UW-Madison and the founding editor of the Forum section of the journal *Political Communication*. He holds affiliations at UW-Madison with the Department of Political Science, the La Follette School of Public Affairs, the Elections Research Center, the Mass Communication Research Center, and the Tommy G. Thompson Center for Public Leadership. A winner of multiple research, teaching, and service awards, his work focuses on examining how the flow of information in various contexts affects public opinion and political behavior. His research appears in outlets such as *Journal of Communication*, *Annual Review of Political Science*, *Human Communication Research*, and *International Journal of Public Opinion Research*.

Mallory R. Perryman, PhD, is assistant professor of broadcast journalism in the Richard T. Robertson School of Media and Culture at Virginia Commonwealth University. Her research focuses on public trust in news with an emphasis on perceptions of media bias. She completed her PhD at the University of Wisconsin in the School of Journalism and Mass Communication and received her bachelor's and master's degrees from the University of Missouri School of Journalism. Her research appears in outlets such as *Communication Research*, *Journalism Studies*, *Review of Communication Research*, *International Journal of Public Opinion Research,* and *Journalism and Mass Communication Quarterly*. Before pursuing her doctorate, she worked as a producer for KOMU-TV in Columbia, Missouri, and for mobile video news company Newsy.

Acknowledgments

CONDUCTING RESEARCH, TEACHING, and engaging in public and disciplinary service are uncommon joys and privileges. We are grateful for the opportunity to work at universities that value all three of these important endeavors. We also appreciate the people using this book in their courses and the students who are reading this book—we hope it is of value to you.

Thinking and talking about this project has resulted in us owning some intellectual and personal debts to Barry Burden, Katy Culver, Kathy Cramer, Claes de Vreese, Lew Friedland, Amanda Friesen, Mike Gruszczynski, Kathryn McGarr, Katie Perryman, Dhavan Shah, Rachelle Winkle-Wagner, #WomenAlsoKnowStuff, and our reviewers listed below.

We are very appreciative of the people who took time out of their own lives to let us harangue them for the DIY Research and How Can I Help? features in each chapter of the book. Thank you: Katie Searles, Jim Crounse, Brian Reisinger, Sen. Adam Morfeld, Steve Smith, Shannon McGregor, Josh Darr, Dhavan Shah, Chris Wells, Sue Robinson, Katie Harbath, Danna Young, Erika Franklin Fowler, Shana Gadarian, Regina Lawrence, Lilach Nir. You are superstars and lovely people to boot.

This book would not have been possible without excellent public-facing research conducted by organizations like the Pew Research Center, the Shorenstein Center on Media, Politics and Policy, and the Wesleyan Media Project. Not only do they do terrific work, they do accessible work that they share with the public. Thank you.

Additional support for this research was provided by the University of Wisconsin-Madison Office of the Vice Chancellor for Research and Graduate Education with funding from the Wisconsin Alumni Research Foundation and the Louis A. Maier Faculty Development Fellow Award.

We also wish to sincerely thank Monica Eckman at CQ Press, for asking us to come along on this adventure and for supporting us through it. We thank Scott Greenan and Sam Rosenberg for their professionalism, good cheer, and helpful editorial hands. We also thank Tammy Giesmann for her quick, professional work that was instrumental in bringing the book to completion. It is a pleasure to work with such wonderful people who are committed to the study of American democracy and to the education of the citizenry.

Mike's acknowledgments: I must personally thank the incomparable Mallory Perryman for agreeing to co-author this book—especially as she was finishing her first year on the tenure track. Collaboration with you is a sincere pleasure. Here's to my glorious Waggle girls, my daughters Eleanor June Winkle-Wagner (11) and Abigail Lucille Winkle-Wagner (8). They are smart, fierce, funny, and kind. Being their dad is the best. Finally, there is no Chez Waggle without Rachelle Winkle-Wagner. This book is sandwiched in between the publication schedule of two of her own. Rachelle, I love our over-extended, yet mindful, life and I love you.

Mallory's acknowledgments: I met Mike back when I was a fresh-faced PhD student at the University of Wisconsin. I spent years asking him questions, and he spent years generously answering them. Today, we're asking questions—and looking for answers—together. I'm fortunate to call him my mentor, writing buddy, and friend. I must also thank my incredible partner, Katie, who was growing our first child while I was writing this book. Thank you, love, for being my rock—and for providing a very motivating deadline!

M.W.W.

M.R.P.

CQ Press wishes to thank the following reviewers for their valuable feedback during the development of this book:

Leticia Bode, Georgetown University

Amanda Friesen, Indiana University–Purdue University Indianapolis

Aaron Weinschenk, University of Wisconsin–Green Bay

Dannagal Young, University of Delaware

Preface

IT'S 6:30 P.M. You are looking for something to watch.
The news is on.
All three channels.

If the network evening newscasts are not doing it for you, you might be able to read the afternoon edition of your local newspaper, tune into a drive-time radio broadcast, pick up a magazine, sit on your front stoop and wait for a neighbor to happen by for a chat. You might even call someone on the phone—they would probably pick up because there was no technology to screen calls.

This was how the communication ecology largely worked in the 1950s, '60s, '70s, '80s, and, in many parts of the United States, '90s. Now, it seems quaint to think about such a severely constrained set of choices. During the 1990s, cable television provided two new opportunities for those looking for something to watch at 6:30. One option was to opt out of learning about political and civic news altogether and watch *SportsCenter* on ESPN or a music video on MTV. Another option, beginning in 1996, was to watch Fox News, which provided a more conservative perspective on the day's news. This option, including the rebranding of MSNBC during the George W. Bush presidency as a cable network providing a more liberal perspective on the news of the day, allows ideologues to select news that fits their point of view.

Research suggests that people who pursue option one have a higher relative preference for entertainment as compared to news. These people are more likely to opt out of participating in politics. When they do participate, their attitudes and voting behavior are more moderate.[1] Those who pursue option two are more likely to be polarized, engaging in more partisan types of behavior.

Since the 1990s and early 2000s, the number of cable channels exploded, the internet became widely available, and social media was born. Now, if you are looking for something to do at 6:30, you could watch that same network news broadcast program your parents might have watched 20 years before, but it is far more likely that you are doing something on your phone or laptop—watching a video, scrolling through social media, texting, looking up directions to dinner, buying something that will be shipped to your home in a day or two, or, on occasion, talking to someone on the phone. Now, the number of news repertoires possessed by citizens is even more complex and varied. Some citizens pursue a conservative news only repertoire while others have a more omnivorous approach, sampling from a wide variety of available options. Even now, however, the television and newspaper repertoire remains top dog of the medium-centric repertoires.[2]

This is quite the sea change in how communication occurs and how it is consumed. Since technological changes do not happen in a vacuum, these changes have been accompanied by changes in how journalism works, how politics works, and how we all react to political communication more generally. As such, it is important for you to understand how different kinds of political communication flow through the modern communication ecology. Having a sense of why the news is the way it is and the different paths communication can flow through will help you put the information you see into a useful context—a context you can use to make decisions about what you want from your government, what you want your society to look like, and what you can do to nudge government and society in the directions you might prefer.

Thinking about the value of attention in our fractured communication ecosystem, the way issues are framed, and how the news media affect elections can also improve how you understand some fundamentals about who gets what, when, and how. This knowledge will improve your own comprehension of the world around you and will, hopefully, give you some ideas for what you'd like to keep the way it is and what you think needs changing.

Knowing how campaign ads work and who they target, the role the news media play in governing, and how structural and individual biases influence both the content of information *and* how we interpret that information can help you check yourself before deciding that the latest terrible thing you have heard (from some source that you cannot remember) about your political enemies is true.

In other words, developing a base of knowledge about political communication in the modern world can help you be a better, happier, more effective citizen. Our goal for this book is to synthesize and provide for you a contemporary, communications-oriented perspective on the central questions pertaining to the health of democracies and relationships between citizens, journalists, and political elites. Our approach marries clear syntheses of cutting-edge research with practical insights explaining how what we have learned from political communication scholarship affects your life.

Why is this our approach? We believe, as many other scholars and citizens alike do, that an informed citizenry improves the likelihood for a healthy democracy. Informed citizens are more likely to have ideologically constrained opinions—that is, their views on one issue are logically connected to their views on other issues.[3] When views are constrained and knowledgeable, it is easier for the mass public to send signals to a country's representatives about what the people want. If the signal is muddled, or worse, random, representation seems impossible.

Sadly, Americans' performance on political knowledge quizzes does not inspire much confidence in their ability to be that well-informed citizenry.[4] For a long time, scholars were worried that this general lack of knowledge spelled doom for the American experiment. However, the past few decades have seen scholars think more deeply about the structure of politics *and* the communication ecology, concluding that even societies that are not filled with a bunch of walking-citizen-encyclopedias can hold elected officials accountable.

More recently, scholars have argued that expecting people to know a bunch of facts about government—such as the name of the Chief Justice of the Supreme Court—are not terribly relevant to the day-to-day work of citizenship in republican democracies. In the book *The Democratic Dilemma*, Arthur Lupia and Mathew McCubbins make the argument that knowledge is really the ability to make accurate predictions about the consequences of different kinds of choices. This means people need some information to make decisions—but they may not need much. Information is valuable to people when it makes their predictions more accurate than they otherwise would have been. People make *reasoned choices* in a low-information environment when they make decisions from limited information that are the same decisions they would make with full information.

For example, you are at a party. You see someone in a Beyoncé T-shirt. You like Beyoncé. You infer from the shirt the person is wearing that you might have something in common, so you strike up a conversation. You begin to date. If you end up partnering with that person, you initially made a reasoned choice. If you end up burning that person's clothes live on Instagram after a devastating break-up, you did not.

People make major choices with limited information all the time. When people vote, some of the races in which people are asked to choose a candidate to represent them contain a list of candidates the people have never seen before. The information shortcut, a *heuristic*, in scholarly terms, that people use most is party identification. If you know which political party each candidate affiliates with, and you know the party you affiliate with, you are likely to select the candidate of your party. This likely maximizes the chance that, of your choices, you have picked the person who is most likely to represent you in ways that you would prefer.

Of course, we do not get more of our information from a ballot. We tend to learn about politics from the news, social media, and our friends and family. To understand how democracy works in a mediated environment like our own, we need to understand how we decide what information we use and how information can change someone's beliefs. Lupia and McCubbins argue that persuasion comes from those we perceive to be both knowledgeable and possessing interests that are similar to our own. If we believe the news media to be fierce arbiters of the verifiable truth, we might well perceive it to be knowledgeable and share our interest in accurate information. But if we distrust *the media* (more on this later in the book) we might seek out more narrowly ideological sources that tell us that our views are right and those with other views are wrong at best and dangerous at worst. We might end friendships with people with whom we disagree. Or we might eschew politics altogether and leave the voting and activism to others.

Lupia and McCubbins' conditions for persuasion leave open the door for some pretty severe manipulation. However, they argue in their book that the conditions for persuasion are reduced when the person trying to do the persuading is likely to be fact-checked and when there are penalties if the speaker is lying. We might think of the news media, along with rival politicians and others, as a group that can verify statements politicians make and provide some penalties—in the way of negative coverage that might increase other pressures—for speakers who do not tell the truth. Of course, if sympathetic media sources and social media accounts provide cover for the lying speaker, lying speakers may be emboldened. In the end, a mix of institutional structures and individual behaviors guide the choices we make and the consequences that flow from them. Learning how to think about those structures and behaviors is something we hope this book will help you do.

How well do citizens make reasoned choices in the contemporary media ecology? Are things better or worse than they were when people had three choices to watch on TV at 6:30? Keep reading.

1

Mediated Democracy

An Introduction

IT IS VIRTUALLY IMPOSSIBLE TO ESCAPE. When President Donald Trump goes on a tweetstorm, you might see it on Twitter. If you don't follow the president, you might see it later on your Twitter feed if someone you follow retweets or replies to the president—perhaps to praise his latest missive as the latest example of how he is draining the swamp to make America great again or to critique his 280-characters-at-a-time thread as the rantings of an unqualified monster who is destroying the political norms that weave civil society together. If you do not use Twitter, you might see a friend share the tweets on her Instagram or Facebook feeds, discuss it in a Reddit forum, joke about them on Snapchat, see them set to auto-tuned music on YouTube, or watch them lampooned by Stephen Colbert on late-night television. You might even learn about them from a more traditional source by watching a television news story or reading a newspaper article about the president's Twitter behavior. If none of these forms of communication reach you, one of your news aggregator apps like The Skimm or Apple News may relay the story to you on your phone. You might even learn about the tweetstorm via a face-to-face conversation with another person!

Democracy in the United States is mediated. This means that what happens in politics and society is not independent of what happens in the news media,[1] social media, and interpersonal communication. Mass communication shapes how we think about what we want, how we evaluate our political leaders, the ways we choose to engage in our society (and check out of it, sometimes), how we think of ourselves, and how we think about each other.[2] Historically, the news media have informed us about a relatively narrow range of issues that we decided were important or not. The way politicians and journalists' framed issues affected how we thought about issues, politicians, and electoral choices.[3] The diversity of the people we talked to contributed to whether we were hardened partisans who distrusted the other side or people who embraced engagement with a wide array of political ideas.[4] These behaviors and choices affected whether we participated in civic life and how we voted in elections.

The twenty-first-century communication ecology looks quite a bit different than it did even fifteen years ago. Then, Facebook was cool and there was barely a YouTube. Twitter, Instagram, and Snapchat did not exist. Both the instantaneousness and worldwide reach of social media communication have fundamentally upended some of what we know about how democracy works. However, and even as their share of the overall communication pie is diminished in this era, classic modes of communication like newspapers, magazines, network television news, and face-to-face conversation still affect what people believe, what their preferences are, and how they engage in civic and political participation in important ways. Unpacking these effects and applying them to your own lives is the central task of this book.

We take a contemporary, communications-oriented approach to studying the health and maintenance of democratic societies and the relationships between citizens, journalists, and political elites. Our perspective marries clear, but detailed, syntheses of both classic and cutting-edge research with practical examples and advice that explain how political communication research matters for your life. We highlight how 1) traditional and new media effects, 2) the behavior of journalists, and 3) the evolution of political institutions are directly related to your opinions on important issues, the civic and political groups you care about, and your own opportunities for civic engagement.

What Is Political Communication?

Political communication is the study of how information flows through society, affecting politicians, political institutions, journalists, and citizens. It also reveals how various communicative platforms and behaviors—among a wide variety of actors—affect policy debates, elections, and political and social systems more generally.

Political communication research is conducted via a wide variety of strategies. Moreover, scholars conduct political communication research all over the globe, allowing for us to compare the effects of different communication strategies and platforms in a variety of political, social, and cultural contexts. The research designs scholars use in their research are often crucially important to the understanding of what their findings mean and how generalizable they are to other situations.

Some scholars use experiments to precisely estimate the causal impact of one thing on another, For example, in Chapter 6, we will look at experiments that vary 1) how different political issues are framed and

2) the nature of the political environment in which the framing occurs (e.g., a polarized legislature vs. a moderate one) in order to learn how framing affects individual political attitudes about issues, groups, and electoral choices. In Chapter 7, we share the results of a variety of experiments that reveal how our own biases and attitudes about others shape what we think of the news media coverage we encounter.

Political communication research also uses public opinion surveys to ask people about their media use, who they talk to about politics, and what they know about politics and current events so that researchers can estimate the effects of various forms of media on opinions and behaviors. In Chapter 5, we will discuss examples of survey research that show how some individuals, often those who are the most politically engaged, choose to engage with news sources that already fit their worldview (think of the conservative who prefers Fox News or the liberal who seeks out MSNBC for political information). In Chapter 9, survey research reveals the differences in voting behavior between those who use ideologically-oriented media as compared to balanced news media, between those who talk to a diverse array of people about politics and those who prefer a more homogenous echo chamber, and between those who live and breathe politics and people who would always choose to watch Netflix over reading the newspaper. Scholars also are grappling with how the mode of the survey—in person, on the phone, or via the internet—can affect who participates in a survey, how they answer the questions, and, more fundamentally, how representative the sample is of a larger population.

Other political communication research analyzes the content of various sources of information. Chapters 2, 3, 4, and 9 attack questions like, how much issue content is available in newspaper coverage of politics as compared to network television (NBC) and cable television (CNN)? Is news coverage of presidential candidates mostly positive or negative? How ideologically or structurally biased are different news sources? What kinds of political conversations take place on Twitter and Facebook? How successful are politicians at getting their way of looking at an issue reported in the news or shared on social media? Some of this content analysis is done by human coders, but increasingly, scholars are turning to natural language processing, artificial intelligence, and other contemporary strategies to analyze larger corpuses of data. Computational approaches to political communication research allow scholars to analyze a truly amazing amount of communicative messages (think terabytes, petabytes, and exabytes), while possibly sacrificing a more nuanced, and human, understanding of the messages in the process.

Another strategy favored by some political communication researchers is one that focuses on individual and small group conversations between citizens. Sometimes, the citizens are part of naturally occurring groups that researchers analyze to understand how people make sense of the political world around them while in other situations researchers arrange focus groups comprised of people who do not know each other to talk politics. Other researchers talk to those who report the news or make the news. In Chapter 10, we explore some of these studies that use elite interviews to shed light on how public policies are made and stories are covered.

Researchers can also contribute to knowledge in political communication by doing theoretical work—that is, making detailed arguments about how political communication ought to be expected to work. Theoretical articles and books provide a framework from which to do empirical research—both quantitative and qualitative—by encouraging researchers to ask particular questions, apply them to specific populations or contexts, or be mindful of other factors that might be expected to mediate or moderate a hypothesized effect.

In this book, we will take time in each chapter, via our DIY Research feature, to interview a scholar of political communication, who will describe a well-known research project they conducted. The researchers will explain how they developed their research question, the theory they used to shed new light on an important problem, the data and research design they used to test their arguments, the results of their study, and how you can conduct research in the same area.

Why Political Communication Matters

While you might win points with family members at the holiday dinner table by dismissing *the media* as an awful, monolithic entity that is making our lives worse, developing a rich, nuanced understanding of how political communication works is important for several reasons. First, the study of political communication helps us understand and evaluate the functions that the news media serve. Second, a focused study of political communication helps us understand how we can apply those functions to building our own expectations of the political system, our political compatriots, and our political rivals. Finally, political communication research reveals a wide variety of important outcomes affecting all levels of our lives.

Functions of the News Media

Much of the indignation directed at *the media* stems from critiques of the ways in which news organizations perform their basic functions. Political communication pioneer Doris Graber has written that there are four major functions of the mass media: surveillance, interpretation, socialization, and manipulation.[5]

One major function of the news media is to inform their audience of current events. This function is called *surveillance*. Since you probably did not wake up this morning, clap your hands together and ask yourself, "How do I hold my government representatives accountable today?" journalists convey to people which events are important and which are not via the topics they choose to cover. At its core, surveillance is about journalists' sense of what is newsworthy. Typically, newsworthiness is determined by how timely, proximal, familiar, conflict-filled, violent, or scandalous a topic or event is. Surveillance is closely connected to the concept of *gatekeeping*—the power the news media have to convey to the audience what is important and what isn't. Which bill working its way through the state legislature merits the most public attention? Should the public be made aware of a protest that took place in your town? Which issue positions of a candidate for president deserve the most scrutiny? What concerts are coming to town next month? Surveillance is public in the sense that it calls attention to public officials, organized interests, and their actions, and it is private in that it helps provide you an avenue to stay informed. Some critics argue media gatekeeping excessively focuses on the discourse of political elites and ignores the challenges and issues facing everyday citizens. Others accept that the news media will spend most of its attention on public figures, even if they might object to the amount of coverage some politicians, parties, and ideas receive as compared to others.

For example, in the 2016 presidential primary season, Donald Trump dominated news coverage. In scores of news articles and a growing number of scholarly examinations, the news media were criticized for showering Trump with near constant attention. Media scholar Thomas Patterson wrote, in a treatment of the volume and tone of the news coverage of Democratic Party nominee Hillary Clinton and Republican nominee Donald Trump, "The volume and tone of the coverage helped propel Trump to the top of Republican polls."[6] *New York Times* columnist Frank Bruni wrote, in a piece titled, "Will the media be Trump's accomplice again in 2020?" that the news media was seduced by covering the latest thing Trump said, to the point that they spent the Republican primaries asking other candidates to simply react to what Trump had done. He continued,

> "Trump basically ran on blowing the whole thing up," said Nancy Gibbs, who was the top editor at *Time* magazine from 2013 to 2017. "So what was it that the country wanted? It's critically important that we find ways to get at what it is people imagine government should be doing and that we really look at what kind of leadership we need." Nicknames have nothing to do with it. So let's not have much to do with them.[7]

Many journalists, like *Time*'s Molly Ball (then working at *The Atlantic*), countered the criticism, arguing that the news organizations reporters work for do not have a vote in the primary and general elections and that media attention is not the same thing as positive media attention. Trump's attention—like that of most people running for president most of the time—was far more negative than positive.[8] Ball's counterpoint is an important reminder that choosing to cover some topics or people instead of others is not the only major function of the news media. *How* the media interprets the news matters as well.

Interpretation is the media function that puts an issue into context. While surveillance informs the audience what news happened, interpretation tells the audience what news *means*. For example, *The Atlantic*'s article "Bill Barr's Dangerous Claims" goes beyond informing readers that US Attorney General William Barr claimed that the government was spying on Donald Trump during the 2016 presidential election. The article argues that Barr's use of the word *spying*, which does not have a legal definition in the intelligence community, could negatively affect public perceptions of how intelligence officials and officers do their work.[9] The interpretation function was also on full display on its post-2018 midterm election analysis article, "Why Democrats' gain was more impressive than it appears."[10] The article noted how the structure of the 2018 midterms (more Democratic seats in danger in the Senate and a relatively small number of competitive seats up for grabs in the House) favored the Republican Party, but the Democrats took the majority in the House of Representatives away from Republicans. The surveillance function noted the results of the election; the interpretation function framed the election as a bigger win for Democrats than Republicans.

Returning to Molly Ball's point that the tone of coverage is important to consider when assessing the news media's campaign coverage, we can see that it was clearly the case that coverage of the 2016 presidential candidates was overwhelmingly negative. Figure 1.1 reveals that more than three-quarters of Donald Trump's media attention was negative while 64 percent of Hillary Clinton's media attention was negative. One interpretation of these results is that there was a bias that the news media had in favor of Clinton. However, a closer look at the topics that generated positive and negative coverage for each candidate reveals that the news media's interpretation of events on the campaign trail are highly predictable and largely governed by professional norms that reporters apply to all candidates.

While Clinton enjoyed more positive coverage than Trump during the general election campaign, Figure 1.1 shows why. Horse race stories—coverage examining campaign strategy and who was winning and losing in the polls—were more positive for Clinton. That is, since most polls showed Clinton in the lead among likely voters, the coverage of the polls was more positive for her. Notice that even though Clinton led in the polls for most

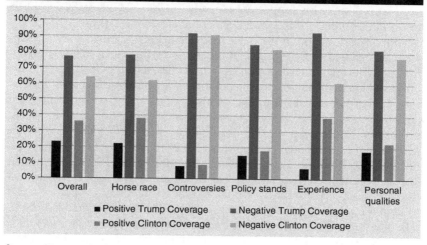

Figure 1.1   Percentage of Positive and Negative News Coverage for Donald Trump and Hillary Clinton, 2016 General Election

Legend:
- Positive Trump Coverage
- Negative Trump Coverage
- Positive Clinton Coverage
- Negative Clinton Coverage

Source: Shorenstein Center on Media, Politics, and Public Policy, 2016, https://shoren steincenter.org/news-coverage-2016-general-election/.

of the campaign, her horse race stories were still *negative* by a 2:1 margin. When it came to stories about controversies, personal qualities, and policy stands, Trump and Clinton received very similar coverage from the news media. The other area in which Clinton had an advantage was in stories about experience. This is not surprising either as Clinton had been a US senator and the secretary of state while Trump had famously never held elective office or served in a presidential administration.

Graber's third media function is *socialization*. This is the function in which the mass media help citizens learn the core values and social behaviors that prepare them to live in their society. For example, there is no law demanding that there be only two political parties in the United States. However, the news media tend to cover the two major political parties and largely ignore third parties.[11] When third parties earn coverage, it is usually to speculate about which of the major parties might lose votes to the "spoiler" third party. News coverage helps socialize Americans to accept the two-party system of government and see important differences between the parties.[12] Broader, cultural socialization can come from the mass media as well; notable examples include changing attitudes about premarital sexual behavior, sexual orientation, gender identity, and racial attitudes. An example of socialization on display in 2016 occurred when then-candidate

Donald Trump claimed he would not automatically accept the results of the election if he lost to Hillary Clinton.[13] After Clinton and scores of news outlets criticized Trump, socializing their audiences to expect that the loser of the election accept the results, he turned the socialization function on its head, appealing to his supporters at a rally in Ohio, "I will totally accept the result of this great and historic presidential election . . . if I win."[14]

Finally, a function of the news media is to engage in what some scholars call *manipulation*. While manipulation might mean many different things, including journalists engaging in *muckraking*, the digging up of dirt on government behavior designed to force lawmakers to "clean up their act," Graber notes that manipulation also can mean the sensationalizing of facts to try to increase an audience's interest in a story to boost ratings and profits, and it can even mean the media surreptitiously advocating for the positions of some politicians or trying to alter the preferences of other politicians. One example of manipulation occurred in 2019 when President Trump commented on the National Aeronautics and Space Administration's (NASA) plans to send astronauts back to the moon (as part of a plan to land a human on Mars). As seen in Photo 1.1, Trump criticized NASA's talk of going back to the moon. News outlets and social media users had a field day tweaking the president. Some outlets, like *The Guardian*, claimed that the president thought Earth's moon was a part of Mars. Others, like ABC News, CNN, and others, aired several stories about the *confusion* created by the president's tweet.

It is clear that his tweet's claim "including Mars (of which the Moon is a part)" is not claiming Mars is part of the moon itself, but that a trip to the moon is part of plan to land a person on Mars. Rather, his tweet is about what he thought NASA should be *talking about*—which, in his mind, was Mars, defense, and science, and not returning to the moon.

In some ways, we can see this tweet and the reaction to it as a way to think about how the four functions of mass media interact with each other. Some news organizations simply reported that President Trump tweeted about NASA's public communication regarding a return to Americans landing on the moon (surveillance). Outlets more critical of President Trump *interpreted* the tweet as evidence the president was unaware that the moon and Mars were not parts of each other. Other news sources *interpreted* the tweet as something that created confusion among those less familiar with the president's communication style—which often uses one word (Mars in this case) as a shorthand for a more complicated concept (the steps involved in landing an American on Mars and bringing them back home safely). The episode is an example that the public is being socialized to accept tweets from political leaders as official forms of communication. Some news organizations manipulated the public to believe the president did not understand what the moon was made of as compared to what comprises Mars.

Donald J. Trump ✔
@realDonaldTrump

𝕏

For all of the money we are spending, NASA should NOT be talking about going to the Moon - We did that 50 years ago. They should be focused on the much bigger things we are doing, including Mars (of which the Moon is a part), Defense and Science!

♡ 125K   12:38 PM - Jun 7, 2019   ⓘ

Photo 1.1 President Trump's NASA Tweet That Seemed to Be Willfully Misinterpreted by Some Media Sources

Graber's functions provide us with a useful framework to approach our study of political communication and citizenship in the twenty-first century. Many scholars think about the functions of the news media with respect to whether news coverage enhances the prospects and performance of democratic citizenship. In other words, we can study whether, when, and how different media functions help to make us better or worse citizens. A number of scholars have pointed out that it may be rational for voters to ignore much of the political information around them. Rational choice theorists, following the lead of Anthony Downs, argue that the benefits derived from reaching a *correct* decision on a candidate or policy may not be worth the costs the voter must pay in order to learn the information.[15] It might take a long time to learn the details of a political candidate's health care, student loan, and foreign policy positions whereas it takes far less time to 1) learn which party a candidate represents, and 2) compare that party to the party you personally favor.

It is rational, from this perspective, for the voter to take a number of information shortcuts, such as relying on someone else's judgment or voting according to one's established party identification. Political scientist Samuel L. Popkin uses the analogy of *fire alarms* versus *police patrols* to explain how most people view political information.[16] Instead of patrolling the political *neighborhood* constantly to make sure there is not something going on that requires one's immediate attention, most citizens rely on others to raise the alarm when something truly important happens. Television news and newspaper headlines may be enough to set off alarm bells for the average citizen, signaling them that they need to spend some time looking into a story.

Michael Schudson, a sociologist of news, argues that a good citizen does not have to be fully informed on all issues of the day but that she, he, or they ought to be *monitorial*.[17] That is, good citizens scan the headlines for issues that might be important enough about which to form an opinion or on which to take some action. We will return to this issue later in the chapter. Political scientist John Zaller argues for a *burglar alarm* standard of media coverage in which reporters regularly cover nonemergency but important issues in focused, dramatic ways that simultaneously entertain and allow traditional newsmakers like political parties and interest groups to express their views about the issue.[18]

The Alarm–Patrol Hybrid Model

Political communication scholar Amber Boydstun argues that while the alarm-style reporting captures a great deal of the news-generation process, it does not account for everything. Her conceptualization of an *alarm/patrol hybrid model* places modes of news generation into four general categories. Sometimes, news media cover stories in a pure alarm mode, generating a brief explosion of coverage around an issue or event. A second category is a pure patrol mode. This is when news organizations produce an extended period of coverage to an issue. Beat reporting is an example of this *timed media explosion* that occurs with regularity.[19] A third category is noteworthy for the general lack of coverage an event or issue receives. In this case, neither the alarm nor patrol mode is fully engaged. The fourth model is termed the alarm/patrol mode; this style of coverage is usually characterized by short bursts of alarm reporting followed by continuing the surge of coverage for a long period of time. Boydstun calls this a *sustained media explosion*.

Thinking about these four types of coverage can help us build expectations for how different events and issues might get covered. For example, President Trump's nomination of Neil Gorsuch to the US Supreme Court was an example of pure patrol coverage. When his nomination was announced, there was a mini-explosion of coverage about Gorsuch's jurisprudence, the selection process, and reactions to the nomination. The confirmation process in the US Senate was fairly typical and there were no major bombshells that required sustained attention to Justice Gorsuch. While there was certainly strong disagreement about Gorsuch between Republicans and Democrats, compounded by Democrats' anger that Barack Obama's final nominee to the Supreme Court, Judge Merrick Garland, was not even given a confirmation hearing by the Republican-majority Senate, the coverage was routine.

On the other hand, the nomination of Brett Kavanaugh to the high court set off an explosion comparable to the one Gorsuch's nomination did in the beginning—but accusations that Kavanaugh had sexually assaulted a woman when he was a teenager caused the initial alarm to generate explosive patrol coverage as well. Coverage reached a fever pitch and stayed there for weeks. Stories about Professor Christine Blasey Ford's wrenching testimony, in which she described her memory of how Kavanaugh tried to rape her, before a Senate panel riveted the nation, energizing the wildly popular hashtag #WhyIDidntReport about why people who were victims of sexual assault did not report the crime to authorities. After Dr. Ford's powerful testimony, deemed credible by lawmakers and the general viewing audience alike, Judge Kavanaugh returned to answer questions before the Senate committee. His fiery statement was widely lampooned, most famously on Saturday Night Live, when actor Matt Damon was cast as the judge, whom he portrayed as an enraged, juvenile, highly emotional beer-guzzler. Stories about Kavanaugh prompted follow-up stories that connected to the wider range of issues being discussed as part of the "Me Too" movement—spurred by the viral success of the #metoo hashtag where thousands of people shared their stories of enduring sexual violence, seeking healing from their experiences, and, often, naming their assailants.

Applying Graber's four functions to the alarm–patrol hybrid model is an example of how understanding political communication is important to how we make important decisions in our lives. Surveillance of the Judge Kavanaugh nomination and the accusations Dr. Ford raised started overnight while various interpretations of what the accusations meant[20] (Were they accurate? Should and would they sink Kavanaugh's nomination? How would voters react to the eventual outcome of the nomination?) lit up the airwaves and filled column inches of print articles. While misogyny, sexual harassment, and sexual violence in the workplace had been an issue that was often part and parcel of daily life for much of American history, the coverage of the Me Too movement appears to be playing a socializing role in American culture now, suggesting that these behaviors are no longer welcome, are likely to be reported, and are likely to have professional, if not legal, consequences. Manipulation can also be found in the Kavanaugh coverage. While Dr. Ford's testimony was widely viewed as highly credible, other people pitched reporters, sometimes successfully, with their own accusations about Kavanaugh. Even though many of these claims were less credible than Ford's, some news organizations reported them as fact before all the facts were known. Despite the power of Ford's testimony and the initial reaction to Kavanaugh's defense, most Republicans came around to believing Kavanaugh while most Democrats believed Ford.[21] The Senate behaved in much the same way, confirming Kavanaugh on a 50–48 vote. All 49 Senate Republicans voted for Kavanaugh while 48 of 49 Democrats (and independents who caucus with the Democrats) opposed him.

Examples of pure alarm coverage include the coverage given to most natural disasters. One thing that makes alarm coverage distinct is that there are typically only a few interpretations available for the event or issue. When an earthquake strikes, there are not a variety of claims coming from multiple political perspectives about the cause of the earthquake. Instead, the stories tend to focus on the size of the earthquake, who was killed or injured, what businesses were damaged, how life will immediately change, if at all, where the earthquake took place, and the estimated cost of the clean-up and renovations.

Recall that Boydstun's final category of news coverage in the alarm/patrol hybrid model includes stories that do not neatly fit into either category. These stories do not usually have a major triggering event, do not receive much interest from policymakers, have few available interpretations, and exist when the media agenda is already fairly congested. Most human-interest coverage fits into this category. The stories are often valuable and popular, but they typically do not cause media explosions, generate enormous public concern, and capture the interest of lawmakers. Crime stories often fit this category as well as they are typically reported on one or two times before the reporter and news organization moves onto something else.

Political Communication Helps Determine Winners, What We Know, and What We Think About

Political communication scholars have spent considerable time and attention on understanding how communication affects political outcomes. Most research into elections focuses on how party identification and the state of the economy are the most important predictors of who is victorious on Election Day.[22] When it comes to elections, political scientist Lynn Vavreck's book *The Message Matters*[23] shows that how candidates build their message around the state of the economy is an important factor in determining who wins and loses presidential elections in the United States. When the economy is strong, a president running for reelection or a candidate from the same party as the outgoing president should focus on campaign messages about the economy. When the economy is weak, the challenger should highlight the weakness of the economy in their messaging. If the state of the economy is disadvantageous to you (i.e., it is in bad shape and you are the incumbent or it is in good shape and you are the challenger), you should seek to shift focus to other issues to try and blunt the advantage the economy gives to your opponent. Vavreck finds that candidates who campaign on the economy strategically are more successful than those who do not.

Other forms of political communication matter to elections as well. Seeing campaign ads on television is associated with citizens being more knowledgeable about the election, more interested in the campaign, and more likely to vote.[24] Candidates are even rewarded by voters for being strategic in how they present their ads. For issues associated with being more feminine, voters find ads voiced by women more credible than ads voiced by men. The same is true for when the electorate has substantially more women than men.[25] We will have more to say about this in Chapter 8.

What We Know

Using panel survey data, in which the same people were interviewed at multiple points in time, a group of political communication scholars found that both mass and interpersonal communication can improve political knowledge.[26] Moreover, the amount, breadth, and prominence of news coverage of specific political issues is associated with increases in policy-specific knowledge among citizens, even when controlling for important demographic characteristics like one's level of education. The interaction between the education level of a news user and the amount, breadth, depth, and medium (newspaper or television, for example) can often exacerbate gaps in political knowledge. Educated individuals tend to learn more from newspaper reporting than less educated people do. In South Korea, the greatest knowledge gap was between educated heavy newspaper users and less-educated individuals who read the paper.[27] In the United States, Jennifer Jerit found that when experts commented on the news, knowledge gaps increased, but when reporters provided more contextual information (e.g., historical background) to their stories, those gaps diminished significantly.[28]

In short, news coverage we encounter and conversations we have about political issues can influence what we know. Of course, one reason we want to know things is so that we can decide what we think. It turns out that political communication can affect our attitudes as well. We will return to these issues in Chapter 3 and Chapter 9.

What We Think

Political communication has the potential to affect how we think in at least three important ways. First, news coverage and political conversations can affect what we think is important. Second, political communication can affect our actual attitude about an issue. Third, the ways political issues are communicated can influence whether and how we think about particular issues and attitudes when we are making political choices.

As political communication scholar Natalie Jomini Stroud notes, "Our attention is a fixed resource."[29] When we are paying attention to one thing, we are not paying attention to all of the other things vying for our attention. What keeps the attention of our eyeballs has the power to influence what we think is important. Classic research in political communication finds that when news organizations give more attention to a particular issue, we tend to find that issue to be more important than we did before. This *agenda-setting* effect is one of the most studied phenomena in the social sciences. In the contemporary communication ecology, groups of individuals can even set elements of the news media's agenda based upon what they are interested in searching for on platforms like Google.

Google searches signal to news organizations what issues are on people's minds, encouraging more news coverage of those issues.[30]

While simply covering an issue helps people understand what might be important, the way that issues are framed in news coverage has the potential to affect what people actually think about the issues. Early research in framing found individuals to be quite susceptible to changing their attitudes based upon which elements of an issue were highlighted in news coverage. For example, if a proposed community rally by the Ku Klux Klan was framed as a free speech issue, people were more supportive of the KKK holding the rally than if it was framed as a public safety issue. However, as framing studies matured, exploring what happens when frames compete against each other in the same news story—as they do in real life—scholars found that framing effects often disappear . . . leaving people's prior attitudes as a strong predictor of their response to a news article with competing frames.[31] More recent work examines how bundles of issue frames appeal to Democrats and Republicans in different ways, affecting attitudes and partisanship over time. Frames that were more policy oriented were associated with changes in Democrats' attitudes while more symbolic frames were correlated with Republicans' opinions.[32] We will spend more time with framing in Chapter 6.

Who Participates

Beyond what we find important and what we think, communication plays a crucial role in both making political participation possible and motivating us to engage in it. Of course, some elements of the communication ecology influence us directly, like political conversations we have with others, while other facets, such as television watching, affect us indirectly.[33] A study of an Israeli political campaign found that those who exhibit the highest level of political interest are more likely to develop deeper political information repertoires that include using digital and traditional ways of searching for political information. Importantly, these individuals and groups engage in higher levels of political knowledge, efficacy, and participation.[34] We give these issues greater attention in Chapter 9.

Twenty-First Century Political Communication, Democratic Citizenship, and You

What does it mean to be a good citizen in a republican democracy? In the now-classic book *The Good Citizen*, Michael Schudson argues that, in the United States, there have been four eras of civic life, each of which had its own definition of good citizenship.[35] In the early years of the republic, citizens left the important decisions to political elites. Good citizens placed their faith in their leaders. In the middle of the nineteenth century, citizens involved themselves in civic life through participation in strong political party organizations in their communities. In the late nineteenth century and into the twentieth century, good citizenship was defined via one of two major models—one growing out of Progressive reforms focusing upon a professional, objective, nonpartisan press and experts' role in governing and the other focusing upon citizen deliberation. Schudson argues that from the 1950s forward, citizenship began becoming more *rights-conscious*. Some people focused on individual rights while others fought for collective rights.

You might have noticed that being an *informed citizen* was never on Schudson's list. In fact, he argues that while being informed is still something that folk theories of democratic politics hold in high regard, a more realistic expectation is for citizens to be, as noted above, monitorial. Some scholars argue that such a view, while reasonable, might sell the people—and by extension, democracy—short.

Beyond what is theoretically expected of citizens, you have probably heard more than one person decry *millennials* as part of an older person spewing existential angst about all that is wrong with the current generation as compared to years past. Journalistic stalwarts like *60 Minutes'* Morley Safer have called millennials "narcissistic praise hounds" while a *Time* magazine article referred to millennials as the "me me me generation."[36] Evidence about millennials' conceptualization of citizenship and participation in democratic activities tell a different story.

In East Asia, millennials are strong supporters of democratic attitudes and also participate regularly in politics, but their conceptions of citizenship differ from those of their elders.[37] In the United States, millennials' voter turnout increased from 22 percent in 2014 to 42 percent in 2018. Generation Z (who began turning 18 in 2014) turned out at 30 percent—about seven points higher than Generation X and millennial voters did when they were first old enough to vote. Together, Gen Z-ers and millennials cast a quarter of all votes in the 2018 American midterm elections.[38] Millennials are the first generation to grow up in a digital world. They, and Gen Z folks, tend to be more educated than other generations, dislike hierarchy, and are unusually focused on transparency.[39]

So, if the younger generations are not taking us all to hell in the proverbial handbasket, what might we expect from them, and all citizens in a twenty-first-century communication ecology? Typically, scholars think about four key agents of socialization in public life—family, school, media, and peers. Each of these groups help teach people what mass communication scholar Dhavan Shah and colleagues call communicative competencies. Communication competencies help to socialize young adults into democratic public life, teaching them to navigate the swamps, chasms, and barricades facing those seeking to practice democratic citizenship. These groups help young people explore and engage with new ideas, process information, and think about public affairs, and develop within them the ability to form arguments, share opinions, disagree, and see the world in more complex ways. Shah and colleagues claim that these skills are required to effectively engage in civil society.[40]

Communication competencies develop early and are guided by the ways in which parents and children tend to communicate. The information and behaviors students learn in school have been shown to affect communication skills and civic attitudes. For example, being exposed to the teaching of controversial public issues can increase students' engagement in politics.[41] If you worked at your school paper or participated in extracurricular activities like student council, you are more likely to participate more in democratic life. Why? To participate in these kinds of activities, you had to monitor current events, discuss potentially contentious issues, and find solutions to challenging problems. You were also more likely to encounter adults who were high participators. Honestly, choosing to take the class that has you reading this book probably means you are more informed and participatory, on average, as compared to your fellow students.

In general, open, active parent–child communication and deliberative, civically oriented school activities help to foster the internal motivations and outward skills necessary for engaging in effective political information acquisition, expression, and exchange—that is, communication competence. Discussions about controversial issues with family members are foundational to both students' participation in deliberative discussion in the classroom and interpersonal political talk about politics with family and friends.

Communication and Civic Competence in the Twenty-First Century

While these socialization patterns were shown to play an important role in developing communication competence and civic competence in the 1990s, times have changed. The contemporary media ecology affords people the opportunity to deeply engage in the news that affirms their worldview, use news that challenges their opinions, or choose to avoid civic news altogether. Recent research led by Stephanie Edgerly finds that more than 50 percent of 12-to-17-year-olds tend to ignore news content, whether it is from traditional news sources, both online or offline.[42] They also tend to eschew news available on social media platforms like Facebook and Twitter. Not surprisingly, those who avoid the news are less interested in politics and participate less in political activities. If these young people do not find a route into communication and civic competence as they age, the likelihood diminishes that a robust democratic society will persist.

On the other hand, about half of young citizens are really into the news. Edgerly and her colleagues found that they clustered into three distinct groups. Some youths prefer traditional news—television, print, and online news. Individuals who prefer these sources tend to be younger and are more likely to be interested in politics. Other teens use a great deal of curated news that caters to their particular interests. Other young people are news omnivores; they seek out news across all kinds of platforms. News omnivores tend to be the most participatory.

Clearly, the news young people use is critically important to what they know, what they think, and how they participate in democratic life. The contemporary media ecology affords a variety of new ways to participate that weren't available when the Shah study was conducted. Now, news organizations and civic groups can get immediate feedback from their audiences on platforms like Facebook and Twitter.

This ability has fundamentally changed elements of how political communication operates in democratic societies. Political communication scholar Chris Wells argues that organizations using digital media to communicate with young citizens about civic action face interesting challenges about how to encourage participation.[43] Recall that millennials and Generation Z generally do not like hierarchies. Wells argues that hierarchical modes of communication from civic organizations (such as using Facebook to tell people how they can participate) are communication strategies that can leave young people feeling disaffected and disconnected. Movements like Occupy Wall Street, which began in 2011, used digital technologies to self-organize, seek advice from would-be participants, share information, and deliberate. Many young people were drawn to engage in courageous civic behavior via modern communication platforms.

Figure 1.2 reveals generational differences in the communication tools used by different generations. Data from the Pew Research Center showed that more than nine out of ten millennials (92 percent) own smartphones, compared with 85 percent of Gen Xers (aged 40 to 55), 67 percent of baby boomers (aged 56 to 74), and 30 percent of the Silent Generation (75 and older). Not surprisingly, having the tools of the modern communication ecology correlates with using the platforms of twenty-first-century communication. A large majority of millennials (85 percent) say they use social media. Moreover, significantly larger shares of millennials use relatively newer platforms such as Instagram (52 percent) and Snapchat (47 percent) than older generations have.

That same Pew study found that no matter the generation, the vast majority of those who go online think the internet has been good for them. *However,* younger internet users are a bit more likely than older Americans who use internet to say the internet has had a positive impact on society

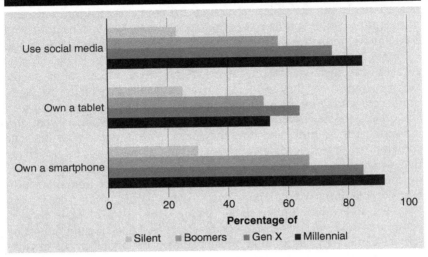

Figure 1.2   Generational Use of Contemporary Communication Tools

Use social media

Own a tablet

Own a smartphone

0   20   40   60   80   100

Percentage of

Silent   Boomers   Gen X   Millennial

Source: Pew Research Center: https://www.pewresearch.org/fact-tank/2018/05/02/millennials-stand-out-for-their-technology-use-but-older-generations-also-embrace-digital-life/

as a whole: 73 percent of online millennials say that the internet has been mostly a good thing for society, compared with 63 percent of users, still a solid majority, in the Silent Generation.

The "How Can I Help?" feature in each chapter engages in a lively Q&A with a citizen engaging in practical communication research. Political operatives like Brian Reisinger, who helped Wisconsin Senator Ron Johnson shock the political world by winning reelection in 2016 despite being behind in all of the polls from the summer to Election Day, will talk about political communication and the practice of running political campaigns in the twenty-first century. Katie Harbath, who works for social media giant Facebook, will discuss how political leaders are learning to use contemporary social platforms to communicate with voters. This feature is designed to give you an idea of the many different careers for which a deep understanding of political communication will be professionally valuable.

From Research to Real Life

The modern communication ecology is huge, unwieldy, immediate, cloistered, cross-cutting, and polarized. People can select from a near-infinite number of news sources that reinforce their own views, while people who do not live and breathe politics can easily avoid politics altogether on their phone, laptop, and television. Politicians keep trying to find new ways to influence us to change our attitudes and participate. Our own partisan glasses color what we know, what we do, and who we trust. This book is designed to help you use both cutting-edge research and practical professional skills to skillfully navigate the information environment so that you can be as productive a citizen as possible.

One way in which this book can be useful to you is as an inoculation of sorts. If you become more acutely aware of how various communication effects operate, you might be more likely to use your awareness of potential effects to potentially mitigate the substantive outcomes of them. Additionally, building a broad base of knowledge about mass communication effects can help you to more effectively and efficiently communicate with others to advance your own social and political goals. Finally, simply becoming more aware of what broad claims people often make about *the media* are true and which are empirically suspect or outright false should help you become a more critical, careful, and useful citizen.

DIY Research

Regina Lawrence, University of Oregon

Dunaway, J., & Lawrence, R. (2015). What predicts the game frame? Media ownership, electoral context, and campaign news. *Political Communication, 32*(1), 43–60.

Regina Lawrence is among the most respected and productive scholars of political communication in the world. She is the associate dean of the School of Journalism and Communication Portland and the director of the Agora Journalism Center. Her research examines political communication, civic engagement, gender and politics, and the role played by the news media in public discourse about politics and policy. She has won the Doris A. Graber Outstanding Book Award from the American Political Science Association's Political Communication section and has served as chair of that same section. She has also been a research fellow at the Joan Shorenstein Center on the Press, Politics and Public Policy at the Kennedy School of Government at Harvard University. Her article, coauthored with Johanna Dunaway, examines the factors that predict the news media's use of the *game frame*—a style of news coverage that treats politics as a game, eschewing more substantive coverage.

(Continued)

(Continued)

Wagner and Perryman: Your coauthored article about what predicts the game frame finds that "news organizations' choices to rely heavily on game-frame election stories are dependent on both news-making and political contexts." What do you mean by that and how does that affect how readers of this book should evaluate game frame news coverage?

Lawrence: One point Johanna and I wanted to make with that study was that game-framed coverage is "over-determined": There are many factors that lead news outlets to produce so much game-framed coverage of elections. News-making factors include the degree of competition an outlet is facing (in highly competitive news markets, there may be more perceived pressure to produce "entertaining," poll-driven coverage) and budgets (in newsrooms with shrinking staff and budgets, game-framed coverage is relatively cheap and easy to produce compared with analysis of candidates' policy ideas). Political factors include the competitiveness of electoral contests: Highly competitive races (note how we all use that term "races"!) readily lend themselves to lots of coverage of who's pulling ahead and falling behind.

The purpose of focusing our research on game framing is to remind us all that this is not the only form of election coverage that's possible—it's often just what's easiest and cheapest to produce.

Wagner and Perryman: What are the next big things for scholars and citizens to be mindful of, when it comes to political communication in democratic societies? What will the Agora Journalism Center be doing to apply these lessons in ways that help us civically engage in the future?

Lawrence: I think the 800-pound gorilla in the room is the evolution of the "post-truth" era. So many of the assumptions that grounded political communication scholarship for decades don't hold anymore. We can't assume, for example, that presidents seek to communicate via the news media in order to bolster their policy agendas and their own legitimacy: Today we have a president who plays jujitsu with the media to further his own particular brand, and seems almost completely uninterested in winning over a solid majority of voters to support his policy agenda. And in a larger sense, the whole notion of truth is under assault. Meanwhile, public trust in the news media has steeply declined and it's not clear how journalism is going to regain the authority and legitimacy it once enjoyed. The contribution I hope Agora's work can make is to help solve that puzzle: How can we reboot the relationship between journalism and the public, not by exhorting the public to simply trust the media, but by fundamentally reforming how journalists go about their work?

Wagner and Perryman: For students reading this book who have an interest in conducting research in political communication, what is your advice for how they should get started?

Lawrence: Start with something that intrigues you, something that puzzles you, something that bugs you about the way we think and talk about politics. Lots of good research begins with intuition.

Wagner and Perryman: Over the course of your career, what are some of the behaviors that you have noticed that the best students do when learning about political communication and applying the lessons from those classes over the course of their lives?

Lawrence: Curiosity is important, of course. If you don't remain curious, you'll get bored with your research—and your research will become boring! Resisting the temptation to give up when it gets tough is another important quality in successful students. Empirical research rarely works out as neatly as we imagine, and every project will present unanticipated challenges. Being a ravenous reader and learner is also important: The best students, in my experience, keep training themselves over the course of their careers and are constantly improving their work by incorporating new ideas. Finally, in my opinion, keeping an eye on the practical impact of your work can be really important, to keep your research grounded, and to hopefully make some difference in the world.

Wagner and Perryman: How do you think about the ways in which your scholarship is connected to the mission and activities of the Agora Journalism Center?

Lawrence: The opportunity to lead the Agora Journalism Center was very attractive to me precisely because it offered a way to do work that might make a difference in the world. Building a research agenda at the same time as you are trying to learn about and develop new approaches to doing journalism can be tough, however. Practitioners and scholars often don't speak the same language, so there's a lot of translation required. And scholarly journals aren't always interested in research that is grounded in practice.

With that said, my long-term goal is to connect the threads in my own academic career in ways that matter. I've always been deeply interested in the power that news has to shape the public's perceptions of the world and to either amplify or marginalize different societal voices. I've moved from looking at news purely from the outside, as an academic, to gaining much more insight on how journalists go about doing their everyday work. I've moved from focusing on national politics to looking at how local journalists cover their communities. And I now have the opportunity to help learn from and shape the work of journalists around the country who are trying to fundamentally change daily news practices. The common thread is the question of power: The power to speak, to be heard, and to represent.

How Can I Help?

Michael W. Wagner, University of Wisconsin-Madison

A former journalist and congressional campaign press secretary, Wagner (one of the authors of this text) is a professor in the School of Journalism and Mass Communication at the University of Wisconsin-Madison. A winner of five teaching awards and two awards for public outreach, Wagner regularly gives dozens of talks a year to community organizations and in public forums where he discusses his research examining politics and the media. Wagner also edits the Forum in *Political Communication,* which aims to connect scholarly research to wider audiences and is an expert source for hundreds of political journalists around the globe. He is the founding director of the Center for Communication and Civic Renewal at the University of Wisconsin-Madison. Funded by the Knight Foundation, the center seeks to improve understanding of how communication can improve democracy at the local and state levels.

Perryman: So, why are we interviewing you? Not getting enough say as a coauthor of this book?

Wagner: Ha! We thought it was important for our readers to know about the value of taking the knowledge learned in these pages, and from other relevant experiences and studies, and bringing them back to the community. Where I work, and where you earned your PhD, we believe deeply in something called the Wisconsin Idea: the notion that what is learned within the confines of the university should be spread throughout the community, state, nation, and world in order to help improve society. Living that idea is why I give a few dozen public talks—usually fifteen to twenty in Wisconsin and another ten to fifteen around the world—each year. It is also why I try to be responsive to reporters seeking expert sources on issues related to American politics and the news media. So, we want students to know that a career path in the academy can be an opportunity to share what you know with broad audiences. We also want students who go on to other careers to consider that giving back your knowledge and expertise to others is a great way to spend some of your time.

Perryman: What have you learned about the value of sharing research, like the research students will read in this book, with community audiences?

Wagner: I've learned that even in a deeply polarized country, there are lots of people clamoring to not only make sense of it all but seeking to figure out what they can do to help make things a little bit better. Coming together on a rainy weeknight to talk about how well our republican democracy works and what we can do about it can be inspiring . . . and it always teaches me something that I didn't know before. I bring what I learn back to my classrooms and my own research.

Perryman: Is there any evidence that giving these sorts of talks, where you share research findings about politics and the media, has any effect on the people who come to listen and share their own ideas with you in the Q&A?

Wagner: Yes. For the past few years, when I give a public talk, I also give some of the attendees a survey about their experience. Of course, people who come to talk politics and the media on a weeknight are already highly likely to be voters, so these talks don't seem to have any effect on voter turnout. However, people who come to the talks report a greater willingness to talk to people who hold different ideas than they do about politics, volunteer in their communities, and share their own opinions about politics on social media.

Perryman: What should readers of this book take away from what you have learned while giving talks across the country and the world?

Wagner: First, I think students reading this book should think about how their own life path might carve out time to find a way to take what they learn in this book to pay that knowledge forward. Helping your friends be more critical consumers of information, more tolerant deliberators, and more engaged citizens has a real value that pays off over and over again. Helping people think about what kind of country they want to live in is a worthwhile thing to do. Second, I hope readers of this book come to see the value of talking with those who are different than you. The goal of conversations with people who are different than you should not always be to persuade them to your way of thinking. Rather, talking with others is a chance to share *and* to listen. We learn a lot when we listen. Whenever I give a talk, I insist on having the same amount of time for a conversation with the audience as there is for my talk itself. The real learning, in my view, happens in the exchange of ideas, not in the preaching from one side to another.

CHAPTER

2

Why the News Is the Way It Is

REPORTING THE NEWS IS A TOUGH JOB. One day, you might be covering a Supreme Court decision for the morning paper that affects the long-term rights of a traditionally marginalized group while in the next you might post a story on your news organization's website about the internal workings of a presidential campaign before filing an update to yesterday's Supreme Court story before finally recording a podcast that sifts through the details of a dense budget proposal. A dizzying array of responsibilities increasingly fills a reporter's day—a reporter for an online-first newspaper in Madison, Wisconsin, told a class of ours that she typically writes four stories a day while working on a cover story and a weekly podcast. Despite this variety, the news we use tends to be produced in a predictable, replicable structure no matter the format and platform. Why is this the case? Why is the news the way it is?

Some of the reasons are structural. For example, journalists must meet unbending deadlines. After all, if you have been assigned the lead story at the local TV station you work for, and the newscast starts at 5:30 p.m., it's either you or dead air that awaits the viewer who tunes in to learn what happened in her community that day. Viewers do not care if your sources did not call you back, but you can be sure that some will call to complain if you only report a quote from one major political party and not any others—no matter who returned your calls. If all you get in response to a request for an interview is an emailed statement and you quote that statement, you are sure to hear from the other side that you are a shill for their political opponents, uncritically regurgitating their talking points.

Some of the reasons relate to professional concerns. Journalists worry about fairness. As compared to everything else that is going on, is the story newsworthy? Have they given the major players in a story a chance to express themselves? How should reporters frame claims sources make that do not match the verifiable truth?

Some of the reasons are market based. Journalists, and their bosses, think about their audience. Who reads the paper? Are they generally aware of this story or do they need some background to understand what is going on? Who watches the 4 o'clock local news? What interests them? Who tunes into the 11 o'clock news? What will they already know about the story by the time they flip on the Nightside news? What percentage of the audience are reading updates on their phones? What do they need to know? What will people click on? What will they share on social media?

Due to these and other considerations journalists sift and winnow through when doing their jobs, a great deal of news coverage fits into fairly predictable patterns in terms of the topics covered, people quoted, and perspectives shared. In this chapter, we describe the major conclusions from research examining why the news is the way that it is. We'll find that the structure and content of the news is guided by journalists' routines, constraints, and models; the systematic indexing of elite opinion; how journalists perceive themselves, those they cover, and the audience they serve; market forces; and changes to the contemporary communication ecology.

Journalistic Models, Routines, and Professional Norms

Models of Making the News

In Chapter 1, we described Amber Boydstun's alarm/patrol hybrid model, which describes the news media as it is, not how we might wish it was. Recall that news coverage can operate in a pure alarm mode, with a short explosion of coverage around an issue or event. It can engage in a pure patrol mode, with extended, regularized coverage of an issue. It can engage in neither an alarm nor patrol mode and it can operate in the alarm/patrol mode with short bursts of alarm reporting followed by continuing the surge of coverage for sustained periods of time.

Boydstun's model does a good job describing how news coverage works. Other models of newsmaking offer more normatively oriented views of what journalism might look like. The *mirror model's* advocates argue that journalism should work like a mirror does and reflect what is happening back to the world. As such, the news should dispassionately and fairly report the important things that happen on a given day. Described in this way, the mirror model sounds a bit like the surveillance function of the media described in Chapter 1. Critics of the mirror model point out that journalists are gatekeepers, regardless of how hard they might try to simply reflect the important stuff back to the audience. With 7.5 billion people on planet Earth, it is impossible for the news to cover every important thing that happens, let alone do it well. Beyond what makes it onto the agenda, stories get framed (see the interpretation function of the media described in Chapter 1 and the research on framing described in Chapter 6) in ways that are not pure reflections of what happened. Moreover, it is worth asking whose reflections are most likely to be reported upon. If reporters are mostly white and well educated (which, as you will see below, they are), should we expect them to do as good of a job reflecting what is happening in communities they are not as familiar with? In practice, it should not come as a surprise that the mirror model falls short of wholly reflecting reality.

A second model is the organizational model. Supporters of this perspective argue that news is influenced by the organizational processes and objectives that exist between reporters and their sources, ideals of the organization they work for, and practical considerations. We will unpack some of these factors later in the chapter. Other organizational features that influence how journalism is practiced include the publication schedule (daily or weekly newspaper or newscasts) and the population size and demographic features served by the news organization.

The professional model considers making the news to be something that is done by skilled professionals who curate important and exciting stories for their audience. As Doris Graber and Johanna Dunaway point out, "There is no pretense that the end product mirrors the world."[1] Some call this model the economic model of news as considerations of the audience are centrally important to determining what gets covered.

The political model assumes that media organizations cover the news in accordance to their political views. As such, the news is a reflection of the partisan and ideological biases of reporters and the political environment in which the coverage is occurring. Indexing, which we describe below, has roots in this model of news coverage.

The mirror, organizational, professional, and politics models of coverage comprehensively account for how the news is made. An interesting exercise is to see how each of these models might fit into the alarm/patrol hybrid model of news coverage. Regardless of the model guiding how the news gets made for the audience, another set of important factors influencing why the news is the way it is are journalistic routines and professional norms.

Journalistic Routines and Professional Norms

Journalistic routines are the rules and behaviors that reporters are trained to follow by people like the authors of this book along with editors and news organization executives that affect what is covered and how it is reported. These routines are designed to help prevent bias from creeping into practice of news gathering and writing, but organizational routines can bias the news even without intending to.

In order to climb the professional ladder, reporters quickly learn what kinds of stories earn clicks, approval from editors, and compliments from their colleagues. Producing a lot of clickable content, fast, is prized in the contemporary media ecology.

Even though the digital environment has increased the number of organizations providing news to various publics, it is still the case that news organizations pay close attention to what major east coast newspapers in the United States choose to cover. *The New York Times*, *Washington Post*, and *Wall Street Journal* continue to drive a nontrivial portion of what other news organizations cover. As such, the potential sources, ways of framing a story, and possibilities for follow-ups are often driven by what the most elite news organizations choose to do. Lance Bennett outlines three major incentives that reporters face that have the consequence of homogenizing their reporting habits: 1) cooperating with and responding to pressure from their sources; 2) the rhythms and pressures of their own organization; and 3) their regular working relationships with other reporters.[2]

Cooperation(?) with Sources

Theoretically, reporters have an adversarial relationship with official sources. However, many interactions that reporters have with politicians and other civic leaders follow reliable formats. Journalists are trained to incorporate the 5Ws and an H (who, what, when, where, why, and how) into the leads of their stories. For example, when President Trump kicked off his reelection campaign on June 18th, the *New York Times* story began (our emphases in the parentheses):

> President Trump (who) delivered a fierce denunciation of the news media, the political establishment and what he called his radical opponents (what) on Tuesday (when) as he opened his re-election campaign (why) in front of a huge crowd of raucous supporters (where) by evoking the dark messaging and personal grievances that animated his 2016 victory (how).[3]

These *pseudo-events*, to use Lance Bennett's term, come with formulaic scripts that do not provide much in the way of hard information to the public. Rather, easy-to-understand images tend to be what people recall. Of course, later in the book we will discuss how voters can make reasonable democratic decisions with fairly limited information, but we will also review how uninformed most folks are about most things more of the time.

It is certainly the case that journalists can and do ask tough questions of politicians while covering these kinds of events. It is also true that it is newsworthy that the president of the United States is going to run for reelection. While journalists and politicians do not share the same goals, they need each other. An example of how all of these things can happen at once took place in June 2019 when ABC's George Stephanopoulos was grilling President Trump in the Oval Office about whether Trump would accept an offer of information about a political rival from a foreign government and if Trump would tell the FBI about the offer. Trump said that he would certainly want to listen to the information and that he might tell the FBI even though he thought the FBI director was wrong when he said that presidential candidates should always tell the FBI if a foreign government or national is trying to affect an American election. ABC's chief political correspondent was factual, firm, and direct in his questioning of the president, an example of the adversarial relationship. During the tense back-and-forth, Trump's chief of staff coughed. Trump, annoyed, stopped the interview and offered to go back and do an answer again so that the cough would not get picked up on camera and be heard in a soundbite, an example of cooperation. Stephanopoulos agreed and the chief of staff was kicked out of the Oval!

Organizational Pressures

Reporters also face pressures from their own news organizations to standardize their work. Since editors at newspapers and online outlets and assignment editors and news directors at television stations hold the keys to professional advancement, their preferences for how stories should be covered can greatly influence how journalists do their jobs. Standardized news has benefits for the news organization, the most important being that it is safe. When news organizations take risks to do original or risky work, they know that they will have to explain to the higher-ups why their coverage looks so different from their competitors'. While one might think that originality would be prized in the mainstream media environment, pack journalism—the tendency for reporters at different organizations to cover issues in similar ways—often wins out.[4]

Perhaps the most important standard is the size of the news hole itself. A thirty-minute local television newscast has between eight to twelve minutes of commercials. The remaining time is divided between local news, national news, weather, sports, and feature stories. This means that many of the decisions about a reporter's story are made before the reporter has conducted their first interview. These include the length of the story, its likely placement in the newscast, and who the sources will probably be.

Most news organizations operate on a beat system, where a reporter is assigned to cover a particular topic, like education, city government, or arts and entertainment. The reporter then cultivates sources in that area, responding to events (e.g., a city council meeting, a presidential candidate visit, or an upcoming concert) and generating their own stories based upon their knowledge of the beat, their sense of what is newsworthy, and what their editors and audience might respond to. The officials who the reporter regularly sees as part of their work on the beat—at meetings, hearings, press conferences, and public events—are the people who reporters are most likely to end up calling for comment.

The Reporters in the Pack

The organizational routines described above often result in journalists covering the same beat moving in packs throughout each workday. Statehouse reporters tend to congregate in the state capitol's pressroom, campaign reporters travel together on a bus or plane, and education reporters see each other at school board meetings. Because they spend so much time together—chasing breaking news, waiting (and waiting) for events to start, and covering the same meetings and key players—they often feel very close to each other. As Alexandra Pelosi documented in the 2000 presidential campaign film *Journeys with George*, reporters endure the same turkey sandwiches, same campaign speeches, and same travel problems at every campaign stop.[5] Certainly, reporters work independently to get scoops, original quotes, and unique stories, but they also compare notes, corroborate evidence, and bounce ideas off of each other. Many become good friends. Some become romantic partners. These behaviors foster some homogeneity in news coverage.

In his famous book chronicling the 1972 presidential campaign called *The Boys on the Bus*, Timothy Crouse called this tendency toward sameness in coverage *pack journalism*.[6] The increasing consolidation in media ownership of local television stations and newspapers has created a second kind of pack journalism—one that seems to be driven by the preferences of management. Sinclair Broadcast Group, the nation's largest local television station owner, requires their stations to carry some opinion pieces from Boris Epshteyn, who the *PBS NewsHour* called a "surrogate for [President] Trump on their station's air,"[7] even famously requiring their anchors to read the same script that accused the national news media of spreading fake news. Media scholar Lewis Friedland noted the dangers that accompany the fact that the "most trusted news source of most Americans (local TV news) is going to be allowed to be turned into an opinion organization."

Feeding Frenzies

Packs also attack. We might be able to predict with some accuracy how most issues will be covered most of the time, but it is not hard to find a politician who will tell you that they do not receive the coverage they would prefer. Political scientist Larry Sabato has dubbed pack attacks on accusations of politicians' personal failings, malfeasance, and the like *feeding frenzies*.[8] Like sharks sensing chum in the water, reporters have a nose for when politicians are in trouble. Frenzies can expose corruption, leading to resignations and prison time and they can be overdrawn soap operas that help cable television stations fill the hours with talking heads who speculate about what might happen next.

An example of a textbook feeding frenzy began in March 2016 during the American presidential race. It was revealed that Democratic candidate for president and former secretary of state Hillary Rodham Clinton used a private email server to conduct official government business when she was serving in President Barack Obama's cabinet. Previous holders of her office, like Republican Colin Powell, had done the same, but Clinton's behavior was deeply criticized by the then-director of the FBI, James Comey. In an extraordinary news conference, Comey said,

> Although we did not find clear evidence that Secretary Clinton or her colleagues intended to violate laws governing the handling of classified information, there is evidence that they were extremely careless in their handling of very sensitive, highly classified information.[9]

One of the issues was whether Clinton had not taken proper care of classified documents on her private email server. Another was the possibility that she could avoid sharing with the public the contents of her private emails, making her service as secretary of state less transparent. While most of the emails that were released were innocuous (details about scheduling, emails about family life), the fact that some emails were not shared gave reporters and Clinton's political opponents something to talk about—framing Clinton as untrustworthy and incompetent.

Reporters asked Clinton about her emails several times a day on the campaign trail. Even her major primary opponent, Senator Bernie Sanders of Vermont, grew tired of the questions about the controversy, exclaiming in a primary debate with Clinton, "The American people are sick and tired of hearing about your damn emails," though in a later debate, he said it was a serious issue.[10]

Fox News' Chris Wallace asked Clinton about her emails in one of her general election debates with Donald Trump. Trump and his supporters hammered Clinton's use of a private email server relentlessly. In an unprecedented campaign moment, Trump literally asked Russia to find Clinton's missing emails, saying, "Russia, if you're listening, I hope you're able to find the 30,000 emails that are missing, I think you will probably be rewarded mightily by our press."[11] This had the effect of starting another frenzy—this one aimed at Trump—for asking a foreign government to involve itself in the US presidential election.

Clinton's own supporters tried to turn the issue on its head on social media using hashtags like #ButHerEmails. This was used to mock people who showed support for Donald Trump. When Trump was revealed to have told *Access Hollywood's* Billy Bush that he felt empowered by his celebrity to sexually assault women, Clinton supporters shared the story with the #ButHerEmails hashtag.

A feeding frenzy more directly involving the twenty-first-century communication ecology began in 2011. New York congressman Anthony Weiner was reported by conservative media baron Andrew Breitbart to have sent a lewd and sexually suggestive photograph to a 21-year-old woman. Weiner denied that he sent the photo, saying that while the photo might be a doctored photo of him, he did not send it. A few days later, another photo surfaced and Weiner held a news conference to admit that he had taken and sent the pictures. He claimed to have engaged in sexually inappropriate conversations on social media with several women over the previous few years. The press coverage was intense, the ridicule from late-night hosts was abundant, and Weiner faced calls to resign from Republican and Democratic leadership. Less than a month later, he resigned.

Later, when he tried for a comeback—this time in the race to be mayor of New York—he sexted women under the moniker Carlos Danger. The frenzy began anew and uncovered that Weiner sent lewd photos to young women while lying in bed next to his toddler son. Weiner pled guilty to a charge of transporting pornographic material to a minor. His wife, top Hillary Clinton aid Huma Abedin, filed for divorce. However, Weiner's relationship with Abedin led FBI investigators to discover emails on Weiner's laptop that were deemed pertinent to Clinton's email controversy, opening that case back up in the months right before the 2016 presidential election, something Clinton blamed for her loss to Trump.

The reporters in the pack covered these controversies relentlessly. However, most of their work is outside of the frenzy-zone. Reporters covering politics tend to follow the routines and norms described above in ways that shape how the public thinks about the level of conflict between elected officials and between elected officials and the news media itself.

Indexing

The most prominent explanation of the relationship between the news media and the government—and how that relationship affects the content of the news in the United States—is W. Lance Bennett's indexing hypothesis. The indexing hypothesis maintains that news coverage of political issues tends to be dominated by official sources and the views expressed in mainstream government debate.[12] This gatekeeping behavior effectively opens or closes admission to being reported on in the news media for citizens, activists, and the like in a way that is based upon how well their perspectives fit into the conflict between elected officials and well-heeled organized interests. Research provides a fair amount of evidence supporting the idea of indexing, but there is also plenty of evidence that reporters can and do more than cover the news as indexing stenographers, more closely fulfilling the democratic requirement that a free press provides a variety of critical perspectives on issues,[13] though, of course, journalists often fall short of this ideal.[14]

Reporting based on official or authoritative views tends to index those views in ways commensurate with the magnitude and content of conflict. Stories about abortion policy tend to provide one reliably *pro-choice* perspective and one equally ardent *pro-life* perspective. Opinion about abortion is far more complicated than the *life/choice* framing that dominated news coverage for decades. Most Americans support some version of abortion rights—from always supporting them to supporting them to favoring the right to an abortion when the life of the mother is at risk or when a woman became pregnant after rape or incest. These nuances are indexed when elites, like the Supreme Court, rely upon those nuances, but they are often absent from coverage otherwise. Stories detailing other important issues relating to abortion, such as what a person seeking one must go through (government-mandated counseling, an unwanted ultrasound, driving hundreds of miles to the nearest clinic), are far less common.

Even so, deviations from indexing are plentiful during times when there is conflict between official sources within the same party or conflict between official domestic sources and the preferences of foreign voices.[15] When neither inter- or intra-partisan conflict is present, criticism of government activity need not come from other official sources to be recognized by the media. Research exploring this idea often focuses on a crisis, often a foreign policy issue such as the 2003 US-led war in Iraq.[16] Indexing is more difficult when it comes to reporting on foreign policy issues, as the government is in greater control of information flows on these issues. More sources are typically available for comment on domestic issues, making indexing—and two-way flows of information—easier.

As new media outlets apply their own interpretations to events, traditional outlets follow suit.[17] Danish political communication scholar Claes de Vreese argues that this is an indicator of the *mediatization* of politics, wherein the autonomy of politics as primarily the domain of political elites has given way to a politics with media as central players.[18]

Indexing has even found a way to survive in the era of infotainment. Even as event-centered reporting declines, reporters often find issues that fit within their conceptions of political conflict and, as Bennett argues, "create their own issues and recycling past developments" to fill the news space until real issues emerge.[19]

Journalists' Perceptions of Themselves and Their Jobs

In 2019, newsrooms in the United States had nearly forty thousand reporters fewer in them as compared to 2000.[20] Researchers David Weaver, Lars Wilnat, and Cleveland Wilhoit investigated whether these changes have affected reporters' demographic characteristics, political and professional attitudes, and professional behaviors.[21] Their survey of more than one thousand US journalists interviewed print, broadcast, and online journalists in 2013. Figure 2.1 shows that the percentage of journalists working for daily newspapers dropped about 16 percent from 1971 to 2013. The percentage of reporters working for weekly newspapers rose by 12 percent over the same time period. Television news has been a growth industry for journalists while radio is about half as large as it was when Richard Nixon

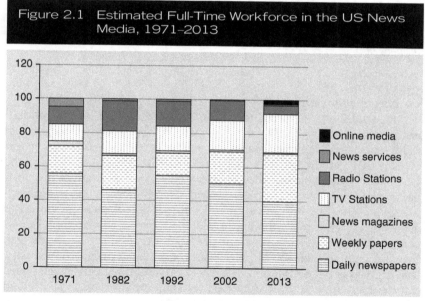

Figure 2.1   Estimated Full-Time Workforce in the US News Media, 1971–2013

Source: David H. Weaver, Lars Wilnat, G. Cleveland Wilhoit, "The American Journalist in the Digital Age: Another Look at U.S. News People," *Journalism & Mass Communication Quarterly 96*(1): 101–130.

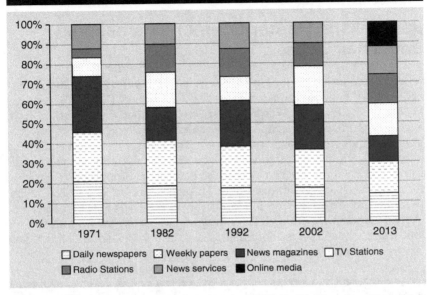

Figure 2.2 Percentage of Women Journalists in News Organizations, 1971–2013

Legend: Daily newspapers · Weekly papers · News magazines · TV Stations · Radio Stations · News services · Online media

Source: David H. Weaver, Lars Wilnat, G. Cleveland Wilhoit, "The American Journalist in the Digital Age: Another Look at U.S. News People," *Journalism & Mass Communication Quarterly 96*(1): 101–130.

was president. Just over 2 percent of all US news media professionals were working in online media.

Figure 2.2 highlights changes in the representation of women journalists in American media. Notably, the percentages of women working in radio, television, daily newspapers, weekly newspapers, and news magazines in 2013 are higher than they were in 1971. However, 1992 was the best year for women in weeklies and news magazines. The largest sustained gains have been made in radio (but recall from Figure 2.1 that radio journalists are only about 5 percent of all journalists). Women are closest to achieving parity in television and weekly newspapers (both about 42 percent women in 2013). Weaver and colleagues reported that the pay gap between men and women in journalism continues to plague the industry. The gap was about $7,000 in 2012, a $2,000 (and three percentage point) improvement from 2001. The average man in journalism made $53,600 in 2012 while the average woman made $44,342.

Table 2.1 reveals changes in the percentage of self-identified racial and ethnic minorities in journalism. While there are gains across the board, they are extraordinarily modest, especially when compared to the demographic

Table 2.1 Representation in News Organizations by Racial and Ethnic Groups, 1971–2013

	1971	1982	1992	2002	2013
African American	3.9	2.9	3.7	3.7	4.1
Hispanic	1.1	0.6	2.2	3.3	3.3
Asian American	NA	0.4	1	1	1.8
Native American	NA	NA	0.6	0.4	0.5
Jewish	6.4	5.8	5.4	6.2	7.6
White and other	88.6	90.3	87.1	85.4	82.8

Source: David H. Weaver, Lars Wilnat, G. Cleveland Wilhoit, "The American Journalist in the Digital Age: Another Look at U.S. News People," Journalism & Mass Communication Quarterly 96(1): 101–130.

NA = Not Applicable due to too small of a number of respondents.

totals of groups such as African Americans and Hispanic/Latinx Americans represented in the population as a whole.

Of course, the individual identity that media critics point to the most when seeking to criticize the news media for being biased is party identification. Figure 2.3 shows that the majority of journalists identified themselves as independents in 2013. However, for most of the years that similar surveys were conducted, Democrats were the largest group. Just over 28 percent were Democrats in 2013 while only 7 percent identified as Republicans—an 11-point drop from 2002. This was the lowest percentage of journalists identifying as Democrats in the forty-two years of surveys conducted by those studying American journalists. The same was true for the percentage of reporters who were Republicans. In terms of their political ideology, almost 39 percent said they leaned to the left, about 44 percent described themselves as *middle of the road*, while only 12.9 percent said they leaned to the right. In terms of their partisanship and their ideology, American journalists do not look like the rest of the country—especially with respect to the number of conservatives and Republicans in their ranks.

Some worry that this is a problem, believing that a reporter's individual political views will affect the fairness with which that reporters does their job. After all, the argument goes, people's core political values affect what they think is important, reasonable, and right—it would be difficult to imagine how journalists could divorce their own views from their reporting. On the other hand, others counter this argument by noting

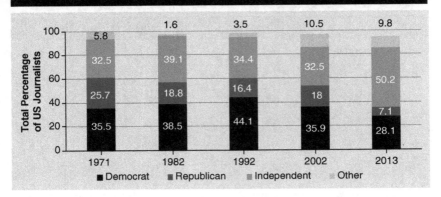

Figure 2.3   Political Party Identification of US Journalists, 1971–2013

Source: David H. Weaver, Lars Wilnat, G. Cleveland Wilhoit, "The American Journalist in the Digital Age: Another Look at U.S. News People," *Journalism & Mass Communication Quarterly 96*(1): 101–130.

that there are liberals, moderates, and conservatives in every profession. People tend not to ask their airline pilot if they are going to fly the plane in a conservative or liberal way or their surgeon if they should be worried about their doctor's views on the capital gains tax before an emergency appendix surgery.

Why is it that there are fewer conservatives in journalism? It might have to do with their general orientation toward authority. Weaver, Wilnat, and Wilhoit report that 78 percent of reporters said investigating government claims is "extremely important." Questioning authority is something that liberals tend to prefer as compared to conservatives. Psychologists Jesse Graham, Jonathan Haidt, and Brian Nosek found that conservatives tend to endorse five *moral foundations*: authority/respect, purity/sanctity, harm/care, fairness/reciprocity, and ingroup/loyalty. Liberals tend to only endorse two (harm/care and fairness/reciprocity).[22] Since journalists have to question authority and strive to the verifiable truth as compared to an ingroup they favor, liberals may be more likely to self-select into the profession as compared to conservatives. Others have suggested that since a high percentage of media jobs in the United States are on the coasts where liberals are a larger share of the population, that part of the explanation is geographic; another explanation is that journalism professors like us, who are more likely to be liberal than conservative, train reporters to adopt a liberal orientation to their work.[23] There is less support for the latter two explanations in the research literature, but it is also the case that there has not been much work done to debunk these possibilities.

Besides questioning those in power, what else do journalists say is an extremely important part of the gig? Sixty-nine percent say the same about providing analysis of complex problems. Just under half believe it is extremely important to get information out quickly to the public. Journalists, as a whole, do not see being an adversary to government (22 percent) or business (19 percent) as very important parts of the job, nor do they think they should be setting the political agenda (2 percent) or be entertaining (9 percent).

Despite heavy workloads and the general precariousness regarding the health of their profession, over three-quarters of journalists in the United States say they are satisfied with their jobs. One area in which journalists perceive less than exciting changes in their jobs is the autonomy they have. Over the past forty years, fewer journalists report that they can choose what to work on or how they want to frame their stories.

In terms of journalists' views about ethical behavior in their reporting, few say it may be justified to use personal documents without permission (25 percent), pay people for confidential information (5 percent), agree to protect confidentiality but then not do it (2 percent), or claim to be someone else (7 percent). More than half of reporters believe it may be justified to use confidential public documents without permission.

Journalists are also adapting to the digital environment. An online survey experiment of working US journalists conducted by Shannon McGregor and Logan Molyneux found that journalists who use Twitter less in their jobs tend to dismiss information their colleagues who are Twitterfiles find to be newsworthy. They also find reporters who use Twitter as a regular part of their reporting routine believe that tweets are as newsworthy as headlines from the Associated Press wire. On the one hand, Twitter can push back against indexing and include more voices into the news agenda. On the other hand, heavy-Twitter-using journalists may be more likely to behave as a pack, quickly coming to conclusions about topics based on their use of Twitter as compared to other tools in the reporter's toolkit.[24]

Journalists' Perceptions of Their Audience

In the digital era, we assume that journalists can know their audiences better than ever, given all of the tools at their disposal to measure clicks, time spent reading a story, the number of times a story was shared on social media, analyzing the comments on the story, and so forth. Notably, a Tow

Center report for the *Columbia Journalism Review* concludes that little has changed since the print era, though journalists appear more open to learning about their audiences than reporters were in the 1970s.[25]

Previous work from the print era concluded that journalists' perceptions of their audience were grounded in ideas about the institutional audience of the publication they worked for, their professional peers, their sources, and people who were important in their own lives (family, friends). In 2019, the report found that "while journalists are open to engaging with readers, the ways in which they form audience perceptions remain largely unchanged despite the rise of audience metrics and analytics."[26] This, of course, is partly because journalists are more interested in the news than they are interested in their audience.[27] This is not to say that journalists do not value their audience—after all, providing news to the audience is a foundational principle of news reporting. Journalists often fear that being too open to audience feedback could harm their news judgment.

Today, journalists can learn from their audience directly via social media conversations, for example. They can also learn about their audience by using data: the metrics and analytics that are used to infer what it is the audience likes, knows, and wants. Of course, social media platforms like Twitter can be echo chambers for journalists as well.[28] Other times, audience response on social media can be downright frightening. Journalists have been harshly and vulgarly criticized and even threatened on social media. The murder of a Roanoke, Virginia,[29] television reporter and cameraman on-air in 2015 and the mass shooting that killed five in the Capital Gazette newsroom in Maryland[30] contribute to the sense of unease that can accompany getting closer to the audience.

The Tow Center report concludes,

> Perhaps one of the ironies of the digital era may be that the most persistent and vivid reader perceptions are still based on actual personal contact, a fundamental human connection that virtual communication—be it through numbers, graphs or even email—struggles to replicate.[31]

How might journalists go about improving their understanding of the audience in order to shift the audience they imagine into the audience that actually exists? It is difficult to say. The Tow Center report suggests that asking reporters what audiences they want to impact is not enough. News organizations will need to figure out who they want to target with particular stories and use contemporary analytics and metrics to investigate whether they actually reach them. Choosing to empower the audience a bit is another suggestion, but how this would work in concert with journalistic norms and routines discussed earlier in the chapter is unclear. Finally, since so much of how journalists perceive audiences comes from their peers and their friends, newsrooms need to seriously focus on diversifying. Recall Table 2.1. Newsrooms are not diverse places. Studies show that people of different backgrounds and experiences can fundamentally alter what kinds of stories get covered and how they are reported. Of course, diversity is not enough—changing routines, habits, and poorly-rooted preconceptions about the news is required as well.

Market Forces and the News

Another major set of factors affecting the content of the news is the market itself. Johanna Dunaway's research reveals that there are important differences in agenda, tone, and slant when comparing corporately owned media to privately owned firms and by contrasting the news coverage of small media companies to enormous media conglomerates. For example, both large newspaper chains and public companies print more negative campaign coverage than privately owned news outlets. Moreover, corporately owned news organizations are less likely to cover political issues than news outlets owned by smaller companies.[32] Chain-owned papers also print more letters to the editor and editorials that are critical of major institutions.[33] Robert McChesney's research provides numerous examples of how corporately owned news organizations limit the issues, voices, and perspectives presented in their pages.[34]

Indeed, there is evidence that journalists' behavior is responsive to economic concerns favoring corporate and commercial interests. Journalists cover elections as a horse race and policy battles as a game, in part, because it sells.[35] Regina Lawrence's research into how news organizations cover stories shows that game framing is more likely as a debate approaches a decision on an issue carrying electoral consequences.[36] James Hamilton's book *All the News That's Fit to Sell* shows that there is more local news coverage of politics in media markets that have higher subscription rates to *Time* magazine. When markets have higher subscription rates to *People* magazine, local news organizations provide less hard news to their audiences.

The limitations regarding the small range of perspectives the market often encourages can even be applied to the editorial voice of the news organizations themselves. Newspapers typically have an editorial section of the paper that is produced by different people than the various news sections of the paper. The editorial section is designed to provide a range of views, through regular opinion columns, syndicated columnists, invited or submitted op-eds, and the paper's own editorials, which are typically unsigned. In the past, mainstream national and local television outlets also provided regular commentary. Today, a handful of stations have local editorials while the stations owned by media giant Sinclair Broadcast Group carry commentaries they require their stations to air.

Sometimes, the market can push papers to keep their editorial perspective quiet. The *Cleveland Plain Dealer* decided to endorse a presidential candidate in 2004, and the *Milwaukee Journal Sentinel*, bruised after making an endorsement in the contentious recall election of Wisconsin governor Scott Walker, declined to make an endorsement in the 2012 presidential race. Kimberly Meltzer argued that this decision to "toe the owner's political line" was one reason, along with pleasing readers, that editorial endorsements might be predicted by knowing who the publisher prefers, something that is more likely for private companies than publicly traded ones.[37]

Beyond the quality and content of coverage itself, market forces simply and directly affect whether news organizations can exist. Between 1970 and 2016, around five hundred daily newspapers went out of business. Several others reduced their publication schedule, shrank their news hole, or moved to an online-only production plan.[38] Newsrooms that have survived often are living with smaller statehouse, Washington, and foreign bureaus.

Media critics worry that our ability to govern ourselves is severely diminished, or even destroyed, if we do not have easy access to independently produced information that informs us about the issues of the day and the behavior of those in power. Social media makes it easier than ever for public officials to jump over the scrutiny of reporters and communicate directly with their constituents, react to news stories (even if they were not willing to comment in the stories in the first place), and shape public debate. What scholars have called the contemporary *hybrid media* system allows for people like President Trump to not only tweet to his followers but also have his tweets breathlessly covered by the news media. A team of scholars, led by Chris Wells, found that a strong predictor of news coverage of Donald Trump, when he was seeking the Republican Party nomination for president in 2016, was his behavior—and the behavior of his followers—on Twitter. When Trump's media attention was lagging, he was more likely to go on a *tweetstorm*. When his followers retweeted his missives in higher numbers, news organizations were more likely to write stories about him.[39]

Tweeting for news coverage is not something that restricts itself to presidents. When the Republican Party surprisingly lost a state legislative seat in a special election that took place several months before the governor's election, then Wisconsin governor Scott Walker sent a series of tweets (Photo 2.1) aiming to energize his supporters and generate news coverage. Several state news organizations covered the tweetstorm, amplifying the governor's message to his supporters.[40]

What can be done to stop the decline of newspapers and usher in a new era of robust news coverage that holds public officials to account while informing the public? Former *Washington Post* editor Leonard Downie, Jr.,

Scott Walker □
@ScottWalker

Senate District 10 special election win by a Democrat is a wake up call for Republicans in Wisconsin.

10:24 PM · 16 Jan 2018

Following

Scott Walker ✓
@ScottWalker

Tonight's results show we are at risk of a #BlueWave in WI. The Far Left is driven by anger & hatred -- we must counter it with optimism & organization. Let's share our positive story with voters & win in November.

7:50 PM · Apr 3, 2018 · Twitter Web Client

Photo 2.1 Tweets From Wisconsin Governor Scott Walker After Republicans Lost a Special Election Eleven Months Before Walker's Reelection Bid

and media scholar Michael Schudson proposed forcing broadcast companies, internet service providers, and those of us who use their services to pay into a fund that would be used to pay for local journalism across the United States. Many other nations already do this. Canada has provided more than $600 million for local journalism. Great Britain has taken $10 million from the British Broadcasting Corporation's (BBC) budget to give to local journalism outlets. In New Jersey, a state fund set up to pay for quality journalism and media start-ups was set to kick off in 2019.[41]

State support might be necessary, even in the digital age. Matthew Hindman's book *The Myth of Digital Democracy* shows that, far from being a power-flattening equalizer of information provision, internet clicks tend to go to sites operated by traditional media and aggregation sites that link to content provided by old media.[42] Moreover, the digital-only organizations that dominate web traffic are a relatively small number—just as there are a small number of companies that dominate mainstream media.

Opponents of state-funded news organizations generally pursue two lines of argument—the first is that the news should be a self-sustaining business. If news organizations cannot earn enough to stay afloat, it must mean that they are not doing a good job meeting the needs of their audience. A second line of argument is fueled by worries that news organizations would become beholden to their funders, in this case the government. If corporately owned newspapers, for example, produce less issue coverage than other newspapers, perhaps government-funded papers would be less willing to hold government officials and institutions to account.

Research suggests that in advanced industrial democracies, these concerns are misplaced. Audiences continue to trust public news outlets in the United States and abroad. The Democracy Index, produced by the magazine *The Economist*, rates democracies based upon how their government functions and protects civil liberties, and how citizens participate, among other factors. The top six countries have some of the most robust public funding of journalism in the world.[43] The United States, which funds public media to a much smaller degree than the top six nations ranked in the Democracy Index, ranks eighteenth.

Audience Demands and Behavior

Since news organizations have more measures of the behavior of audiences at their fingertips than ever before, it stands to reason that some of these measures would be used to affect the kinds of stories that get covered and how they are framed.

Building upon Boydstun's alarm/patrol hybrid model of journalism, researchers have studied how what we search the internet for on Google can affect what news organizations put on the agenda. The theory of *agenda-uptake* provides explanations for when we should expect: 1) the mainstream media's agenda to influence niche media's agenda or the public's agenda; 2) niche media's agenda to influence the mainstream media's agenda or the public's agenda; and 3) the public's agenda to influence the mainstream media's or niche media's agenda.

For issues receiving patrol coverage, like the abortion issue, public attention to the issue tends not to shift based on mainstream media coverage, nor is it affected by niche (i.e., partisan cable news or narrowly focused digital outlets). People who are interested in abortion politics are already interested and seek to follow news about the issue regularly. The mainstream news media, however, is reactive to what more narrowly targeted news outlets are doing. That is, they are more likely to cover abortion politics when niche organizations are paying more attention and when the public does show an interest, based upon their Google searches about the topic. Niche organizations also are more likely to cover abortion when the mainstream news media cover it and when people are searching for information about the topic.

Issues that received patrol coverage and regularized alarm attention as well affect the public and news agendas a bit differently. Issues like the state of a nation's economy get regular attention from news organizations but also earn routinized punctuations in coverage around releases of monthly reports, major changes in the stock market, and election seasons. The public's agenda regularly takes up mainstream and niche coverage of the economy. Niche organizations do not affect the mainstream media's coverage of economic news but traditional news organizations are influenced by public searches about economic issues. Niche organizations are not affected by mainstream coverage, but they follow public interest as well.

One example of alarm issues that tend not to become patrols are scandals, which tend to generate a great deal of attention for a short amount of time. Sometimes, as with the Watergate scandal in the 1970s, coverage builds slowly over time, causing the scope of the scandal to grow as investigative journalists learn more. But, most scandals are relatively short-lived in the media ecology. Typically, mainstream coverage is driven more by the availability of new information to reporters and niche media's attention to the scandal. Since a scandal usually focuses on one side of the political spectrum (e.g., Democrat Bill Clinton's inappropriate sexual relationship with White House intern Monica Lewinsky or Republican Donald Trump's attempts to thwart a government investigation into his presidential campaign's dealings with Russia), niche news is more responsible to public attention as they are in the position to provide the "red meat" of scandal coverage to their audience when it is the other side that is in trouble.

Beyond Google searches as a measure of the public agenda, scholars have shown that social media behavior also can influence what news organizations choose to cover. For ten of the twenty-nine issues studied, traditional news coverage led to social media conversation about political issues. For seventeen of the issues studied, social media activity led to mainstream news attention to political issues. The largest effects were for gun control.

One example of how the fact that social media conversation can affect news coverage matters can be found by looking at social media conversations about gun policy in the wake of mass shootings. An ambitious study of Twitter discourse about fifty-nine mass shootings from 2012 to 2014, led by Yini Zhang, highlighted the importance of social discussions about major issues. Zhang and her colleagues found that tweets about *thoughts and prayers* immediately follow mass shootings. There is typically conversation about gun control that persists for a few days as well. Importantly, tweets about increased gun rights dominate social media coverage for *forty* days after each shooting.[44] Future research is seeking to understand whether the frames used in social media conversation have any relationship with the frames used in news coverage of the same issue.

The Future of News

Legacy News Adapting

The increasingly fragmented media environment, albeit with traditional powerhouses still demanding a great deal of attention, is the major story of the past two decades of mass communication research. While widely mocked when awarding the "Person of the Year" to You in 2006, the focus on individual content creators did not go far enough in announcing the changes coming to global communication. Personalized mass media is here.

Traditional media are modernizing. Their power has been meaningfully reduced, but they still control a nontrivial portion of the most popular news production and distribution outlets. Technology has made it far easier to do much more traditional reporting. Enormous, searchable databases now hold exabytes of data, making computer-assisted reporting easier and more immediate. The distribution of news has flattened as well.

Local newspaper websites can stream live video of something happening halfway across the world. Broadband technology has reduced delays in when news is shared with the audience. As technological changes help reporters do their jobs, they also can cost some reporters their jobs. Newsrooms are shrinking and reporters who hold onto their jobs are being asked to write more stories across more platforms while also maintaining an active social media presence.

Meanwhile, traditional media also remain under attack. Newspapers, local broadcast stations, and cable television are all competing with what the web can provide. In addition to competing with a new slate of hungry and nimble content providers, traditional sources are also competing with the explosion of streaming services like Netflix, Amazon Prime, Hulu, and Roku—all of whom provide scores of binge-worthy entertainment options with a few simple clicks. While traditional media have maintained much of their power, local news has been suffering. The growth of *news deserts*—communities without dedicated local media coverage, usually due to newspaper closures—are associated with increased polarization, lower political knowledge about one's own representatives, and the further nationalization of political news.[45]

Technology and the Truth

A major element of news' future is likely to be wrapped up in deciding what is true. Over the past decade and a half, fact-checking journalism has exploded. Digital-only sites like Politifact and FactCheck.org hold equal or greater prominence to *The Washington Post's* fact-checker in the United States. The International Fact-Checking Network now certifies fact-checking organizations across the globe based upon the frequency of fact-checks organizations produce, how transparent they are about their funding, reporters, fact-checking process, political activism, and corrections policies. Rather than reporting claims from competing political perspectives and *leaving it there* before the commercial break, fact-checking organizations directly tell their audience whether claims newsworthy people make are true.

Technological advances are making it easier for people to engage in *deep fakes*, which use artificial intelligence to combine images and video from one or more sources to make it look like evidence of another source engaging in that rhetoric (imagine one of the authors of this text recording themselves saying that the Minnesota Vikings are the greatest franchise in NFL history, but using deep fake technology to make it look like Green Bay Packers quarterback Aaron Rodgers was saying it . . .). As deep fake technology improves, it is likely that it will be used to try and embarrass political enemies in campaigns and other contexts. News organizations will be on the front lines of helping citizens determine what is real and what is not. It is not hard to imagine fake video potentially derailing a major political campaign, nor is it hard to imagine real video of nefarious activities passed off as a deep fake (e.g. Anthony Weiner initially claimed the lewd photos he shared were pictures that were stolen and altered).

More Interactivity

It is no secret that information flow is no longer one-directional. Digital media is interactive and is likely to remain so. Even traditional outlets are now encouraging feedback from their audience. Beyond how interactivity affects the news, the internet has been used as an effective tool to drive support and fundraising for a variety of causes. Political candidates raise $25 to $50 at a time from hundreds of thousands of web donors.

Interactivity also affects how people experience the news and newsworthy events. Second screening political news coverage has been shown to influence political participation. In particular, during the 2016 presidential campaign, those who second screened newscasts and had positive attitudes about Donald Trump were more likely to report engaging in political participation than second screeners who did not like Trump.[46] In a study examining second screening and the American and French presidential debates in 2012, political party–associated Twitter accounts helped shape discussion of the debates in real time, moving the spin room from backstage onto social media. In France and the United States, political and media elite accounts were heavily retweeted. In the United States, humorous tweets—such as those seeking to produce memes—also received a boatload of attention on Twitter.[47]

From Research to Real Life

How is an understanding of news models, journalistic norms, journalists' backgrounds and beliefs, and market forces and the news relevant to your life? First, understanding journalistic routines and models of newsmaking can help you understand why stories you encounter in the news media look the way that they do. More importantly, it can help you think about how you might want to pitch stories to reporters to get them interested in a topic that is personally important to you. Understanding elements of newsworthiness and how the beat system works can make you a more effective communicator with reporters that you are trying to get to cover a story.

Second, understanding who journalists are and how they approach their job can help you prepare for interviews you or the people you work with, represent, or are promoting will have. What kinds of things journalists are likely to ask about can be more accurately predicted by understanding the content of this chapter.

Third, for those of you looking to disrupt the system—it is crucial to understand what you are seeking to upend. What routines and norms would you want journalists to keep in the media company you might wish to start? Which ones would you jettison? What would you want to replace them with so that your own vision for a modern journalism might be reached?

In other words, understanding how the news is made will make you a more skillful user of the news and a more effective advocate during the times that you want to shape how a particular event is understood by reporters and their audience.

Conclusion

Despite a rapidly changing information ecology, a great deal of what becomes the news continues to be shaped by long-standing journalistic norms and organizational routines. Who reports the news that is seen by the most people, who gets covered, and what range of views are given the most attention have not changed at the rate many early adopters of the web predicted. Of course, there are now myriad alternatives to legacy media available for people. These sources serve a variety of needs from demographic representation to deep concerns with particular social problems. On the one hand, the media ecology is fragmenting. On the other hand, media power continues to be concentrated in a relatively small set of conglomerates.

News is shaped by all of these factors and more—including the demographic make-up of those reporting the news, audience demands and interactivity, and market forces. There is no singular reason for why the news is the way it is. That fact is one reason it is so difficult to change.

DIY Research

Kathleen Searles, Louisiana State University

Searles, K., & Banda, K. (forthcoming). But her emails! How journalistic preferences shaped election coverage in 2016. *Journalism*. Online First.

Kathleen Searles is a political communication professor in the Department of Political Science and the Manship School of Mass Communication at

Louisiana State University. Searles has published more than thirty academic journal articles, many of which are cited in this book, examining issues ranging from how journalists cover politics to how various communication devices affect how we pay attention to the news to how campaigns use emotional appeals in advertising. She is an editorial board member of the terrific site #WomenAlsoKnowStuff, which makes it easier for journalists and scholars to locate women experts in political science to cite in research and quote in news stories. Her article, written with Kevin Banda—a political science professor at Texas Tech University who studies how candidates interact, campaign advertising, and the influence of partisan polarization on public opinion— examines coverage of the 2016 presidential election to understand how journalists prioritize newsworthy information. The article is new, innovative, and sure to be influential for political communication scholars, and, hopefully, journalists, in the years to come. Our Q&A with Searles, conducted over email, is below:

Wagner and Perryman: In an election season where the stories that focused on qualifications, experience, and ideas all favored Hillary Clinton, what does your research show were the reasons why coverage, in your words, ended up with a "balance of news stories that favored Trump"?

Searles: In this article we wanted to better understand the *preferences* of journalists, in other words, beyond picking and choosing stories, how do journalists rank-order the stories they cover? To that end, we compared the relative volume of three types of news stories for each of the two major party candidates during the 2016 US presidential election—horse race, issue, and scandal. Unsurprisingly, we found that media outlets were more likely to cover the horse race for both Trump and Clinton, suggesting an overall journalistic preference for such stories. However, we also found that media outlets were disproportionately more likely to cover Clinton's scandals relative to Trump's scandals. We conclude that, inasmuch as scandal coverage is not positive for candidates, an overall balance of stories that emphasized Clinton scandals may have inadvertently favored Trump.

Wagner and Perryman: What are some of the major questions you were left with about how journalists prioritize their work after wrapping up this research article?

Searles: The model we pose of *rational journalistic preferences* proved explanatory in an American presidential election context. However, in ideal circumstances we could test this same model for other election years, for other election types (e.g., gubernatorial, state), and in other countries. Our results

(Continued)

(Continued)

also bring up more normative questions regarding how news outlets invest in scandal coverage. While we theorize (and the data support) that media outlets assign resources to frontrunners because such an investment allows them to economize with limited budgets, in 2016, this means that two major party candidates—both plagued by scandal—received different coverage. How news organizations can avoid such issues in the future remains an open question.

Wagner and Perryman: What kinds of things could students interested in your work do on their own to try and advance knowledge in this area in a small-scale way?

Searles: Sponsored by the Shorenstein Center, Dr. Thomas Patterson has produced wonderful reports on media coverage of the 2016 presidential election that are publicly available and written for a lay audience (authors' note: we rely on this data for much of our discussion of the 2016 election in Chapter 9). Students can also use the model we pose as a jumping-off point for thinking about other subject areas they find of interest that also may be shaped by journalistic preference, for example, science coverage or crime coverage. A cautionary note: This model does not dictate that journalists always behave rationally (none of us do!) but gives us a framework for generating predictions given complex circumstances. Once you think of it that way, the possibilities are seemingly endless.

Wagner and Perryman: What is your advice for students assigned to group projects who are coauthoring research papers for their class?

Searles: First, find a subject matter that interests you and second, think through the *how* you would test a possible research question. There are many projects we would like to do (this is true for all of us!), but there isn't available data, or we don't have the right skill sets to test that question. In other words, balance the needs of your intellectual curiosity against the constraints of the task!

How Can I Help?

Rosario Dominguez, Univision Chicago

A child of immigrants to the United States, Rosario Dominguez is a reporter for Univision Chicago. Earlier in her career, she served as the David Maraniss

Fellow at the *Capital Times* newspaper in Madison, WI, an intern at CNN En Español, and a television reporter at CBS 31 (WMBD-TV) in Peoria, IL. A bilingual journalist with print and online experience, Dominguez now tells stories in English and Spanish for television news audiences. We interviewed Dominguez over email.

Wagner and Perryman: What drew you to broadcast journalism as a career?

Dominguez: Watching Spanish news was a daily routine for my family and I while I was growing up in Chicago. I always enjoyed being informed and staying up to date with current events. While I was pursuing my undergraduate degree (Dominguez later earned a MA degree in Journalism), I learned about storytelling through video and found myself producing short videos about my Mexican community, to a predominantly white classroom. My passion for video and storytelling seemed to draw me to broadcast journalism.

Wagner and Perryman: How did you get your internship at CNN En Español? What should students expect to do on internships?

Dominguez: I applied to multiple internship positions at CNN without really believing I would get it. I had met a CNN recruiter at a conference. I followed up with her to let her know I had applied. It is still unclear to me if she had an influence, but I believe networking is very important for landing an internship like this one. Students should expect to have to push to do more than shadow or sit on a desk and do minimal work. Use this time to meet as many people as you can and work hard to do more than what they ask you for.

Wagner and Perryman: What are your favorite stories to tell?

Dominguez: My favorite stories to tell are of those who are in the margins, whose story is not often told. I love stories that focus on humans and the impact they are making. I also enjoy telling stories that help break stereotypes and barriers. Most importantly, I like to inform my audience of people or events going on, that they otherwise wouldn't hear from because they are not part of their world.

Wagner and Perryman: What are the similarities and differences involved in reporting a TV story in Spanish as compared to one in English?

Dominguez: The news-gathering phase of reporting in Spanish and English is basically the same. A main difference is that a story has to be modified depending on the audience. Some sound bites can be more relevant for a Spanish-speaking audience than for an English-speaking audience.

(Continued)

(Continued)

Challenges come when you have written the script in one language and have to translate it. It is a process that can take time to produce accurately. Often times, news managers don't understand how time consuming it can be. They are treated as one single story when in reality, it's two separate stories.

Wagner and Perryman: What advice do you have for students looking to have a career in TV news?

Dominguez: Set foot in a newsroom as soon as you can whether it's an internship or part-time job. This will help you see what it entails, and you will know if this is really something you want to pursue. Work on a video reel showcasing your on-air presence and reporting skills because it's what will help you land a job. Most importantly, build a strong support network with mentors and family members and always take care of yourself no matter what!

3

The Communication Ecology

Information Flows and Public Opinion

"FALSEHOOD FLIES, AND THE TRUTH COMES LIMPING AFTER IT." These words, written by Jonathan Swift in 1710, highlight the importance of how information flows through our communication ecology. If false information spreads faster than true information, the implications for what we know and how we behave are both vast and worrisome. Swift's words appear prescient in the age of social media. For example, just after the 2016 presidential election, Eric Tucker—an Austin, Texas, man with about forty Twitter followers—took a photo of what he thought were paid protesters being bussed to grouse at President-elect Donald Trump, tweeting a series of photos of buses as evidence of #fakeprotests.

Though the buses were for a conference hosted by a company called Tableau Software and had nothing at all to do with protesting Donald Trump, people immediately began sharing the conspiracy theory on sources like Reddit. Later that evening, some of the 300+ commenters blamed the busses on liberal billionaire philanthropist George Soros. The next morning, the conservative discussion forum Free Republic linked to the Reddit thread about Tucker's tweet. The post was shared thousands of times.

Reporters started catching wind of the story, but they quickly learned there was a problem with the bussed protestors narrative. The bus company said that they had no involvement at all in any potential protests. Even so, the story then made its way to Gateway Pundit, a popular conservative blog. After that, the President-elect of the United States weighed in himself, on his favorite social media platform.

The next day, a spokesperson for the software company told local news reporters that the buses were connected to a conference, not protests. Tucker, to his credit, posted again—this time to clearly note that his original message was false. All the while, the original, inaccurate post was still being shared all over Facebook and the conservative blogosphere. After thousands of retweets and shares to what ended up being false information that stoked the partisan ire of Trump supporters, his correction tweet earned less than thirty retweets.

Donald J. Trump ✔
@realDonaldTrump

Just had a very open and successful presidential election. Now professional protesters, incited by the media, are protesting. Very unfair!

6:19 PM · Nov 10, 2016 · Twitter for Android

| **Photo 3.1 Trump Tweet**

When false claims like the one Tucker shared flow through the communication ecology, it can shape attitudes in multiple ways. After all, the story appeared on Twitter, blogs, and conservative news outlets before being corrected by more traditional news sources—though research shows that naming the false claim as it is being debunked can backfire so that people believe the false claim anyway. People sharing the information believing it to be true are likely to believe that future protests against President Trump are phony as well. They might also believe that there is not a meaningful opposition to the president since what they might remember from the bussed-in protestors blip is people on the other side have to pay fake protestors to criticize the president.

In this chapter, we will work to unpack how information flows in the contemporary communication ecology. Then, we will explore the current lay of the land and describe various news platforms, paying attention to who uses them and to what effect. Finally, the chapter will examine how information flows through different networks—those of journalists, political leaders, and the public—to develop an understanding of how where people are situated in the communication ecology influences what they believe, what they want, and how they participate.

The Twenty-First-Century Communication Ecology: An Early Check-In

Twentieth-century political communication research largely conceived of mass media effects as top-down, unidirectional processes. Politicians and other important actors would create messages that filtered through a small number of elite mass media sources to influence the public. Despite the fact that interpersonal communication had the power to moderate media effects, something that can be traced as far back as the *two-step flow* from Lazarsfeld et al., in the 1940s, scholars in the second half of the century tended to discount or even outright ignore the role of interpersonal communication. But toward the end of the last century, after major changes in technology that fundamentally altered how people could choose to engage, or not, in political communication, scholars developed a renewed interest in the intersection of mass and interpersonal factors. By doing so, they offered an important corrective that recognized that media influence is mediated by message flows among elites, as well as the audience, both face-to-face and online.

However, our contemporary communication ecology has changed in some pretty radical ways, necessitating a more significant rethinking of the nature of information flow and mass communication effects. In particular, researchers argue that the changes demand greater consideration of interpersonal communication processes and how that interacts with the news media ecosystem.[1] The emergence of the internet and social media are enormously consequential changes to the communication ecology, influencing the flow of news content, the increasingly conditional nature of media effects, and the ability of the audience to generate content on their own. The potential of digital media users to become content producers in their own right shifts, at least in part, the focus of mass communication research from what the news media do to people to what people do to the media.[2]

As noted in Chapter 2, what constitutes *the news media* has changed in a number of significant ways over time and continues to vary in the minds of anyone we might ask to define it. Digital media have shifted the emphasis of news media from providing information toward providing entertainment and opinions.[3] For example, cable television outlets that cover politics are producing a smaller number of traditional TV news packages and replacing them with formats featuring live discussion among partisan advocates and, occasionally, experts.[4] These experts have regular spots on TV and maintain active social media profiles where they interact with their audiences about current events.

These kinds of changes ushered in a set of newer media practices that carry with them a number of political implications. The clear line demarcating mainstream and alternative media that characterized the twentieth-century model is blurry in the twenty-first century. The news media itself are generally moving from serving mass audiences to niche audiences.[5] As such, its content is less likely to be building consensus-oriented messages. Instead, contemporary news media messages are developing an orientation toward exclusive, conflict-oriented messages.[6] Some news organizations have abandoned traditional norms of news objectivity, neutrality, and fact-based reporting in favor of a focus on partisan opinion, ideological expression, and dramatic conflict.[7] While scholarly critics of the news media spent the twentieth century criticizing the news media for failing to adjudicate the truth,[8] a variety of news outlets, especially those on the far right and left, now actively construct the *truth* to align with their partisan leanings. Others engage in fact-checking journalism that involves journalists directly weighting in on the veracity of statements made by political elites. The media's power remains strong, but it is decentralizing, with political blogs' content, niche news sites, audiences' information search patterns on platforms like Google and traditional mainstream news coverage helping to set the news agenda.[9]

As the news media system continues evolving in rapid and meaningful ways, the nature of media audiences is changing too. In the twentieth-century media system, audience members were generally information receivers. They did not have a large set of choices from which to select their news or talk back to their content providers. Moreover, market pressures generally led news organizations to provide relatively homogenous news, producing a shared common knowledge base. Typically, audience members received messages in isolation from other audience members. If they responded to a reporter or news organization, it was in a letter to the editor or a private phone call.

Today, media exposure is much more fragmented and selective. Audiences can actively seek content that fits their motivations and predispositions, though they do not always do so.[10] Media content is commonly experienced online, with audience members reacting and sharing their interpretation of events in real-time on Facebook, Twitter, or Snapchat. Contemporary news media appear to track and respond to these dynamics.[11] Audience members now create and send messages to one another, solidifying relatively homogeneous social networks—though research suggests that those who have more heterogeneous networks are less polarized and are more likely to split their tickets when they vote.[12]

As with most developments in communication technology and media behavior, changes in audience involvement with the information ecology raise some concerns for scholars. The expanding set of information options and the partisan nature of news media have led many audience members to attempt to tailor their news repertoires to messages that are consistent with their own political predispositions.[13] As the media choices and content exposure of audience members have withdrawn into more ideologically homogeneous niches, examples of divergent realities have emerged for important issues, such as climate change. Under the twentieth-century media system, media users from different ideological perspectives were more likely to share a basic set of facts that they generally believed constituted reality. This is not to say that people always agreed with each other or did not engage in motivated reasoning as they processed the information they consumed (see Chapters 6 and 7). Partisan audiences have always, and continue to, view balanced news coverage as hostile to their views—even believing that the coverage does not affect them as much as it does others.[14]

In the past, political elites followed party-established platforms, disseminated information that was indexed (see Chapter 2) by the mainstream media, and set the public's agenda.[15] Now, even in a deeply polarized elite environment, partisan politicians cultivate and mobilize online followers to amplify their message, a change from how they used to behave online.[16] In short, while the flow of information through the communication ecology was once top-down and unidirectional, it can no longer be characterized so simply.

Centralized news media gatekeeping and unidirectional agenda-setting have been replaced by more decentralized processes and platforms that take some power away from media as the main arbitrators of shared reality. Today's communication ecology is more geared toward a system governed by partisanship, selective exposure to ideologically favored sources, activism, and conflicting realities. Expression and other kinds of political participation now play important roles of both cause and effect with the news media. In order to understand information flow in the contemporary ecology, then, it is important to understand how information flow is structured.

The Structure of the Communication Ecology

While it is certainly true that the communication environment has changed a great deal in the last twenty years, many foundational elements of the communication ecology remain in place, even if they are not as dominant as they once were.

Newspapers

Newspapers are probably the most critical part of the communication ecology. Newspapers, in print and digital form, provide impressive depth of coverage across several topics important to audiences who want to be engaged citizens of a republican democracy. They also, more often than not, are the first mover in terms of setting the rest of the news media's agenda.

About thirty-one million people read a daily print or digital paper in 2017.[17] This is about a 10 percent decline from 2016. About thirty million fewer people read the daily paper than did so in 1980. While the numbers are only about ten million less than in 1940, a time before television took off, the US population was not even half as large as it is today.

In other words, the percentage of people who read a paper was extraordinarily higher in the mid-twentieth century than it is today.

The economics of newspapers are changing as well. While advertising revenue generated almost $50 billion for the newspaper industry in 2000, that was down to less than $16 billion in recent years.[18] Concomitantly, newsroom employment dropped 23 percent over the past decade.[19] Over the past fifteen years, more than one in five papers have closed. About half of the 3,143 counties in the United States have one newspaper, usually a weekly, trying to cover the news for its audience.[20] Nearly two hundred counties do not have a newspaper and many papers that do survive are *ghost papers* that have minimal, at best, coverage of local and regional politics.

Who owns the papers that do survive? The twenty-five largest newspaper companies own two-thirds of the nation's daily newspapers. Recall from Chapter 2 that these papers are systematically less likely to provide issue coverage and more likely to cover politics negatively. This is important as, traditionally, newspaper use has decreased gaps in political knowledge for the less educated. That is, when people without college degrees read newspapers regularly, they know about as much about politics as moderately educated people who use newspapers regularly. Across a variety of issues, the volume of media coverage, as well as the breadth and prominence of that coverage, contribute to positive changes in the level of issue-specific knowledge among the American public.[21]

Higher newspaper use is also associated with greater political participation.[22] Research also finds, however, that those with higher education learn more about politics from newspapers than the less educated. In high coverage environments, as compared to environments with little newspaper coverage, the gap between what the highly educated and less educated know about politics *increases*, though both scores go up.[23] Whether these findings will continue to replicate if the newspaper audience shrinks is an open question.

A major report to the Federal Communications Commission addressing the critical information needs of the American citizenry, and whether they are being met, concluded that traditional media outlets have yet to find a solid business model and remain on a downward path. Even so, traditional media like newspapers are still providing the bulk of the news that circulates through the media ecosystem.[24]

Radio and Podcasting

The audio news sector of the American media ecology is growing. Radio consists of terrestrial (AM/FM) radio, satellite radio, and digital podcasts. Ninety-two percent of people over the age of twelve listen to AM/FM radio each week. More than half of the public listens to radio online at least once a week. Podcasts are growing in popularity as well. Nearly half of the public has at least listened to one and about a quarter of the public do so on a monthly basis.[25] While newspaper revenue is declining, radio station revenues are largely flat over the past decade. Even so, automation and other factors have led to a decrease of around nine hundred radio jobs since 2004.

As is the case with newspapers, radio stations are mostly owned by a small number of giant corporations like Entercom, CBS Corp., Hubbard Broadcasting, and the Sinclair Broadcast Group. Many of these stations air hours of *outrage* talk radio each day where hosts use emotional language and an in-your-face style to keep their audiences in a lather. In Wisconsin, for example, more than eighty hours of conservative talk radio are on the air, across various stations of course, over the course of any single weekday. Research from Sarah Sobieraj and Jeffrey Berry[26] finds that conservative talk radio engages in a high percentage of *outrage* content, something that Chapter 9 addresses in more detail. How does this kind of programming affect what people know? As is often the case, the answer is that it depends. On the one hand, active talk radio listeners tend to have higher levels of overall political knowledge. On the other hand, frequent conservative talk radio listeners were also more likely to believe misinformation.[27] Talk radio is an important component of the conservative media ecosystem.[28] Liberals, on the other hand, tend to enjoy public radio programming. Even so, liberals and conservatives were found, in a 2008 study, to have somewhat similar media repertoires.

Local Television News

Per usual, local television remains the most likely source for Americans to get their news. Even so, local TV news audiences are declining—even as local TV stations generated more revenue on the backs of advertising dollars from candidates seeking office in the 2018 midterms.[29] Late local news audiences dropped eight hundred thousand viewers across the country from 2016 to 2018. Advertising revenues continue to inch higher in election years and remain relatively stable in nonelection years.[30]

As of 2018, 703 local TV newsrooms created news for 1,072 local TV stations.[31] The actual number of hours local TV news airs is on the rise as many local stations are adopting a late afternoon newscast to go with their two newscasts that are sandwiched around the network evening news and their late local newscast. As with newspapers and radio, local TV stations are owned by a small number of large corporations. In 2018, 144 local stations were sold, mostly to larger companies—a $4.7 billion (and thirty-seven station) increase over the previous year.

Local news is a critical resource for citizens in the communication ecology. Research shows that the more attention local journalists devote to a political campaign, the more competitive it tends to be. Of course, journalists are more likely to cover competitive races, so the association may not be a causal one.[32] On the bright side, the more competitive the congressional campaign, the more likely that reporters cover candidate issue positions, which could help foster greater knowledge and participation among voters.[33] This is important, as a study from Danny Hayes and Jennifer Lawless found that a diminished news environment literally depresses civic engagement. Citizens who saw a lower volume of local coverage were less able to evaluate their representative in the House, less likely to express opinions about candidates for Congress in their districts, and, remarkably, less likely to vote. These results held for individuals regardless of levels of political knowledge, revealing that the damaging consequences of a decline in local coverage are widespread and not merely something that happens to less interested and attentive people.[34]

Regarding the critical information needs of the citizenry, the report to the FCC mentioned above notes that, in general, local television news is not meeting the critical information needs of the public. In fact, there is reason to think the provision of critically important issue coverage is on the decline. Combining your knowledge of the organizational and deadline pressures on journalists that were described in Chapter 2 with the increase in the number of hours of information local news stations are airing, something has to give. What is giving, apparently, is coverage of important issues. Given the importance of local television to civic engagement, this is particularly troubling.

Network Broadcast Television

Not to sound like a broken record, but network TV news audiences declined from 2016 to 2018 as well, though the rate of decline seems to be flattening out.[35] By network television, we mean NBC, ABC, and CBS national news. Each network airs newscasts on a national morning show and during a half-hour evening news broadcast. For decades, network TV news was king, bringing in more than 10 to 15 million viewers per night on each station.[36] Now, network newscasts garner a few more than five million sets of eyeballs each night. Advertising revenue has been steady for the past five years. Watching network news on the web is growing in popularity.

A Pew Research Center study in 2017 revealed that 37 percent of younger adults who like watching the news instead of reading it prefer to do so online. Still, television continues to be used more than mobile phones by citizens across the globe seeking to follow politics.[37] A study led by Stephanie Edgerly showed the young people watch network television news more than they read national and local newspapers, watch satirical cable programs like *The Daily Show*, visit news aggregator sites on the web, and receive news via social networks.[38]

Cable Television

Cable news channels like CNN, Fox News, and MSNBC cater to narrower audiences than the networks do. As such, their viewership is smaller. The 2019 State of the News Media report from the Pew Research Center showed that the average viewership in primetime for a cable news channel is just over a million people.[39] Even the highest rated programs, such as Fox News' *Hannity*, have about three million viewers per night.

Cable television has a more complicated relationship with the notion of objectivity that drives newspaper reporters and local TV and network TV reporters. Some journalists working at cable networks do their jobs in much the same way as reporters at more traditional outlets. However, cable television, especially in prime time, is a host-driven medium. Show hosts like Rachel Maddow on MSNBC and Sean Hannity on Fox News are not bound by the same norms of objectivity that reporters working on the same networks work under in their jobs. Certainly, we should expect the hosts to say things that are true, producing evidence for the opinionated claims that they make. But, the nonpartisan gloves are off of cable TV hosts as they are often advocating for a particular ideological and partisan perspective—one shared by the lion's share of their audience.

Figure 3.1 highlights demographic differences between local TV, network TV, and cable TV news consumers. Column one of the figure shows that local TV earns the highest percentage of viewers, even though it is still not approaching a majority of adults in the United States. Women watch more local news than men and there is a pointed demarcation in viewers by age. Forty percent of those between 50 and 64 watch local news often while 57 percent of those at retirement age and older watch local news. Not quite one-fifth of people between 18 and 29 are avid watchers of local television. Nonwhite adults are more likely than white adults to watch as well.

It is easy to see how television viewing is a bit of a knowledge gap closer for the less well educated. Those who stopped schooling at or before high school are nearly twice as likely to watch local TV news as those who graduated from college. Remember that those without a college education are more likely to reduce the knowledge gap with the well-educated when they regularly use local news. Finally, there is not much of a partisan difference in local TV news viewing.

The middle column of Figure 3.1 shows that fewer people are regular viewers of network TV as compared to cable TV. Moreover, slightly fewer people reported watching network TV often as compared to cable news. Additionally, more Democrats than Republicans watch network TV news (30 to 21 percent). In Chapter 7, we will spend more time on biases exhibited by media audiences, but for now, it is enough to know that conservatives and Republicans are less trusting of mainstream media than liberals and Democrats. As such, it is not surprising that they are less likely to

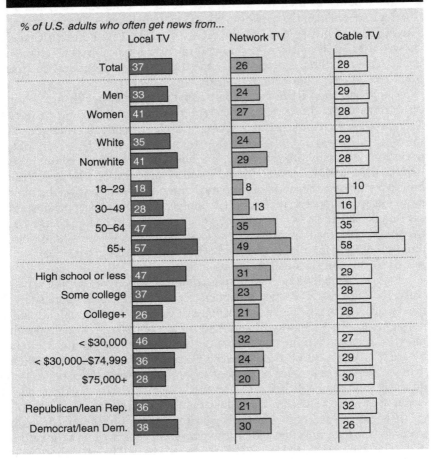

Figure 3.1 Demographics of Television News Viewers

% of U.S. adults who often get news from...

	Local TV	Network TV	Cable TV
Total	37	26	28
Men	33	24	29
Women	41	27	28
White	35	24	29
Nonwhite	41	29	28
18–29	18	8	10
30–49	28	13	16
50–64	47	35	35
65+	57	49	58
High school or less	47	31	29
Some college	37	23	28
College+	26	21	28
< $30,000	46	32	27
< $30,000–$74,999	36	24	29
$75,000+	28	20	30
Republican/lean Rep.	36	21	32
Democrat/lean Dem.	38	30	26

Source: https://www.pewresearch.org/fact-tank/2018/01/05/fewer-americans-rely-on-tv-news
-what-type-they-watch-varies-by-who-they-are/.

watch network news. Nonwhite people are a bit more likely to watch network news than white people.

Network TV is on life support with 18-to-29-year-olds whereas about half of people 65 and older watch regularly. Once again, there is an education gap with network TV news viewing. About one in three people without any college experience watch network news while about one in five college graduates watch often. As with local news, those with lower incomes are more likely to watch as well.

The third column of Figure 3.1 reports who watches cable news. Notice that the gender gap, education gap, white/nonwhite gap, and income gaps generally disappear for general cable viewing. Young adults are still the least likely age group to watch cable news. Republicans watch more cable news than Democrats. In particular, they watch Fox News.[40]

A 2014 Pew Research Center survey found that individuals who held conservative views on both economic and social issues chose Fox News (47 percent) as their main source of news. Radio came in second at 11 percent. For those with the reverse set of views, those who were liberal across both economic and social issues, CNN was number one (15 percent), but National Public Radio (13 percent), MSNBC (12 percent), the New York Times (10 percent), and local TV (5 percent) were close behind. People with a more mixed set of preferences watched CNN the most (20 percent), with local TV (16 percent), Fox News (8 percent), Yahoo News (7 percent), and Google news (6 percent) close behind.[41]

The results about which sources these different ideological groups trust are noteworthy as well. Consistent liberals had more trust than distrust for most mainstream, web, and cable sources, except for Fox News. Conservatives distrusted NPR, PBS, the three major TV networks, CNN, USA Today, The New York Times, The Washington Post, and several other sources. The only source all groups exhibited more trust than distrust for was The Wall Street Journal and the only source all groups expressed more distrust than trust for was Buzzfeed.

Hispanic and African American News

While the fragmentation of the media ecology has meant that there are fewer opportunities for all citizens to see the same news at the same time, it has also expanded the opportunities for news organizations who seek to serve a particular racial or ethnic population. Viewership for Univision and Telemundo (the United States' two largest Spanish-speaking stations) earns nearly the same number of viewers each prime time period as Fox News, CNN, and MSNBC do. Hispanic-serving newspaper circulation has decreased slightly over the past five years in Los Angeles, but has generally held steady in other locales like Miami and New York.[42]

Black-oriented newspapers have a long tradition in the United States. Papers like the Chicago Defender, founded in 1905, played an important role in the "Great Migration" of Black Americans from the South to the more urban North of the United States. There are about 170 members of the Black Press trade association but circulation numbers for each are hard to come by. The 2019 State of the Media report from the Pew Research Center shows considerable variance in the health of black-oriented newspapers. Papers such as the Michigan Chronicle and the Chicago Defender have grown in circulation over the past decade while others, like the New

Pittsburgh Courier, have seen circulation drop. Regarding Hispanic and African American presence in newsrooms, the Pew study mirrors the study examined in Chapter 2, showing a relatively flat line of representation for both groups over the past twenty years.[43]

Digital News

Ninety-three percent of adults get at least some news online. Unlike most other major sources of news, the advertising revenue for digital news continues to grow. The average number of unique visitors to digital-native outlets was about three million people more in 2017 than it was in 2014. At the same time, the number of newsroom employees in digital-native news outlets is on the *rise*—almost twice as high in 2017 as it was in 2008. A majority of the highest-traffic digital-native news organizations has apps for either iOS or Android (or both)—the two main mobile platforms. Just as a few large companies control a majority of the nation's newspapers, local TV, network TV, and cable TV outlets, a small number of companies dominate the digital sector. Facebook gets about half of mobile digital display advertising revenue, for example.

Just as with any other resource, there is a divide with respect to who has access to digital news. A 2011 study found that socioeconomic status was more strongly related to the informational use of the internet than with that of the traditional media, especially newspapers and television. Even more noteworthy, the differential use of the internet was associated with a greater knowledge gap than that of the traditional media.[44] Internet access and online exposure to election information were shown to be consequential for political knowledge and participation as well.[45]

Social Media

Social media has fundamentally changed how information flows in democratic societies. That said, it is important to remember that social media users are not perfect proxies for the public at large. While over two-thirds of the American public has a Facebook account, just over 20 percent use Twitter. Of those, about 10 percent of Twitter users account for 80 percent of the content on the platform.[46] Moreover, most of the information shared on these sites via links comes from more mainstream outlets. Figure 3.2 shows that Facebook, YouTube, Twitter, Instagram, Snapchat, and LinkedIn users report that they get a fair amount of information from the traditional sources we described above. News websites are the most used sources of information by social media users across the board. Local television news is also a fixture of information seeking for social media users. Not surprisingly, those who use social media report getting less of their information from newspapers, but keep in mind it is hard to measure

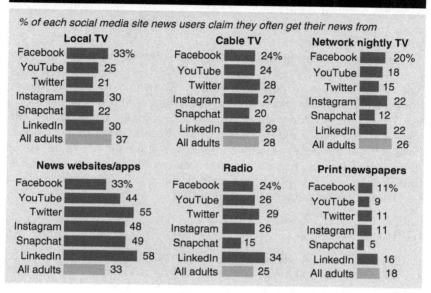

Figure 3.2 Use of Traditional News Platforms by Social Media Users

% of each social media site news users claim they often get their news from

Local TV		Cable TV		Network nightly TV	
Facebook	33%	Facebook	24%	Facebook	20%
YouTube	25	YouTube	24	YouTube	18
Twitter	21	Twitter	28	Twitter	15
Instagram	30	Instagram	27	Instagram	22
Snapchat	22	Snapchat	20	Snapchat	12
LinkedIn	30	LinkedIn	29	LinkedIn	22
All adults	37	All adults	28	All adults	26

News websites/apps		Radio		Print newspapers	
Facebook	33%	Facebook	24%	Facebook	11%
YouTube	44	YouTube	26	YouTube	9
Twitter	55	Twitter	29	Twitter	11
Instagram	48	Instagram	26	Instagram	11
Snapchat	49	Snapchat	15	Snapchat	5
LinkedIn	58	LinkedIn	34	LinkedIn	16
All adults	33	All adults	25	All adults	18

Source: https://www.journalism.org/2017/09/07/news-use-across-social-media-platforms-2017/.

Note: Reddit, Tumblr, and WhatsApp not shown.

newspaper use as survey respondents are often not sure if you are asking about trading a hard copy of a paper or its web version. For example, if you read the *New York Times* online today and the Pew Research Center called you tonight to ask if you read a newspaper today, would you say yes or no?

How do people use social media if they are interested in the news? A Pew exploratory study of 176 people who took a survey and allowed Pew to look at their tweets found that although most people do not tweet that often, more than half tweet about the news on occasion.[47] Of those folks, about 48 percent of their tweets were about the news. In general, people tend to create original content on Twitter, but those who also tweet about the news do more retweeting—that is, sharing news with people who follow them. News tweeters are also more active users of Twitter in general, have more followers, and follow more people. They also provide more links to URLs, include more photos, and use more hashtags than the general Twitter-using population. What news gets shared the most? Entertainment and sports news got shared more often than political news.

Social media use is also related to political engagement and participation. A study of 113 million Facebook status updates found that those living in battleground states are more likely to discuss politics than Facebook users in uncompetitive Electoral College states. In short, variation in the political environment in which people live affects day-to-day changes in how people experience politics, especially on social media. Posting political status updates was significantly related to voter turnout as well.[48] Another study revealed that seeing your friends share "I voted" status updates make you more likely to vote.

In addition to using social media more than in the past, people are using their mobile devices to keep up with the news. But is watching the *NBC Nightly News* or reading the *Wall Street Journal* on your phone having the same effects on you as if you were using those sources in the traditional way? In a word, no. Innovative eye-tracking research led by Johanna Dunaway and Kathleen Searles finds that people's attention to news on mobile devices is not the same as attention to news on computers.[49] While mobile phones or tablets may be some people's only opportunity to get some news, these devices curb people's attention, muting some of the positive effects that reading or watching the news can bring.

Talking Politics

Of course, before all of the available forms of news and social media existed, there was talking to others. Even in a mediated, interconnected world, there is still talking to each other. People talk about politics. Research examining political discussion networks has found that people living in cross-cutting social and political networks—living and working around, and talking with, people with whom individuals disagree politically—is related to holding more ambivalent political views. This can discourage political participation. Additionally, that politics is controversial can threaten social relationships.[50]

In her three books researching citizens who talk to each other about politics, political scientist Katherine Cramer has argued that by talking with and listening to people about politics, scholars can learn their perspectives, rather than just their preferences.[51] Her research for her book *The Politics of Resentment* led her to create the concept of rural consciousness—the identity some have as a rural person (no matter where they are from or end up living). Rural consciousness involves a strong perspective that distributive politics does not benefit you or your identity. It is also made up of resentment of cities and those who live in them, political and cultural elites, people of color, and partisan polarization. When one element of the resentment gets tapped into by a politician, it can activate other resentments that can be deployed by strategic politicians in electoral environments. Her example was Wisconsin governor Scott Walker, who sometimes communicated in ways that blamed people in cities and people of color for the problems rural people perceived.[52]

Consistent Conservatives More Likely to Have Close Friends Who Share Their Political Views

% who say . . .

- ■ Most close friends share my views on government and politics
- ▨ Some close friends share my views, but many don't
- ☐ I dont't really know what most close friends think

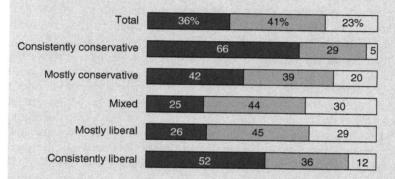

Total	36%	41%	23%
Consistently conservative	66	29	5
Mostly conservative	42	39	20
Mixed	25	44	30
Mostly liberal	26	45	29
Consistently liberal	52	36	12

But Consistent Liberals More Likely to Drop a Friend

% who stopped talking to/being friends with someone because of politics . . .

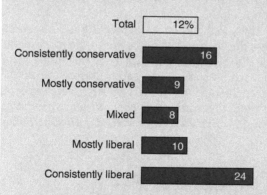

Total	12%
Consistently conservative	16
Mostly conservative	9
Mixed	8
Mostly liberal	10
Consistently liberal	24

American Trends Panal (wave 1). Survey conducted March 19-April 29, 2014. Q44, Q46. Based on web respondents. Ideological consistency based on a scale of 10 political values questions (See About the Survey for more details).

Source: https://www.journalism.org/2014/10/21/political-polarization-media-habits/

Walker himself was viewed so contentiously in the state, over one-third of people reported that they stopped talking to someone because of their views about the effort to use a recall election to remove Walker from office (it was unsuccessful).[53] Figure 3.3 shows that, nationally, those who have consistent preferences on both social and economic issues tend to have the most homogenous networks of political talk. Consistent liberals, though, were the most likely to end a friendship over politics.

"News Finds Me"

A prominent explanation for how people can be somewhat informed despite avoiding traditional news sources is the "news finds me" (NFM) orientation.[54] People who think news finds them believe they are well-informed about the news even though they do not actively follow it. They think that crucial information will find them through their general internet use, social networks, and general media use. People that news finds need not be uninterested in current events. Rather, they believe they do not need to actively seek news because their other behaviors end up giving them all the news they need to be informed. However, early research into the effects of NFM finds correlations between passive information receivers and low political knowledge. Potential dangers of thinking you are well-informed when you are not include being susceptible to conspiratorial thinking.[55] Recall that Russia made major efforts to stoke conspiracies and spread misinformation in the 2016 presidential race. For those who think that social media use, among other things, will help people stay informed, it is possible that they will be learning things from the news that finds them that has the virtue of being false.

Still, the increased selectivity and audience fragmentation of the modern media environment alters the agenda-setting power of the mass media via NFM behaviors as well. One experimental analysis that took place over time examined whether mainstream media can influence the public agenda when channeled through social media. Those who were exposed to political information incidentally, through Facebook, had their issue agendas affected via increasing the perceived importance of specific policy issues.[56]

Hybridization and Information Flow in the Communication Ecology

Information flow in the contemporary media environment is complex. Andrew Chadwick has found that the elements of what we think of as the *new* online media are hybridized with what is the supposedly *old* broadcast and print media. This *hybridization* affects power relations among those in the news. Integrating regular people into the construction of news at multiple points in the lifespan, or cycle, of an issue or story are now important characteristics of political communication.[57] Twitter is a newly important factor in generating and shaping news stories, but it is still largely directed by journalists and politicians as compared to citizens.[58]

In some instances, candidates for office use an individual, rather than partisan, style of social media campaigning. In Norway, the individual style was associated with more Twitter use but less Twitter influence from the candidates.[59] In 2016, in the United States, Donald Trump's hybrid media campaign revealed Trump to be enormously influential at generating media coverage on the heels of his Twitter audience retweeting him.[60] When Trump's news attention diminished, he was more likely to go on *tweet storms* that energized his audience, sending a signal to news outlets that there was something to cover here.

Events like political debates have become hybrid media events. Nontraditional political actors proved to be prominent hubs of spreading memes during the 2012 presidential debates. The memes became parts of news stories themselves, highlighting how viewers can be media objects as well.[61]

Political protests are also changing in the hybrid media environment. Communication is an important part of protest groups' organizational structure. In the hybrid media environment, scholars argue that two kinds of *logic* are at play. The first is the traditional logic of collective action. This is associated with high levels of organizational resources that work to form collective identities among protest group members. The second, the logic of *connective action*, is rooted in the sharing of personalized content across different mediated networks. Sharing is the crucial lynchpin of connective action.[62]

While sharing is crucial to connective action, sharing is not always done equally. When exposed to information about racial disparities, black and white individuals expressed different intentions to share the information on social media.[63] White students were less likely to express an intention to share information about racial disparities that affected black students. Black students see and share more content about race on social media as well.

Journalism in a Hybrid Media Ecology

In the era of instantaneous, online information, models of news are in flux.[64] What Alfred Hermida calls the *ambient journalism* that can come from *Twittering the news* raises questions for how journalists should use Twitter. Routine Twitter use has been shown to affect journalists' news judgment, which could result in them ignoring information that journalists who are not on Twitter would deem newsworthy. On the other hand, Twitter use among journalists has the potential, via their witnessing of social media sharing, to increase the diversity of opinions included in journalists' stories.[65]

Eli Skogerbø and Arne Krumsvik described intermedial agenda-setting in their research examining the relationship between social media and traditional news organizations in Norwegian elections. They showed that Facebook, Twitter, and YouTube are rarely used by professional journalists as source material for campaign stories whereas Norwegian parties were skilled at earning news stories in newspapers by creating local media events. While Norwegian campaigns use social media, journalists still rely on traditional behaviors associated with newsgathering.[66] Once again, an American counterexample to this is the 2016 campaign of Donald Trump. Trump's hybrid campaigning style generated coverage with traditional behaviors like campaign events and interviews, but his tweet storms and relationship with his followers mattered as well. Whether this is a Trump effect or the dawn of a new era of journalism and political campaigns remains an open question.

Twitter also affords journalists a chance to share a bit about who they are with their audience. Americans desire a strong connection between local journalists and the communities they serve. However, most people, especially Republicans, do not think that journalists should share their personal opinions about local issues on Twitter. There are also major partisan differences over whether criticism from reporters keeps elites from doing things that shouldn't be done. Thirty-eight percent of Republicans say such criticism keeps political leaders in line, compared with 82 percent of Democrats who favor journalists to play a watchdog role.[67]

Media Geography and Information Flow

Despite the affordances of modern technology, geography still affects what kind of news people are exposed to.

Figure 3.4 shows that urban dwellers are far more likely (61 percent) than rural residents (41 percent) to think that local news media cover the area where they live as compared to another area. Moreover, urban residents are more likely to think that the media is influential in their community as compared to rural residents as well. Even so, rural residents want journalists who are personally engaged in their communities at the same levels that urban and suburban residents do. Interestingly, there are not major differences in the issues that people wish to see the news media cover in their communities. However, there are major differences in how people view the importance of the internet in getting news, with 37 percent of urbanites claiming the web is the most important way to get local news as compared to 26 percent of rural folks.[68]

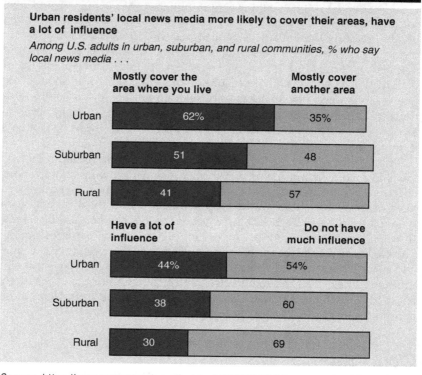

Figure 3.4 Geography and Perceptions of Local Media Attention

Urban residents' local news media more likely to cover their areas, have a lot of influence

Among U.S. adults in urban, suburban, and rural communities, % who say local news media . . .

	Mostly cover the area where you live	Mostly cover another area
Urban	62%	35%
Suburban	51	48
Rural	41	57

	Have a lot of influence	Do not have much influence
Urban	44%	54%
Suburban	38	60
Rural	30	69

Source: https://www.pewresearch.org/fact-tank/2019/04/12/for-many-rural-residents-in-u-s-local-news-media-mostly-dont-cover-the-area-where-they-live/.

Note: Respondents who did not give an answer are not shown.

Why the difference? One reason might be that rural residents are more likely to struggle with access to high-speed internet. A quarter of rural residents said it was still a major problem in 2018. Additionally, only 65 percent of rural residents own a smartphone as compared to 83 percent of urbanites and 78 percent of suburban residents.[69] Rural areas are also more likely to be home to news deserts, something we discuss in greater detail in Chapter 11.

From Research to Real Life

How do people know which media sources to seek out to learn something about a topic that matters to them? Understanding the roles played by different mediums of news in the information ecology can help you understand when you should be tuning into the local 10 p.m. television newscast, reading a national online outlet, or looking for a feature story in a monthly magazine for information about the topic that is on your mind.

Moreover, if you are looking to communicate with people in your own social network about the things you care about, understanding what types of news they are more likely to be using can help you understand how to meet people where they are at. Local television news watchers who avoid national news might need you to give them more information about major national issues while cable news junkies might need to hear about other points of view and how they might be relevant to the topic at hand. Additionally, understanding how information flows within a communication ecology can help you keep better tabs on which voices are being centered in important conversations and which ones are being left out.

Finally, being mindful of what your local communication ecology looks like can help you be on guard against some of the more deleterious effects that occur in particular environments. For instance, if you live in a news desert, you are now aware that you might be more likely to engage in more partisan polarized reasoning when asked to make political decisions. If, when given time to reflect, you do not prefer extreme partisanship, the knowledge of your place in the communication ecology can give you time and space for meaningful reflection. If you are one who has views that significantly differ from the status quo, you might embrace the opportunity afforded by living in a news desert to try and shape the attitudes of those around you to more closely match your own.

Conclusion

Within an individual's personal communication network, similar kinds of *curation* are undertaken by a variety of actors—not just traditional newsmakers but everyday media users, advertisers, and even computer algorithms. Understanding how these actors compete, intersect, and overlap is critical to understanding how information flow in the media ecology affects public opinion.[70]

DIY Research

Dhavan V. Shah, University of Wisconsin-Madison

Zhang, Y., Shah, D., Foley, J., Abhishek, A., Lukito, J., Suk, J., ... & Garlough, C. (2019). Whose lives matter? Mass shootings and social media discourses of sympathy and policy, 2012–2014. *Journal of Computer-Mediated Communication*, 24(4), 182–202.

Dhavan V. Shah is the Louis A. & Mary E. Maier-Bascom Professor at the University of Wisconsin-Madison where he directs the Mass Communication Research Center and is the scientific director for the Center for Health Enhancement System Studies (CHESS). His research focuses on how electronic and digital media affects social judgments, civic engagement, and health support. In some ways, all of the elements of his research agenda are on full display in the article we explore here. Shah and his collaborators analyzed social media responses to mass shootings from 2012 to 2014, finding that while the number of victims and child deaths predicted public outpourings of grief and calls for more gun control, mass shootings also consistently predicted social media calls for gun rights. Moreover, lives seemed to matter in differential ways—when black lives were the ones lost in mass shootings, there was less general sympathy expressed online and less policy discourse as well. Our conversation with Shah explored this article and examined ways to make collaborative research—a hallmark of Shah's career and of the MCRC he directs—fruitful.

Wagner and Perryman: One of the most striking findings of your coauthored study is that gun rights advocates outlast gun control supporters when it comes to social media discourse. What are the implications of that finding for gun policy?

Shah: It speaks to the difficulty of moving forward with gun control measures. The defense of gun rights on Twitter was more persistent than the demand for gun control, signaling to politicians and journalists that the gun rights advocates have a more passionate and active base of supporters. To maintain a persistent voice on social media presumably requires organizational effort. This finding suggests the critical importance of activists organizing themselves on social media to project a clear and strong voice.

Wagner and Perryman: How did you gather and code the data for this project? What would you say was the most important decision you made in the research design phase of the project—in terms of how that choice influenced what you found?

Shah: We collected Twitter data for this project through an archive that collects 10 percent of the global Twitter stream. We selected a set of keywords relating to mass shootings and gun policy discussions and then searched for all tweets containing one of those keywords.

The most important decision we made in the research design phase was distinguishing different discourse spurred by mass shooting events. Among the many different streams of related discourses, such as expressions of frustration

(Continued)

(Continued)

and anger, discussions about mental illness, and updates of breaking news, we decided to focus on expressions of sympathy in the form of *thoughts and prayers*, calls for more gun control, and defense of gun rights. We did so because they were the most prominent discourses, though other discourses merit attention as well.

Wagner and Perryman: If a student reading this book wanted to conduct an analysis of social media conversation on Twitter for a class research paper, what would you recommend they do to get started?

Shah: The social media conversation on many topics is often very large in volume. Sampling a small set of content and going through it first to develop a general idea of the scope of the different discourses. Besides understanding the content of the conversation, it might also be worthwhile to dig into the drivers of the conversation, including who the most prominent actors are who are generating the discourse. This can usually be measured by the number of retweets a particular post accumulated.

Wagner and Perryman: For students in group projects in their class—this article was a team effort, the calling card of MCRC research. What advice do you have for students beginning a collaborative project about how to work together to produce the best possible result?

Shah: First, each person should be given sufficient time to express their thoughts on the project. This not only creates a comfortable and intellectually stimulating environment but also benefits the project itself because different students see different aspects of a question and can offer insights that others cannot. Second, each person should try to contribute their expertise. A person does their work best when it is what they are interested in pursuing. This is also how students can best learn from each other. Third, planning and leadership are key to moving a project forward. Regular meetings with assigned roles and coordination are key to ensuring progress.

How Can I Help?

Jim Crounse, Ambrosino, Muir, Hansen, and Crounse: Political Consulting and Direct Mail

A top Democratic Party mail consultant, Jim Crounse directed the team that did direct mail for President Barack Obama in 2008 and 2012. Crounse also created direct mail for President Bill Clinton, US Senators Evan Bayh, Kent

Conrad, Byron Dorgan, Chris Dodd, and Jack Reed, among others. In 2008, Crounse led the transition team to confirm the nomination of Cabinet Secretary Timothy Geithner and US Trade Representative Ron Kirk. Crounse gives talks around the country about the art of direct mail advertising in politics. A Nebraska native, Crounse, along with his wife Patsy, founded a lecture series at the University of Nebraska that honors the late Congressman Peter Hoagland. Crounse served as Hoagland's Chief of Staff in the 1980s. Wagner spoke with Crounse over the phone and has produced an edited transcript of our conversation.

Wagner: What makes a direct mail piece effective?

Crounse: Many things go into defining a campaign, but I think there are three things that are especially important to think about. Number one, direct mail is a good option for some Senate races and House races and lower office races that are in television markets that are super expensive like Los Angeles, Chicago, and New York, so campaigns are not able to buy as much TV time as they would need to make it effective. Second, when campaigns are in cheaper media markets where they can air more ads, direct mail can help target voters who might be tuning out of all of the TV advertising. Third, you need to think about an identified target that you have found in polling. You might find out that women from 30 to 60 are a highly sought-after target and direct mail becomes a direct, efficient way to get at that group. You can do that with the internet, TV, and radio somewhat, but with mail you have a list of registered voters with voter files, giving you lots of ways to pick and choose who you mail.

Wagner: What have been some of your favorite direct mail pieces that you created for political candidates?

Crounse: I did a piece for Evan Bayh when he first ran for the Senate (in Indiana). He'd been governor for two terms and it was the year Mark McGwire and Sammy Sosa were having that home run battle. Sometimes, popular culture can be used to get people to pay attention to a campaign. The mail piece had a vintage baseball picture on the cover, saying "he broke all the records." Bayh had these amazing statistics of job creation and taxes and such. Each panel in the piece featured a worker like it was a baseball card that featured each different accomplishment. I got him to pose in a baseball bat and the final panel said Washington needs senator to hit a home run for them. He had a lot of people asking him to autograph that mail piece!

Wagner: Besides your award-winning (and campaign-winning) work in political advertising, you have served as a chief of staff for Democratic Senator

(Continued)

(Continued)

Max Baucus of Montana and the late Democratic Representative Peter Hoagland of Nebraska. What skills were most important to being effective in that job?

Crounse: Those jobs were different for a couple of reasons. I had a long personal relationship with Peter and it was my hometown and it was the House. Each of those three things meant the job was different than in the Senate. You've got to have a good relationship with the principal. You need leadership skills; you have to be able to motivate staff. Finally, you have to have a good understanding of the state and the city. I had that with Hoagland and Omaha. I had to learn that about Montana, and it was fun. I got to go out there a lot and learn the state and fall in love with it. You have to understand the rules of each of those institutions so you can get things done and in both of those instances, we were lucky enough to have Democrats in the majority, so we got some big things done.

Wagner: What advice do you have for people thinking about a career in politics?

Crounse: Dream big. You have to be willing to start at the bottom and be willing to work hard. If you are working hard, you have a better chance of being in the right place at the right time when opportunities come along. For example, I needed an assistant on a campaign and hired a young man who was doing some good work in local campaigns. He did a phenomenal job for me, which led me to recommend him for a position with Bill de Blasio (the Mayor of New York and a Democratic presidential candidate in the early 2020 primary season), which he received. Second, you have to have a good, clear answer for why you want to work in politics and what you want to do in politics. This helps me, and people like me, know which of my contacts in the business to connect you to, given your goals.

CHAPTER

4

Are Media Biased?

ARE NEWS MEDIA BIASED? The public certainly seems to think so. In a 2017 Gallup/Knight Foundation poll, a majority of Americans said they could not name an objective news source, nearly half (45 percent) said there is a great deal of political bias in news coverage, and 65 percent said that "too much bias in the reporting of news stories that are supposed to be objective" was a major problem.[1] When Gallup first asked its media trust question back in the 1970s, over 70 percent of Americans had confidence in the media. Today, nearly 70 percent say their trust in news media has declined over the past decade. When given the opportunity to explain why they do not trust certain news sources, 42 percent explicitly mention biased, slanted, or unfair reporting.

But is the widespread perception that media are biased accurate? In other words, are the people right? Are media indeed biased? And if so, how? To really answer these questions, we need to start with some definitions. In research, we'd call it *operationalizing* our key variables. In layman's terms, it means we all have to get on the same page about what it is we're talking about. We begin this chapter by defining both *media* and *bias*. We then turn our attention to understanding different types of bias and how it sneaks its way into news stories, or, in the case of openly partisan news, is deliberately employed to advantage a political perspective. We end with a discussion on fake news and how it has impacted perceptions of news media.

Defining Media

Let's start with the obvious. What do we mean by *media*? Recall from Chapter 1 that there is no such thing as *the media*.[2] The news industry is not monolithic. The first clue is that we use a plural verb when speaking about media. We ask, *are* media biased, not is "the media" biased. Journalists do not have a governing entity, a central means of communication, or a single boss blasting out instructions about which stories to cover and what that coverage should look like.

75

According to Pew Research Center's 2017 estimates, there are 88,000 reporters, editors, photographers, and videographers staffing US newsrooms across newspaper, radio, broadcast television, cable, and digital news outlets.[3] Think about your local media market. You likely have at least one daily or weekly newspaper, one or more local TV stations, some radio stations that provide news, digital news outlets, and possibly topical (politics, business) or community-oriented publications.

For national news, you have morning and evening programming from major broadcast TV networks (ABC, NBC, CBS), radio organizations such as NPR, cable news (CNN, MSNBC, Fox News), national newspapers (*The Washington Post*, *The New York Times*), wire services (Associated Press, Reuters), native online publications (The Huffington Post, Buzzfeed, Politico), and news magazines (*The New Yorker*, *Time*). Today, there are news podcasts, apps, aggregators, and video news services that stream only to YouTube or a smart TV. Factor in international news options, and there are hundreds, if not thousands, of news media outlets.

So what is the definition of media? Even terms meant to refer to a specific group of news outlets—terms like *mainstream media* or *major news outlets*—do not necessarily have a clear, shared meaning. Table 4.1 shows examples of the question wording that major polling agencies use when measuring public attitudes toward media. As you can see, even among researchers, there is not an agreed upon way to refer to the news industry.

Further complicating this puzzle is the fact that even if researchers agreed on what constitutes *the media*, it is unlikely that every consumer would be on board with that definition. You may immediately think of CNN and NBC's *Today Show* when you think of news, but how many people would say the same? With so many news choices today, it could easily be the case that each news consumer is thinking of their own preferred media outlet when they are asked to evaluate the news industry in a general sense.

In fact, it appears that people do not think of their own preferred news outlets when prompted to think of media. For example, in an experiment, one team of researchers found that media trust was much higher when respondents were asked to evaluate their preferred news outlets compared to when respondents were asked to evaluate unspecified media outlets. If people naturally thought of their preferred news outlets when evaluating *media*, we would not have seen that difference.[4]

The gap between evaluations of *own media* and *other media* is also evident in survey data. For example, Pew Research Center surveys repeatedly show that trust in local news organizations is higher than trust in national organizations.[5] Data from the Media Insight Project shows that even while people are skeptical of the media in abstract, they are far more positive about the media they personally use. The instinct to like your own version of something and dislike the general version of that thing is common in democratic societies. In the United States, the US Congress has incredibly

Table 4.1 Measuring Media Trust

Survey	Question Wording	Answer Choices
General Social Survey	I am going to name some institutions in their country. As far as the people running these institutions are concerned, would you say you have a great deal of confidence, only some confidence, or hardly any confidence at all in them? (Institution: the press)	A great deal, only some, hardly any
American National Election Studies	How much of the time can you trust the media to report the news fairly?	Just about always, most of the time, only some of the time, almost never
Pew Research Center	How much, if at all, do you trust the information you get from national news organizations?	A lot, some, not too much, not at all
Gallup	In general, how much trust and confidence do you have in the mass media—such as newspapers, TV, and radio—when it comes to reporting the news fully, accurately, and fairly?	Great deal, fair amount, not very much, none at all
Knight Foundation/ Gallup	What is your overall opinion of the news media in the United States today?	Very favorable, somewhat favorable, neutral, somewhat unfavorable, very unfavorable

low approval ratings despite most people also saying that they like their congressperson.[6] In fact, liking your own news sources may actually exacerbate perceptions that the media in general is biased. A study based on Wisconsin news consumers found that consuming like-minded news was linked to the perception that other media—the media *out there*—is biased. When people are evaluating *the media* as a whole, they do not appear to be basing their evaluations on the media outlets they use and trust.[7]

So what *are* people thinking about when they think about the media? Without a window into the mind, it is hard to know for sure, but it never hurts to simply ask. The Media Insight Project found that news consumers most often name cable news (48 percent) or broadcast TV (37 percent) when asked to name the media organizations that come to mind when they think about *news media*. Far fewer name local news (18 percent), national newspapers (16 percent), or social media (3 percent). When we asked people in our own research what they think of when they hear the words, *the media*, we found similar results, shown in Table 4.2. We first asked this question of a sample of US adults in a study from 2016, then asked it again in 2018. Note that hardly anyone mentioned local news, even though that is the news source people use and trust the most often (though local TV news use is declining).[8] As you can tell by looking at Table 4.2, cable news outlets were the most commonly named sources, especially CNN. Considering the audience size for cable news programming is around 3.5 times smaller than the audience size for nightly network TV (ABC, NBC, CBS), it may be the case that cable news has an outsized effect on perceptions of *media* as compared to the number of Americans actually using it.

With so many definitions of media, it's critical to clarify which *media* we're talking about when we investigate news bias. Many researchers focus on bias in individual news stories or coverage from a particular outlet. Others take a more holistic approach, assessing bias across a particular group of outlets such as nightly TV news programs, major newspapers, or local news organizations. Bias can also be examined for a particular news event, like a presidential election, across a sample of news outlets.

Table 4.2 Percentage of Respondents Mentioning Various News Sources

Source	2016	2018
CNN	40	41
MSNBC	2	14
Fox News	19	40
NBC	15	18
ABC	11	16
CBS	7	13
Newspapers	13	24
Local news	3	18

Notes. N = 885 for 2016 data, 845 for 2018 data.

It should be clear that the definition of media is flexible, making it difficult, if not impossible, to declare whether the US news industry as a whole is biased in any particular fashion—in terms of ideological orientation, level of commercialization, or anything else. What is more manageable is an investigation of individual news stories, coverage on a particular topic from a specific outlet or group of outlets, or news coverage across outlets on a particular topic during a specific time period. You will be looking for a long time if your goal is to find a reputable study that states: "We looked at all the political news coverage ever published and concluded that media are biased against Republicans." Rather, researchers might say: we examined a random sample of political news coverage on CNN, Fox News, and MSNBC in three presidential election years and found that Fox News tends to use words and phrases popular among Republican politicians, while MSNBC tends to use words and phrases popular among Democratic politicians.[9] The latter isn't as splashy, but it captures the nuance required in assessing media bias.

Defining Bias

The term *media* is tricky. *Bias* isn't much clearer. The term generally indicates a prejudice toward a particular person, group, or idea. It brings to mind a sense of unfairness or favoritism, something that seemingly contradicts the traditional journalism ideal of objectivity. Someone who claims a news story is biased may alternatively have said it was one-sided, played favorites, or was written with the intention of propping up one side. For example, a journalist who includes only the Republican perspective for a story on a proposed tax policy should not be surprised when accusations of bias start rolling in.

But such an obvious case—where a news practitioner completely omits one side while reporting on an important issue—is hardly the most common form of media bias. Bias also exists if a journalist uses a story frame favored by one political party (e.g., *undocumented* vs. *illegal* immigration), spends more time covering one political candidate than another, or demonstrates a preference for sensational stories over substantive ones. How much does a story have to favor one side before we label it *biased*? And what do we mean by *favor*—how do we quantify it? What if reality favors one side? A story about Super Bowl champions will not spend much time discussing the Minnesota Vikings. A story about Oscar winners is unlikely to mention Tara Reid. You'll probably find it unsurprising that there is no single way to define bias or measure it.

Partisan and Structural Bias

There are two major forms of journalistic bias: partisan and structural. Let's start with partisan bias, since it's the most familiar. Partisan bias occurs when a journalist's or news organization's political orientations result in the unequal treatment of the sides in a political conflict. This sort of bias might take the form of a gatekeeping bias, where editors devote more time or space to stories that benefit a particular party, candidate, or side of an issue. It could also result in a content bias, where the copy or structure of a story is seemingly unequal. *Unequal* is a tricky word here—and the next section will discuss how that term has been defined—but even with disagreements as to what constitutes unequal treatment, there is a general agreement that partisan bias is politically motivated unfair treatment of one *side*.

Republicans have been particularly skeptical about journalists' ability to report in a nonpartisan fashion. Data on journalists' political affiliations is hard to come by, but one team has tracked affiliations over decades.[10] The latest figures from 2013 indicate that a majority of journalists identify as Independents, 28 percent as Democrats, and just 7 percent as Republicans. That combined with evidence that when journalists donate to a political candidate, that candidate tends to be a Democrat,[11] provides fuel for the idea that there is a left-leaning bias across all US news outlets. The implication is often that because journalists are generally more liberal than conservative, their political values must be influencing their coverage (i.e., a partisan bias).

Critics argue that partisan bias is intentional. Seeing a week's worth of coverage on a story that reflects negatively on a Republican gubernatorial candidate, news consumers may believe liberal journalists are knowingly crafting stories to support their personal ideological preferences while delegitimizing alternative positions. But any observed partisan bias is just as likely to be unintentional. Creating news stories requires dozens of decisions regarding who to interview, who to quote, which quotes to use, how information is ordered, word choice, story length, etc. While journalists are trained to go about this process in a way that minimizes the chance of bias (e.g., gather as many perspectives as possible, lead with the most recent information, include quotes from multiple sources, fact-check all claims regardless of source), any one of those choices could introduce an unintentional bias into a story or coverage in general. For example, when a local mayor calls for a property tax increase to fund public schools, does the headline read "Mayor Proposes Property Tax Increase" or "Mayor Proposes Restoring Pre-Recession Property Tax Rates"? The mayor would certainly prefer the latter, so if a journalist uses the phrasing, have they committed partisan bias? Does intention matter, or just the outcome?

Research on partisan bias is mixed. One study revealed that the issues on which political parties have a better reputation (taxes for Republicans, for example) are issues where that party gets more coverage.[12] Political scientist Danny Hayes found that presidential candidates tend to get more favorable coverage on issues *owned* by their party.[13]

In a widely discussed study that tried to come up with a purely objective measure of media bias, political scientist and economist Tim Groseclose and economist Jeffrey Milyo argued that the mainstream news media are overwhelmingly liberal in their coverage of national and international affairs. The measure they invented to demonstrate this claim is a comparison of how often members of Congress cite particular think tanks when they are speaking in the House or Senate to how often the news media use those same think tanks in their reporting. Groseclose and Milyo found that media outlets are far more likely in their reporting to use think tanks favored by Democrats compared to those favored by Republicans.[14] Even the *Wall Street Journal*, a paper with a conservative editorial page, printed news coverage using think tanks favored by Democrats compared to those cited by Republicans.

Political scientist Brendan Nyhan has argued that Groseclose's evidence is not persuasive as liberal members of Congress tend to favor quoting nonpartisan think tanks, which feeds in to the media norm of balance in news coverage, while conservative lawmakers tended to cite think tanks with a clearly communicated conservative point of view. Nyhan argues that this is not evidence of media bias but a difference in lawmakers' preference for their sources of evidence.[15]

In contrast to partisan bias, structural bias refers to unequal treatment that can be explained by journalistic news values, newsroom routines, the commercial nature of the news business, limited resources, and everyday obstacles that journalists face when gathering information. An interview with a political candidate may be missing from a story because the candidate did not have time for an interview before the print deadline; a story on the Democratic primary race may receive far more coverage overall than the Republican primary because news organizations perceive it as more competitive; and a TV journalist may not include all the details on a viewpoint because it was too complex for a ninety-second story. Even following strict journalistic standards, the news production process can naturally result in unbalanced coverage. For example, independent and minor party candidates get much less attention in news coverage of elections.[16]

Even though they come about in very different ways, it is difficult to untangle structural and partisan bias. The outcome can often look the same, especially to a partisan reader who spies—what they believe to be—an unfair report.

More on Structural Biases

The commercial nature of news combined with journalistic norms produce a few notable nonpartisan, or structural, biases. The most obvious bias is toward what is new. Recent developments get more attention, and journalists are mindful about appearing current. You may be thinking, well, of course . . . news is *new* after all! But this seemingly logical preference may be responsible for frustrating aspects of coverage. For example, there is a well-documented bias toward horserace polling instead of substantive issue coverage during elections.[17] Knowing that newsrooms value new developments, is it any wonder that journalists opt for the latest polling data over a story repeating a candidate's plans once in office? Issue positions warrant coverage when they are first announced, when they are attacked, or when they are particularly controversial, but in the absence of updates, they are sure to fall from the headlines. Of course, time and resource restrictions also help explain why journalists shy away from issue-based stories and favor the low-hanging fruit of polling news.

Even polling stories can contain partisan biases. A study comparing when several television news organizations conducted polls about presidential approval and when they chose to report the results revealed differences in how the major television networks and Fox News behaved. Tim Groeling found that ABC, CBS, and NBC were more likely to cover increases in public approval of President Bill Clinton (D) and decreases in approval of George W. Bush (R), whereas Fox News engaged in the opposite patterns. Fox also was more likely to report on other news organizations' polls when the news was bad for Democratic presidents and good for Republican ones.[18]

Negative News Bias

A second structural bias is toward negativity, or *bad* news. How often do you see a series of headlines about all the good things that happened that day? Or an evening news anchor leading the newscast, "Tonight . . . several airplanes landed safely at their destinations." The saying "if it bleeds, it leads" is an old one, but it's never been truer. Data scientist Kaleve Leetaru, for example, analyzed news articles over several decades and found that coverage has become increasingly gloomy.[19] US political coverage in particular has grown increasingly negative. Scholars point to the 1970s as the start of a shift toward the press as vocal critics of public leaders as coverage of the Watergate scandal and growing public anger at American engagement in Vietnam.[20] You can read more about negative election coverage in Chapter 9.

The negativity bias may also be driven by audience demand as much as journalistic norms. Research from various disciplines reveals a tendency for people to give more weight to negative information than positive information when making economic choices,[21] forming impressions of other people,[22] and evaluating political information.[23]

News consumers may find negative news more useful than positive news because it allows them to surveil possible threats. Indeed, back when

Pew Research Center performed weekly tracking of the types of stories the public said it was following closely (1986–2012), categories like war and terrorism, bad weather, and disasters regularly topped the list. In an unscientific but nevertheless interesting experiment, Russian news site City Reporter reported only good news to its readers for a day. The result? It lost two-thirds of its normal readership that day. As Marc Trussler and Stuart Soroka point out, "The relationship between demand and supply [for negative news] is almost certainly reciprocal."[24] Still, some research suggests that for certain media behaviors, consumers may prefer good news. For example, analyzing six months' worth of stories on *The New York Times* most emailed list, researchers at the University of Pennsylvania noticed that readers tended to share stories with positive themes in addition to long articles on intellectually stimulating topics. These two preferences are not necessarily mutually exclusive; people may have a preference for consuming negative news but sharing positive news (after all, who wants to be seen as a Debbie Downer?).

Another structural, nonpartisan bias in news is a bias toward unusual or sensational events. Someone who dies of a rare disease is more likely to have their story told than someone who dies of common heart failure. Plane crashes get more attention than car crashes. And as we witnessed in the 2016 presidential election, unusual candidates tend to attract attention.

Real Versus Perceived Bias

The second distinction that should be made is actual bias versus perceptions of media bias. Bias can be both an inherent and an ascribed aspect of reporting. That is, for any given news article, there is presumably some objective process for determining whether the content deviates in some measurable way from a point of true neutrality (inherent bias). This objective process typically takes the form of a content analysis, a research technique where trained coders systematically evaluate definable features of content: the presence of certain words or phrases, evaluations of tone, length of story, etc. Think of a content analysis as an unbiased assessment of media bias, if you will (though as you'll soon see, evaluating news stories for bias is challenging—even the Groseclose and Milyo measure discussed above has been subject to numerous criticisms). At the same time, media bias is an ascribed trait—a label assigned by the audience. When audiences encounter news, they conduct their own, informal content analysis—an analysis based on past experience, heuristic cues, personal preferences, and instinct. Because audiences and researchers are not using the same tools to measure bias, it should hardly come as a surprise that audience-based and research-based assessments of bias do not always match up.

Measuring Real Bias

To determine whether actual unequal treatment has occurred in news coverage, scholars have taken a variety of approaches, but typically, they rely on content analyses to make this determination. The first step is usually to collect a random sample of news stories. Researchers then create a measurement tool for evaluating bias and use trained coders or machines to assess the news coverage in a predetermined way. The coders are not looking for bias, per se; they are counting or assessing elements within the story. They might count the number of times a particular side is quoted in an article, for example, or make a judgment as to whether an article's headline is negative or positive about a candidate. For example, looking at headlines after the first debate in the 2020 Democratic primary, where reporters could choose from several angles, some opted for negative frames (e.g., "Sanders Admits He Would Raise Taxes on the Middle Class to Pay for Programs," Yahoo News); others, for positive ones (e.g., "Kamala Harris Breaks Out," Politico).

Prominence

The story elements researchers look at to assess bias generally boil down to *prominence* and *tone*. For prominence, researchers are looking at the elements such as the volume of news coverage received and the placement of that coverage (e.g., front-page news, top of a newscast, first person quoted in a story). For example, reviewing local TV newscasts, Sue Carter, Frederick Fico, and Jocelyn McCabe counted the order in which the sides were presented, the total time given to each side in the story, whether visuals of the candidates or campaign were included, and whether candidates were given soundbites or paraphrased by reporters or anchors.[25] Prominence bias has been measured by physical space within a newspaper or the number of photographs in which a candidate is featured. Measuring prominence generally requires counting elements that exist (number of words dedicated to a viewpoint, length of soundbites for various points of view), but some scholars have attempted to measure bias by looking at what's missing. For example, controlling for actual economic data, one study examined whether newspapers were more likely to report negative economic news when the president was a Republican or Democrat.[26] Quantifying the prominence given to various viewpoints in a news story or in news coverage in general is tricky—but it's an important step to exploring political bias in news.

And yet, even if you counted the number of words dedicated to opposing sides across all the news stories in a given day, those figures still need to be interpreted. Is there a magic threshold at which coverage becomes biased? Perhaps not . . . unless the criteria for bias is that each side must be *exactly* the same. Indeed, that is precisely the standard proposed in some content analyses. You can see the appeal for researchers; because US politics is dominated by two major parties, it is reasonable to assume that fair, unbiased coverage would give these competing campaigns equal time. For example, some supporters of 2016 Democratic presidential candidate Bernie Sanders alleged there was a "Bernie Blackout"—that is, that media did not split time equally between Sanders and eventual-nominee Hillary Clinton. An analysis from Harvard's Shorenstein Center shows that the gap in media coverage between the two candidates was fairly narrow in the months before Super Tuesday. If the candidates got similar, but not equal, levels of coverage during a critical point in the primary, does that refute the notion of a Bernie Blackout? Or does any deviation from a balanced 50/50 split in coverage indicate bias? It might help to think of a similar situation on the other side of the aisle: the Shorenstein Center report shows Republican candidate Donald Trump dominating coverage, and a report from *The New York Times* suggests he may have received the equivalent of $2 billion worth of free media. Does a lopsided amount of attention translate into bias on the part of news organizations? If so, is the bias structural or partisan in nature?

Moreover, what should we expect of the news media in multiparty systems? In countries with proportional representation—where the percentage of votes a party gets in an election results in the party getting that percentage of seats in the legislature—is fair coverage proportional?

Deciding whether disproportionate media coverage should be labeled *biased* is complicated by the fact that prominence cuts both ways. There are certainly times when targets of news coverage would say it's actually *excessive* attention that's biased. Hillary Clinton thought the press paid too much attention to her email scandal in 2016. Donald Trump believed news outlets were unnecessarily fixated on Russian interference in the election. Considered on its own, the volume of media coverage does not necessarily indicate a partisan bias. If two candidates receive exactly the same amount of airtime but one candidate's coverage is overwhelmingly negative, we would hardly say the candidates received equal coverage.

Tone

Because volume of coverage doesn't tell the whole story, researchers often consider prominence alongside the *tone* of news coverage. This generally requires that researchers code content as either negative or positive in tone. For example, one study determined the slant of news coverage during Senatorial campaigns by judging whether news articles were positive or negative, and the number of criticisms about each candidate.[27] The Shorenstein Center's report shows that 71 percent of the news coverage in the 2016 presidential election was negative. If you find yourself wondering how they knew coverage was positive or negative, you're asking the right question! Take a look at the sentences below—which one would you say is positively toned and which one is negatively toned?

Until you pay your fines, you will not receive your diploma.

Once you have paid your fines, you will receive your diploma.

You likely thought of the first option as negative, but can you explain why? The idea of coding content as positive or negative assumes that sentiment is embedded in our language. That is, words convey both meaning and feeling. By categorizing words as negative or positive and creating a *valence dictionary* of sorts, you are then able to count the number of negative and positive words associated with each viewpoint in a given news story. This task can be left up to human coders, but you can imagine it might take a long time to code the positive and negative elements in more than a handful of news stories. Today, researchers are experimenting with automated sentiment tools that define content as negative or positive based on a preprogrammed lexicon. Many private companies offer automated tone analysis (e.g., Media Tenor, Crimson Hexagon), but there are also free options available for political researchers (e.g., Lexicoder).

Then again, would it be safe to say the candidate with the negative coverage received *biased* coverage? Perhaps the candidate's campaign simply experienced more scandals than the competitor, or consistently trailed in the polls, or continued to announce positions that were wildly unpopular. Those stories would very likely be categorized as negatively toned. As you can see from Figure 4.1, the Shorenstein Center classified a majority of news coverage about Trump and Clinton as negative (note that, for the full election, including the primaries, 56 percent of Trump's coverage and 62 percent of Clinton's was classified as negative). *The Washington Post's* Glenn Kessler, who runs the paper's fact-checking unit, has tracked down more than ten thousand false or misleading statements made by Donald Trump.[28] Is it the fault of fact-checkers that President Trump tells so many lies? Of course not. If President Obama told ten thousand lies and fact-checkers did not call him out on the misstatements of fact, that would be bias.

In other words, can you infer journalistic bias from negative coverage? To be sure, excessive negative coverage *could* indicate a partisan bias, but it does not *necessarily* do so. Professional ethics dictate that journalists be fair in their coverage, and many would consider the idea that rival viewpoints receive coverage that is equitable in volume and tone to be *false equivalence* or *false balance*. A newspaper editor would not neglect to print a story about a presidential candidate's disastrous meeting with a foreign leader, for example, simply because the paper had run another negatively toned

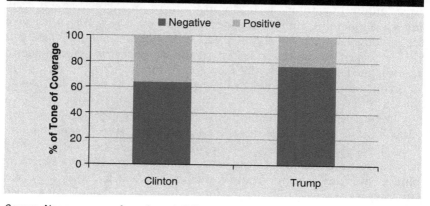

Figure 4.1   Tone of 2016 US Presidential General Election Coverage

Source: News coverage from August 8-November 6, 2016. Excludes neutral coverage. Data from Media Tenor/Shorenstein Center, https://shorensteincenter.org/news-coverage-2016-general-election/.

story about that candidate the previous day. However, you can easily see how that editor might be biased if she regularly published negative stories about one candidate and neglected to publish equally important, negative stories about others.

Phrasing

Another creative way that researchers have measured media bias in political news coverage is to assess the extent to which a reporter uses the same partisan phrases as politicians. Advocates, lobbyist groups, and political parties are quite effective at using language to communicate how their stances reflect their values. For example, when those who oppose abortion use the term *pro-life*, it connects their position on the issue to a universal value (respect for life). Those who support abortion, on the other hand, might prefer to call the opposing group *anti-choice*, highlighting the universal value they would prefer to emphasize (individual liberty). For example, in a study about news coverage after gun violence, Emma Mcginty and her colleagues examined whether stories were more likely to mention *dangerous weapons* or *dangerous people* with serious mental health issues.[29] Similarly, a 2012 study looked at how local and national news sources framed arguments in favor of an anti-immigration bill, finding that certain outlets were more likely to discuss the bill using conservatives' preferred framing (public safety and economic opportunity).[30]

In a popular study, Gentzgow and Shapiro compared mentions of certain phrases in four hundred daily newspapers in 2005 to oft-used phrases among congressional Democrats and Republicans.[31] Some of the phrases were intuitively partisan, such as *worker's rights* for Democrats and *death tax repeal* among Republicans. Other phrases favored by the parties were far less obvious, such as *national forest* for Republicans and *fuel efficiencies* for Democrats. When researchers used the *phrase-matching* technique to measure media bias on cable TV, their conclusions matched up with partisan reputation: Fox News was to the right of CNN, while MSNBC was to the left.[32]

One issue with this method is that it assumes that, ideally, reporters will use (or include via direct quotes or soundbites) Democratic and Republican phrasing equally. But it could also be the case that one party is simply more consistent with its communication strategy–repeating phrases over and over to clearly communicate their focus. Wagner and Gruszczynski showed that, over a forty-year period, Republicans tended to get more sources quoted on abortion, taxes, and foreign policy while Democrats earned more quotes on energy policy.

Organizational Factors

The bias-detecting tactics we've addressed so far focus on news content. Alternatively, when the question focuses on whether a particular news source is biased, researchers may look at organization-level features rather than news content. The FCC, for one, has taken the position that "there is a positive relationship between viewpoints expressed and ownership of an outlet. The Commission has sought, therefore, to diffuse ownership of media outlets among multiple firms in order to diversify the viewpoints available to the public."[33] Gentzgow and Shapiro found no evidence that newspaper slant was related to owner ideology (operationalized by campaign contributions). Other research finds that the slant and content on the editorial page of newspapers is affected by ownership. When conservative media titan Rupert Murdoch purchased the *Wall Street Journal*, their editorial page became more conservative in terms of how it treated Democrats (more negatively) and Republicans (more positively); it also became less supportive of government intervention in the economy.[34]

Audience Ideology

It may also be tempting to infer the partisan leanings of a specific news outlet by looking at the makeup of the audience. In a 2014 study on media habits, the Pew Research Center placed news outlets along an ideological continuum based on the average ideology of the outlet's consumers.

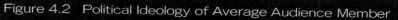

Figure 4.2 Political Ideology of Average Audience Member

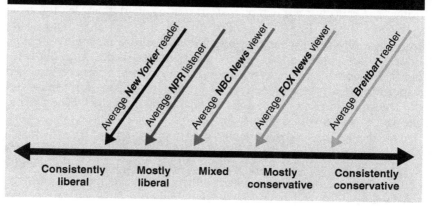

| Consistently liberal | Mostly liberal | Mixed | Mostly conservative | Consistently conservative |

The results largely align with the outlets' reputations (see Figure 4.2). For example, the average consumer of MSNBC and NPR tended to be more liberal and the average consumer of Fox News and the Rush Limbaugh Show tended to be more conservative. If the audience for a news outlet tends to be of a particular political orientation, is it reasonable to conclude that outlet shares their political slant? That assumption rests on the *selective exposure hypothesis* (see Chapter 7), which reasons that individuals prefer attitude-confirming news sources. But it could also be the case that liberals and conservatives are attracted to different, nonpartisan features of these outlets—story format and length, accessibility, host personalities and individual reporters, style and branding, geographic region of coverage, or topical focus. Another possibility is that news outlets have partisan reputations, and thus when consumers are asked to report their media habits, they report using sources they think of as ideologically consistent.[35]

Perceptions of Media Bias

That news outlets have a reputation for being liberal or conservative illustrates another key component of media bias: public perceptions of bias. Media researchers gauge perceptions of bias by asking news consumers to indicate levels of media bias for individual news stories, news coverage of a particular topic, a specific news outlet, or in news media overall. These perceptions of bias do not necessarily indicate actual bias; in fact, there is considerable evidence that news consumers tend to overestimate unequal treatment in media. To understand how news consumers interpret media content, look no further than the results of this classic study called

"They Saw a Game." In the 1954 study, researchers asked Princeton and Dartmouth students to watch film from a football game between the two teams. The game was a rough one—Dartmouth's quarterback left the game with a broken leg, Princeton's ended up with a broken nose, and Princeton ultimately won. When the students watched the game film later, the Princeton students counted twice as many penalties as the Dartmouth students. Perhaps this comes as no surprise to anyone who has ever watched a sporting event with a friend rooting for the other team, but it illustrates the crucial notion that perceptions are shaped by individual values, group allegiances, and predispositions.

Much like the football fans in the "They Saw a Game" study, media consumers on different sides of a contentious issue often come to different conclusions about media coverage of that issue. Researchers have carefully crafted objective, neutral news pieces only to find that competing partisans have wildly different perceptions of the content—with each side believing the story to be biased against their side. This phenomenon, called the *hostile media perception*, happens primarily among those who are said to have high involvement with an issue in the news. Involvement in this sense means a person has formed a clear opinion or attitude about the topic at hand. For example, strong supporters of a particular political candidate are more likely to sense undesirable bias in news coverage about that candidate, compared to folks who are undecided. The hostile media perception is especially curious given the human tendency to interpret information as supportive, rather than hostile, to our beliefs. That is—we usually look for ways in which new information supports what we already think. The hostile media perception is the opposite—media messages tend to be judged as hostile to our existing beliefs and preferences. Scholars have observed this phenomenon on a micro level—such as when political rivals both sense a news story is hostile to their view—and on the macro level—such as when Republicans accuse the *mainstream* media as being against them. We have much more about the hostile media perception and how audiences interpret media coverage in Chapter 7, but suffice it to say, in the quest to determine whether media outlets are biased, audiences' perceptions should be taken with a grain of salt.

So, Are Media Biased?

It should be clear by now that there is no single definition of *media* or *bias*. Media can refer to a single outlet, outlets of a particular medium (TV, newspapers), geographic location (local, national), or prominence (high circulation newspapers, big three TV networks, web-only sites). Bias can be structural or partisan in addition to being real or perceived. It can manifest as a preference for which stories are told, the language used to tell those stories, which sources are given time and space, and what information is vetted and included. Operationalizing bias, and attempting to figure out where it originated (opinionated journalists? heavy-handed owners? revenue models? newsroom routines?) is a massive challenge in understanding political bias in the US news industry.

The results of studies examining political bias in media are best described as inconsistent. Considering the variety of ways researchers have defined media and bias, inconsistency is not entirely surprising. Studies that have noted a Republican bias[36] are met with studies showing a Democratic bias.[37] Others have found that even when bias exists in a particular outlet, it doesn't necessary always favor the same party—for example, one study found that newspapers may favor Senate candidates that their editorial page has endorsed, regardless of party.[38]

Overall, a 2000 meta-analysis of fifty-nine studies exploring media bias in election campaigns concluded that there were no significant signs of bias in how news outlets cover Democrats and Republicans. Specifically, David D'Alessio and Michael Allen found that Democrats and Republicans were granted the same amount of attention in television, newspaper, and magazine election overage.[39] The study notes that equity was consistent across studies included in the analysis—that is, regardless of which race was being studied or which media outlets were being examined, the findings consistently showed that Republican and Democratic voices were generally balanced. Of course, that analysis is a few years old by now, and the media landscape has shifted significantly since then, but it is fair to say that scholars have not identified a consistent partisan bias among major US news outlets.

Partisan News

Of course, there are overtly biased news sources. In fact, the growth of partisan news sources represents one of the major shifts in the news industry over the past few decades. This development comes after a long streak of strict adherence to the journalistic notions of objectivity—so it may come as a surprise that partisanship, not objectivity, has actually been the norm in American journalism history. The newspapers of the nineteenth century were openly committed to a political party and presented news solely from that party's perspective. Parties were major financial backers for newspapers, and it wasn't uncommon for editors to work part-time in government. So open were newspapers about their partisanship, historian James L. Baughman explained in his essay on the rise of the partisan press, that when Democrat Grover Cleveland won the presidency in 1884, "the Republican *Los Angeles Times* simply failed to report this unhappy result for several days."[40]

Scholars offer several explanations for the industry's shift toward objectivity. The most popular of these focus on technological advancements and economic incentives. For example, many historians credit the telegraph for the adoption of a factual literary style and news wire services for the shift toward mass appeal.[41] Other scholars focus on the money. When party dollars were no longer covering the bills, papers turned to advertising revenue. Advertisers understandably wanted broad audiences.[42] Those audiences, especially in the middle of the twentieth century, would be described as moderate by modern standards; partisanship was less intense, party divisions not as stark, and on a host of key issues, the public was more united than divided. In other words, both supply (advertising dollars) and demand (American news consumers) pointed a path toward a neutral press. The move toward balanced, objective reporting was helped along by the fact that the latest entry into the media landscape—broadcast television—was forced through regulation to be even-handed. The Fairness Doctrine, enacted in 1954, required broadcast networks to devote time to contrasting views on issues of public importance (it was abolished in 1987).

Historian Michael Schudson challenges economic and technological explanations for the objectivity norm.[43] Instead, he traces the emergence of nonpartisan reporting to the professionalization of the industry. Reporters in the 1920s increasingly integrated interviews into their stories, took pride in the accuracy and speed of their work, and sought to distinguish themselves from public relations professionals. Newspaper editors created national associations and adopted codes of ethics. Journalism schools emphasized factuality and service to audiences, rather than publishers.

From a consumer perspective, if you wanted the news, you either tuned in for the evening TV broadcasts or waited for the paper the next morning. There were still choices, of course—the 1980s saw Dan Rather (CBS Evening News), Peter Jennings (ABC's World News Tonight), and Tom Brokaw (NBC's Nightly News) competing for the nearly forty million American households who tuned in to the evening broadcasts. But the audience was largely unsegmented, meaning, both journalists and advertisers had an incentive to appeal to a diverse group of viewers.

Starting in the 1950s, the press had widely adopted objectivity as its mantra. Partisan sources were hard to come by, a radical change from the turn of the century. And yet, only a few decades later, partisan news sources reemerged. What changed in the 1990s and early 2000s that ushered in the return of partisan journalism? An obvious place to point fingers: technology. The rise of cable television made it a lot easier to engage in two distinct behaviors: 1) selecting a news source that told you that your side is right and 2) watching something other than the news altogether—something like SportsCenter or a Lifetime movie.[44] News junkies could self-select into partisan news more easily and entertainment junkies could have the television on at 5:30 p.m. central time and watch something other than the news.

Accessibility to the internet made information even easier to find than ever before, revolutionizing the news industry. Twenty years ago, the vast majority of humans couldn't simply begin their own TV news program or start their own newspaper, but today, you can have your own news outlet up and running in less than an hour. How would you compete for a slice of the information-weary audience? A report from Axios shows that a majority of the digital outlets founded from 1993 to 2016 were partisan. Why would this be the case? Why not just start a traditional, nonpartisan news outlet? You can imagine that some of the partisanship of digital news sources was an attempt to stand out. Major news outlets that had their start on other mediums (*The New York Times*, CNN, NPR) were getting into the online game as well, so a nonpartisan startup would have been in direct competition with the websites of legacy media outlets.

Changing Revenue Models

The partisan nature of online news outlets may also be partly attributable to the impact that the digital revolution had on the news revenue mode. Advertising is still the main source of revenue for news, but once introduced to the online world, ad dollars that once fueled the news industry were redirected to digital news sources, and eventually, to major tech companies like Facebook and Google. Today news outlets are fighting over fewer ad dollars.

One solution is for news organizations to turn to subscription-based revenue, which requires delivery of a product that people are willing to pay for. Consumers are accustomed to paying for newspapers, but the online version of slotting a quarter into a vending box has been a hard sell. If consumers can get something for free, why would they pay you for it? One option for capturing ad dollars in today's news environment: if you can't deliver a large, broad audience, instead deliver a specific audience that advertisers are interested in. Advancement in audience metric technology has created an opportunity for advertisers to target slices of the public, and partisan-focused online outlets can offer specific audiences that advertisers seek. Indeed, some news outlets that cater to a specific audience, like Fox News did with conservatives beginning in 1996, have been incredibly successful. Fox News has long reigned as the ratings leader among its cable news competitors CNN and MSNBC. Even so, the most-watched program on Fox, *Hannity*, usually only gets three million viewers, less than 1 percent of the country. The three major network newscasts, on the other hand, earn about twenty million viewers a night between them.[45] A little more than half a million viewers in the coveted 25 to 54 demographic watch *Hannity* on a typical night while about four million watch network news.

Whether a news outlet's revenue model (subscription vs. advertising) is connected to media bias is an open question. There are plenty of traditional, objective news sources that rely on advertising, just as there are plenty of traditional, objective sources that rely on subscriptions. One team of researchers who looked into the connection between revenue model and bias found that subscription-based revenue models *may* increase news bias if editors are incentivized to give the audience what it wants.[46] Another study shows that advertising may alleviate or exacerbate that tendency; advertisers who want broad appeal and a large audience would prefer outlets that offer that to diverse audiences, while other advertisers may target outlets that serve up an audience whose political preferences tend to correlate with specific product purchases (e.g., conservatives are more likely to buy pickup trucks, liberals are more likely to buy a Prius).[47]

Changing Audiences

Of course, it's not just the news industry that's changed. The news audience has changed as well. Congress has become increasingly polarized, and as the two major parties became more ideologically defined, the gap between them has widened substantially. Though today many people commonly claim they are political Independents, Americans on either side of the political divide are colder toward *the other side* than ever before.[48] Political scientists describe this era as one marked by deep polarization driven by identity politics and divides over issue preferences.[49] If the American public is clearly divided into *teams*, does it not make sense that news outlets would arise to cater to those affiliations?

The link between partisan news and partisan audiences is complex, possibly even cyclical. On the one hand, we know that people are attracted to news outlets that—at least in terms of reputation—share their political views (see Chapter 7 for more on the concept of selective exposure). For example, Pew Research Center data shows that the audience for Fox News, a source popularly thought to have a conservative bent, tends to be more conservative.[50] On the other hand, perhaps it is partisan news sources that are creating more partisan audiences. One intriguing study from political scientist Gregory Martin and economist Ali Yurukoglu studied the impact of watching cable news on voting preferences. They estimated that in the 2000 election, nearly 60 percent of Fox viewers who started out as Democrats changed to supporting Republicans. That rate was 27 percent in the 2004 election, and 28 percent in 2008. CNN and MSNBC did not have effects of that magnitude (for example, MSNBC convinced only 8 percent of initial Republicans to switch to the Democratic ticket in 2008). Aside from cable news, researchers have found that consumer demand explained 20 percent[51] of the variation in the partisan slant of newspapers, leading them to conclude that outlets have an economic incentive to tailor content to the political leanings of their audiences. The situation may be such that partisans are generally attracted to *news that fits their views* and that consumption of such news strengthens their partisanship.

For the folks who venture over to news *from the other side*, certain partisan news sources may have a persuasive effect (however, there is also plenty of evidence[52] that people are resistant to information that counters their views— see Chapter 7 for more on motivated reasoning and confirmation bias).

Changes to Reporting and Presentation Style

Aside from the growing number of openly partisan news organizations, journalistic style changes and story formatting changes may contribute to the perception that news—on the whole—is more partisan. Indeed, a quarter of Americans say it is difficult to sort news from opinion in media, and just over 40 percent say they see opinion creeping into news content.[53] Some of the confusion may be due to media formats. Imagine for a moment that you flip on CNN and see a panel discussing an immigration bill. There's an anchor holding court with a nonpartisan analyst, an immigration advocate, and representatives for the major political parties. Halfway through the segment, they bring in a reporter for a live shot in front of the White House, or briefly cut away from the panel for a quick interview with a senator. Who are the journalists in this scenario? Who are the pundits? Is this an opinion segment, a debate, a news report, or something else entirely? There has also been a gradual change from a detached, *just the facts* style of reporting to more interpretive and analytical journalism. Some journalism scholars would describe the distinction as one of passive and active journalism. As an example, a reporter practicing passive journalism might write a story on global warming and note that some people believe humans are not responsible for climate change. An active journalist would be sure to include the fact that the scientific consensus is that humans are a major cause of global warming, and may even point out the lack of evidence for competing views.

Moreover, individuals have a difficult time remembering where they learned information. In a study led by mass communication scholar Emily Vraga, researchers varied whether information was presented online in simple (more traditional) or difficult (where information from one source was then critiqued by another source) ways; people were less able to remember the source of the information in the more difficult condition.[54] If it is difficult to remember the source of where you learned something in the body of a single news story, it is probably even harder to remember the source of information that you might encounter in your Twitter feed.

Conclusion

Keep in mind that journalists have very little regulatory oversight from government or within the industry itself. Most of the *rules* in journalism are established through professional norms: journalism schools, newsroom routines, and a shared identity among journalists. As the industry changes due to technology, audience demands, and revenue challenges, journalists must wonder whether the norms of the next era will persist in the modern world.[55] While most traditional roles are likely to persist—the duty to hold public officials accountable and to deliver timely information to the public—how those norms are put into practice is an ever-evolving question. It isn't as simple as deciding whether journalists should be openly partisan or not. Rather, journalists are tasked with considering questions like: What is objectivity? Is it a strict adherence to reporting only what others are saying with no interpretation or analysis (i.e., parroting, passive), or is a process that describes the routine of gathering information, examining it thoroughly, and being open about that process with the public (i.e., interpretive, active)? The lines between reporter and activist, skeptic and partisan, analytic and biased are not always clear. Of course, even if journalists have a shared definition of nonpartisan objectivity, the audience also brings its own views to the table. When Gallup partnered with the Knight Foundation to ask Republicans and Democrats to name an objective news source, 60 percent of Republicans who could name a source offered up Fox News. The cable giant didn't make the cut for Democrats. Instead, they named sources like CNN (21 percent) and NPR (15 percent).

Fake News

If you were reading a book in this class that was written a few years ago, you wouldn't have found the phrase *fake news* in the index. Today, it's a term that's hard to ignore. Indeed, it was Collins Dictionary's word of the year in 2017. *Fake news* as you probably understand may be:

1. A derogatory term for the US news industry
2. News stories that a political leader or group believes to be biased or uncomplimentary
3. Inaccuracies or misstatements reported by traditional news sources
4. Lies or falsities in general
5. Deliberately false reports posing as legitimate news

Technically, only the fifth definition is what experts would typically describe as fake news. But words have never been very good at staying shackled to their dictionary definition, and *fake news* is a prime example of how phrases can be imbued with fresh meaning.

What Is Fake News?

In an article titled, "I Helped Popularize the Term 'Fake News' And Now I Cringe Every Time I Hear It," Buzzfeed journalist Craig Silverman explains why he was tweeting about fake news back in 2014.[56] He was running a research project exploring the spread of misinformation online and he—reasonably—used the term to describe websites that were created for the sole purpose of creating and spreading falsities. He regrets his use of the term, writing, "I should have realized that any person, idea, or phrase—however neutral in its intention—could be twisted into a partisan cudgel." But Silverman was simply applying a new label to a type of misinformation. The crux of fake news—lies, conspiracy theories, propaganda, disinformation—are not new concepts, even if they are being lumped together under a new name.

Silverman's initial definition of fake news is exactly how researchers think of the concept: "News articles that are intentionally and verifiably false, and could mislead readers."[57] Outrageous headlines such as "Hillary Clinton Adopts Alien Baby" may come to mind, but fake news can also be subtle. The phony headline "Pope Francis shocks world, endorses Donald Trump for president" was the most shared false news story of 2016, with Buzzfeed reporting it garnered 960,000 engagements. Those engagements are another key part of today's fake news—the stories rely on the viral nature of social media to spread. They don't necessarily need to be believed, just shared (or liked, retweeted, or commented on). Sharing a fake news story could qualify as a form of misinformation ("the inadvertent sharing of false information") or disinformation ("the deliberate creation and sharing of information known to be false") depending on intent.[58] In fact, intent may be an important dimension of fake news, depending on how you want to define the concept. Does intent matter? Consider, for example, *satire* and *parody*. These information formats spread false information, but it is not intended to deceive people. When comedians Colin Jost and Michael Che deliver the week's news from an anchor desk on *Saturday Night Live*, they intend it as satire, not as a serious competitor for NBC *Nightly News*. When *The Onion* publishes an article called, "Red Cross Installs Blood Drop-Off Bins for Donors' Convenience," the satirical website doesn't intend for people to take it seriously. On the flip side, *The Washington Post* once interviewed a content creator who has written stories about California instituting sharia law or former president Bill Clinton becoming a serial killer—not to trick people, but to see how outrageous his headlines can be before people will stop believing it. His site even features a disclaimer: nothing on this page is real.

Contemporary fake news varies on two dimensions: intent and payoff. Most of the fake news headlines you've come across are not attempts at trolling. They *are* intended to deceive. This desire—to deceive the public

Table 4.3 Fake News Headlines

Headline	Source
Obama signs executive order banning the pledge of allegiance in schools nationwide	abcnews.com.co
Pope Francis shocks world, endorses Donald Trump for president, releases statement	Ending the Fed (now-defunct site)
McDonald's employee fired for putting his mixed tape in children's happy meals	Huzlers.com
Girl Scouts of America approved to sell marijuana edible cookies at dispensaries	Now8News.com
Taylor Swift shocks music industry: "I voted for Donald Trump"	Lifeeventweb.com
FBI insider: Clinton emails linked to pedophile sex ring	yournewswire.com
Jay Z and Beyonce trying to purchase rights to confederate flag	thesource.com

under the guise of real news—is nothing new. From the *yellow journalism* of the 1890s where partisan papers would routinely publish rumors about their political rivals to the Nazi propaganda used to drum up anti-Semitic attitudes in the 1930s, misinformation disguised as news has been an effective tool of deception. The motivation for spreading misinformation then is the same as it now: the payoff is either political, financial, or both. Websites that spread misinformation for political gain tend to spread a mix of fact-based and false information. For example, while online liberal site Occupy Democrats does feature some fact-based articles, it also shares memes that claim things like, "House GOP attacked for passing bill that makes it legal to fire single moms," which Politifact reported to be entirely false.

Partisan sites may accidentally share false information or they may do so intentionally to fire up their audiences, but the end product—information dressed as a news story but containing false information—is the same regardless of intent. Indeed, some stories that seem like they're being spread for partisan gain—for example, website WTOE 5's story claiming the Pope had endorsed Donald Trump in the 2016 election—are actually spread for financial gain. These sources are created for the sole purpose of running digital ads: raking in money by racking up clicks.

WHAT MAKES IT FAKE NEWS?

▶ Content is styled to mimic the features of legitimate news sources

▶ The information provided is veritably false

▶ The source has a questionable or spotty track record of publishing factual stories

If you performed a search of academic articles on fake news, what you'd find is a more nuanced typology: news satire and parody, news fabrication, photo manipulation, advertising, and propaganda. What you won't find are many attempts to categorize sloppy journalism or reporting errors as fake news.[59] News organizations make mistakes—sometimes even egregious mistakes, such as when multiple news outlets (including NPR, CNN, Fox News, and Reuters) erroneously reported that Congresswoman Gabby Giffords was killed in a shooting in Arizona. More often, mistakes are mundane—a misspelled name, an incorrect data point, or a fact that warranted additional context. The proper recourse for any mistake is, of course, to publish a correction. But with growing concern among audiences about bias, fake news, and the integrity of the news industry, even the mildest reporting error can further erode trust between the public and the press.

How Does Fake News Spread?

If fake news and other types of misinformation are nothing new, why is there such a robust public conversation about disinformation happening today? The answer probably won't surprise you: social media and the online world more generally have greatly facilitated the spread of false information. Robots, or *bots* as they're commonly called, make disinformation's journey into your newsfeed even easier. An estimate from 2017 shows upwards of 8.5 percent of all accounts on Twitter were bots, as were up to 5.5 percent of accounts on Facebook and over 8 percent of the accounts on Instagram. That's close to two hundred million bots across social media channels. One research team working to unmask online bots found that one way they help spread fake news is to make content appear more popular than it really is, capitalizing on a human bias known as the *bandwagon effect* (see more on this in Chapter 7).[60] They found that bots accounted for around half of the shares in the first few seconds of a fake news story's life on Twitter. Another bot strategy they uncovered: bots target influential Twitter users, hoping to score an endorsement that would give the story far more reach than even an army of bots could. By simulating a version of

Twitter where ten thousand suspected bots were weeded out, the researchers concluded they could stifle the spread of fake information by as much as 70 percent. Hoax Twitter accounts can even make their way into news stories. In their study, Josephine Lukito and Christopher Wells searched the content of thirty-three major news outlets and found that thirty-two of those outlets featured tweets from the Russia-backed Internet Research Agency in at least one story.[61]

But we can't place all the blame on the bots. Humans share fake news as well. In fact, some research suggests that people might be more likely to share fake news than real news. Fake news is splashy, sensational, and novel—and unlike real news articles, these stories are carefully crafted to be shared rather than read. And before you judge your fellow Netizens for falling for absurd stories such as "Morgue Employee Cremated by Mistake While Taking a Nap,"[62] keep in mind that in an era of information overload, a lot of people never get past the headline. In fact, according to one study, half of Twitter users who retweeted an article never clicked the link to read it. Many others don't even notice the source of information or take the time to check if it's legitimate.[63]

Who is most likely to fall for—or share—false information? Some research shows falling for fake headlines is associated with cognitive styles: low levels of analytical thinking and high levels of dogmatism and religious fundamentalism.[64] Another study found that partisanship may also play a role, at least in the context of the 2016 presidential election. Researchers

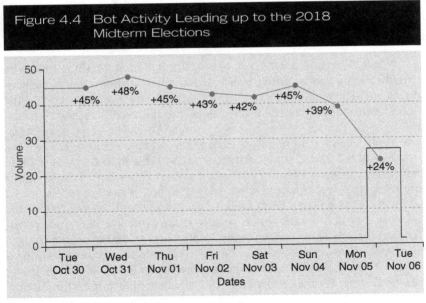

Figure 4.4 Bot Activity Leading up to the 2018 Midterm Elections

Source: Data and visualization from the Social Media Observatory at Indiana University.

found that about 60 percent of the visitors to fake news sites came from the 10 percent of people with the most conservative online information diets.[65] Another study found that across political ideologies, adults age 65 and up are more likely than their younger counterparts to share false information online, which the authors reason is due to a lack of digital literacy.[66]

Finally, it probably comes as no surprise that people are more likely to share fake news if it confirms their prior beliefs. Take the infamous Pizzagate debacle, where an armed man showed up at a Washington, DC, pizzeria to investigate whether the restaurant was headquarters to a secret child trafficking ring run by presidential candidate Hillary Clinton. The rumor started online—via sites like Reddit, 4chan, and Twitter—where most people recognized it for the outrageous conspiracy theory that it was. But some with far-right ideologies weren't so quick to dismiss the claim, likely because it confirmed their worst fears about a politician they strongly disliked. The tendency to be less skeptical of information that supports your own beliefs—a flavor of confirmation bias—creates an open lane for fake news to flourish. For example, when a team of researchers asked people about the accuracy of fake news headlines, they found people were much more likely to say a headline was accurate if it favored their own party compared to when it favored the opposing party.[67] Another recent study of both British and American news consumers found that partisanship played a powerful role when consumers were asked to determine whether stories were credible.[68]

Has the Term *Fake News* Been Weaponized?

During a press conference in 2018, President Trump refused a question from a CNN reporter by telling the crowd "CNN is fake news—I don't take questions from CNN." Though he wasn't the first to use the phrase, Trump can be credited with popularizing *fake news* as both a way to discredit certain news reports and disparage the wider news industry. He didn't begin using the term until after his election, but his use steadily increased in the first few years of his presidency, especially on Twitter. An analysis of his tweets shows that he mentioned *fake news* over three hundred times in the first two years of his presidency. His regular use of the term to dismiss negative news about his administration has led many critics to the conclusion that Trump's definition of fake news may simply be *uncomplimentary news*. If that is his definition, he's not alone. A 2018 poll from the Knight Foundation and Gallup found that 40 percent of Republicans say accurate news stories that cast a politician or political group in a negative light should *always* be considered fake news. Statistics such as this suggest that—at least for some—the term has simply become another tactic for describing dissatisfaction with the news industry, à la the now-passé *lamestream media* insult among Republicans or the *corporate media* moniker sometimes used by the political left. It is such a common phrase now that it has even transcended its political meaning to become general slang. The forecast called for snow but you got only rain? Fake news. Email says the document is attached but it's not? Fake news. Whether it's being weaponized for political gain or used (either seriously or in jest) to refer to the media industry, today's definition of fake news is a far cry from its original meaning.

The term *fake news* has become so politicized that there have been plenty of calls to stop using the term entirely; even some Republican leaders have asked President Trump to retire the phrase. As *The Washington Post* media columnist Margaret Sullivan wrote in 2017, "Instead, call a lie a lie. Call a hoax a hoax. Call a conspiracy theory by its rightful name. After all, 'fake news' is an imprecise expression to begin with."[69] The British government has gone so far as to ban the term from its official documents, stating that it is "a poorly-defined and misleading term that conflates a variety of false information, from genuine error through to foreign interference in democratic processes." Recent evidence suggests such concerns over the use of term are not unfounded. In an experiment, researchers discovered that mere exposure to the term *fake news* can cause harm.[70] Both liberal and conservative participants who were exposed to political leaders' tweets about fake news later had a hard time differentiating between real and fake news. They also had lower levels of trust in media in general compared to those who were not exposed to tweets about fake news. The authors ask an intriguing question: is discussion about fake news actually more detrimental than fake news itself?

OK, So It's Not a New Problem, but Isn't Fake News Still a *Big* Problem?

Fake news is certainly something people *think* is a problem. A 2018 Monmouth poll found that three in four Americans believe major TV and newspapers report *fake news*. More than 30 percent believe this happens regularly.[71] Data from a 2016 Pew Research Center study shows that two-thirds of Americans believe *completely made-up news* has caused a great deal of confusion over basic facts.[72]

But the research gives us mixed results as to whether fake news is as big a problem as commonly perceived. On the one hand, there is evidence that a lot of people fall for fake news. A study from Buzzfeed found 75 percent of people fall for fake news headlines.[73] A study we mentioned earlier found that people are actually more likely to share fake headlines than real ones.

But other investigations have turned up evidence that sharing fake news is rare. For example, one study that examined activity among 3,500 Facebook users found only 8.5 percent shared a fake news article during the 2016 presidential election. One analysis revealed that only about 1 percent of Twitter users accounted for 80 percent of exposures to fake news content during the 2016 election cycle.[74] Another study, also focusing on the 2016 election, tracked more than 2,500 Americans' online activity and found that articles on fake news sites made up only 2.6 percent of the total hard news stories that people read (specifically, 40 percent of Trump supporters and 15 percent of Clinton supporters were exposed to at least one fake news story).[75] Exposure to fake news was down even more in the lead-up to the 2018 midterm elections, with only 7 percent of the public reading an article from a fake news site.[76] Those studies also show that the amount of traffic to fake news websites coming from Facebook is declining, suggesting the company's tactics to limit the spread of false information may be working.

News consumers report seeing fake news far more frequently than those numbers would suggest. Only a quarter of Americans told Pew that they *hardly ever* or *never* see fake news. And what's more—news consumers are confident that fake news won't fool them. A 2018 study from IPSOS found that 65 percent of Americans believe they can identify fake news from real news. Pew Research found similar numbers—only 15 percent said they lacked confidence in their ability to recognize fake news. How do we reconcile widespread concern about fake news with evidence that it makes up a small slice of total news consumed and that consumers aren't duped by it all that frequently? This particular conundrum may be yet another example of the third-person perception—the tendency to believe media's effects happen to *them* but not *me*. In other words, people *are* concerned about fake news, not because they're worried they'll fall for it themselves, but because they're worried that other people will! We'll discuss the third-person perception more in Chapter 7.

Fighting Fake News

Regardless of whether you consider it an overblown or serious problem, whose job is it to stamp out fake news? Is it up to individuals to be savvier information consumers? Should governments create harsher penalties for those fabricating stories? Should the social media giants refine their algorithms to recognize fake news faster and stop it sooner? The public is split on whose responsibility it is to stamp out fake news. Participants in a Pew Research Center poll believed news audience, elected officials, and social networking sites all shared responsibility for stopping the spread of false information.

There are several ongoing bot-fighting efforts that could at least slow the spread of fake news.[77] Google has said it is committed to getting fake news out of its search results, and has unveiled fact-checking tools that promote credible news sources. After catching criticism for its role in allowing disinformation to spread in the 2016 election, Facebook implemented changes that appear to be working—engagements with known fake news websites are down on the platform.[78] That doesn't appear to be the case on Twitter, where the number of fake news shares are up. Mass communication scholars Rebekah Tromble and Shannon McGregor argue that social media companies are too interested in "moving fast and breaking things" than "slowing down and fixing things"—something they could do if they enlisted the help of social scientists who studied these issues.[79] Aside from the tech companies themselves, teams of researchers and advocacy groups are working on projects that will help detect and eliminate bots, educate consumers on how to critically evaluate information, and provide browser add-ons to help identify misinformation in real time.

Most of the conversation about government stepping in to help stop the spread of fake news has focused on regulating social media companies, especially after revelations about Russian disinformation campaigns on social media in the 2016 presidential election. Congress has been interested in how Facebook, Twitter, and Google can stop foreign interests from targeting voters. But any attempts at government regulation of social media will be met with concern from First Amendment advocates. Indeed, any attempt to combat fake news may have unintended consequences. For example, Malaysia passed, and then later repealed, an Anti-Fake News Act in 2018. It had outlawed sharing "any news, information, data and reports, which is or wholly or partly false, whether in the form of features, visuals, or audio records or in any other form capable of suggesting words or ideas." Critics of the rule pointed out that leaving it up to the government to determine what is *wholly or partly false* unintentionally gave political leaders the power to silence dissent.

Fake News and Media Bias

Recent survey data points to the possibility that fake news has become just another synonym for *biased*. Earlier we noted a survey that showed 40 percent of Republicans say accurate news stories that cast a politician or political group in a negative light should always be considered fake news, which is just one example where audience members are using "fake news" as a catch-all description of undesirable news. A Monmouth poll found that only a quarter of Americans say fake news refers *only to* stories where the facts are wrong. Rather, 65 percent told the polling firm that fake news also applies to how news outlets make editorial decisions and which stories they report (earlier in this chapter, you learned that we'd call that a selectivity bias). Over 40 percent in the Monmouth poll also think outlets report false stories in order to push an agenda, whereas 72 percent in an Axis/SurveyMonkey poll around the same time period believed that news sources *often* or *sometimes* report news they know to be fake, false, or purposefully misleading. It seems that the murky and varied definition of *fake news* has led many to the conclusion that it is a form of journalistic bias, where journalists are reporting unverified facts for political gain.

From Research to Real Life

So what does this mean for you—someone who consumes news and someone who, by virtue of reading this book, knows a little more than the average person about media and politics? How can the information in this chapter help you become a savvier news consumer, and, hopefully, a stronger advocate for quality journalism?

First, it is important to identify your own ideas about what constitutes *the media*. When you talk about the news with others or hear people talk about news in a general sense, dig into exactly what it is you are talking about. Did a particular news agency make a decision you disagree with or run a story you wouldn't have published? Or are you getting a sense that *the media*, or a particular type of news media, is talking about a candidate or issue in a way that you think is unfair? Where exactly are those impressions coming from? Question yourself and others. Even in a world of media indexing, it is unlikely that every single major news organization is addressing a topic the exact same way, and it's decidedly unfair when consumers paint *the media* with a broad brush because of an issue with a specific outlet, journalist, or story.

Of course, criticism is fair—and often healthy! But one thing that you can do to help journalists do a better job while not contributing to the deterioration of media trust is to be specific when criticizing news. It should go without saying that using politically loaded terms like *fake news* is unhelpful and, as you learned in this chapter, likely harmful to legitimate news organizations.

It should also be clear from this chapter that people have a great deal more trust in their local news outlets, but for whatever reason, they don't think of home-based journalism when they evaluate the media writ large. But the truth is that a vast majority of journalists in the United States work for local newspapers, TV stations, and radio stations. National media may make a bigger splash, but most of the day's headlines are crafted by local journalists covering what's going on—as NBC *Today's* Al Roker would put it—"in your neck of the woods." Perhaps more importantly, most people use local television—a source they tend to trust—more than any other source to learn about the world.

We've also covered how difficult it is to objectively measure bias. How many times should Democrats and Republicans be quoted in a story for it to be perfectly balanced? Must soundbites from competing parties be exactly the same length? What if one side is making an argument in bad faith—is it biased to point that out, or should journalists just present the information as it is and let the audience decide? Researchers do not agree on one way to measure news bias, and as you've learned about hostile media perception (more about that in Chapter 7), allowing the audience to gauge bias is an imperfect tactic as well.

To be sure, there is always a risk that a journalist's' own political preferences might inform their coverage, but you've learned from this chapter that a lot of the issues that audiences have with journalism are borne from structural biases: deadlines, lack of resources, and an adherence to traditional news values. Any journalist will tell you that objectivity, fairness, independence, and a commitment to truth are fundamental to good reporting. What those values look like in practice—and how they're interpreted by the audience—is ever evolving.

DIY Research

Shannon C. McGregor, University of Utah

McGregor, S. C. (2019). Social media as public opinion: How journalists use social media to represent public opinion. *Journalism*, 20(8), 1070–1086.

Shannon C. McGregor is assistant professor of communication at the University of Utah. McGregor is the author or coauthor of more than twenty articles, book chapters, and books in the field of political communication. Her work examines how social media is represented as public opinion, how social media companies shape and approach modern campaign communication, and *big data* in political communication research. She won the Lynda Lee Kaid Outstanding Dissertation Award, National Communication Association in 2018. She has organized several leading conferences in political communication, including the Badass Ladies of Communication meeting after the 2019 International Communication Association conference. Her article uses a content analysis of 2016 news stories and interviews with journalists to understand how journalists use social media posts—even though social media users are a skewed sample of public attitudes—to represent public opinion.

Wagner and Perryman: You found that journalists use social media to reflect public opinion. What are some consequences of that behavior?

McGregor: Twitter can only represent opinion on Twitter—it doesn't represent the opinions of people across the country. So, when journalists include metrics or posts from Twitter or Facebook to showcase public opinion, it presents a very particular opinion—one that is likely more partisan and polarized than the US public as a whole. Opinions on Twitter are also not limited by national borders and people's identity cannot be easily verified. During the 2016 election, more than thirty news outlets included tweets in their stories as public opinion that we now know were part of the Russian-led disinformation campaign.

Wagner and Perryman: You engaged in multimethod research, content analyzing news coverage of the 2016 election and interviewing journalists themselves. How did using those two strategies together inform what you discovered in your article?

McGregor: In this case, the content analysis guided the interviews. I examined social media as public opinion in news stories first—this gave me an idea of the scope and terrain of this emergent phenomenon. I then culled a list of journalists to interview from the bylines in my content analysis, allowing me to hear from journalists in their own words about how social media data shaped their reporting on public opinion. Together the two methods allow me to understand the processes that led to what I analyze in the news content, instead of making assumptions about journalistic routines.

Wagner and Perryman: If a student reading this book wanted to conduct a research paper for their class that examined how journalists used social media to reflect public opinion, where would you recommend they start?

McGregor: Start by consuming lots of news! If you attune yourself to all the ways social media is mentioned to bolster arguments, describe public opinion, and shape coverage, you will undoubtedly find many new avenues for research in this area. For instance, I observed that many times social media used to represent public opinion in stories that made fun of a candidate—exploring the role of humor would be interesting.

Wagner and Perryman: What do you wish you had known about political communication research when you were an undergraduate?

McGregor: I wish I knew more about it! I was a journalism undergrad, but we didn't learn a lot about all the things that shape the news. Political communication research offers critical insight into all of this. It's so important for folks who may go on to be journalists or strategists to understand research—it's not just for those who want to go on to become researchers.

How Can I Help?

Dannagal G. Young, University of Delaware

Danna Young is associate professor of communication at the University of Delaware. She is also an improv comedian. She has published dozens of articles examining the effects of political satire and the psychology of humor as well as political psychology and political communication and public opinion more generally. Her new book *Irony and Outrage: The Polarized Landscape of Rage, Fear, and Laughter in the United States* is a major contribution to our understanding of communication and the world we live in. Besides her award-winning scholarship and teaching, Professor Young performed at Comedy Sportz in Philadelphia—a playful, highly informative talk show that explored the psychology of media, politics, and popular culture. She also cocreated vMOBilize—gamifying civic learning and engagement. We asked her about those two initiatives over email.

Wagner and Perryman: What was the philosophy behind "Dr. Young Unpacks"? How do you think about what roles social scientists can play in civic life?

Young: After twenty years studying political communication theory, I started feeling as though our field kept covering the same territory over and over. I felt like what we actually needed to effect change among the public and among journalists was not oodles of new ideas, necessarily, but for the public and journalists to be aware of the ideas we've already got. Ideas relating to media economics, media psychology: the ways that media industries work and why news looks the way it does, combined with an understanding of how and why our brain works the way they do and what happens when media content (shaped by profit and ratings motives) interacts with the natural processes of our brains. My thought was that bringing these issues to life in the classroom has profound effects on the ways that students interact with—and are critical of—their mediated worlds—so why not the public? Why not just people out in the world who are curious about the way media affect viewers? If people are able to consume media content aren't they also able to (and shouldn't they) start thinking about how and why that content looks like it does and what effects it might have on them? This was the spirit behind Dr. Young Unpacks: Making information about media industries, effects, and psychology playful and fun and accessible for audiences. The shows also featured interviews with expert guests who responded to questions on a particular topic or study. These interviews relayed new social science findings, but also had a lot of laughs.

Wagner and Perryman: What kind of feedback did you get from audiences?

Young: My favorite part of the show was hearing from people outside of academia. Folks who are interested in news and current events, but maybe haven't taken classes or read books about these issues from an academic standpoint. They loved acquiring new terminology and language to describe some of the phenomena that they are experiencing in their worlds. There were the "ah-ha!" moments for them as I covered some habit or tendency of news, and explained how and why it looks the way it does. For me, that was a giant win. For the graduate students and political communication scholars in the crowds, they reported learning new ways to explore and teach these ideas that relate to media industries and political communication. Many talked about wanting to integrate the examples from the comedy club into their college classes.

Wagner and Perryman: While readers of this book aren't likely to host public events where they unpack some of social sciences' mysteries for a live audience, what are ways that young scholars of political communication can use their knowledge for good?

Young: Every single person that we meet in the world every single day would benefit from the knowledge that political communication scholars have: understanding the habits and pressures that guide the behaviors of news organizations, understanding how political polarization shapes society, how motivated reasoning and selective perception affect how we come to know what we (think we) know. Once you start learning these ideas and start to grasp the significance of these phenomena on individuals, society, and democracy, you can *unlearn* it. You can't *unring* that bell. You are no longer a Muggle. You are now a Wizard. And as a wizard, you now have an obligation to use those powers for good. Without being condescending or arrogant, you can help the people you love (family, friends, parents, grandparents) start to better understand their world, too.

Wagner and Perryman: What is vMOBilize and how did it work?

Young: vMOBilize is an online social networking that Matt Baum (Harvard) and I created to try to put political communication theory to work. The game was designed to facilitate political engagement, attention, efficacy, knowledge, and participation among college students by *gamifying* civic behaviors—making them fun and easy in an online game context. Students played the game throughout the semester as a supplement to course instruction. The game issues weekly challenges that students can complete in exchange for points and virtual badges. Points were tallied at the end of

(Continued)

the semester and extra credit was awarded based on the rate of participation in the online game. Challenges included things like reading or viewing a news story and answering questions, filling out brief public opinion surveys, *checking in* at political events, and uploading politically relevant photos. Through a controlled study completed in 2016, we found positive effects of gameplay on voter registration, virtual political participation (following a candidate on Twitter, liking a candidate on Facebook, and watching debates), and consumption of public affairs information (including National Public Radio, non-NPR political talk radio, and online news aggregator sites). We were also encouraged by the finding that the students with the least political knowledge at the start of the game were the ones who benefited *most* on many of these dimensions of political engagement. The best part was that the students really seemed to enjoy the game: 79 percent of participants reported being very to somewhat pleased if they were asked to play the game again.

Wagner and Perryman: What did your research's findings about knowledge suggest to you about how teachers should think about educating young people about their civic rights and responsibilities?

Young: One of the risks of political engagement or other informational campaigns is that they tend to benefit the people who need the information the least. We know from research on the Knowledge Gap that the people who learn the most or are most affected by health and political informational campaigns are the people who are already in the know. Our study shows that if you change the currency of the campaign—where the currency isn't informational, but is playful (like *points* for a game that are rewarded with extra credit)—you avoid the *top benefits most* pitfall. In a sense, what vMOBilize does is reduce the barriers to entry by changing the motivational incentives to engage politically. Instead of appealing to civic duty or democratic obligations, the game is just about competing with friends and classmates in a low-stakes environment in which the political engagement just happens almost by accident. Just like parents who put spinach in a blender and feed it to their kids baked into a chocolate cake, so too can games and other entertainment content quietly integrate democratically healthy information in a way that benefits audiences.

CHAPTER

5

The Politics of Attention

FOR LINCOLN, IT WAS NEWSPAPERS. For FDR, radio. For Kennedy, television. And for Trump, Twitter.

The technology may change, but the desire among politicians to communicate with the masses has not. For much of American history, the press was the primary bridge between office-holders and those they served. The entire nation wasn't present for Lincoln's Gettysburg Address, but within a few days, it had been telegraphed and printed on the front page of newspapers across the country. Even today, as Trump tweets directly to his constituents, his remarks are picked up, analyzed, and amplified by the press.

Though it's somewhat of a tradition for politicians to wrestle with the press, there's also a sense that these two oft-competing pillars of democracy need one another. The cynical view is that journalists need lawmakers for ratings and lawmakers need journalists to try and schmooze the public. The *healthy democracy* view is that journalists see it as part of their professional mission to shine a light on government, and lawmakers see the press as a pesky but necessary way of truth finding and public accountability.

The tension between those who govern and those who control the microphone has been further complicated by the fact that it's now easier than ever for members of the public to talk back—and to tune out voices they don't want to hear. Constituents no longer have to show up at a town hall meeting to voice their displeasure with their representative; now they can just fire off an ALL CAPS tweet. Someone who doesn't want to hear about the president's remarks can simply change the channel, unfollow, or unsubscribe.

Had we written this chapter even a decade ago, the focus might have been solely on how politicians communicate with the public through the media, a style of communication where media are the megaphone. Today, that communication is more like a telephone conversation: no longer top-down, centralized, or one-sided. Politicians now communicate directly with the public. The public talks back. The press is often somewhere in the middle, listening to the conversation and deciding when to turn up the volume, mediate, or interpret. This chapter focuses on the flow of communication between the public and lawmakers—and the news media's role in that discussion.

How Politicians Communicate With Media

Lawmakers have many incentives to communicate with journalists. The journalists aren't really the intended audience, of course, the endgame is getting their message to the public, but news media are a convenient avenue for visibility. In our political system, visibility matters. Research shows that people are more likely to vote for (and are generally more trusting of) politicians they are familiar with.[1] News coverage is where most people learn about politics.[2]

Interviews

Whether it's a sit-down with *60 Minutes* or a quick sound bite in the local news, politicians most often appear in the news because at some point, a journalist thought to ask them a question. Those questions are sometimes asked in a prearranged setting where a politician sits down with a journalist to discuss a range of issues, or they may be volleyed at a lawmaker as he exits the room after an important meeting or event.

Granting interviews is strategic. Lawmakers will happily accept interview requests when they're seeking support for a new bill, want to be seen as an authority on some topic in the news, or are in the midst of campaigning. At the higher levels of government, lawmakers have media relations teams that field these requests and make connections with reporters. When caught up in a scandal or reeling from negative publicity, lawmakers and candidates are likely to be far more selective about their interviews. For example, when an old college yearbook revealed that Virginia governor Ralph Northam may have once worn blackface, the governor didn't respond to every outlet's request for comment. Instead, he did a sit-down interview with CBS' Gayle King. Northam's team likely thought about how the format and reach would impact public reaction. He was in hot water, so a sit-down setting where he would have more time to explain himself was favorable. King is respected and nonpartisan, lending more credibility to his statements than if he interviewed with someone seen as sympathetic. And of course, CBS has a large, national audience—an attractive factor for public figures.

Northam not only picked an advantageous interview setting, he also likely spent time preparing for the interview. Indeed, learning how to talk to journalists is an increasingly important skill in governing. At the most basic level, simply being willing to talk to journalists goes a long way. There are go-to folks in a journalist's contact list—sources they know they can rely on for a statement or a quick quote. Those are the people who will get the first call.

While there is a popular perception that politicians tend to dodge questions in interviews, press conferences, or during debates, research shows that this is not often the case. One study looked at fifteen years of presidential Q&A sessions and found that presidents rarely (3 percent of the time) outright refused to answer a question and that they never answered a question by pivoting to a totally different topic. Instead, they almost always stuck with the topic at hand, even if they didn't fully answer the question.[3] Rather than *changing the subject*, it's more common for politicians to give an on-topic answer, even if that answer is a bit ambiguous. One study shows that this type of *artful* dodge can be effective. A series of experiments shows that audiences are not very good at catching when politicians avoid answering questions as long as the answer they do provide is on-topic.[4]

In 2014, the magazine *Governing* asked public officials to rank the order in which they would respond to local media requests for interviews.[5] Nearly half ranked TV outlets first, 37 percent ranked newspaper first, and only 7 percent said their first callback would be to an online-only outlet. There's not much of a mystery as to why politicians prefer TV—local and network TV is still the number one source for news for most Americans. Over five million televisions are tuned in to the networks' evening newscasts every day, while 3.3 million TVs tune in for their local early evening news shows. Cable news pulls in about 1.2 million TV sets a night.[6]

Television also offers many alternative settings to the traditional hard news interview. Interviews on entertainment television shows like *The Daily Show, The Ellen DeGeneres Show,* or *The Tonight Show* are a regular stop on the interview circuit, especially during elections. Research shows it can be an effective strategy—one study found that people are able to remember more about a candidate after watching them on a political comedy show compared to when watching them on cable news.[7] Another study found that people who watched an opposition candidate on a talk show (like *Oprah*), found them more likeable.[8] There is even some evidence that *Late Show* host Stephen Colbert's old program, *The Colbert Report*, affected campaign donations for Democrats who appeared on his show.[9]

Press Conferences

Instead of interviewing with one journalist at a time, why not talk to the entire press corps at once? In a press conference setting (also known as news conferences), lawmakers read a statement to the press, often allowing a Q&A with a gaggle of reporters. It's a useful tool during campaigning, or when big news breaks and lawmakers feel the need to respond.

Journalists don't typically prefer the format; if the interviewee says something newsworthy, it's not exclusive and it may not have been in answer to their particular question (though anything said during a press conference is fair game). But they're often the only opportunity for reporters to ask questions of public figures, especially at the presidential level. Data from the American President Project shows that presidents today give far fewer press conferences than in the past.[10] For example, FDR averaged over seventy conferences a year. Obama averaged twenty. When possible, reporters try to pull the participants in a press conference off to the side for a more exclusive exchange.

The Anonymous Interview

Political figures may also be interviewed under the condition of anonymity. This is less typically the case for political leaders, but rather, people within the political sphere. You might see them identified by where they work, for example, "White House advisors," or in general terms like, "a person familiar with the matter." Similarly, political sources may talk to reporters off-the-record, meaning the information can't be published, even if attributed to an anonymous source.

The anonymity works for the source, not the journalist. Journalists would always prefer sources go public, but fear of retribution or unwanted publicity can sometimes mean a journalist must choose between having the story at all and having an anonymous source. The payoff can be worth it when sources bring an important story from the shadows into the light. It can also go the other way, such as when a *New York Times* reporter fabricated an unnamed police source when reporting on the 2002 DC sniper case.

Why would a political figure leak information, either by acting as a quotable, anonymous source or forking over desired documents? You may recall when Edward Snowden leaked highly classified NSA documents, or when pages of Trump's 1995 tax return randomly showed up in reporters' mailboxes. Whistleblowing occurs when someone leaks information because they think it's of public concern. The most famous example of a source turning to reporters to reveal government secrets may be Watergate. Known only as "Deep Throat" until 2005, former FBI Associate Director Mark Felt aided *The Washington Post's* Bob Woodward and Carl Bernstein by leaking key details about the Nixon administration's behavior.

Secret-spilling that leads to public awareness of misbehavior is one category of leaks, but more common are leaks that offer (sometimes embarrassing) peeks behind the curtain. Rather than sharing classified information, leakers sometimes tell journalists unauthorized information. Trump grew so frustrated after the *Times* ran an editorial penned by an anonymous source claiming to part of the *resistance* within the president's administration that he floated several ideas for hunting down the source of the leak.

The Espionage Act and other federal laws, however, only allow prosecution for sharing certain national security information. He certainly isn't the first president to try and punish leakers—Obama's administration prosecuted several cases against whistleblowers.

Professional journalism guidelines do not forbid the use of anonymous sources or the use of leaked info, but they do encourage reporters to be careful. It's entirely possible that political figures would speak anonymously to damage an opponent or discredit a news agency. One step journalists take to make sure they aren't being misled is to independently verify a source's claims; that is, they seek out other evidence that supports the information, or find others who will verify the information (even if that's also anonymously). For example, a *Times* story about the Trump administration once attributed information to "six White House aides." A consistent story from several sources offers more confidence in the information.

How common is the use of unnamed sources in political journalism? In a content analysis of over 1,200 newspaper articles from 1958 to 2008, one study showed that the use of anonymous sources peaked in the 1970s (nearly half of examined articles included an unnamed source) and was less common by the twenty-first century (only a quarter of articles in the 2008 sample used unnamed sources).[11] It may seem like anonymous sources are on the rise once again, but more recent content analyses are not available. It's unclear whether unnamed sources are being used more often in reporting on the Trump administration, or whether it's just a popular topic of discussion on social media. Either way, some publications have cracked down on the practice. In 2016, for example, the *Times* said its new guidelines resulted in a 30 percent decrease in the use of unnamed sources.[12] Editors said they made the change after readers complained about the practice, and there is some research that suggests readers find stories with unnamed sources less credible.[13]

Reporters may offer alternatives to sources that can encourage them to go on-record. One good practice is to be open with political sources about the purpose and parameters of an interview. No one wants to be on the receiving end of a *gotcha* line of questioning. It should be noted, though, that sharing exact questions ahead of time is generally considered unethical in the news industry. Another way journalists wrangle reluctant sources is to offer quote approval—agreeing to give the source access to (and sometimes veto power for) quotes. Many publications forbid quote approval, and even though most journalists would consider it unethical for purposes other than checking the accuracy of a statement, it does happen.

Becoming a Preferred Source

There are patterns to the types of political figures that journalists tend to interview. The journalistic value of *balance* does not necessarily mean that all lawmakers or political candidates receive the same amount of attention. Factors such as accessibility, a willingness to work with publication deadlines, and eloquence all make candidates or office-holders more likely to be interviewed. But beyond a willingness to participate, there are some inherent factors that help determine whether journalists will offer up a slice of the spotlight.

First, it's generally the case that incumbents dominate news coverage, a phenomenon known as the *incumbency bonus*. Researchers analyzing twenty years' worth of news coverage in Denmark found that incumbents were mentioned twice as often as challengers. They reason that in nonelection contexts, journalists are focused on their watchdog role and thus less likely to pay attention to people who are not in power. Alternatively, as election contests heat up, the notion of balance is more relevant and challengers receive more attention.[14]

Similar to the incumbency bonus, journalists tend to seek out sources with authority on a topic, or *official* sources. Many scholars have observed that this means journalists are highly reliant on elite opinion, to the extent that issues may not even get coverage unless politically powerful people are in disagreement.[15] This is called indexing theory (see Chapter 2)—the idea that the views expressed by political elites will be the views that get media attention (i.e., without a powerful figure backing a view, it will not be *indexed* in coverage).[16] You might imagine this being a perfectly fine system when the spectrum of opinions available on Capitol Hill are reasonable, responsible, and reflective of the citizenry. You can also imagine this being quite a problem if elite views become extreme, illogical, or out of touch. Later in this chapter we'll discuss the tug-of-war between the press and politicians to control which issues are discussed and which views are heard.

Aside from these structural factors, characteristics of individual politicians also help account for media attention. One study found that being less agreeable and more extroverted tended to garner politicians more media coverage.[17]

How Politicians Communicate With the Public

Sometimes it's more efficient to skip the middleman! Whereas direct communication with the public used to be limited to speeches and debates (and even those tend to be filtered through news media), today political figures have more options than ever when it comes to talking directly to the public.

Your mind may immediately jump to Trump's use of Twitter— and that's a good example that we'll discuss—but first let's focus on the traditional ways that politicians communicate with constituents. In other words, besides watching the news, when do you hear directly from politicians? One avenue is through political advertising. Especially while in campaign mode, candidates will flood the airwaves, your inbox, and even your mailbox with direct communication. We don't want to spoil Chapter 8 for you, but suffice it so say that advertising isn't all that effective at changing minds. Still, it directly communicates a candidate's issue priorities and other branding and personality elements to voters (e.g., a *change* candidate, a policy wonk, a champion for workers, etc.).

Another traditional avenue for communicating directly with the public is to hold public events. During election season, these take the form of rallies, where a politician will deliver his or her *stump speech* slightly tailored for that particular audience. The size of a political rally is often fodder for pundits and analysts in news coverage, but it's important to keep in mind that rallies tend to attract enthusiastic and politically active folks. According to a 2018 Pew Research study, only 11 percent of Americans had attended a political rally in the past year.[18]

Outside of election season, public events are more likely to take the form of *town hall*–style meetings. These forums generally take place during Congress's August recess, and they can be a flashpoint for voter frustrations. The 2009 town halls are a good example. *Politico's* headline at the time, "Town halls gone wild," refers to a series of town hall meetings where Tea Party protestors raised a ruckus about healthcare reform. The number of town hall meetings has fluctuated ever since, with *Politico* reporting that 550 took place in August 2014, 450 in 2016, but only 180 scheduled for 2018, when a majority of House members didn't have any town halls on the books.[19] The traditional town hall Q&A format has also been co-opted by news media. By June 2019, CNN, Fox News, and MSNBC had cumulatively hosted over thirty town hall–style events. Some lawmakers host *virtual* town hall meetings on social media platforms. Lawmakers can reach larger groups who tend to be satisfied with the interactions with their representatives.[20]

Texting

Today, texts from political campaigns are commonplace—and depending on who you ask, annoying. But when Barack Obama texted potential voters in 2008, it was game changing. *Slate* even called text messaging the Obama campaign's *secret weapon*.[21]

Obama was the first candidate to harness the power of mass text messaging. His New Media division collected three million phone numbers from supporters, and cell phone users could text "HOPE" to subscribe to texts from the campaign. Obama's texts reminded people of important

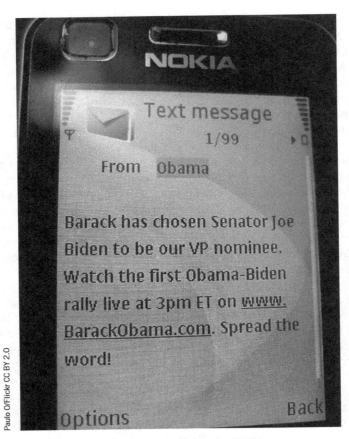

| Photo 5.1 Text Message From Obama Campaign Announcing VP Pick

deadlines and events (e.g., debates, registration deadlines), recruited volunteers in specific zip codes for phone banking or door-to-door canvassing, and made important campaign announcements. In fact, the campaign brought in a slew of new subscribers when it promised to make its VP announcement via text message (which it did . . . at 3 a.m.). Obama continued to be the *new media* candidate into the 2012 election, where he became the first to accept donations via text.

There is some evidence that texting is a more effective tool than other impersonal communication methods like robocalls or mass emails. One study from the 2006 election found that Election Day texts increased turnout by as much as 3 percent.[22] Another study—this one from local and statewide elections in 2009 and 2010—confirmed that text reminders to vote can increase turnout, but mostly among people who had voted in previous elections.[23] The results from these studies are somewhat surprising considering studies generally find that in-person tactics (phone banks or voter-to-voter conversations) are far more effective than impersonal tactics like direct mail or emails.[24] Some researchers have reasoned that texts are more effective simply because voters are likely to read them (even if they immediately delete).

Facebook

Obama's *new media* prowess was not limited to texting. He was also hailed as the Facebook king, with 1.7 million supporters on the platform. This may not seem impressive by today's standards—Obama now has around fifty-five million Facebook fans—but it was remarkable compared to the three hundred thousand *likes* his Republican opponent John McCain had back in 2008. Obama actually had more supporters on Myspace than McCain had on Facebook.[25]

Much to some users' dismay, Facebook is now a common arena for political talk. A lot of political discussion is user-to-user, but Facebook is now firmly a part of the arsenal of communication tools that politicians use as well. One arm of research focuses on the *supply side*—how politicians use Facebook to communicate with the public. Several years ago, the question would have been: which politicians use Facebook and why? Now, the social media platform is so enormous that elected officials feel compelled to use these platforms even if they do not believe they impact voters.[26]

The question has now become: how do politicians use Facebook? When asked, elected officials and political campaigns say they use Facebook to connect with voters and market themselves.[27] In practice, Facebook is more of a one-way communication channel. Interactive tools such as replying to comments are underused.[28] Politicians also use Facebook to share news articles, though an analysis of congressional Facebook posts by the Pew Research Center found that over half of the news articles shared by members of Congress were from sources predominantly linked to by members of one party.[29]

Facebook posts generally seem to fall into the category of simple information sharing, but one analysis of 2015–2016 posts found that roughly 10 percent of Facebook posts by members of Congress were strongly negative (demonstrating *indignant disagreement*) toward the opposing party. Those negative posts tended to come from congressional members with highly ideological voting records.[30] Another analysis of 2017 congressional Facebook posts showed that Democrats' posting activity surpassed Republicans' activity after the 2016 election, suggesting the out-of-power party may be more likely to engage with constituents via Facebook. These posts were overwhelmingly critical of Trump and Republicans—71 percent targeted the president, while 41 percent targeted Republicans.[31]

Few candidates seem to amass huge followings on Facebook. Even some well-funded, well-organized campaigns do not necessarily play well on Facebook.[32] In fact, only 25 percent of Americans say they follow a politician on social media.[33] One study found that the volume of media coverage and polling numbers—indicators of offline electoral success—does not correlate with social media popularity. Rather, candidates for open seats and those running in the out-of-power party seem to attract more followers, suggesting Facebook and other social media can be helpful in bucking the incumbency advantage enjoyed in offline campaigning efforts.[34] Members of Congress with the most liberal or conservative voting records also tend to have larger followings and get higher engagement on their posts.[35]

Users are more likely to interact with campaigns' posts about policy compared to posts that are purely promotional.[36] Users are also more likely to engage with posts that attack an opponent, publicize an endorsement, or call attention to a new TV ad than they are to engage with posts asking for donations.[37] One study showed that users respond to posts that communicate negative emotions, personal stories, or a call to action.[38] Another study—this one from the Pew Research Center Center—also confirms that negative posts get more traction. Pew looked at negative Facebook posts by members of Congress and found that posts that showed overly negative (or *indignant disagreement*) got twice as many likes and shares, and three times as many comments as posts which featured no disagreement.[39]

Tweets

Only 22 percent of American adults have Twitter accounts, and those who do tend to be younger, more likely Democrats, and more educated than the general public.[40] Despite the platform's smaller audience, you're unlikely to find many politicians without Twitter accounts.

Frequent tweeting is more common among candidates involved in competitive races and those with strong ideological positions. Content analyses reveal that most politicians use Twitter to post about campaign activity or share links to their websites, and rarely to discuss policy issues or differences. In fact, much like Facebook, studies show that politicians are mostly engaged in one-way communication, rarely interacting with constituents.[41]

A new trend in Twitter research focuses on Trump's use of the platform. In his first year as president, he sent out over 2,500 tweets—about seven a day. Analysis shows what might be obvious to anyone who follows Trump's Twitter activity—his style is grandiose, dynamic, and informal.[42] Or, as one researcher phrased it: amateurish but authen-

Donald J. Trump @
@realDonaldTrump

Follow

So funny to watch the Fake News, especially NBC and CNN. They are fighting hard to downplay the deal with North Korea. 500 days ago they would have "begged" for this deal-looked like war would break out. Our Country's biggest enemy is the Fake News so easily promulgated by fools!

9:30 AM - 13 Jun 2018

38,354 Retweets   153,190 Likes

♡ 49K   ↻ 38K   ♡ 153K   ✉

Photo 5.2 Trump tweeted about fake news 182 times in 2018.

tic.[43] While Trump rarely interacts with voters, he regularly goes head-to-head with celebrities or other politicians. His most popular tweets have been accusations of media bias and attacks on his Democratic opponents.[44]

Trump's tweets are rarely about bipartisanship. Rather, his account serves mostly *red meat* to his base. But while his base is responsible for the large number of likes and retweets on his messages, it's the journalists in his audience that really amplify his messages. About a quarter of Twitter users are journalists.[45] Rather than Trump tweeting in response to news events, his tweets during his candidacy have frequently directed news coverage—that is, when Trump tweets, journalists tend to cover either the tweets themselves or the topics they address.[46] We'll discuss the ability of politicians to direct media attention (i.e., agenda-setting) later in this chapter.

How the Public Talks Back

Direct Communication

In a 2018 survey, 23 percent of Americans said they had contacted an elected official in the past year, and 40 percent said they had done so in the past five years.[47] Though a majority do not try to directly influence their representatives, a sizeable percentage of citizens do call, email, or, more recently, tag them on social media.

Political experts say contacting lawmakers via traditional methods is not a waste of time. In a panel for *Propublica*, congressional insiders recommended writing letters, making phone calls, visiting district offices,

Donald Trump/Twitter

attending town hall meetings, writing op-eds for the local paper, and working with advocacy groups.[48] There are congressional staffers whose job is to read letters and field phone calls from constituents, entering the data into a constituent-management system. That data isn't publicly available. According to the Congressional Management Foundation, constituent communication takes up 20 to 30 percent of a congressional office's budget. Anecdotal and research data suggests that lawmakers are moderately responsive to constituents who want to talk. In one experiment, researchers sent nearly five thousand emails to lawmakers across forty-four states. More than half (55.6 percent) received responses.[49] Even so, many citizens fear they won't get much help from a representative they might contact if that representative is not a member of the citizen's political party.[50]

The extent to which direct communication influences lawmakers is unclear. Congressional staffers say personalized emails, letters, and editorials in local newspapers are more likely to influence a lawmaker's opinion than a phone call. Unless, of course, that phone call is part of a *flood* of opposition.[51] For example, the week of January 30, 2017—the first week of Trump's presidency—the Senate got an average 1.5 million phone calls a day. Those calls are more likely to be successful if they are unscripted and are from people who live in a lawmaker's own district.

One recent study is pessimistic that constituent contact has much of an effect on lawmakers. In an experiment, researcher John Cluverius divided hundreds of state lawmakers into groups and asked them what they would do if they received 1) six constituent emails about gun control, 2) six emails about genetically-modified foods, 3) sixty emails about gun control, or 4) sixty emails about GMOs. Lawmakers who got either six or sixty emails about gun control said it wouldn't affect their support for the bill, suggesting elected officials aren't likely to budge on deeply partisan issues. Lawmakers who got sixty emails supporting GMOs, on the other hand, said it would actually lower their support for the bill. Cluverius interviewed lawmakers to try and understand that result and found that while many elected officials say they want to hear personal stories, they are also frustrated by what they see as *artificial advocacy*. Cluverius concludes that because of polling abilities and clearly defined party ideologies, direct communication may fail to influence lawmakers because elected officials tend to believe they already know what people want.[52]

Other research shows that direct constituent lobbying efforts make a difference. For example, one study found that email lobbying influenced politicians' voting behavior.[53] As with many phenomena in political behavior, the likelihood of changing a lawmaker's mind through direct communication is largely context dependent. Constituents are more likely to be persuasive when they speak from personal experience, live in the official's district, and are contacting the lawmaker about an issue that isn't a deeply entrenched partisan issue.

Protests

Protests are an indirect, collective way of putting pressure on elected officials. A staple of political activism, protests have often been part of political movements that sparked radical change. The Boston Tea Party in 1773 helped kick off the American Revolution, the 1911 Triangle Shirtwaist fire protests paved the way for workplace safety laws still in place today, and the 1963 March on Washington built broad support for the Civil Rights Act. Hindsight allows us to see how those events made a big impact, but are they outliers, or do protests typically lead to political change?

It's tough to measure the immediate and long-term effects of protests, but researchers in this area have gotten creative. One study, for example, compared white Americans living in counties where peaceful civil rights protests took place in the 1960s to whites who live in counties where protests did not take place. The results showed that white Americans living in counties where protests took place were less racist, more likely to support affirmative action, and more likely to identify as Democrats.[54] Another notable study looked at the efficacy of the 2009 Tea Party protests by comparing support for the movement in areas where it rained on the protest day versus areas where it didn't rain. Areas where it didn't rain should have had higher protest turnout. Sure enough, the Tea Party seemed to have gained more ground in areas where it didn't rain—suggesting well-attended protests were influential.[55]

In their study of thirty years of both liberal and conservative protests, Daniel Gillion and Sarah Soule conclude that vote share for the protesting party increases in districts where protests take place, and that protests create an opening for challengers. They conclude, "When legislators are not attentive to the issues raised by protest behavior, a fertile ground is fostered for challenger candidates to underscore the sitting politician's failure to address constituent concerns, leading to a greater number of quality challengers."[56]

Of course, not all protests are equally as effective. Some evidence suggests that protests are twice as effective when they are nonviolent.[57] One experiment showed that when fictional antiracist protestors were said to act violently against a white nationalist group, people were not only less supportive of the antiracist protesters, they were more supportive of the white nationalists.[58]

| Photo 5.3 Civil Rights March on Washington, DC

Despite academic and historical evidence that protests can be effective, the public largely believes they don't work. For example, a 2016 poll shows that only 7 percent of white Americans and 19 percent of black Americans believe protests will improve racial equality.[59] Of course, people said the same thing back in the civil rights era. In 1961, Gallup asked Americans whether they believed sit-ins at lunch counters, freedom busses, and other demonstrations would help or hurt the civil rights movement. A majority (57 percent) believed it would hurt it. They might say differently today!

How journalists cover protests can also influence public perception of collective action. Protests tend to get media coverage when they are deviant and socially significant.[60] Coverage tends to focus less on the issues at the heart of the protest and more on the actions of the protesters, conflict with counter-protesters or those in power, and unusual or new protest tactics. In his experiment about citizens' reactions to news coverage of protester–police confrontations, Douglas McLeod summarizes several ways that journalists undermine protests movements:[61]

- Emphasizing violence and ignoring peaceful action

- Gathering soundbites or quotes from police and not the intended target of the protest (e.g., government, corporation), thereby framing the story as protesters versus police

- Protesters either not interviewed or not given enough space to make their case

- Police often shown to be restoring order, implying the protest needed intervention

- Focusing on protest actions, not the issues being protested

- Selective use of quotation marks, such as when "peace march" is used to describe an anti-war demonstration

Some scholars have argued that negative media coverage of social protesters—and the tendency to cover protest behavior as deviant—may limit which ideas are seen as legitimate in the public sphere. Several experiments have shown that how journalists frame protests in news coverage impacts how people see protesters and the movement itself. Of course, Americans tend to have unfavorable views of protesters to begin with. Only 27 percent of Americans, for example, thought the residents of Ferguson, Missouri, were *reasonable* in their protests after the police shot and killed Black teenager Michael Brown in 2014.[62] Still, Americans largely believe in maintaining the right to protest. In a 2017 poll, 79 percent said the right to nonviolent protest was *very important* for democracy.[63]

And even with the popular perception that protests don't work, a good chunk of Americans have participated in one. According to 2018 Gallup data, a little over a third of Americans say they have felt the urge to participate in a protest at some point in their lives. Protests have been particularly popular since 2016. A 2018 *The Washington Post*-Kaiser Family Foundation poll found that one of every five Americans had participated in a rally or protest since Trump's election. The 2017 Women's March is currently the largest US protest of all time.

Talking Politics Online

The arrival of the internet, and with it, social media, opened up a new avenue for political participation. Citizens can now express their political views by liking political pages, displaying preferences via profile pictures, discussing politics in posts or comment sections, tagging politicians or using political hashtags, and organizing protests or rallies. As the online world gives folks more opportunities to participate in the political process, researchers have explored whether social media might *reinvigorate* the democratic process, creating a virtual public sphere for deliberation, discovery, and putting the pressure on elected officials.

The evidence as to whether social media has been a *good* thing for political participation is a mixed bag. On the one hand, studies find that people who use social media in certain ways (e.g., for seeking out information or news) are more likely to be civically engaged and participate in politics both offline and online.[64] Other scholars have found social media to have a negative impact on participation, such as one field experiment which showed that users tasked with maintaining a Facebook account for six months reported being less likely to engage with politics.[65] Especially for those that want to use social media as a form of escapism, seeing politics on their timelines can be frustrating—or, as one study found, can lead to apathy and cynicism.[66] In the midst of the 2016 election season— 37 percent of Americans said they were worn out by political posts and discussions on social media.[67] A 2019 poll showed that 57 percent of Americans believe social media divides us—though that doesn't appear to be a deterrent for using the platforms: 69 percent say they use social media at least once a day.[68]

One explanation for the inconsistent findings about the overall effects of using social media for talking politics is the diversity of methods and measures that researchers use to examine the issue. Some scholars look at specific social networks, while others look at social media use overall. Some studies focus on behavioral outcomes like whether social media use makes people more likely to vote, while others focus on attitudes, such as whether social media use makes people more understanding of others' views. Different methods, like panel analysis (repeated observations of the same people over time), cross-sectional surveys (one-shot surveys), or experiments sometimes yield different results.

But what is clear from the research is that for many users, social media *can* be a tool for positive political participation. To be sure, new platforms for deliberation also have notable downsides. It's important to recognize both the good and bad of politics on social media. Knowing these can help you maximize the value of your own social media use for political purposes.

Connections and Discussions

Imagine the internet as a ginormous town square. You can join in on the millions of groups having conversations. Or you can listen to the person with a megaphone at the center of the square. Or you can ignore it all and opt to watch cats in the corner.

A lot of people opt for the cats. Some scholars argue that the expansiveness of the digital town square has allowed more opportunity to opt out of political participation online, instead using digital access for entertainment and nonpolitical purposes.[69] At the same time, there is also evidence that people are increasingly reliant on their online social networks for political information.[70] During the 2016 election, for example, 44 percent of Americans said they had learned something about the election in the past week from social media. On Facebook, a lot of that exposure is incidental—from friends and family members sharing political information. Some researchers argue that one way social media enhances political participation is that it increases the size of a users' friend network, allowing more opportunities for exposure to political information and chances for participation.[71]

According to self-reports of activity on social media, only 9 percent of users *often* discuss, comment, or post about politics on social media, though an additional 23 percent say they *sometimes* do.[72] And even though younger people are more likely to use social media in general, those 50 and older are just as likely as those under 50 to talk politics online. Those who do talk politics online tend to be less sensitive to rejection, that is, they've got thick skin![73]

When you imagine the audience for a political post online, you realize that a diverse network of friends, coworkers, family members, etc., will see it. That can discourage participation for a lot of folks. Indeed, young people who post about politics on social media tend to rank low on scales of conflict avoidance—that is, "Some individuals posting about politics enjoy being provocateurs, posting not *in spite of* the potential for disagreement but *because* of it."[74]

Seeing political discussions, even disagreements, can lead to an assortment of effects. Some research has shown that the more frequently people witness political expression online, the more likely they are to participate themselves. Others find that exposure to political disagreement may lead to unfriending (though, this is actually pretty uncommon).[75] Others worry that coming across dissenting political opinions on social media can stifle political expression[76] (i.e., spiral of silence theory). It's also unclear whether exposure to differing political views via social media does much to change political opinions: only 14 percent of Americans say they have changed their mind on an issue because of something they saw on social media.[77]

While a sizeable portion of internet users talk about politics sometimes, a much smaller percentage of social media users take on the role of political influencers. One study found that 12 percent of those in a national sample were what the authors call *prosumers*—users that are highly engaged in consuming, producing, and sharing political content via social media. These people see themselves as opinion leaders.[78] This opinion leadership is easy to see on Twitter, where 50 percent of all tweets are now retweets (back in 2012, it was only 20 percent).[79]

Who are these active political personalities? They're likely to be the same people who are active in offline political activity, as studies have shown that political activism online is generated by the same folks heavily involved in politics offline. Those with consistently liberal or conservative views are more likely than those with mixed views to say they frequently talk about politics.[80] But social media may also open the door for some quieter voices, as people from marginalized communities show high levels of political participation on Twitter.[81]

Filter Bubbles

When social media allows you to talk politics with anyone, who do you reach out to? That can go one of two ways: users can use the online world as an opportunity to expand their network and connect with a variety of different voices or they can hunker down, boxing themselves into an *echo chamber* of like-minded voices.

The idea that people might use the filtering and networking power of the online world to build havens of homogeneity has long been a concern for scholars, pundits, and even citizens. The idea is that instead of fostering a public sphere with diverse voices, the internet has actually made it easier for people to be exposed only to like-minded information. Chapter 7 discusses this concept in terms of news exposure. Selective exposure is the idea that people build news diets of only like-minded media, especially online. But the idea of filter bubbles—also called echo chambers—tends to refer to a situation where people build like-minded networks of *people* online. Being drawn to like-minded others is a concept called *homophily*.

On Twitter, researchers have found that liberals and conservatives tend to be segregated into ideological clusters. One study found that liberals were more likely to retweet liberals and conservatives were more likely to retweet conservatives (though liberals were more likely than conservatives to retweet someone from the opposing ideology).[82] Other studies have also shown that conservatives are more likely than liberals to build Twitter networks of like-minded users.[83]

On Facebook, people also tend to be connected with people who share their ideology (though, of course, this is partly because people tend to be friends with people who share their political leanings offline). One study of 10.1 million Facebook users who included their ideological preference on their profiles concluded that about 20 percent of the friend networks for liberals and conservatives were made up of people from the *other side*.[84] If you ask people directly, they say that most of their friends share some, but not all, of their beliefs.[85]

When people do discuss politics online with people they disagree with, it may not have the effect of broadening their perspective. A vast majority (64 percent) of Americans say that these types of discussions cause them to realize they have less in common politically that they thought.[86] One study found that when Republicans were exposed to Twitter bots that retweeted messages with liberal political views, they became more conservative (Democrats also became slightly more liberal when exposed to conservative tweets, but not significantly so).[87]

A similar concern to echo chambers is the idea that these like-minded networks will have the effect of promoting more extreme voices. One study found that even though extreme conservatives and liberals made up only 16 percent of sampled users, extreme liberals accounted for 28 percent of all retweets about the 2012 election and extreme conservatives accounted for 38 percent.[88]

But researchers have also pushed back on the idea that social media creates filter bubbles at all. Some studies have shown that users' friend networks on social media are more diverse than they realize.[89] Others have found that the more users engage with others on social networks, the more likely they are to be exposed to diverse political news[90] and to share political news from sources across the political spectrum.[91] One study attempted to quantify the number of people living in filter bubbles on Facebook, concluding that between 10–27 percent of Facebook users fit that profile, depending on the method used to define *filter bubble*. Similarly, despite widespread concern that personalized algorithms will feed users only one-sided political information, some evidence suggests these concerns are overblown; several studies have shown that Google News recommends similar articles to liberals and conservatives, with about 70 percent of the recommendations coming from only five major news outlets.[92]

Incivility

The internet gave people more opportunities to talk politics—and inevitably, more opportunities to argue about politics. As you've probably noticed, it's not always a polite conversation. Scholars call this uncivil online discussion "an extreme form of polarized discussion in which discussion participants use disrespectful statements or attacks which clearly demonstrate disrespect or insult toward an opposing political party or its members."[93] You might have heard of it as *flaming* or *trolling*, though those terms are usually associated with attention-seeking, rather than sincere, uncivil posters.

A majority (53 percent) of Americans say their online discussions are less respectful than offline, and 49 percent say they are less civil.[94] Content analyses back up that perception, with studies showing that talking politics online tends to be more uncivil than talking politics in person.[95] A content analysis of Twitter and Facebook responses to posts from the White House concluded that responses are more uncivil on Twitter than Facebook, partly because of differences between users of the two platforms.[96]

Who participates in uncivil dialogue? Anonymous users are the most likely suspects. Results from one experiment show that anonymous users wrote nearly twice as many uncivil comments compared to non-anonymous users.[97] Even places that would seemingly attract similar audiences sported differences in anonymous and non-anonymous comments. For example, comments on *The Washington Post's* website—where there is anonymity—are more uncivil than comments on the *Post's* Facebook page—where there is less anonymity.[98]

Other determinants of making uncivil comments online include personality traits—people who are lower on agreeableness and openness to experience are more likely to see uncivil comments as acceptable responses.[99] People who witness uncivil comments online also become more likely to contribute uncivil comments themselves.[100] Overall, data on the frequency of uncivil comments on social media is hard to come by, but a content analysis of comments on news articles suggests about 20 percent are uncivil.

While only a small fraction of users may make uncivil comments online, lots of people who aren't involved in the discussion are still exposed to it. What sort of effects does exposure to uncivil political talk have? First, uncivil comments can understandably cause anger and other unwelcome emotions. On the one hand, this can be defeating . . . discouraging discussion and making people think less of those on the other side of the argument. On the other hand, anger can be motivating, and there is some evidence that uncivil discussions can be more engaging than civil conversations.[101]

Another risk of exposure to uncivil political discussion online is the impression it gives people about the state of public opinion. One study found that, while uncivil comments don't cause people to become more extreme in their own attitudes, they do lead to a belief that the public is extremely polarized. In other words, witnessing uncivil disagreement online makes you think the public is hopelessly divided.[102] This can be problematic since people already tend to think the United States is more polarized than it really is.[103] Believing the public is divided also contributes to an *us versus them* mentality.

Another possibility, at least for uncivil comments in the context of news stories, is that seeing uncivil discussion regarding news articles can influence perceptions of the news itself. For example, one study found that being exposed to uncivil comments on a story about an emerging technology made people think the technology was riskier.[104] Uncivil comments may also lead users to think the accompanying news story is negative and biased.[105] Concerns about the effects of uncivil online discussions have led several news outlets to shut down comment sections on their articles.

Uncivil, vilifying, or violent comments can also be associated with support for political violence. Political scientist Nathan Kalmoe ran an experiment where he found that exposure to mildly violent political metaphors ("fighting for our future") increased support for political violence among people with aggressive personalities. That is, aggressive people become even more likely to support political violence when they are exposed to violent political rhetoric.[106]

Scholars have also studied how President Trump's words have caused audiences to behave worse than they otherwise would. In national experiments from 2016 and 2017, political scientist Brian Schaffner found that exposure to Trump's uncivil, and what Kalmoe and many others have called racist, comments about Mexicans during his campaign led individuals to be more likely to write offensive statements toward Mexicans and other groups.

Hashtag Politics

Online political action is sometimes referred to as hashtag politics, a descriptive term, to be sure, but also one that can imply *lazy* or *ineffectual* political action (the term *slacktivism* is also popular to refer to online political activism). A 2018 survey found that more than 70 percent of Americans believe that social media makes people believe they're making a difference when they're really not.[107] There is research that counters that assumption—one study of Israeli internet users, for example, found that political participation online (e.g., signing petitions, *liking* political content) was a positive predictor of offline participation.[108]

Americans also see a lot of positives for online political movements. A majority say social media movements are important for getting elected officials to pay attention to issues and creating sustained movements for social change. Black Americans, in particular, see social media as a tool to amplify underrepresented voices and highlight important issues.[109] Movements like #blacklivesmatter and #metoo undoubtedly found a footing in public dialogue through trending hashtags. Hashtags raise participants' voices to a volume louder than they could achieve alone. And with approximately five hundred million tweets sent per day, hashtags do the mundane but important task of organizing a very big conversation because they are uniquely searchable.

There's also evidence that lawmakers notice when there's an avalanche of social media activity on a given issue. In a 2015 report, nearly half of surveyed congressional staffers said that ten to thirty similar comments on one of their social media posts will grab their attention. More than 70 percent said a flurry of social media posts would have at least *some* effect on an undecided representative or senator.[110]

Communicating Which Issues Are Important

In the months leading up to the Affordable Care Act, we did not all just wake up one day and collectively decide that it was time to talk about health care. Nor is there a control panel somewhere on Capitol Hill where lawmakers crank up the dial on immigration one day and healthcare the next. The day's top issues and concerns do not necessarily arise organically, with concerned citizens suddenly able to make the entire nation care about a particular cause—nor are they handed down from on high, the public's priorities being controlled by a political puppet master.

The public agenda emerges from an informal negotiation between the public, lawmakers, and journalists. The political issues people are thinking about, discussing, and taking action on emerge from the communication flow between these groups. Journalists write stories about issues that people are talking about, and people talk about issues in the news. Lawmakers draw reporters' attention to certain stories, and lawmakers must address issues that journalists are reporting on.

Scholars explore "what's on the public's mind and how did it get there" in areas of research called *agenda-building* and *agenda-setting*. The basic premise of agenda-setting is that when news media pay more attention to an issue, the public begins to believe that issue is important. Agenda-building research, on the other hand, focuses on who tries to influence the news agenda and their methods of doing so. A third, emerging area of research—called agenda-uptake—focuses on the multi-directional transfer of issue salience between the digital publics, mainstream news, and niche news outlets.

Agenda-Setting

Maxwell McCombs and Donald Shaw introduced agenda-setting theory in 1972 in a study that demonstrated that what voters in the 1968 election thought of as the most important issues were the same issues covered extensively in media.[111] It's one of the most heavily cited pieces in the field of mass communication, spurring hundreds of follow-up studies.

Agenda-setting imagines news outlets as the ultimate gatekeepers of the public's agenda. It argues that without media attention, it is difficult to sustain public interest in an issue. While the public are able to impact which stories media cover, extensive research has shown that, most of the time, it's media coverage that's directing public attention, not the other way around.

Can agenda-setting effects survive the new digital environment? With more media choices than ever before, a small group of major news outlets would seemingly have a harder time setting the agenda. Some scholars have argued that, because news audiences can simply tune out of news they aren't interested in, "the key problem for agenda-setting theory will change from what issues the media tell people to think about to what issues people tell the media they want to think about."[112] Other studies have shown that traditional agenda-setting persists, despite the growing number of choices for news.[113]

There are several forces working to preserve a centralized agenda-setting function. First, as we will discuss in Chapter 7, selective exposure may not be as common as once feared. That is, most people still consume news from popular, traditional sources.[114] The nightly newscasts on ABC, NBC, and CBS are not as popular as they once were, but those outlets are still consumed by a large swath of the public. The audience, even with myriad media options, isn't as scattered as it could be.

Second, mainstream news outlets often set the agenda for *other* news outlets. Studies of intermedia agenda-setting explore how media outlets influence one another's coverage. Journalists share news values that attract them to the same stories, and reporters frequently follow up on scoops reported in other media. Major reports from news giants like *The New York Times* have the potential to kick-start extensive coverage on an issue, such as when the *Times* started a public dialogue about sexual harassment with its story detailing decades of abuse by Hollywood's Harvey Weinstein. Rather than diversify topics in the news, research has shown that stories across outlets are largely redundant—that is, people may be using different sources, but they're still pretty much hearing about the same stories.[115] News wires like the Associated Press also contribute to story redundancy, as multiple outlets draw from the same pool of information.

Does a pattern of different-outlets-same-topics persist on social media? Sort of. One study looked at whether Twitter simply rehashes what's in the mainstream media, or whether there are enough Twitter-specific discussions to suggest the platform has its own agenda independent of media. The study concluded that traditional media is very influential on Twitter: around 37 percent of tweets directly referenced mainstream media. However, there were also several popular Twitter topics that didn't receive any mainstream coverage. The findings suggest that Twitter doesn't have much influence on traditional media, but that the platform is a home for topics that don't receive mainstream attention.[116] Indeed, one important way that the public uses social media is to push back on the agenda set by traditional media. Opponents of California's Proposition 8, for example, found a voice on YouTube once coverage of the issue faded headlines in traditional media.[117]

Other researchers have looked at agenda-setting on Facebook. One interesting study began by asking two groups of participants to indicate whether they thought a variety of issues were important to society. Then, in an experiment, one group was asked to follow a Facebook page that shared nonpolitical news to their newsfeeds, while another group was asked to follow a page that regularly shared political news on a few specific topics. After seventy-five days, the researchers again measured whether participants thought certain topics were important to society. Those who were in the condition where they saw news stories about the topics were more likely to now see those topics as important.[118] The experiment showed that news communicated through nontraditional channels such as an online newsfeed can still convey the news agenda.

Besides the rise of social media, the proliferation of media sources has also led to an increasing number of openly partisan outlets. Have partisan outlets influenced the sorts of stories told in traditional media? Some evidence says yes, partisan media is impacting traditional media. One study found that partisan media was particularly good at leading coverage of stories that would eventually gain widespread attention. The authors suggest this may be because partisan media are more aggressive, writing, "Compared with the traditional media, partisan media are less bound by journalistic conventions such as objectivity and balance, allowing them to post information almost immediately."[119]

Unfortunately, partisan media also seem to be particularly responsive to deliberately false news stories that circulate via social media. In a study of fake news from 2014 to 2016, results showed that fake news and partisan media often responded to one another—and on many topics, fake news predicted coverage on partisan media. The authors worry that, if fake news can influence the agenda of partisan news, and partisan news can influence the agenda of traditional news, fake news could indirectly influence the mainstream news agenda.[120]

Agenda-Building

Lots of folks would love the chance to control what makes the front page or the top of the newscast. In fact, there are entire professions dedicated to trying to influence what journalists cover and how they cover it. Whether for commercial or political purposes, when outside forces attempt to shape the public agenda, it's called *agenda-building*.

Elected officials, candidates for office, think tanks, interest groups, and political activists are all looking for opportunities to influence the public agenda via news coverage, whether by putting an issue on journalists' radar (first-level agenda-building) or helping to frame a political issue (second-level agenda-building). They use *information subsidies*—press releases, videos, social media content, or speeches—not only to talk directly to voters, but also to influence reporters.

Evidence suggests these tools are fairly effective at directing media attention. In a study that looked at the association between media coverage and press releases in the 2012 presidential race, researchers found a modest correlation between the issues pushed by campaigns and the issues that received attention in the news.[121] Associations have also been noted between issues that receive attention in media coverage and campaign websites,[122] election advertising,[123] and political speeches and issue platform statements.[124] Journalists who work for smaller publications[125] and who are geographically distant from Washington, DC, or their state's capital[126] are more likely to use information subsidies to shape their coverage.

When it comes to politicians influencing the media agenda, there is no greater force than the presidency. Because of the news value *prominence*, and the possibility for every presidential action to impact citizens, journalists pay attention to presidents. The State of the Union and other policy speeches provide a direct look at the issues that presidents would like to focus on.

And yet, studies show the president has a limited ability to direct media attention. One study of forty presidential speeches across six presidents found that only 35 percent of presidents' national addresses resulted in increased media attention to the issue at hand, and only 10 percent did so for more than a month. Other studies show that presidents are typically more likely to respond to coverage than to guide it.[127] The evidence suggests the agenda-setting power varies by president. For example, an analysis of State of the Union speeches found that Nixon's 1970 address directed the media agenda but that Carter's 1978 and Reagan's 1985 addresses were mostly responsive to media coverage.[128]

Presidential influence on the media agenda has gotten renewed attention in the Trump era. Trump is regularly credited with changing the media conversation via a flurry of Twitter activity. There's evidence that it's effective, too. Christopher Wells and his colleagues found that news coverage didn't predict Trump's Twitter volume, but the number of Trump retweets predicted the volume of news coverage.[129] In other words, the more attention Trump got for his tweets, the more likely journalists were to pay attention. However, another study of pre-election activity suggests Clinton's Twitter activity was more likely to predict issue coverage in the media than Trump's tweets.[130] That finding may be due to the fact that the study focused on actual political issues like education, employment, and healthcare, whereas Trump's tweets were not often about the issues. For example, in 2016, the word *economy* appeared in twenty-three of his tweets, while *Clinton* appeared in 377.

One avenue for future research will be to see whether other elected officials can leverage Twitter to impact media coverage, or whether the effect is unique to Trump because his relationship with Twitter has become a news topic in and of itself. If we look at pre-Trump studies of Twitter as a platform for agenda-building, findings suggest the outlet could be useful for lawmakers looking to influence news coverage. In one study, for example, a researcher interviewed journalists about how they use political sources on Twitter. Reporters acknowledged that they used the platform to generate story ideas—though they said tweets from bloggers, think tanks, and interest groups were more useful for finding issues to cover than were tweets from political leaders. Interview subjects also expressed a reluctance to rely on tweets that read like mini press releases, and that they were more likely to follow up on a tweet that linked to an analysis or additional information.[131] A separate study found that journalists are more likely to use tweets to inform their coverage when the tweet is quotable.[132]

Of course, the reverse of this relationship is also true: media coverage affects what politicians care about[133] and which issues they focus on.[134] You can probably think of a recent example where reporting helped make an issue relevant to lawmakers. Coverage of refugees being held at the United States-Mexico border, reporting on sexual assault and harassment by powerful men, and investigative reporting on the opioid crisis are all instances where enterprising and prolonged news coverage made it difficult for politicians to ignore the issue. Still, while research suggests media coverage impacts what lawmakers *say*, there's less evidence that it influences what they *do*. As one overview of political agenda-setting points out, media coverage has been shown to influence political actions like speech-making or holding a hearing, but very few studies look at whether media coverage impacts political actions like law-making, issuing executive orders, or altering budgets.[135]

Agenda-Uptake

Agenda-uptake describes the dynamic flow of information between niche media, mainstream media, and the public. It aims to explain

- "the mainstream media's agenda to influence niche media's agenda and/or the public's agenda,

- niche media's agenda to influence the mainstream media's agenda and/or the public's agenda, and

- the public's agenda to influence the mainstream media's and/or niche media's agenda."[136]

Those issues which are always on mainstream media's radar can be thought of as *patrol* issues. When major sources give an update on the economy, or abortion, or any other regularly reported on issue, it's not likely to cause a spike in public interest. These are issues that are already familiar to citizens, and they aren't likely going to go out and Google a topic they hear about all the time. Niche outlets, on the other hand, see an opening in mainstream news coverage. They are more likely to increase coverage of an issue when it's getting mainstream attention. On the flip side, discussions about patrol issues among niche outlets and the public drive mainstream coverage. For example, a ubiquitous issue such as the economy has a certain base value of newsworthiness—it's always important. If the public or niche sources suddenly start talking about the economy, it gives mainstream media an excuse to pick it up as well.

Alarms represent another category of issues. These issues receive a sudden burst of mainstream media attention (e.g., scandals) and may or may not be followed with sustained patrol-style coverage. The agenda-uptake model suggests media attention for these issues influenced the public's agenda, but only when the coverage is sustained. Mainstream outlets may be more likely to sustain coverage of scandals or other alarm issues if niche outlets are pushing for coverage, thereby giving niche outlets the ability to influence the mainstream agenda. Mainstream outlets may also uptake alarm stories from the public, assuming those issues are pushed long enough to make it into the news cycle.

Overall, the agenda-update model outlines a process where niche media, the public, and mainstream sources contribute to building an agenda. Context and longevity are the keys to determining when salience for one group will be transferred to another—issues must be valued by the uptaking agent (i.e., must be newsworthy, be an issue of public interest) and must stick around long enough for someone else to notice and act on it (e.g., a three-hour Twitter trend isn't likely to receive mainstream news coverage). More research is needed to understand the various psychological and sociological mechanisms that lead individuals to search for information and reporters to be responsive to audience behavior and the work of their competitors on different platforms.

So, Who Leads the Tango?

Who decides which issues grab the public's attention? Most evidence points to the news media as the primary keeper of the public's priorities, and journalists make decisions about who and what to cover by relying on news values—prominence, timeliness, proximity, impact, conflict, novelty, and human interest. Still, outside forces are capable of pulling journalists' attention toward their preferred issues, and they're more likely to find success if they understand journalists' routines and values. As technology provides new ways for the public and elected officials to try and directly influence the agenda, the gatekeeping power of mass media may fade, but so far, the agenda-setting power of news media remains a powerful force.

From Research to Real Life

We've come a long way since Barack Obama's VP text announcement was cutting edge. Who knows? Maybe someday soon we'll have politicians appearing as holograms in our living rooms (sorry for putting that idea into the universe!). No matter the technology, lawmakers will continue to try and find new ways to command citizens' attention—and citizens will find new ways of trying to make their voices heard.

One thing you've hopefully picked up from this chapter is the difficulty of capturing attention. Politicians can blast out an email, tweet, post to Facebook, hold a rally, stream a speech on YouTube, and grant several interviews to journalists and *still* not connect with many voters. In a space crowded with messages, it is increasingly difficult to convince someone to allot attention to yours. Keep an eye out for how campaigns and public figures innovate in how they connect with the public. And while today's innovation (The first candidate with a Snapchat account! The first campaign ad on YouTube!) will seem outdated in no time, each addition to the communication toolbox can tell us something about how people connect with one another. For example, campaign-to-voter texts prompted research into the sorts of information people will allow to *bombard* their personal devices—an area of inquiry that can now be applied to mobile push notifications and smart watch alerts.

It's inevitable that whatever the technology, people in positions of power will attempt to use it. But as you've seen in this chapter, much of the research on social media and other new avenues of communication focus on how everyday people use media to talk back. Has social media given the public a voice? Or has it led to deterioration of civil discussion? With millions of users vying for attention online every day, how are netizens able to make their voices heard? The next time you find yourself reading a friend's political post on Facebook, checking out photos from a protest on Instagram, or noticing a new political #hashtag trending on Twitter, ask yourself: which voices are part of the conversation, who's talking the loudest—and who's listening?

DIY Research

Chris Wells, Boston University

Wells, C., Shah, D. V., Pevehouse, J. C., Yang, J., Pelled, A., Boehm, F., . . . & Schmidt, J. L. (2016). How Trump drove coverage to the nomination: Hybrid media campaigning. *Political Communication*, 33(4): 669–676.

Chris Wells is an assistant professor of journalism in the College of Communication at Boston University. Wells has written more than fifty books, articles, and book chapters examining civic engagement, social media, and citizenship in political communication research. Wells is the 2018 recipient of the International Communication Association's Young Scholar Award. His coauthored article that we feature here is one of the most downloaded articles in *Political Communication* since it was published in 2016. The article examines then-candidate Donald Trump's use of conventional campaign communication behavior and his unconventional behavior on Twitter to understand the news coverage he received in the primary election season. Our Q&A with Wells, conducted over email, is below.

Wagner and Perryman: You and your coauthors find that Donald Trump's hybrid campaigning helped drive his coverage to the Republican presidential nomination. What does this imply about news coverage of contemporary political campaigns?

Wells: As the title of our article suggests, one of our most basic findings was the hybrid nature of attention attraction in our media system. Trump garnered news media attention through both conventional *information subsidies* (rallies, election events) and his well-known Twitter activity (and others' amplification of that). It also speaks to the hybridity and pressures being felt by journalists as they cover politics. Journalists and news outlets covering the campaign are now highly attentive to who is generating attention in multiple spaces, including social media, and they are doing it while becoming intensely aware of the size of audience they are reaching with every story. Of course, commercial media have always shaped their content with an eye to attracting viewers, but with the metric revolution we have entered the nuclear age of audience measurement. I think we are only beginning to appreciate the implications of this for the quality of communications in the public sphere.

Wagner and Perryman: What was the most important decision you and your colleagues made in the design phase of this study and how did that decision influence what you discovered in this article?

Wells: A couple of decisions that were important include our selection of a lag length of one day for time series modeling. Without a lot of prior research telling us how long effects move from the social media-news media system, we had to kind of take a guess, so we chose the shortest lag length that our data could support. Another choice we made was the set of news media we tested: we really tested from the heart of the media system, rather than considering partisan outlets. These are both limitations that we have explored in more detail in subsequent work. I would emphasize, though, that these are two of dozens of significant decisions.

(Continued)

(Continued)

Recently I was working with a graduate student on a related project, and he marveled at how many choices we had to make. This is really the nature of working with these large and aggregated datasets. Our approach right now is to reason through each decision we are making, keep track of all of them in notes and code, and where feasible run alternative model specifications.

Wagner and Perryman: If a student reading this book wanted to research a hybrid media campaigning issue for their class, where would you recommend they start?

Wells: A few places I would recommend beginning are: first is exploratory research, which often has a qualitative flavor. Although the study we are talking about is quantitative, it's hard to get a grasp of dynamics of communication without looking at quite a lot of data, which is what we did in earlier stages of this project. That means looking at a variety of news sources and having a sense of how they are covering issues in a given campaign over time. Same for social media. Second, there are some tools that can help a scholar move from a grounded idea of what a campaign is about to a more quantitative, broader view of its dynamics. One is mediacloud.org, a tool made by a team at Harvard and MIT that collects an enormous quantity of news media content. They have a pretty good dashboard that researchers can use to search on particular terms and graph some results. Third, for researchers with some—really even a little—proficiency with R, there are a number of good packages for accessing Twitter content according to user, hashtag, or keyword. One I would point students to is the rtweet package, created by Michael W. Kearney of the University of Missouri.

Wagner and Perryman: This project is a collaborative one. What advice do you have for students working on group projects in political communication research so that the research process goes as well as possible?

Wells: Have great colleagues! That sounds glib, but I think it's really about having a culture of collaboration and idea sharing. It is helpful to have a group that can combine open-ended conversations with times when the job gets done. Reading and talking about published material works well. So does asking analysts to create presentations of preliminary analyses of data. When it comes to research ownership, it is helpful to have some clarity about what role (and author order) each contributor will take early in the research process. And remember that any one study is rarely the last—there is always another chance for someone else to lead, or explore that further analysis that just doesn't fit in the first article.

How Can I Help?

Catasha Davis, FrameWorks

Catasha Davis is a researcher at the FrameWorks Institute in Washington, DC. FrameWorks conducts social science research to help organizations figure out how to frame public discourse on social and scientific issues. Dr. Davis studies how the news media and entertainment media affect how the public thinks about, feels, and acts toward various social groups, especially communities of color. While working on her PhD, which she earned from the University of Wisconsin-Madison, Davis was a fellow with the National Cancer Institute at the National Institutes of Health, where she worked on health communication. There, her research focused upon how marketing techniques can be used to help African Americans make more informed decisions about enrolling in clinical trials related to health. Outside of FrameWorks, Dr. Davis has published her research in the *American Journal of Public Health* and the *International Journal of Public Opinion Research*. Our conversation took place online.

Wagner and Perryman: How did your educational background prepare you to use political communication theories and methods to try and solve real policy problems?

Davis: My educational background provided me with a substantial background in research design and methods. I came into my current position with a great deal of knowledge and experience working in both qualitative and quantitative methods and this knowledge helped me examine all kinds/types of research and policy questions.

Second, a communications degree is interdisciplinary by nature. Throughout my time in the School of Journalism and Mass Communication, I studied history, social psychological theories, media effects, Black studies, and political theory. This vast background gave me an appropriate amount of knowledge to tackle a variety of issues in the policy realm. Regardless of the specific topics in which I am conducting research, my background, in theory, gives me a good foundation to tackle research projects.

Wagner and Perryman: What is similar, and what is different about publishing academic research in political and health communication as compared to doing policy work in those areas?

Davis: One similarity between academic research and nonprofit policy work is that people want to see work that is theoretically driven and well researched.

(Continued)

(Continued)

On the other hand, advocates may have different concerns and priorities in comparison to their colleagues in academia, which means that some research questions are less interesting in the nonprofit space and therefore publishing in policy space is more applied than in the academic space.

Publishing in nonprofit or policy world is also different because people want to get things out as quickly as possible. Many advocates do not want to wait eighteen months or two years for research to be completed and a report to be ready.

Wagner and Perryman: You have done really important work studying traditionally underrepresented groups—groups that have not received enough attention from scholars or our lawmakers. Are there particular things people should have in mind if they'd like to follow in your footsteps and do work with similar populations?

Davis: Research with socially disadvantaged or historically underrepresented groups should include the voices of those being discussed. I like to think of people as experts in their own experiences and therefore I firmly believe that it is necessary to engage them in the development of any work on policy.

Second, when doing work that pertains to socially disadvantaged or historically underrepresented groups, it is vital that the work is attuned to language including how and why you are using a specific name for a group and also how groups are discussed. Lawmakers and researchers often misname or unintentionally talk down to groups, which can lead to mistrust and resentment.

Wagner and Perryman: What advice do you have for undergraduate students thinking that they might like to use mass communication skills in the policy world?

Davis: Spend time honing your skills. Having an undergraduate degree is not enough to stand out; you need to continue to expand your skillset. I consistently watch online courses for skill-building and read articles related to research.

Second, be flexible and willing to work in unexpected areas and on unfamiliar topics. I am often asked by my friends in academia to talk to their graduating seniors and surprised about how rigid some undergraduates can be about their futures. They talk about only being open to one path and not interested in others. I came to Washington, DC, as a fellow at the National Cancer Institute. I had no previous experience working on cancer research but was open to a new opportunity. It turned out to be an amazing opportunity for growth and helped me began the process of building a professional network, which is essential to working on policy issues. Unexpected opportunities have the chance of being the best opportunities, so be flexible.

Framing the News

When and How It Matters to the Audience

WHERE DO OUR PREFERENCES COME FROM? Understanding how our attitudes form, harden, and, under some circumstances, change are fundamental tasks for political communication researchers, and for human beings on planet Earth for that matter. The study of preference formation and attitude change is an important part of all of the major social science disciplines. Each general area of study tends to focus on a different aspect(s) of the origins of what we say we want our government to do. Scholars train their gaze upon social structures and interactions (sociology); emotions, cognitions, and behaviors (psychology); individual self-interest (economics); and how political elites both shape and respond to our preferences (political science). In our study of political communication and democracy in a mediated environment, it makes sense to pay special attention to the origins and nature of our attitudes, something that is most commonly explored through analyses of *framing*.

A frame is classically defined as a *central organizing idea* that provides an audience a way to understand an issue or unfolding series of events. James N. Druckman's simple and generalizable definition is a good one: frames are verbal or nonverbal statements that clearly emphasize specific considerations.[1] The more success you have at getting people to think about the considerations you want them to think about when they are asked to express some kind of preference, the more likely you will get what you want. If you want to go for pizza with some of your classmates after class ends, you might engage in some strategic framing to persuade your friends to crave pizza as well. In Madison, Wisconsin, you might try to get pizza and only pizza on your friends' minds by saying, "Hey, do you want to go to Pizza Brutta, Ian's Pizza, or Roman Candle?" No matter the option that's chosen, you get to have your pizza. Or, you might try to get them to consider cost. "I'm nearly broke, but I can afford a slice at Ian's." Alternatively, you might frame the issue as one of harmony. "Elena doesn't like Indian food and Marquise is allergic to shellfish and I'm sick of sandwiches. What if we get pizza? Everyone likes pizza." In other words, there are a variety of ways to frame an issue that can lead to the expression of the same preference.

Political elites, journalists, and citizens in conversation with others frame issues every day. How frames find their way into news coverage can affect what people think and how they participate over time. The frames we encounter about political issues and political candidates can affect how we form, harden, or change our attitudes and how we make voting decisions. In spite of, or perhaps because of, framing's importance, scholars approach the study of framing and its effects in many ways. Because of this, framing research is often described with phrases like "a fractured paradigm"[2] where scholars lack "conceptual clarity and consistency about what exactly frames are."[3]

Framing is a concept that is commonly and widely used in the social and behavioral sciences. The origins of framing as we use it as scholars of political communication research are rooted in both sociological and psychological traditions.

In the sociological tradition, the work by Erving Goffman is foundational. He argued that frames help us make sense of the world. Frames help by reducing the complexity of our everyday lives. In psychology, the work by Daniel Kahneman and Amos Tversky (which we will address later in this chapter) is often cited as foundational. Their "prospect theory" argues that new information is evaluated very differently depending on whether it is accompanied with a gain frame or a loss frame.

In this chapter, we will review what a preference is; explore different types of frames and their general effects and limitations; examine how framing operates in competitive, partisan environments in the United States, Western Europe, South Korea, and Latin America; and consider the future of framing research.

Preferences and Frame Types

What Is a Preference?

A preference is a rank ordering over some set of attitude objects. For example, a voter in England might prefer a full Brexit (completely exiting the European Union) to a "soft Brexit" (maintaining membership in the EU's single market and customs union) to remaining in the EU. An American voter in 2016 might have preferred Libertarian Gary Johnson to Republican Donald Trump to Democrat Hillary Clinton to the Green Party's Jill Stein. Some scholarly disciplines, most notably economics, treat the rankings as transitive and invariant. That means that if someone prefers Johnson to Trump and Trump to Clinton, he must prefer Johnson to Clinton as well, no matter the order of how you ask ("Are you voting for Johnson or Clinton/Trump or Clinton/Clinton or Johnson?").

Our preferences come from making comparative evaluations of what psychologists call attitudes—a general evaluation of something. For example, when deciding whether to support a full, partial, or no Brexit, British voters might decide if they have a relatively favorable evaluation of Brexit to remaining in the EU. Psychologists often think of attitudes via the expectancy value model.[4] An attitude toward something, called an *attitude object*, is made up of the weighted sum or a variety of evaluations about the object. Formally, $Attitude = \Sigma v_i {}^* w_i$, where v_i is the evaluation of the object on a particular attribute (i) and w_i is the salience weight ($\Sigma w_i = 1$) associated with that attribute, that is, how much that evaluation matters. For example, one's overall attitude, A, toward a proposed football stadium might consist of a combination of negative and positive evaluations, v_i, of the project on different dimensions i. An individual may believe that the stadium will be good for the local economy (i=1), good for the team the stadium is being built for (i=2), but be bad for the environment (i=3) and cost too much (i=4). Assuming our individual places positive values on the economy, the football team, the environment and low cost, then v_1 and v_2 are positive and v_3 and v_4 are negative. The individual's attitude toward the object will depend on the relative magnitudes of v_1, v_2, v_3, and v_4 discounted by the relative weights ($w_1 \dots w_4$) that correspond to each attribute.[5]

A voter might prefer Hillary Clinton to Donald Trump if the most relevant consideration is political experience, but that same voter might support Trump over Clinton if the most important consideration is outsider status. The same logic holds true for whether people support particular policy remedies for important problems. For example, caring whether an African American had personal experience as a slave (a personal involvement consideration) as compared to being concerned with how the social structure created by slavery affected generations (a sociological consideration) affects whether one believes African Americans ought to be eligible for government reparations over enslavement.

Frames in Thought

Druckman calls the dimensions (the "*i*'s" in the equation) that contribute to a person's evaluation of an attitude object a frame in thought. Democratic primary voters using head-to-head polls comparing how various candidates fare against Donald Trump would be in an electability frame of mind. If that same person was more concerned with which candidate held issue positions that were closest to the person's, we might say they were in a policy representation frame of mind.

All of these examples of frames shift the emphasis of what one is thinking about when making some kind of political choice. Emphasis frames are also called issue frames, value frames, and evolutionary frames. What matters, in terms of understanding what causes a preference to form, is the weight one gives to each emphasis.

There is a second type of frame called an equivalency frame (sometimes also called valence frames). While politicians use emphasis frames that aim to change the dimensions of what their audience is thinking about (pro-choice vs. pro-life on the abortion issue, for example), equivalency frames cast the exact same information in different ways. The classic example of how equivalency frames work in social science research comes from the work of Amos Tversky and Daniel Kahneman. They asked people in an experiment to imagine that a population of six hundred had a disease problem. People needed to choose between two strategies aimed at fighting the disease that could affect the six hundred people. Participants were assigned to one of two scenarios. In one condition, participants were asked to choose between Program A, which will result in four hundred deaths, and Program B, which has a one-third probability of resulting in zero deaths and a two-thirds probability of resulting in six hundred deaths. In the second condition, Program A results in two hundred people being saved and Program B results in a one-third probability that six hundred people will be saved and a two-thirds probability that zero people will be saved.

Notice how the math is equivalent (four hundred deaths out of six hundred is the same thing as two hundred lives saved. A one-third chance that six hundred people will be saved is the same thing as a one-third chance that no one dies). What matters is the valance—the lives are being saved (a *gains* frame) or there are deaths (a *loss* frame). When in a saved frame of mind, people are more likely to pick Program A (a sure saving of two hundred lives) while they tend to go for Program B (which is riskier).[6] The authors replicated their work across several issues and in a variety of different contexts.

You might be wondering about the usefulness of equivalency frames—thinking that politicians are not terribly likely to engage in equivalency framing battles, opting instead to choose a version of the facts that suits them best and engage in emphasis framing. However, there are many relevant examples of how equivalency frames affect people's attitudes in the real world, such as frames about the percentage of criminals there are as compared to the percentage of people not committing crimes or the percentage of a bag of chips being advertised as 95 percent fat free instead of 5 percent fat.[7]

Frames in Communication

The frames in thought rattling around in our heads, shaping our attitudes, have to come from somewhere. Attitudes are influenced by our past experiences, religious faith, upbringing, schooling, the state of relevant attitude objects in the world, and even our biology. But perhaps the most relevant factor comes from communication about frames. Think back to the example of getting pizza after class. There, the *frame in communication* occurs in conversation. Politicians frame issues in interviews and news coverage, social media use, and paid advertising. While frames in thought are focused upon what we are thinking about, frames in communication focus upon what is being said (or shown visually) by a relevant communicator.[8] A framing effect is when a frame in communication affects a person's frame in thought.

When thinking about what is and what is not a frame in communication, it is useful to think back to Graber's four functions of the news media described in Chapter 1. A story engaging in the surveillance function might report a statement of fact like "an evangelical Christian baker refused to make a wedding cake for a gay couple." That statement might affect a frame in thought, but it is not a frame in communication. Frames in communication "place clear emphasis on particular considerations."[9] The interpretation function of the media might report a frame in communication that the baker believes that "her religious freedom allows her to refuse to serve gay people because she has a religious objection." Frames in communication can influence frames in thought. They can also fail to affect an individual's frames in thought.

How Frames in Communication Affect Frames in Thought

Frames in communication can influence frames in thought when the dimensions of those frames in communication are available, accessible, and applicable.[10] For a consideration to be available, it must be in our memory and able to be retrieved from our memory so that we can use it when constructing an attitude. How might a baker's decision about who to serve be related to religious freedom or the wedding couple's right to be treated equally? If a person is unable to understand the significance of a consideration, it is not available.

While the availability of considerations is stored in one's long-term memory, accessibility comes from an unconscious process that occurs automatically. The more one uses a consideration over time, or when a frame in communication brings a consideration to mind, it can be accessible. Repetition of frames in communication matters. The more individuals hear that tax cuts increase individual freedom, that women have a right to choose what happens to their bodies or how many lives might be saved when using Program A versus Program B to stop a disease can cause frequent information processing, which can increase a frame's accessibility. Indeed, when frames in communication make it clear over time that the two major political parties in the United States have divergent views on the same issue people are more likely to have an attitude that the two parties have important differences between them.[11]

The applicability of a consideration that is available and accessible also affects how we evaluate attitude objects. Concern that the baker might face protests for failing to bake a cake for a gay couple might be available and accessible, but the individual doing the evaluating might not care about the likelihood of protests and therefore not place any weight on that consideration when expressing an attitude about the baker's decision. However, people do not always consider applicability when forming preferences as it requires people to be consciously processing the information in the consideration. People who are motivated to develop accurate attitudes are more likely to think about the applicability of a frame. Think about how parents rarely find "But everyone else is doing it" an applicable consideration to let you stay out all night at a high school party. Frames in communication often compete against other frames in communication, making it harder to determine what is applicable.[12] Those without the personal motivation or living in a competitive environment are more likely to rely without deep thinking on the considerations made accessible through exposure to a message. That is, sometimes, applicability or appropriateness do not matter as people base their preferences on whichever frames are accessible.

Frames in communication can also backfire. When President Bill Clinton was accused of having an inappropriate sexual relationship with a White House intern, pundits were shocked to find Clinton's approval rating improve as the scandal wore on, culminating in Clinton being impeached by the House of Representatives but not convicted and removed from office by the Senate. Many concluded that the scandal just did not matter to the public. In the terms of framing research, the scandal must not have been applicable, accessible, and available when it came time for people to judge the job the president was doing in office. A set of scholars led by Dhavan Shah found that the news coverage of the scandal as something that was politically motivated by conservatives, the growing economy, and Clinton's general policy performance led to higher approval ratings for the embattled president.[13] Notably, they concluded that the sustained support for Clinton was a backlash to frames in communication that focused upon the strategic motives of conservative politicians. Why might people respond in this way? Experiments led by political communication researcher Nam-Jin Lee found that when presented issue frames that deal with strategic concerns on controversial issues, people were less likely to use their partisanship to guide their preference formation, looking to other considerations instead.[14]

Framing Effects and Citizen Competence

The early history of framing effects in political communication research told a story of human preference formation that was not very attractive.

People's attitudes seemed to be led around willy-nilly, following most any frame in communication they might encounter in news coverage. Whether people chose the safe or risky option in the disease problem rested upon whether the issue was framed in terms of saving or dying. The implication for equivalency framing effects like these is that they make interpreting people's real preferences impossible. If people prefer an economic proposal that results in 95 percent employment but oppose the *exact same* program when the frame in communication is that it will result in 5 percent unemployment, it is impossible to know if people support or oppose the program.[15] What should a politician do, if she wants to represent her constituents, when she cannot know with any degree of accuracy what it is her constituents want because their answers change depending upon how the very same problem is framed? Worse, political elites could use the knowledge that citizens can be led around by the nose by some carefully calibrated frames in communication to manipulate public opinion for their own ends.

The implications stemming from emphasis-framing research were not much better. When exposed to a single frame in communication about freedom of speech in connection with a hate group's attempt to hold a rally in a community, people tend to favor the group's right to hold the rally. When exposed to a single frame about public safety in rallies held by hate groups, people are less supportive of the group's quest to hold the rally.[16] On the one hand, people were not changing their preferences in response to an equivalent set of considerations. On the other hand, if emphasis framing effects work through the accessibility of specific considerations, there is little citizens can do to defend themselves against elites who seek to manipulate them.[17]

The Limits of Framing Effects

Despite these worries, there is evidence that citizens are not saps to all equivalency frames. Those who have higher cognitive ability,[18] have strongly held attitudes,[19] and think for a moment about their decision[20] are less likely to experience equivalency-framing effects. Additionally, if a person has to provide a rationale for their decisions, they tend to not undergo a framing effect.[21] Finally, even the classic Tversky and Kahenman disease problem does not produce a framing effect when participants are told it is a statistics problem and not a math problem.[22] Equivalency framing effects are also probably limited in political contexts as politicians tend not to feel inclined to frame issues in equivalent ways. Moreover, people often know which party supports which issue position. Since they have an idea of what they think about that issue and which party has a view closer to their own, they are less susceptible to framing effects in news coverage as news coverage tends to reveal which party the source of the frames are coming from.[23]

There are limits to emphasis framing as well. Despite worries that emphasis frames work through accessibility, direct research examining this question found no effects.[24] Scholars have, however, uncovered five moderators of emphasis framing effects: predispositions, citizen deliberation, political information, source credibility, and competition. Kimberly Gross found people tend to generate counterarguments when they encounter a frame that violates their own predispositions.[25]

Deliberation can affect one's susceptibility to framing effects. Of course, the point of deliberation is to arrive at the best opinion possible after carefully considering a variety of options. So, if deliberation does lead to framing effects under some circumstances, the implications are not as necessarily negative.

Information affects emphasis framing's effectiveness as well. Donald Kinder and Lynn Sanders found that those who know less about politics, generally speaking, were more likely to be affected by frames about affirmative action.[26] Just as knowledge matters, familiarity with an issue is important as well. The more familiar people are with an issue, the less likely they will change their attitude about the issue simply because they encountered a frame about it.

Of course, in politics, frames in communication compete. For example, news stories about those who prefer an end to legal abortion tend to frame abortion as though the issue turns on the sanctity of human life; in contrast, advocates of legal abortion tend to frame the issue as revolving around a woman's right to choose what happens to her body—importantly, both perspectives are included in most news stories. Recall from Chapter 2 that journalists regularly index coverage to focus on the positions of competing partisan elites. Most of the first few decades of framing research did not take competition into account. Once they did, many effects that were found when only one frame in communication was present in a story disappeared when a competing frame was also offered in the same story.[27]

A little more than a decade ago Chong and Druckman accurately asserted that the "literature on framing effects has virtually ignored perhaps the most typical communications environment in which competing sides promote alternative interpretations of an issue" (p. 638).[28] Since then, however, framing studies take the effects of competing communications seriously.[29] These works show that framing effects are often contingent on the strength of frames, the sources of the frames, whether the frames are examples of cheap or costly talk, and the values that the frames highlight.

Partisan Framing Effects in Competitive Environments

Still too often absent from these treatments of framing is an examination of how these frames work in an environment where real-world political battles take place between Republican and Democratic elected officials, and sometimes even between lawmakers in the same party. When partisan sources are provided for emphasis frames, research shows that individuals have significantly higher levels of issue constraint; that is, people with liberal (or conservative) positions on one issue tended to have liberal (or conservative) positions on other issues.[30]

Partisan polarization can also affect how framing influences opinion formation. In an influential study, James Druckman, Erik Peterson, and Rune Slothuus showed that when people in the United States are in a polarized environment and emphasis frames compete in the same news story, people tend to form preferences about issues that follow the frame in communication from their preferred political party.[31] In fact, people tended to express more confidence in weaker arguments made by their own side when the environment was polarized.

However, the same frames, in environments that were not polarized, had different effects. Then, stronger arguments performed better than weaker ones. If the weak argument was offered as a frame in communication from a political leader in one's own party, individuals were more likely to form a preference based on the better argument—even though it came from the other side.[32]

Slothuus, working with political communication scholar Claes de Vreese, found that people in Denmark were more likely to follow a frame from their party, especially when the issue being framed was at the center of conflict between major parties and the individuals encountering the frames are more politically aware.[33] Lene Aarøe found, over the course of three inventive studies, that partisan cues in frames in communication can trigger contrast effects (pushing citizens to form an opinion that is different than the one advocated by a partisan elite) when the elite is not likable.[34]

The source of the news is often thought of by significant portions of the news audience as something that is partisan as well. Recall from Chapter 7 that partisans often experience a hostile media perception that is relatively enhanced when the source of information is one that has a partisan reputation. In an inventive experiment, political scientist Joel Turner recorded a professional broadcaster reading news stories from Fox News and from CNN. Turner varied whether folks thought the Fox (CNN) script was airing on Fox News or CNN. When liberals thought they were watching Fox News, no matter the actual source of the news, they perceived it to be more conservatively biased. When conservatives saw stories on CNN, no matter who actually wrote the story, they thought it was liberally biased. When liberals saw the Fox story as though it was on CNN, they thought it was a middle of the road story. Conservatives reacted the same way to watching the anchor read Fox's story as if it was on CNN.[35] As such, frames matter in partisan environments, but the cues provided by the sources of the news matter as well.

Framing Effects Over Time

So far, we have mostly described framing research that occurred in a single-shot experiment. That is, participants came into a lab or logged online, answered some survey questions, read a randomly assigned news story with one specifically chosen frame (or competing frames) or another, and answered some more questions about their attitudes about the attitude object in the story. Experimental research is extraordinarily valuable in research as it can allow scholars to isolate particular elements (such as a freedom of speech frame or a public safety frame) to see if it causes some kind of change in an attitude expressed by an individual. Of course, in the real world, people are not randomly exposed to one frame or another. Moreover, when we encounter a news story, we bring with us everything we have experienced up to that point in our lives (albeit with different degrees of accessibility, applicability, and availability). When researchers find a framing effect in a study, one obvious implication is that the frame has caused a change in one's attitude, perhaps a durable change.

However, most framing studies do not follow up and investigate whether framing effects last. This is especially important when thinking about how politics works outside the lab for many reasons. First, political elites sometimes change how they frame issues. Political leaders who support legal abortion might frame abortion at *time 1* as an issue about a woman's right to choose, but they might shift their rhetorical strategy later, as President Bill Clinton did, to a frame such as abortion should be "safe, legal and rare." Still others might try to tie abortion to reproductive issues more generally (birth control, cost, etc.). How do framing effects found in the lab hold up over time?

The honest answers are that 1) it varies and 2) we are not sure. Some evidence suggests that effects that occur in the lab are in one ear and out the other after a few weeks away from the research process. One reasonable criterion for assessing the effectiveness of frames over time is to investigate whether people respond to elite frames in communication in a way that is consistent with their own core values. A group of scholars used a panel survey (interviewing the same people at two different points in time) to show that, regarding opinions about a political campaign dealing with questions of naturalizing immigrants, framing the issue so that people should have the final say in the naturalization process only affected the opinions of those who held core values related to social order, tradition, and security. For those who cared deeply about fairness, the framing from the opponents—which focused on a fair process—was more persuasive.[36]

Lene Aarøe and Carsten Jensen discovered that when citizens have prior exposure to a value frame, it improves people's ability to respond to a frame in communication in a way that is consistent with their deeper values. Importantly, this was most true for citizens with lower levels of political sophistication.[37] Sophie Lecheler led a study that explored what happened to classic framing effects over a day, a week, and two weeks. They found framing effects to be surprisingly persistent over time, especially for those with moderate political knowledge. Framing effects on those with lower political knowledge faded much faster.[38]

On the other hand, value frames highlighting ethical concerns about the nuclear developments in North Korea did not affect opinions about US government policy about North Korea. Opinions about the nuclear crisis with North Korea were generally aligned with people's general political attitudes. This was especially true when the ethical frame, rather than a material dangers frame, was used.[39]

In addition to exploring connections between frames and values, scholars have hypothesized that being exposed to repeated frames might affect opinion formation. Lecheler and deVreese investigated this question experimentally, showing that framing effects are stronger when the time between repetitive exposure to a frame in communication is short.[40] Once again, knowledge mattered with respect to how framing effects operated over time. The highly knowledgeable were less influenced by how recently they saw a frame, but they also showed stronger signs of a cumulative framing effect (by seeing the same frame repeated over time).

A strategy that scholars use less often, because it is incredibly labor intensive, is to code frames in news articles over long periods of time and merge the prevalence of particular frames at specific points in time with public opinion data. Paul Kellstedt found, in a several decades-long study of American civil rights attitudes, that when news frames focused on egalitarianism, public mood toward racial issues was more liberal while when it focused on individualism, public mood on race was more conservative.[41]

Michael Wagner (one of your authors) and Mike Gruszczynski coded four decades of issue frames found in American news coverage about two issues, abortion and taxes, finding framing effects on attitudes about the issues when the issues were framed consistently by partisan politicians. They also found that frames used by Republicans, Democrats, *and journalists* were associated with changes in partisanship over time. The prevalence of policy-specific liberal frames was associated with more liberal attitudes and Democratic partisanship while symbolic conservative frames were associated with more conservative preferences and Republican partisanship.[42] Regarding party identification, the consistency of frames appeared to matter. For example, people who held a position on the abortion issue, and saw a consistent set of frames over time explaining each party's position on the issue were more likely to adopt a party identification that matched the party who shared their views on abortion. The substantive effects on attitudes, not partisanship, were greater for the economic issue of taxes than for the social-cultural issue of abortion. In particular, frames from Democrats that highlighted policy preferences and frames from Republicans that focused on symbolic conservatism tended to work in the way the partisan politicians using the frames intended.[43]

Framing Research Outside the United States

Most, but by no means all, of the framing research discussed to this point has been conducted about framing effects in the United States or on US populations. Framing scholars, however, do great, theoretically motivated, and empirically sophisticated work all over the globe. Many advances in framing theory have come from Western European scholars. For example, using a survey experiment, a trio of scholars from the University of Amsterdam found that position emotions serve as mediators of framing effects on immigration opinions.[44] Their results also suggested that frames that face competition from other frames in communication in news coverage can cause strong emotional responses from individuals, responses that mediate the effectiveness of frames.

In a multimethod study of the effects of the framing of the 2004 enlargement of the European Union, scholars advanced framing theory about risk and opportunity, showing that those exposed to the opportunity frame about enlarging the European Union were more supportive of EU enlargement. Moreover, those with low levels of political knowledge were more likely to experience a framing effect from the risk frame.[45]

Research has also shown limits to framing effects. Issues that are highly important to individuals are not strong candidates for framing effects, in terms of preference formation.[46] This makes sense when recalling the study of issue frames on abortion that were in the news for four decades—when people for whom abortion was important saw the issue framed consistently over time, it spurred changes in individual partisanship for those citizens who had preferences about abortion that did not match their party's.

Framing effects are usually found in preferences about issues, but frames in communication can also affect preferences about particular political leaders. In a creative study focusing on attitudes toward two different South Korean presidents, Youngkee Ju found that news coverage of President Roh Moo-hyun focused on a politics frame whereas stories about President Kim Young-sam focused on a policy frame. Roh was more negatively evaluated and thought of as a politician by the people, whereas Kim was evaluated with respect to his policies by the Korean public.[47]

In Brazil, researcher Mauro P. Porto showed that political advertising in the 2002 presidential race led to important framing effects. Porto found that when people watched the most watched newscast, TV Globo's *Journal Nacional*, voters were more likely to support the frame that was promoted by President Fernando Henrique Cardoso's administration, as well as by the country's. However, exposure to political advertising led voters to reject this same frame, since opposition candidates to the president chose to emphasize Brazil's social problems, especially poverty, hunger, and social inequality as the most important issues, making those issues more available, accessible, and applicable to political decision making during the Brazilian election.[48]

The Future of Framing Research

As we argue throughout this book, the news media serve a vital function in democracies. Kathleen Hall Jamieson notes that information, investigation, analysis, social empathy, public forum, mobilization, and democratic education are all important roles filled by journalists.[49] Frames in communication serve positive and negative aspects to these roles. After all, frames can provide news and useful information that lead to prodemocratic outcomes. Of course, as we discussed in Chapter 3, they can also focus on politics as a game, hinder mobilization, and harm democratic behavior.

Some scholars argue that framing research is too unwieldy to be a useful, singular concept. Expanding framing effects beyond equivalency frames to emphasis frames, the argument goes, leads to overlap with other media effects concepts like agenda-setting. Michael Cacciatore and colleagues argue for a return to a more rigid definition of framing, relying on equivalency frames.[50]

Douglas McLeod and Dhavan Shah argue for thinking about framing effects research in a 2 x 2 typology.[51] One side of the typology pits what they call the idealistic approach (such as the precisely controlled equivalency frame experiments) against the pragmatic approach (such as studies that focus on emphasis-framing effects from the political world). The other side of the typology considers context-specific framing effects that are relevant to the particular case being studied (think Nelson and colleagues' study of the framing of support of a hate group rally) and context transcendent that are universally relevant. Other researchers focus upon politically relevant factors such as the strength of frames in a competitive environment, how that frame strength interacts with partisanship, core values, and different issues that get debated in the marketplace of ideas.[52]

The changing media ecology impacts the future of framing research as well. Recall from Chapter 2 that information flows from journalists to the public, but also from the public to journalists. If citizens can respond in real time to reporting they see by posting on social media, journalists are potentially exposed to new frames that they might use in future work. Indeed, Sharon Meraz and Zizi Papacharissi have shown that frames on social media are now *networked*; this can affect the stickiness, persistence, and spread of frames.[53] Moreover computational social science tools and artificial intelligence tools are being used to conduct automated content analyses of *big data*—opening another avenue for future work on how frames in communication spread, are interpreted, and are responded to by other political actors.

From Research to Real Life

Political scientist E. E. Schattschneider famously argued that in any debate, "the definition of alternatives is the supreme instrument of power."[54] In other words, if we want to understand how power operates in democratic societies, we must understand how issues are framed. While frames are important, they are not all-powerful. Any complete understanding of mediated democracy requires careful exploration of how people form preferences, change them in response to the frames in communication, or stick to them despite persuasive attempts by others whether through exposure by the news media, social media, advertising, and conversation.

Understanding how the scope of conflict is being framed to you by your leaders or by various actors in the news media can help you make better decisions about what you believe. Be on the lookout for the core values at the heart of various issue frames you see espoused by politicians and those who cover them. Think about how those values relate to other ones that are important to you before deciding what you believe. Notice who is being left out of particular characterizations of an issue. Whose lives are being elevated? If people come to believe the arguments advanced in the issue frames they see, what kind of world would we be more likely to be living in? Is that ok with you?

You know from earlier chapters that some people selectively expose themselves to like-minded media *and* you know that the communication ecology is so vast and ubiquitous that it is impossible to avoid information that challenges your worldview. What can framing research tell us about when we are more likely to accept ideas offered by *the other side*—or at least accept the legitimacy of the other side to exist?

DIY Research

Shana Kushner Gadarian, Syracuse University

Albertson, B., & Kushner Gadarian, S. (2015). *Anxious politics: Democratic citizenship in a threatening world*. New York, NY: Cambridge University Press.

Shana Kushner Gadarian is an associate professor of political science at the Maxwell School, Syracuse University. Gadarian studies how the tone and content of the political news media environment affects how people seek information and form preferences. She is a former Robert Wood Johnson Scholar in health policy research and has had her research funded by organizations such as the National Science Foundation, the Robert Wood Johnson Foundation, and the Princeton Policy Research Institution for the Region. Gadarian has published more than thirty books, articles, and book chapters, including *Anxious Politics*, with Bethany Albertson. Their book, winner of the 2016 American Political Science Association's Robert E. Lane Award for best book in political psychology, shows how emotions matter in politics. Our conversation, conducted over email, is below:

Wagner and Perryman: Your book provides scads of evidence that political anxiety triggers engagement in politics in ways that are good and bad for democracy. How does political anxiety affect how we consume political news? Is there anything people experiencing anxious feelings can do to mitigate the negative effects they have on democratic behavior and outcomes?

Gadarian: Anxiety is about feelings of uncertainty, and we find that when people are uncertain about political issues, one of the things that they do is seek out political news. In a world where people are generally uninformed about politics, this seems beneficial, but what we find may be less positive overall. Anxious people seek information, but what they pay attention to and remember is threatening information. This tendency to pay attention to negative, threatening information may help people avoid some dangers but it also skews the way that people think about issues as varied as immigration and climate change by focusing on the potential harms. To mitigate some of these negative effects, people should read widely and also try to actively pay attention to news that focuses on neutral or nonthreatening aspects of a policy or puts the harms in a broader context.

Wagner and Perryman: What was the most important decision you and your coauthor made while designing your research? How did that decision affect what you discovered?

Gadarian: I think that the decision to focus on more than one policy area gave us a broader look at the role of anxiety in political life. We started by looking at the effects of immigration anxiety, and we could have concluded that anxiety makes people support more restrictionist or conservative policy. By including public health, terrorism, and climate change as policy areas we were able to make a larger claim—anxiety makes people want to seek protection and put their trust in policies and leaders who can mitigate danger. Sometimes those protective policies are conservative as in the case of immigration

(Continued)

(Continued)

and terrorism but sometimes, when the Democratic Party is viewed as more expert, like on climate change, anxious people will support liberal policies.

Wagner and Perryman: If a student reading this book wanted to conduct research on anxiety and politics for this class and be able to finish it this semester, how might they get started?

Gadarian: My advice is to always start with already collected survey or experimental data as a first place to develop a research project. The American National Election Studies has a battery of questions about Americans' worries about presidential candidates and several questions on the fear of terrorism. Using Roper's iPoll Databank, students can search for questions about fear in other policy areas that have been asked on surveys since the 1950s. These questions can spark ideas about how you may design your own observational study or experiment or can be used on their own to test your ideas.

Wagner and Perryman: You did this award-winning research collaboratively. For students working on group projects, what advice do you have to make the collaboration as successful as possible?

Gadarian: Collaboration is not always easy but it can make working much more fun and much less lonely. It's important to establish from the get-go what everyone's strengths are and how you are going to divide up each part of the project. Then, as you go, you need to coordinate and communicate each step—literature review, theory building, finding and analyzing data, and write-up. Each person needs to take responsibility for some part but be open to others' ideas and editing. Sometimes you will need to get rid of a part of a project that was your idea and it's challenging. Put all of your cast-off writing and ideas in a separate document and it will feel less permanent.

How Can I Help?

Steve Smith, Civic Nebraska

Steve Smith has done it all. He has covered politics and civic life in newspapers around the country, ran the communications shop for the University of Nebraska, and is the director of communications for Civic Nebraska, a nonprofit that works on youth service learning, civic health, and nonpartisan voting rights to made democracy more *modern and robust* for all Nebraskans.

Our Q&A with Smith, conducted over email, is below. He is a published author and an active mentor in Big Brothers and Big Sisters in Lincoln, Nebraska.

Wagner and Perryman: You've been a reporter, a university communications specialist, author, and are now the director of communications for Civic Nebraska. How has your job influenced how you have framed the messages you have wanted to convey to various audiences?

Smith: I've framed lots of different messages in my career. Each iteration has originated from the values and priorities of the organization I've represented. Every organization has a set of clear values and key audiences that they wish to reach. As a newspaper reporter and editor, I focused on telling stories to older, more educated audiences that would ask a pressing question and then seek to answer it. Then, I would work to write that story in a way that would prompt a reaction from readers—and action from stakeholders. Newspaper editors call that "Writing it strong." Not sensationalizing a topic or event, but describing it in active, emotive terms that get readers invested.

Nebraska U. is a public institution that prioritizes conveying its quality and stewardship to statewide and national audiences. During my days at NU, I focused more on explaining the *why* of different aspects of the university and always, always, *always* highlighted our core values—*the university is innovative, the university is confident, the university is proficient, the university is thoughtful, the university is safe.* Whether publicizing research and scholarship, announcing a new athletic director, or responding to any number of crises that popped up, we based all of our communication on one or more of those messages.

It's a similar process to frame messages for Civic Nebraska, a nonpartisan nonprofit that builds and protects democracy in our state. But it's executed a bit differently and for slightly different audiences. Our organization keeps its lights on through the kindness of donors, so many of our most important messages are with them in mind. We make sure to emphasize exactly what we do with their money—and that what we do *matters and has an impact.* This can take on several different forms: In messages to our core supporters and active volunteers (who, while we are nonpartisan, tend to be left-leaning), our language tends to be urgent and more aggressive. In framing issues for mainstream media, we often build our statements from a "last word" standpoint that is enveloped in expertise, with no official partisan loyalty. If we weigh in on one side or another of a partisan argument—and we do, regularly—it's

(Continued)

(Continued)

with our extended audiences in mind and with the aim of cementing our credibility and authority on a particular topic about our democracy.

Wagner and Perryman: Civic Nebraska pursues youth service learning, civic health initiatives, and nonpartisan voting rights advocacy (www.civicnebraska.org). What are the different ways that communication is involved in the pursuit of these goals?

Smith: Communication is embedded in every one of our programs and initiatives. Beyond our messages that convey what we do and what impact we have, we connect all of our programs by over-emphasizing *why* we do what we do. Through a variety of owned, earned, and paid media, we can reach a wide range of Nebraskans. Whether it's through social media, on our website, in a marketing campaign, or in a mass email, these communications bring more donors, volunteers, advocates, and ambassadors into our camp. We've seen our youth civic leadership programs grow because parents, teachers, and school administrators see *why* building the next generation of civic leaders is so important, and they want to be part of that, to help it grow. A campaign aimed to explain to city leaders *why* housing adequacy is important to neighborhoods, and in turn vital to building democracy from the ground up, was a key part of our successful strategy to get legislation aimed at protecting older neighborhoods in Lincoln passed. And frankly, we rarely have to explain why it's important to protect the right to vote and to remove unnecessary barriers to the ballot.

Wagner and Perryman: What advice do you have for students reading this book who think a career in political and/or civic advocacy might be for them?

Smith: First, be sure that the cause, candidate, or effort with which you're enlisting aligns with your personal values. Sure, you can work in the world of political/civic advocacy if you're kind of academically detached from the subject matter. But ultimately, advocacy work is not for those who are lukewarm about the people, places, and issues involved or the stakes at hand. That's not to say you should live your job—but to truly succeed in and "get" the world of advocacy, your motivations must come from within.

Wagner and Perryman: What kinds of skills and behaviors are most valuable for people just getting their start in political communication-related fields?

Smith: Even in this world of memes, YouTube, and Instagram, you still need to have a strong word skill to convey your key messages. By that

I mean you have to have a strong command of the language and its various nuances—choosing the right words, and making those words count, whether they're written or spoken. Also, always be open to new ways of approaching or doing things. Among the various communication fields, communication around politics and advocacy evolves pretty quickly, simply because of the constancy and import of external events—what was normal or edgy a year or two ago might feel outmoded or ineffectually quaint today. Flexibility and the wisdom to break with established methods is a valuable trait in this fast-moving communication world.

Who's Biased Now?

How People Interpret the Media They Use

CAMPAIGNS CRAFT ADVERTISEMENTS. Journalists write stories. Politicians tweet, deliver speeches, and blast out emails. These very different forms of communication all have a common purpose: to reach an audience. Whether the point of the message is to persuade voters, inform the public, or communicate a position—the defining feature of mass communication is that it does in fact reach *the masses*.

It can be tempting to think of those masses as a faceless crowd—a blob of hapless sheep swayed by whatever message they heard last. Someone flips through the channels and catches the latest ad for the Republican Senatorial candidate . . . maybe they'll now consider him! Later, they crack open the newspaper to find a flattering story about his Democratic opponent . . . now they're leaning back toward her! The next day, they refresh their inbox to find emails from both campaigns touting the candidates' accomplishments . . . now they're really torn—how can they possibly choose between the two candidates when they're getting so many different messages?!

Hopefully you recognize the absurdity of the above scenario. People do not mindlessly react to media messages. Upon hearing a political advertisement, they do not suddenly support that candidate. After reading a news story encouraging them to vote, they do not drop what they are doing and head to the polls. The idea that audiences are mindless sponges soaking up whatever media messages come their way is an outdated communication model known as the hypodermic needle, or magic bullet, theory. It's the idea that people are strongly and uniformly influenced by the media they consume—they are vulnerable *sitting ducks*, just waiting for their next dose of media messaging.

Today, we know that audiences are far more sophisticated and resilient. Messages affect people in different ways, or quite often, not at all. When people encounter media messages, they are never without their own experiences, knowledge, beliefs, and opinions—and all these things play a role in everything from which media messages they choose to how they interpret those messages and what effects they experience because of that exposure. While we have reviewed research examining whether and how news organizations are biased, it is important to remember that, no matter the direction(s) that news sources may be biased, we humans encountering that information have our own sets of biases that we need to understand if we are to paint a complete picture of political communication in a mediated society. The audience is not passive, it's active, which means message creators—whether they are journalists or political operatives—have to account for the fact that each member of the audience may interpret a message in their own unique way. It may come as no surprise that political communication researchers have discovered there are patterns to how audiences choose, interpret, and respond to certain types of messages.

Choosing Media Messages

You can run into mass-mediated political messages anywhere: in a magazine in the waiting room at the dentist's office, on airport TV screens while waiting for a flight, during a commercial break for your favorite show, or on your social media feed when you log in to wish a friend *happy birthday*. But more often, you encounter media messages actively. That is, you choose to follow news organizations, newsmakers, or political figures on social media (or friends who share these messages frequently). You navigate to various news websites for your morning updates. You choose to open the newspaper or flip on the nightly news.

The concept of the active audience begins with the notion that people are active participants in their own media consumption. Though there are times when they encounter media involuntarily (e.g., advertising, which people rarely choose to consume but always seems to find them nonetheless), people generally opt into—or out of—exposure to media messages. Scholars have long been interested in the types of messages people seek out and their reasons for doing so.

Uses and Gratifications

So what kind of mass media messages do people want? According to one theory, that depends on the particular payoff an audience member is looking for. The *uses and gratification theory* of media focuses on understanding the cognitive, affective, personal, and social needs that media consumption fulfills. Gratifications sought can change for any individual media consumer in any given moment, and sometimes may be complex. For example, a liberal may seek out a news article on a Democratic candidate's immigration policy because of a desire to be informed (cognitive gratification) and to be able to discuss the issue among friends (social gratification). If they want to think in-depth about the issue, perhaps they seek out a story in *The Atlantic,* or, if they want the information visually, they seek out a longer video news report from *Vice* or *60 Minutes.* They may also have a desire to surveil what *the other side* is saying, so they seek out an opinion piece in the *National Review.* That piece may frustrate them, prompting a visit to The Huffington Post for a more flattering piece on their preferred candidate (emotional gratification). Because they spent so much time learning about the issue, perhaps they share the story with their friends on social media as a way to persuade others while also appearing thoughtful and well-informed (personal gratification).

There is no central guide to the multitude of gratifications people seek when interacting with mass media. Different scholars use different categorization systems, and the latest studies are always coming up with new reasons why people might seek out certain media in certain contexts, especially as people have more and more ways of accessing media. But all research in the uses and gratification area asks a common question: What is it about the audience that explains their encounters with and reactions to media messages?

Selective Exposure

One characteristic that scholars have hypothesized may play a role in how people select media—specifically, news media—is partisanship. The theory of selective exposure is that people tend to seek out news that fits their political perspectives, that is, the idea that a Republican prefers Fox News and a liberal prefers MSNBC. The outcome of this theory is that partisans dedicate a disproportionate amount of their news diet to like-minded content.

While the idea that people might gravitate toward attitude-confirming information isn't anything new,[1] recent trends in the mass media industry have amplified concerns about how easy it is to turn to *news that fits your views.* The proliferation of news sources, the reemergence of openly partisan sources, and the ability to curate content via social media have certainly made it easier for people to actively seek like-minded political news (selective exposure) or avoid attitude-challenging views (selective avoidance). Studies that provide evidence for selective exposure do so in different ways. One popular tactic is to ask audiences to report which media outlets they use and then determine the partisan slant of those outlets. Of course, as we saw in Chapter 4, determining slant is not entirely straightforward. Researchers have categorized newspapers as left or right based on which candidate the paper's editorial board endorsed, classified cable news outlets based on reputation, and determined the slant of radio talk shows based on the host's political affiliation.[2] Using this technique, researchers look for evidence that audiences self-report exposure to sources that the researchers somehow classify as politically like-minded.

Another popular way of determining whether audiences have selective news habits is to have them choose from among a set of headlines that feature either pro- or counter-attitudinal information.[3] That is, given only two options, which headline does a Republican choose: "Unemployment rate hits 10-year low under Trump administration" or "Unemployment rate falls short of expectations this month"? If Republicans tend to choose the former, that would be considered evidence of selective exposure. Studies that employ this method tend to find that like-minded headlines are chosen more often than attitude-challenging headlines.

However, other research has shown that the notion of selective exposure isn't so simple. One clever study asked respondents to choose from four stories on the topic of abortion: a story marked as having more pro-choice arguments, one marked as having more pro-life arguments, a third marked as having both sides equally represented, and a fourth story marked as featuring few arguments for both sides. Participants were shown an icon alongside the headline that explicitly told them how the stories treated each perspective. The research team found that people tended to choose stories that purportedly favored their side, but that they did not necessarily avoid stories that presented an opposing view (though, the authors found some evidence that Republicans were more likely to avoid attitude-challenging information). Overall, as long as the story was marked so that the participant knew their preferred view would be included, it didn't seem to bother them that the other view was included as well. The authors point out that neither Democrats nor Republicans seemed to prefer news that was heavily weighted in favor of their own side. The takeaway? That when diverse-viewpoint news stories are available, they will often be selected over clearly partisan news stories.[4] Our bubbles may not be so filtered after all.

That's a promising result in light of the reality of the modern news market. Though there is a strong myth of red media or blue media political news market, the vast majority of news sources adhere to traditional notions of objectivity and neutrality (see Chapter 4). While they may display bias from time to time, and may even have a reputation for leaning slightly left or right, the bulk of day-to-day reporting by American journalists is not overtly partisan. To be sure, there are partisan outlets and people do use them—the success of Fox News attests to that—but scholars also point out that people may exaggerate how often they consume partisan news. For example, by tracking media habits instead of having respondents report them, Jacob Nelson and James Webster found that web traffic was heavily concentrated on a few nonpartisan, mainstream outlets like Yahoo and ABC News—and that even more obscure partisan outlets had ideologically diverse audiences.[5] Those findings are a stark contrast to

Pew Research Center's (2020) self-reported audience data, which showed that Democrats and Republicans gravitate toward different sources.[6] Why would this be? It could be the case that people may report consuming news that they perceive to be like-minded in an effort to appear ideologically consistent ("everyone knows that good Republicans watch Fox News!") but that in reality, they don't actually consume much partisan media.

Regardless of the extent to which the public actually engages in selective exposure, the idea of the *filter bubble* or *echo chamber* online is persistent. A 2018 Ipsos study found that 77 percent of Americans *believes* that the average member of the public lives in a filter bubble, looking only for opinions they agree with.[7] That is, they think other people are seeking out like-minded information, yet only 32 percent say they themselves seek out primarily like-minded info. Our own research (see Table 7.1) shows that people have very different impressions of their own and others' media diets. In fact, both Democrats and Republicans believe those on *the other side* are more likely to look for *news that fits their views*. They believe members of their own party are less likely to do so, signaling that they believe their political opponents are close minded.

What's the danger of believing that other people engage in selective exposure? As we'll discuss later in this chapter, people tend to believe that others are very affected by the media they consume. If people believe others are using primarily media that reinforces their attitudes, you can see how it might lead to the assumption that other people are becoming more extreme. As polarized as the US electorate currently is, studies have shown that Americans actually tend to overestimate the polarization of attitudes between Democrats and Republicans.[8] If we overestimate how extreme our political opponents are, we might be less willing to compromise with them.

Table 7.1 Percentage of Democrats and Republicans Who Think They and Others "Always" or "Often" Seek Out "News That Fits Their Views"

	% agreeing that _____ often/always seek out like-minded news		
	You	In-group	Out-group
Democrats	44	56	65
Republicans	52	66	74

Source: Perryman, M. R. & Wagner, M. W. (2019, May). How U.S. partisans perceive their own and others' news habits. International Communication Association (Mass Communication Division), Washington, DC.

Note: N = 815

Additionally, we might be more willing to accept harsher punishments for them, or support restrictions on their political participation and freedom of speech.

Interpreting Media Messages

Do you think the news media is biased? More than 70 percent of Americans do.[9] But biased in which direction? That is something you won't find widespread agreement on. In fact, you'll predictably find the answer split along partisan lines. Democrats are more likely to say media in general, news outlets, or a specific news story news is biased against Democrats. Republicans are more likely to say the opposite.

Hostile Media Perception

The hostile media perception—a phenomenon where rival sides both tend to notice media bias against their own side—is a consistent curiosity in media research. How can a news story declared neutral by impartial observers be seen as undesirably biased by the most committed people on both sides of a controversial issue?[10] And yet, that is what has been observed time and time again when researchers test how competing partisans evaluate news stories about everything from religious and political conflicts, sports, and elections to specific issues like abortion, smoking, genetically modified food, and even the use of primates in research.[11] Take any issue with competing perspectives and have folks from competing camps evaluate media coverage of that issue, and you're more than likely going to find that each side believes they got the short end of the proverbial stick.

The hostile media perception isn't strictly a political phenomenon, but politics are an ideal context to see this perceptual quirk in action. The US political environment is extremely polarized, with clearly defined sides where people feel very cold toward the *other side*.[12] So it should come as no surprise that in the 2004 presidential election, Democrats thought media coverage was biased against John Kerry while Republicans thought it was biased against George W. Bush.[13] Fast-forward more than a decade and the same pattern still holds: Republicans were far more likely than Democrats to believe that the media was biased against Trump. In fact, 80 percent of Republicans thought the media favored Clinton when Gallup polled voters a month before the 2016 election—only 25 percent of Democrats agreed.[14] It's worth nothing that perceptions of bias in election campaigns tend to be mitigated by the perception that your preferred candidate is winning. For example, in the study examining perceived bias in the Kerry versus Bush race, Bush supporters recalled seeing less bias after he'd won the election. Similarly, because Clinton was widely projected to win the 2016 election, it isn't entirely surprising that only 10 percent of Democrats thought media coverage was biased in favor of Trump.[15]

The hostile media perception appears when competing partisans are asked to evaluate specific news outlets, specific news stories, or media in a general sense. What initially caught researchers' attention was when rival partisans each read the same, neutral news story and declared it biased against their interests. We call this an *absolute* hostile media perception. That is, each side sees an absolute bias against their side, so much so that they believe the news content favors the opposing side. This generally requires researches to know the true slant of the news story, either by crafting a news story to be strictly neutral or analyzing articles to determine the slant in order to compare it with readers' perceptions. For example, one team of researchers analyzed the slant of newspaper coverage of the 1992 presidential election.[16] They then measured readers' perceptions of the slant. They found that readers' impressions of newspaper bias had little to do with the newspaper's actual behavior. Instead, partisanship predicted perceived slant, such that Republicans tended to see papers as slanting in favor of Clinton (D) and Democrats sensing that papers slanted toward Bush (R). This was true even when rival partisans were evaluating *the same newspaper*.

But the differences in how competing groups assess media bias are not always so drastic. In what we term a *relative hostile media perception*, competing groups may agree on the slant of the story (or news coverage in general) but disagree on the severity of that slant.[17] For example, Figure 7.1 shows how Donald Trump and Hillary Clinton voters evaluated a variety of news sources.[18] You'll notice that Clinton voters believed that sources like *The New York Times* and *CNN* favored the Democratic nominee, but they believed that bias was slight, while Trump voters thought it was more severe. Similarly, another study found that when subjects were randomly assigned to view either a liberal-slanted or conservative-slanted news program, conservatives perceived more bias in the liberal program compared to liberals, and liberals saw more bias in the conservative program compared to conservatives.[19]

Relative hostile media perception can also appear when partisans estimate levels of media attention. Complaints about media focus are commonplace—too much focus on polls, not enough focus on the issues, too much attention to Trump's rallies or Clinton's emails, too little focus on third-party candidates or trailing primary candidates . . . the list goes on. You might notice that supporters of a candidate often have complaints about a candidate's coverage level (complaints about the Bernie Blackout of 2016—and again in 2020—may come to mind) that seem to baffle nonsupporters. We can chalk up at least some of the divergence in perceptions of how much attention a candidate receives to hostile media perception. For example, in estimating media attention in the 2016 election, Trump voters,

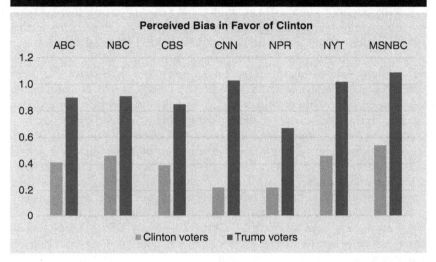

Figure 7.1   Audience Perceptions of Bias in 2016 Election Coverage

Perceived Bias in Favor of Clinton

Clinton voters   Trump voters

Source: Perryman, M. R. (2019). Where the other side gets news: Audience perceptions of selective exposure in the 2016 election, International Journal of Public Opinion Research, Advance Online Publication.

Note: N = 657.

compared to Clinton voters, thought media paid more attention to negative Trump stories like his refusal to release his tax returns, his controversial comments, and possible Russian interference in the election. On the other side of the aisle, Clinton voters were more likely than Trump voters to believe journalists paid attention to her use of a private email server and the attack on the Benghazi embassy—both of which happened when she was secretary of state.[20]

Why Do Hostile Media Perceptions Happen?

One reason this phenomenon interests scholars is because it flies in the face of how people typically interpret information—as supportive of their views. That is, we usually have a bias toward fitting new information into our existing mindset (an assimilation bias). The hostile media perception is curious because it reveals a situation where rival audiences are each interpreting information as being against their views (a contrast bias). The more *involved* a person is with the topic (e.g., having a strong or extreme attitude, finding the issue personally important), the more likely they are to see undesirable bias in news coverage of that topic. In other words, a Republican who deeply cares about immigration is more likely to see liberal bias in an immigration story than a Republican who is not interested in immigration.

Why might this happen? Researchers have tried to answer that question by comparing how people interpret information in a nonmediated format (like a student essay) versus how they interpret that same information in a news story. What they've found is that when people read the information in a student essay format, they see it as supportive of their views—and yet, when that same information is presented as a news article, consumers see it as biased against them. Albert Gunther, who has penned over a dozen studies on this peculiar perception, reasons that it is the knowledge that a message will reach others that triggers a sort of defensive processing. When we see information in a nonmediated format, we know that few others will encounter it, and thus there's no need to be concerned about the content. You might think of it as being on *low alert*. Now think about reading information that you know thousands of other people will see. Might you process that information differently, perhaps in a state of *high alert*?

Researchers have attempted to sort out exactly what's happening in the brain to generate judgments about media content. One possibility is *selective recall*, where news consumers are drawn to information that contradicts their position and therefore they remember more undesirable facts from a news story. Another possibility is *selective categorization*, where partisans tend to categorize ambiguous information in a news story as contrary to their position. A final possibility is the *different standards* explanation, where involved news consumers tend to classify attitude-challenging information in a news story as inaccurate or unnecessary, leading to the conclusion that the story is biased.

Beliefs about news media in a general sense also affect perceptions of media bias in any particular story. Republicans, in particular, are likely to believe media coverage is biased. A recent Gallup/Knight Foundation public opinion survey found that a full 67 percent of Republicans say they see a great deal of bias in news coverage, only 26 percent of Democrats and 46 percent of Independents said the same.[21] Republican accusations of media bias are not a recent development. One study shows that over 90 percent of the public complaints about media bias came from Republicans in the 1988, 1992, and 1996 elections.[22] But it goes back even further than that: complaints about a liberal media bias are easy to track down throughout history—they've come from Republican leaders such as Vice President Agnew, President Eisenhower, Vice President Quayle, and presidential candidate Dole. Though all politicians occasionally wrestle with the press, the modern Republican party has increasingly positioned the press as an adversary. Their *us versus the press* crusade is led by President Trump, who regularly calls portions of the news media the "enemy of the people."[23] Democrats, notably Senator Elizabeth Warren, a candidate for the 2020

Democratic Party presidential nomination, have specifically focused their ire not at "the media" writ large, but at Fox News—an outlet Warren called a "hate-for-profit racket."[24]

It's important not to interpret media bias perception as proof that the sources were actually biased. It simply shows how competing partisans view media, and most of the time, it's difficult to say whether they are right or wrong. On the other hand, the fact that people tend to see bias in news doesn't necessarily mean that partisanship makes it impossible for people to provide useful judgments about news quality or slant. Recent research shows both Democrats and Republicans accurately rate mainstream sources as more trustworthy than hyper partisan or false news sites, and that when *trustworthiness* ratings from an ideologically mixed group of people are considered in aggregate, they tend to match up with ratings from professional fact-checkers.[25] In other words, with a diverse group of people all rendering judgments about media bias, you can at least get an estimate that's close to what experts come up with themselves.

Motivated Reasoning

The hostile media perception focuses on how partisanship affects how people evaluate news messages, but partisanship also impacts how people interpret political information more broadly. The concept of *motivated reasoning* explores how preexisting beliefs guide interpretation of new information. Far from being *cool calculators*, motivated reasoning research shows how emotion plays an important role in interpreting political information. Similar to the concept of cognitive dissonance or conservation bias[26] motivated reasoning challenges the notion of people as rational decision-makers. That is, upon exposure to new information, do people update their beliefs accordingly? Scholars have long argued that affect (emotion) and cognition are inexplicably linked. Psychologist Robert Abelson called it *hot cognition*, hypothesizing that every piece of information in memory is linked to a particular emotion.[27] Thus, when information is made salient, such as when you learn something new about a candidate you've already formed an opinion about, the emotion is triggered as well.

Motivated reasoning research has demonstrated that partisanship, or political preferences more generally, has a powerful impact on how people process and interpret information about political candidates and issues. People readily question arguments that compete with their existing beliefs, but are all too happy to uncritically accept arguments that favor their political attitudes.[28] Even faced with strong evidence that their original political belief is incorrect, people resist being corrected, determined to integrate incongruent information into their current mindset. One startling example of the muscle behind motivated reasoning: Brendan Nyhan and Jason Reifler found that confronting conservatives with evidence that Iraq did not possess weapons of mass destruction in the lead-up to the Iraq War actually backfired, strengthening their original, incorrect belief.[29] Similarly, in certain contexts, supporters may actually become more supportive of a candidate after learning negative information about him or her.[30]

Some scholars have suggested that motivated reasoning explains why people fall for the blatantly false information peddled by *fake news* factories or hyper-partisan sources. The idea is that partisans want the information to be true so badly that they're willing to rationalize questionable—or even outrageous—information. Some scholarship suggests that emotions are not totally to blame for fake news, though: Gordon Pennycook and David Rand recently showed that people with stronger analytical reasoning skills were able to discern between real and fake news headlines even when the headlines aligned with their political beliefs.[31] The authors conclude that lazy thinking may be a major reason why people fall prey to disinformation. On the other hand, the highly educated are often the most guilty of motivated reasoning. After all, they are taught in college how to use evidence to make an argument. As such, it is not hard to understand why the educated might be quite good at finding reasons to keep believing what they want to believe, even in the face of evidence that they are wrong. In other words, we might be teaching you to be a motivated reasoner!

Third-Person Perception

Imagine you trek out to the mailbox and find a snazzy flyer singing the praises of a candidate that you vehemently oppose. The advertisement is beautifully designed, complete with a handsome photo of the candidate and a long list of his accolades and achievements. In fact, it's so compelling that you find yourself looking at your undecided neighbor's house, wondering if it could possibly sway their vote. Would you be tempted to snag it out of their mailbox? Or to strike up a conversation about the election next time you see them to see if the flyer had any effect?

People are routinely concerned about media's effects. Not effects on themselves—of course we're all far too savvy to be affected by something like a political advertisement—but effects on *them*, the third persons. The *third-person perception* is the idea that we believe we are uniquely immune to media's influence whereas others are quite impressionable. If anyone is going to be affected by political advertisements, election polls, or news coverage, surely it will be *them* and not *me*.

This is particularly true for messages where it would be perceived as *bad* to be influenced. For example, we generally believe others are more susceptible to outside influence than we are, but when that outside influence is something like television violence, pornography, or misogynist rap lyrics, we're especially likely to believe others will be affected. There are several studies that have shown a reverse of this trend; first-person effect studies show that, for positive messages, we sometimes think we're more influenced than others. For example, people sometimes say they are more influenced than other people are by public service announcements. The first-person perception hasn't been as consistent as the third-person perception, probably because people generally dislike admitting that they are influenced by outside forces. As one team of scholars put it, people like to believe they are "alone in a crowd of sheep."[32]

Are we correct? Are other people more affected by media than we are? You know what they say: if everyone is unique then no one is! A host of research shows that people tend to overestimate media's effects on others. Why would this happen? It may be due to *biased optimism*—a tendency for people to believe they are less likely than others to experience negative consequences. Alternatively, it may be an *attribution bias*—a tendency to believe our actions are due to situational factors but others' actions are due to their own flawed character traits. We're motivated to protect our own egos, in a way, by believing we can withstand blatant attempts at persuasion. At the same time, we're just more aware of our own capabilities and limitations, whereas we fall back on heuristics like *other people are gullible* when making judgments about how others will respond to media messages.

There are patterns to whom we believe to be most at risk for media influence. First, we tend to think that more socially distant groups are the most likely to fall victim to media's influence. For example, one study found that people believed a political ad for an opposing candidate would have the largest effect on the out-group, a slightly smaller effect on the general public, and at the smallest effect on members of the in-group.[33] Scholars have reasoned that this boils down to basic in-group preferences: we typically have more positive feelings toward groups we are closer to than toward groups we are not a part of. We think more highly of in-groups and in some cases, we even think of them as extensions of ourselves, making us more confident of their ability to withstand media pressure.

Social distance isn't the only factor we consider when thinking about how media might influence others. We also make a quick assessment of how relevant the media message might be to a particular group. For example, Jakob Jensen and Ryan Hurley's experiment found that students believed environmentalists were more likely than their own classmates to be influenced by a news story about the environment since the message was perceived as more relevant to the environmental group.[34] You might think of the implications of this finding in the context of what you've learned so far about political news. As you read in the section on selective exposure, people tend to believe others are seeking out like-minded media, even though evidence suggests that practice may not be as widespread as some fear. If people believe others look for *news that fits their views* and they believe that others are especially susceptible to like-minded messages, it's easy to see how people think others are being brainwashed by *biased* media.

Reacting to Media

Now, think about how you might respond to the feeling that others are being influenced by media. Going back to the beginning of this section and our trek out to the mailbox, our concern for our undecided neighbor might have put a few ideas in our minds: pull the flyer out of his mailbox before he sees it! Strike up a conversation with him later so you can counter the flyer's influence! Give him a flyer for your own preferred candidate!

Influence of Presumed Influence

That's the thing about perceptions—they tend to form the basis for action. That is, we don't necessarily stop at thinking, "Media messages really influence other people!" We often take it a step further: "And I'm going to do something about it." The area of research focused on the consequences of third-person perceptions is broadly called the *influence of presumed influence*. As Gunther and his coauthor J. Douglas Storey explained when introducing the concept, "People perceive some influence of a message on others and then react to that perception of influence."[35]

What are some actions people might take? One possibility is censorship. Remember you wanting to purge the flyer from your neighbor's mailbox? That's censorship. Studies have consistently found that when people believe others are influenced by media, they're more enthusiastic about censorship. One study found that people who believed others were affected by election news stories were more supportive of giving the government power to ban *unfair* news stories and polls.[36] Another found that increasing perceptions of media influence were linked to a willingness to restrict negative political advertising.[37] Fewer negative campaign ads might sound like a great idea to you—but consider, do you want the government involved in determining the sorts of political messages that Americans can be exposed to?

Another possible reaction to perceived media influence is to go on a counteroffensive. This is sometimes called *corrective action,* and a good example would be if you presented your undecided neighbor with a flyer for another candidate, or struck up a conversation about the election to try and persuade him. Researchers have shown that believing others are influenced by messages—and even worse, believing those messages are biased—can lead to online and offline corrective actions.[38] One study found that such beliefs lead people to talk about politics more often and seek out a variety of viewpoints.[39]

A final possibility—probably not a likely one in our mailbox scenario—is that the perception that others have been swayed by media leaves us feeling out-of-sync with public opinion, prompting us to change our own opinion or behaviors. Imagine that all your neighbors have signs for the opposing candidate in their yard. You may be the kind of person who sticks your own candidate's sign in your front lawn in defiance—but social norms are a powerful thing, and you may find yourself complying with what you perceive to be the popular opinion. For example, in an experiment where subjects interacted with people who disagreed with them politically, two-thirds ended up conforming so that they were more in-line with the popular opinion.[40] In a political context, these are often thought of as *bandwagon effects*. One recent study, for example, showed that polling news stories that frame candidates as having *momentum* can actually increase support for the rising candidate.[41] When one of your authors moved to Wisconsin, he was told by neighbors that he should put a "Recall Gov. Scott Walker" sign in his front yard, lest his liberal neighbors think he supported the Republican governor. This was despite the fact that your author moved to the Badger State *after* Walker won the recall election facing him!

But more generally, we tend to adopt attitudes and behaviors that we see as normative. That's why a common way to promote healthy behaviors is to let people know that the healthy behavior is popular (e.g., "95 percent of university students get a ride home when they're out drinking"). How we perceive media can nudge us toward conforming behaviors as well. For example, in another study from Gunther and colleagues, they found that when teens assumed their peers had been affected by pro-smoking media messages, they were more willing to smoke themselves.[42]

Physiological Responses to Media

So far, we've been focusing on what we might call audience psychology: how cognitive quirks and biases help (or inhibit) our understanding of and reactions to mediated content. Another interesting area of research focuses on how audiences *physically* react to media content, and how those reactions reflect underlying emotions and attitudes. Mass communication physiological research focuses on measurable, biological responses to mediated messages. For example, how does the length of a radio ad impact a viewer's heart rate, and what does that physical marker say about how the viewer is processing the advertisement? Do viewers have a stronger physical reaction to negative or positive news?

Answering these types of questions requires measuring physical reactions to media content. This usually happens in a lab setting. Psychophysiology labs feature equipment that can measure things like heart rate, tiny muscle movement in the face, and skin conductance (electrodermal activity). Subjects are hooked up to electrodes that send their biological signals to a computer program that logs the data. Researchers show the subjects media messages (typically, videos or photos) and measure their reactions over time.

What can this biological data tell us about how people process messages? One of the central assumptions that this area of research makes is that physiological reactions are tied to our brain's processing of information. The idea of the embodied brain is that "thinking, feeling, meditation, awareness, and consciousness are side effects of the organ called the brain, which is physiologically connected to every other organ and system in your body."[43] In other words, physiological reactions reflect the thinking and emotional processing happening within the brain.

One important contribution of physiological measures is the opportunity to measure attention. You can ask someone how much attention they paid to something, or you can quiz them to check their memory of the message, but physiology measures allow researchers to gauge attention through heart rate. Researchers believe a deceleration in heart rate indicates that the brain is dedicating more cognitive resources to processing information. If you're watching a campaign ad and your heart rate slows down, you are paying more attention to the information.

For example, one team of researchers wanted to know whether people paid more attention to health news when the story was about a health threat in their town versus a town that was five hundred miles away. They found that subjects who read a news story about a health threat in their town had more pronounced heart rate slowdowns compared to subjects who read about a health threat that was far away, suggesting they were paying more attention.[44] You can see why a nearby threat might cause you to pay more attention than a threat that's five hundred miles away! Similarly, another team of researchers found that heart rate deceleration was more pronounced when viewing negative news story compared to when viewing positive ones, again suggesting that people pay particular attention to negative or threatening information.[45]

Researchers also look for evidence of emotion in how people respond to media messages. This can be a difficult task—how can you tell the difference between sadness and anger, or happiness and nervousness? There are typically two approaches. Some researchers look on the dimensions of valence and arousal—valence being whether an emotion is positive or negative and arousal describing the intensity of the positive or negative emotion. Alternatively, researchers look for markers of distinct emotions like sadness, anger, or disgust. The activation of certain muscles in the face (the zygomatic for smiling, for example, or the corrugator for frowning) gives researchers clues as to which emotion is triggered. Of course, it isn't as simple as "this muscle activation = this emotion." Psychophysiology researchers recognize that all parts of the body are intertwined and usually working on multiple tasks at once (e.g., keeping you alive *and* processing a media message). So instead of just looking at one indicator of an emotion, researchers consider several at once. The discrete emotion of disgust, for example, is marked by activation of the levator labii (which happens when your nostrils slightly constrict and your mouth opens a bit), an initial acceleration of heart rate followed by a deceleration, and heightened levels of skin conductance (a measurement of the level of sweat in the eccrine sweat glands on the palm of the hand or sole of the foot).

Other physiological responses include measuring levels of the stress hormone cortisol, which can be captured by swabbing the inside of the mouth. For example, one group of researchers found that conservative students who watched news coverage about the election of Barack Obama had heightened cortisol levels, indicating stress.[46]

Some researchers have even looked at brain imagining when processing political information. One team used an MRI machine to look at brain activity while partisans processed neutral, positive, and negative information about political candidates. They found that different areas of the brain *lit up* depending on whether the subject was processing information that they had a personal stake in, suggesting that motivated reasoning does indeed activate the parts of the brain that process emotions.[47]

Genetic Effects

A new realm of research suggests that liberals and conservatives may even have distinct physiological reactions when processing information. A team of researchers found that conservatives tend to have longer startle responses to loud noises and spend more time looking at images of angry faces. MRI scans even show conservatives and liberals have distinct brain patterns when processing repulsive images—to the extent that the team could predict a subject's ideology with 95 percent certainty based only on neuroimages. These findings are consistent with questionnaires that show conservatives tend to have higher sensitivity to disgust.[48] One study even found that conservatives were better than liberals at detecting bitter compounds hidden in food![49]

Disgust is not a political value, but rather, an emotion theorized to help protect us from threat. When you see a moldy piece of bread, you lose your appetite. When you smell sewage in your bathroom, you're inclined to call a plumber. Disgust is an automatic tool that helps us avoid threats in our environment.

Researchers have noted that this tool can often malfunction—flagging nonthreats as threats (e.g., people with disabilities, people of a different race). In one study, psychologist Mark Schaller showed that people cued to think about germs tended to be less supportive of their country advertising to people from unfamiliar nations.[50] Can triggering concerns about biological threats increase prejudice? Other research has shown that opposition to immigration increases alongside sensitivity to disgust, so it certainly seems plausible.[51]

The connections between political ideology, emotion, physiological reactions, and the underlying biological predispositions are messy. If conservatives consistently show stronger reactions to negative stimuli (which plenty of research has shown to be the case), then can we conclude that some innate biological difference exists between liberals and conservatives? Even brain patterns differ between the two opposing political camps. Does that not suggest that liberals and conservatives differ on some fundamental level?

Some researchers argue that yes, physiological and broad character traits (such as disgust sensitivity) guide political preferences. This doesn't mean that if you hate bitter vegetables you're destined to be a conservative, but it may mean you're more likely to be conservative than someone who loves broccoli and arugula. Other researchers argue that it is possible that political ideologies actually impact and, over time, help shape the way we process information and emotion—resulting in those differences we see between liberals and conservatives in brain patterns and physiological responses. One research team calls this the "chicken-and-egg problem."[52] Do political attitudes shape physical and psychological characteristics over time? Or do physical and psychological characteristics make us predisposed to a particular political ideology?

From Research to Real Life

Now that you are aware of the many cognitive quirks people use to process media, do you think you are guilty of any of them? Have you ever thought a story was biased when it may have been even handed? Have you been more easily accepting of information that fits your preconceived notions? Perhaps you've assumed a media message would have a huge impact on others—even though it probably didn't? The results of one clever study suggest that you (and the authors of this book, and everybody else) seem to think we are the exception to cognitive biases. Even after being informed that our judgements are not necessarily objective, we tend to believe that they are.[53] We have a proclivity for believing that we alone are not swayed by undesirable internal biases or external forces. But hey—you can take comfort in knowing that at least everybody else is biased too!

What can you do to help? You can start by being wary of sharing information when you are not sure about its veracity. It might feel good to see a headline that shows how a politician you do not like was *eviscerated* by John Oliver or that they are guilty of some sort of terrible personal behavior and think, "I should share this on social media!" But think before you share. If the source is a place you had not heard of and a two-minute trip down the Google rabbit hole reveals that no other sources are reporting the story, it probably is not true. If you still are not sure, submit the story to a fact-checking organization like PolitiFact or FactCheck.org. Let them check it out before asking other people to pay attention to a story that might have the virtue of being false.

Remember that our attention is a fixed resource. If we are paying attention to one thing, we are not paying attention to everything else. As political communication scholar Talia Stroud has noted, "[t]he choices that are available and what is taking place in the broader environment also influence whether people will choose to allocate their attention to the news."[54] Share wisely.

DIY Research

Lilach Nir, Hebrew University of Jerusalem

Nir, L., & McClurg, S. D. (2015). How institutions affect gender gaps in public opinion expression. *Public Opinion Quarterly, 79*(2), 544–567.

Lilach Nir is associate professor of communication and journalism and is also associate professor of political science at the Hebrew University of Jerusalem. She studies public opinion, media effects, and psychophysiology in political communication research and social network effects on our attitudes, thinking, and behavior. Her research has won awards from the International Communication Association and the World Association for Public Opinion Research. Her article, coauthored with Scott McClurg, shows that a variety of country-specific features affect how much one's gender affects one's willingness to express their opinions.[55] They find a "trade-off between gender equality and opinion expressiveness." This is important because people's willingness to engage in the expression of opinions in typical political discussions is crucial to public opinion dynamics ranging from being able to lead opinion to the reaching of a false consensus. We spoke with her about her research over email.

Wagner and Perryman: You and your co-author use a comparative perspective to show how different country-level features affect gender equality and opinion expression. What would you say are the most important things your article discovered?

Nir: To study opinion expression is to study whose voice is heard by other citizens and policymakers. The two most important things we discovered are: (a) gender differences in political expression are explained by institutional differences, and not just individual traits; (b) paradoxically, the rise of

(Continued)

(Continued)

women's education, employment, and income widened, not narrowed, gaps in opinion expression.

Wagner and Perryman: What was the most important decision you and your co-author made in the research design of your study and how did that decision influence what you found in your analyses?

Nir: We analyzed cross-national, cross-section survey data in 33 countries. The most important decision we made in the design was to include democratic countries that vary systematically on important features we theorized as explanations of opinion expressiveness. We also used multilevel modeling to test the relative effect each level of analysis and their interdependence.

Wagner and Perryman: What was the biggest question about gender and opinion expression that you were left with after your article was published?

Nir: The biggest question we were left with is how to explain the *widening* gap in opinion expression in countries where women achieved more *equal* status. One possibility we discuss is that a gender-egalitarian workplace maximizes perceived group threat (see page 563 of our article in *Public Opinion Quarterly*).

Wagner and Perryman: If a student reading this book wanted to conduct their own research, albeit on a smaller scale, about gender equality and opinion expression, where would you recommend they start?

Nir: To conduct a follow-up research on gender equality and opinion expression, think how you would explain the paradox of greater (material) equality leading to greater (expressive) *inequality*. Does intergroup contact in the workplace affect differently men and women's political expression? Are women threatened, are men threatened, or both? What would be the logical mechanism? What experimental or other design will show this mechanism?

How Can I Help?

Karen Lincoln Michel, *Madison Magazine*

Karen Lincoln Michel is publisher and executive editor of *Madison Magazine*, a print and online publication that reaches an audience of 170,000 readers. Michel is past president of the Native American Journalists Association and is a board member and past board president of the Wisconsin Center for

Investigative Journalism. She is a former executive editor of *The Daily Advertiser* in Lafayette, LA, and was the assistant managing editor of the *Green Bay Press Gazette*. She is an award-winning leader in Native American journalism, newsroom diversity, and newsroom leadership. She is a member of the Ho-Chunk tribe in Wisconsin. We spoke online.

Wagner and Perryman: This book has discussed a lot about what has changed in newspaper and magazine publishing over the years. What would you say is still the same?

Michel: Readers are still interested in good stories with strong narratives. When I made the switch from newspapers to magazines in 2015, I was pleasantly surprised that long-form journalism is thriving in an age when many Americans get their news from social media sites and keep apprised of happenings through succinct news alerts. I work for a city-regional magazine and I have found that people will take time to read in-depth stories about their community, especially if they can relate to the subject matter or somehow see themselves reflected in those pieces.

Wagner and Perryman: How did you go from being a reporter to being executive editor and publisher of a popular monthly magazine?

Michel: It wasn't planned. I thought I had found my calling when I landed my first job as a news reporter and figured I would always be a writer. That gradually changed after I became president of a national non-profit organization called UNITY: Journalists of Color Inc., which promoted accurate and fair news coverage of communities color and challenged media companies to staff their newsrooms to reflect the nation's diversity. Through my work with UNITY (which disbanded in 2018) and with the Native American Journalists Association, I realized that many of the changes we sought would come when journalists of color are employed in key decision-making roles within their companies. I was fortunate that when I decided to pursue a path into management, I had support from newsroom leaders and mentors who helped me get the proper training that prepared me for leadership positions. I have approached every opportunity with a reporter's curiosity, and I think that helped propel me to serve as a top editor and publisher.

Wagner and Perryman: Editors can play large roles in deciding whose voices get heard by an audience. How do you approach your job as the editor of *Madison Magazine* in terms of the topics you want to cover and the people you choose to cover them?

Michel: From the outset, I made it clear that my approach as editor was to try to tell the whole story of Madison, including neighborhoods that are

(Continued)

(Continued)

largely ignored by legacy news media. We're very conscious of the stories we choose and look for diversity in our sources and in the subject matter. In 2016, we started a monthly feature called Spectrum Voices, which spotlights people who represent diverse communities and viewpoints. We also strive for diversity in our bench of freelance writers and photographers. Sometimes my editors and designers are more vocal about diversity than I am, and that's exciting.

Just one quick story that speaks to that point is when my former publisher asked me in February 2016 if I noticed that people of color had graced the cover of the last four issues of our magazine. I hadn't realized it, which was great. It meant that covering the whole story of Madison was beginning to seep into our editorial DNA.

Wagner and Perryman: What qualities do you look for in people who are just starting out, seeking a career in writing and reporting?

Michel: I appreciate someone who is inquisitive and has an approachable style because those qualities will help them in the reporting process. In the hiring process, I look closely at cover letters to get a sense of the applicant's writing style and I carefully read clips. I also look for someone who is passionate about journalism and is energized by the chance to uncover meaningful stories that affect and enrich our lives.

Wagner and Perryman: What advice do you have for readers of this book interested in pursuing a career in a mass communication field?

Michel: Journalism is a worthwhile career because at its heart is a quest for the truth. Despite political attacks that label investigative pieces as "fake news," the news media and the truths they uncover are vital to our democracy. The broader field of mass communication is also an integral part of our society and aids in the free flow of information. When we're well informed, we make better choices as individuals, as voters, as consumers, and as Americans.

CHAPTER 8

Political Advertising

WHEN HARRY TRUMAN RAN for president in 1948, he promoted his campaign across thirty thousand miles and half a million handshakes. Only a few years later, Dwight D. Eisenhower found a way to reach millions more voters right in their living rooms. With the launch of his "Eisenhower Answers America" TV ads, modern political advertising was born. The ads were simple. Handpicked citizens asked questions and Eisenhower, who recorded his part of the commercials at a different time than the audience members, answered them in short sound bites.

To be sure, many mediums have been used for campaign advertising. Candidates have taken out newspaper ads, radio spots, and more recently, ads via social media. But for several decades, television ads have been the dominant force in campaign advertising. While we'll discuss other advertising platforms (especially digital), much of the content in this chapter deals specifically with video ads that air on broadcast or cable TV. The Wesleyan Media Project (WMP)—which tracks every ad that makes it onto TV screens across America—is an invaluable resource for understanding the volume of ads, the trends in ad tone and content, and ad sponsors.[1]

Most people will tell you that they do not like television advertising, largely because many of the ads are negative. However, it's important to acknowledge that there's a reason we still focus on traditional TV ads: they very much still dominate campaign advertising. The total volume of ads may dip in a given cycle—for example, ad volume was down in the 2016 presidential election compared to the 2012 race—but other cycles will set new ad records (e.g., the 2018 midterms featured twice as many ads as the 2014 races).[2] Overall, the total volume of TV ads is higher than ever. Because it's been the most prominent avenue for campaign ads, much of the research on political advertising focuses on the content and effects of television ads.

In this chapter, we overview how campaigns create ads, how they pay for them, and how outside groups play a role in the process. We then discuss the substance of ads and dig into why ads have become more negative over time. This chapter wraps up with a discussion about how (or if) ads impact voters.

Creating Campaign Ads

Democratic ad maker Mark Putnam has asked candidates to do some odd things. He encouraged a Senate candidate to assemble an assault rifle while blindfolded. He asked a gubernatorial hopeful to jump into a shower fully clothed. He convinced a presidential contender to dress up like an old Western sheriff. The long-time ad maker told CNN that a political ad "can't look like a political commercial. It has to be compelling. You're just hoping you can break through that den of noise and do something special, that is special for your candidate and that is special for that viewer, that they'll want to pay attention to."[3]

Campaigns and consultants spend a great deal of effort (and money) crafting campaign ads. All elements of the ad—the tone, the message, the visual cues—are carefully considered and tested using focus groups or surveys that evaluate the ad's believability, information value, and potential to persuade. Some of the ad elements that campaigns must decide on include

- Length: Typically, ads are 30 seconds for TV and longer for online videos

- Tone: Negative ads mention an opponent, positive ads focus on the ad's sponsoring candidate, and contrast ads comparing both candidates

- Visuals and audio: Imagery and music can be used to communicate issue stances, evoke emotions, or build associations (such as attack ads where opponents are shown in dark, grainy images). Background music is commonly used to help establish tone—98 percent of ads in 2014 featured it.[4]

Ad strategists will typically begin by trying to identify which voters the candidate could possibly attract. That is, who is the target audience? What do they already know about the candidate? Which issues do they care about? They don't just guess! They use research methods—surveys and focus groups—to help them figure out which audiences might be reachable and what sorts of messages would appeal to those targets. Campaigns then have to arrange to actually shoot and edit the ad, which, depending on the vision, could be an extensive production.

There's no need to, as they say, "throw things at the wall to see what sticks." Research methods like focus groups and online surveys allow campaigns to test which version of an ad has the biggest impact. Technology has made it easier than ever to pinpoint ineffective ads. Dial testing, for example, allows viewers to provide real-time feedback. Viewers are asked to turn a dial while viewing an ad and the dial direction lets the campaign gauge emotional responses to specific parts of the video. For example, a viewer might crank the dial up when they feel interested and down when they feel bored. Alternatively, campaigns can live-test their ads by using a technique called A/B testing: creating multiple variants of an ad and launching them simultaneously to see which version results in more engagement. Donald Trump's 2016 advertising team ran between forty thousand and fifty thousand variants of campaign ads on Facebook daily to gauge what was most effective![5]

Ad Sponsors

Many of the campaign ads you see during an election cycle were not created by the campaigns themselves. In fact, the Wesleyan Media Project estimates that over 20 percent of the ads in 2018 House races and a third of the ads in Senate races came from outside groups, while 80 percent came from campaigns and political parties. The person or group behind an ad matters. As you'll see in this section, different rules exist for campaigns and outside groups in terms of ad funding and content.

Campaigns

Candidates fund ads by spending money they collect as campaign donations. The Federal Election Campaign Act allows candidates to accept donations only from individuals, political parties, and political action committees (PACs). For the 2020 election cycle, the most an individual can donate to a candidate for federal office is $2,800 during the primary and another $2,800 during the general election. Political parties can also help build up a candidate's war chest, with the ability to contribute $5,000 per candidate per election.

PACs are the third source of a candidate's cash flow. These collectives are folks who band together to raise money for candidates or a specific cause, and they're typically focused on a social, business, or ideological issue. For example, some of the top PACs in 2018 were the National Beer Wholesalers Association, AT&T, and the National Association of Realtors. PACs receive voluntary donations from members. So, while companies like Boeing and Blue Cross/Blue Shield have PACs, that money does not come directly from the corporation. PACs are limited in how much money they get to spend or donate to candidates, though the amount differs between state and federal candidates.

Candidates spend a healthy portion of their campaign donations on political ads.[6] And there's good reason to spend money on ads as a candidate, not an outside group. There are some legal perks available to campaigns when they spend their own funds on ads. When outside groups buy ads on a candidate's behalf, they don't get the same bonus. One advantage is access to broadcasters' lowest unit rate. This means that for a certain period of time before Election Day, stations have to provide candidates ad time at the lowest cost normally offered to their preferred advertisers in a given time slot. This low rate is not offered to PACs.[7] At the federal level, campaigns also must be given reasonable access to ad space, meaning stations can't limit the number of available slots or decide to only air ads during certain windows. These are the Federal Communication Commission's reasonable access rules, so they don't apply to state and local candidates.

Rules on equal time, however, do apply to local, state, and federal candidates. The equal time rule means that if time is offered to one candidate in a race, all other candidates must be given an equal opportunity. Stations must maintain a record of all requests for airtime. The rule primarily applies to ads, but has had other implications: when Arnold Schwarzenegger ran for governor in California, his campaign asked the networks to stop airing his movies, lest his opponents demand equal time! There is an equal time exemption for news coverage, so news programs are not required to dedicate equal amounts of space to candidates. The now-defunct Fairness Doctrine dealt with how news organizations treat candidates for political office, but that has not been in effect since 1987.

Another advantage of paying for your own ads: no censorship. Broadcast stations (keep in mind, all these FCC rules apply only to broadcast networks, not cable) are not allowed to refuse to air an ad based on its content. Of course, since they can't turn down an ad, stations also can't be held liable for the content. If a candidate wants to air an ad accusing their opponent of being a foreign spy, and your station has given the opponent airtime, you're required to run it.

Because of the advantages campaigns enjoy when airing ads, a majority of a candidate's ads will come directly from his or her campaign. This ultimately means that campaigns are spending a huge chunk of change on ad buys. In the 2012 election, 45 percent of the Obama campaign's total spending was on local broadcast or national cable TV advertising. His opponent, Mitt Romney, spent 33 percent of his budget just on local broadcast ads. Because Obama had a bigger war chest, he was able to secure better rates on ads (since his campaign was footing the bill), compared to Romney, who was more reliant on the Republican party and interest groups for ads funding.[8] According to data from the Wesleyan Media Project, the average Senate candidate spends 38 percent of their campaign funds on local broadcast TV ad space.

| Photo 8.1 A 2016 Hillary Clinton Advertising Disclaimer

You'll know when you see a candidate-sponsored ad. Since the 2002 Bipartisan Campaign Reform Act, any television ad created by the campaign must receive a blessing from the candidate. That's why you hear, "I'm Donald Trump, and I approved this message." The rules are a bit different when an outside group creates an ad supporting a candidate. Those ads aren't approved by the candidate—in fact, many groups that create ads championing a certain candidate actually cannot legally coordinate with that candidate.

Ads sponsored by anyone other than the candidate must also feature some sort of disclaimer that lets people know who paid for the ad. The rules differ a bit based on whether the ad was approved by the campaign (a coordinated expenditure) or whether it was created independently of the campaign (independent expenditure), but the bottom line is that ads need to clearly communicate who paid the bill.

Parties and Outside Groups

Candidates' campaigns take care of a bulk of the campaign's advertising. Who foots the bill for the rest of the ads? Other ad sponsors include political parties on behalf of a candidate, ads coordinated between a candidate and a party, and ads from outside groups (which are not coordinated with the candidate). Political parties and outside groups tend to direct their dollars to competitive races.

Take a look at Table 8.1 and you'll see that outside groups are accounting for more ads than ever before. The WMP's analysis of TV ads from

Table 8.1 Outside Group Spending as a Percentage of All Federal Airings

Year	Group %
2000	10.14%
2002	5.83%
2004	13.94%
2006	5.54%
2008	6.99%
2010	13.90%
2012	28.93%
2014	28.53%
2016* (thru 8/1)	32.54%

Source: Kantar Media/CMAG with analysis by the Wesleyan Media Project, http://mediaproject.wesleyan.edu/disclosure-report/.

Note: Includes all available primary and general election broadcast television, national network, and national cable television advertising airings for each cycle.

2000 to 2016 shows that in 2004, ads from outside groups made up less than 15 percent of all ads. By 2016, they were responsible for nearly a third of the political ads that aired on broadcast and cable television. The increasing presence of outside group-sponsored ads is evident in midterm elections as well: in a two-week period before the 2018 midterms, for example, outside groups accounted for 17.5 percent of ads for House races and 32 percent of ads in Senate races.[9] Outside groups have now surpassed political parties as the second-biggest spenders on political ads.[10]

When we talk about outside groups spending, your mind probably lands on super PACs (e.g., Priorities USA), which can't donate directly to candidates or coordinate with campaigns but can collect unlimited donations to engage in so-called *independent expenditures*. Because they are not working directly with a campaign, super PACs are able to collect donations directly from corporations or unions (remember, a regular PAC can only collect a limited amount of money and it has to come from individuals). The end result? Super PACs have a lot of money to spend on ads, they just can't coordinate with the campaigns. WMP data shows that by August in the 2016 presidential election cycle, super PACs accounted for nearly 75 percent of all ad spending by outside groups.

Candidates are often accused of trying to indirectly coordinate ad strategy with their Super PACs, such as when 2016 presidential candidate Ted Cruz's campaign complained to Politico about how few Cruz ads were airing in early primary states.[11] It wasn't a direct communication with the super PAC about ad strategy, but it's certainly one way of sending a message.

Dark Money

One concern that often pops up when discussing super PACs is *dark money*. The term refers to money used for election spending that originates from an unknown source. The term is associated with super PACs because—even though these types of PACs have to file financial disclosure forms with the Federal Election Commission (FEC) just like regular PACs—it's fairly easy for dark money to make its way into super PAC coffers. Here's how it works: certain politically active nonprofits collect money from donors. If these groups are classified a certain way by the US tax code, they are not required to disclose their donors. In fact, it's not uncommon for a majority of the dark group's funding to come from a single donor, such as when the 501 (c)(4) group Conservative Solutions Project received a $13.5 million donation from an unnamed donor during the 2016 presidential primary.

The dark money group then goes on to donate unlimited amounts to a super PAC. Some people call it the *Russian doll problem*. We know the names of the groups donating to super PACs, it's just that for certain groups, we don't know where they got that money to begin with.

Dark money within super PACs might be better thought of as *gray money*, since it typically doesn't account for all the money the super PAC spends. Many donors who give to the super PAC are named, so when the super PAC files its disclosure forms, at least some of its donors are publicly known. We call this partial disclosure, hence, *gray money*. However, there are ways to go completely dark. As long as they do not expressly advocate for one candidate over another, a 501c (e.g., Crossroads GPS) or 527 group (e.g., Swift Boat Veterans for Truth) can run ads up until sixty days before a general election without having to report their spending to the FEC.

Sometimes, groups like these can influence elections without airing a large number of ads. In 2004, the 527 group Swift Boat Veterans for Truth aired a series of ads criticizing Democratic presidential nominee John Kerry's service in Vietnam. The ads did not air in may media markets, nor did they air a comparatively large number of times, but they did receive an inordinate amount of free media coverage. That is, over five hundred news stories covered the ads, amplifying their potential impact. In the end, John Kerry's performance in the election polls had gone up and down before the ads aired and after the ads aired, so it is difficult to claim that they altered the election. However, the attention they received on air kept other issues and arguments Kerry would have preferred to make off the air. Recall from Chapters 3 and 5 the importance of controlling the news agenda.

Overall, the Center for Responsive Politics reports that dark money groups spent $181 million in the 2016 election—less than the $308 million spent in 2012.[12] According to the WMP, just over 11 percent of the ads that aired in the 2018 midterm elections were from dark money sources.[13] The WMP notes that even though full disclosure groups account for most of the ad spending by outside groups, the volume of ads from nondisclosure groups has increased over the past few elections.

Ad Spending

According to one report, ad spending in the 2016 election cycle was a whopping $9.8 billion.[14] The bulk of that went to broadcast TV advertisements: $4.4 billion, which is down 20 percent from the 2012 cycle. Radio ads were also down by over 20 percent, costing campaigns $621 million. Where's the money going? Online, of course. Digital advertising hit $1.4 billion in 2016, a massive 789 percent increase from 2012. That's about on-par with what campaigns spent on cable TV advertisements ($1.35 billion).

How do campaigns decide where to spend their ad dollars? The first general principle is that ad dollars increase in competitive races. The bulk of the ads in both the 2012 and 2016 presidential races were shown in battleground states—states that had a real shot of going red *or* blue.

Campaigns must also decide which medium to use. For broadcast TV ads, the allure is eyeballs. According to TV ratings company Nielsen, television reaches 87 percent of Americans over the age of 18. Nielsen data from 2016 shows that the average adult spends over thirty-five hours watching TV each week, eclipsing the eleven hours they spend on their smartphones in the same time period. If you're between the ages of 18 and 34, that fact may surprise you![15] After all, your age group watches far fewer hours of TV on average (twenty hours per week) than those ages 35–49 (thirty-two hours) or 50 and older (forty-seven hours) while spending about seventeen hours per week on smartphones and tablets. Today's viewership data allows campaigns to more carefully target certain demographics, since, as you can imagine, the viewership for *The Big Bang Theory* differs from the viewership for *Empire*. Even with a declining overall audience, the volume of televised campaign ads is going up. Wesleyan Media Project data shows that four million TV ads aired in the 2018 midterm elections—up from 2.5 million in 2014.

The central appeal of television is breadth, and that breadth costs a pretty penny. For example, according to *Variety*, a thirty-second ad airing after one of the 2016 presidential debates came with an approximate

$225,000 price tag.[16] One political strategist who worked on several Democratic presidential campaigns explained that TV consultants who work for campaigns have an incentive to convince candidates to spend their money on the airwaves.[17] Why? They get 10–15 cents for every dollar spent on TV ad purchases.

Digital advertising, on the other hand, offers more affordable opportunities to target a message to a specific slice of the audience. In 2012, presidential candidates Mitt Romney and Barack Obama spent around a quarter of their advertising budgets online.[18] According to the WMP, about 10 percent of advertising budgets went toward digital ads during the 2018 midterms.

Social media accounts for more and more of those digital ad dollars. Donald Trump's campaign went so far as to suggest Facebook ads were the critical difference in the 2016 campaign. While Hillary Clinton outspent Trump on ads overall—she spent $72 million on last-minute TV ads whereas he spent about half that—Trump's campaign spent more on digital advertising in the final weeks of the campaign, most of which was funneled into Facebook ads.

The trend toward Facebook spending has continued after Trump's successful use of the platform. Facebook announced that $400 million worth of political ads appeared on its platform in the months before the 2018 midterm elections. In the first five months of 2019 alone, Trump spent $4.6 million on Facebook ads.[19] His Democratic challengers for the 2020 election also showed movement toward the platform. Joe Biden, for example, spent about $1 million on Facebook ads in the first month of his candidacy. Candidates in the 2018 midterms spent $150–$600 per Facebook ad.

Tailoring

One of the appeals of digital advertising—and Facebook advertising in particular—is the ability to tailor a message to a specific target audience. Campaigns are increasingly tailoring their messages to specific audiences, especially as research shows that different groups tend to prefer different types of messages. For example, women find ads with women's voices more credible than men do, and Independent voters tend to prefer ads featuring average Americans.[20] Running tailored ads comes with a risk—audiences say they don't like the idea of being targeted based on their interests or demographics.[21] Nearly two-thirds of voters in one survey said their support for a candidate would decrease if they found out the campaign was buying information about their online activities and showing them ads based on that info.

Platforms like Facebook make it especially easy for campaigns to target voters based on certain demographics. But beyond simply targeting ads to women, people in a certain age group, or those with a particular interest, there's also the possibility that ads could be targeted to you based on a more intrusive analysis of your personality, interests, voting history, and network. You may recall the scandal where tech company Cambridge Analytica scraped Facebook's data to assemble enough information to compile psychographic profiles of millions of users. Facebook's original strategy to "move fast and break things" prompted political communication scholar Dannagal Young to advise the social media giant to "slow down and fix things."[22] Leading social media researchers Rebekah Tromble and Shannon McGregor suggest that Facebook will not need to fix as many things if they take lessons from the social sciences—like the ones you are learning about in this book—and bring them into the core of how Facebook seeks to innovate technology use in public life.[23]

Facebook has since tightened up access to user data, but the scandal revealed how uncomfortable people were with companies trying to customize their online experience. Perhaps more importantly, Facebook, Twitter, and Google go beyond simply promoting their services and helping campaigns engage in digital advertising. Daniel Kreiss and Shannon McGregor found, via interviews with staff from these platform giants, that social media organizations actively shape campaign communication via their work with staffers of political candidates. Social media companies "serve as quasi-digital consultants to campaigns, shaping digital strategy, content, and execution."[24]

Ad Content

When you think of political ads, what comes to mind? You may think of a guy in jeans and a tucked-in Oxford shirt with the sleeves rolled up. He might be strolling through a corn field or shaking hands with *everyday* Americans while repeating his campaign promises with a slight southern drawl. Patriotic music is almost certainly swelling in the background. Alternatively, you may think of a series of grainy black and white images flickering across the screen, an ominous voice warning you that newly acquired documents show that if elected, Candidate X will murder puppies, ban rainbows, and ultimately destroy the planet.

You've probably seen enough ads to easily recognize the three major types. One type is positive ads, which promote a candidate by highlighting their strengths. Positive ads make no mention of the opponent and tend to focus on biographical information. You may see the candidates with their families, chatting with folks from their hometowns, or reflecting on their time in military service. Biographical ads have gotten more sophisticated in the digital age. A three and a half minute ad for MJ Hegar, a 2018 House candidate from Texas, showcased her life from childhood by moving through all the "doors" she had walked through. The ad was widely acclaimed and garnered over three million views on YouTube.[25]

Contrast ads, the second general type of ad, also feature positive information about a candidate, but they point out how a candidate differs from the opponent. These types of ads tend to include more specific information about a candidate's stance on the issues, especially highlighting where they might hold a more popular position relative to their opponent. In Donald Trump's ad "Immigration," Hillary Clinton's America was painted as one where dangerous criminals and illegal immigrants abuse the system, harming hard-working Americans whereas Donald Trump's America was depicted as one where families were safe, the border secure, and dangerous criminals were kept out.[26] Note that contrast ads need not outline specific policy proposals, though many do.

Finally, the third type of ad is negative ads. These are the most common types of political ad—a fact that is unsurprising to anyone with a pulse and a working TV during an election cycle!

Negative Ads

If you feel like campaign ads have gotten progressively more negative, you're not wrong; campaign ads have become increasingly negative over the two decades. In 2004, only 1 percent of ads sponsored by the Democratic Congressional Campaign Committee (DCCC) and 46 percent of Republican Congressional Campaign Committee (RCCC) ads were negative, but by 2006, those numbers were at 83 percent and 89 percent, respectively. The Wesleyan Media Project, which tracks all federal and state candidate ads, noted that 69 percent of 2018 midterm election ads were negative.[27] That's a 61 percent increase in negativity from the 2014 midterm elections. Today, negative ads are far more popular than positive ones.

The avalanche of negative campaign ads isn't lost on voters. More than 70 percent of Americans described the 2016 presidential campaign as too negative, up from 51 percent in 2012 and 43 percent in 2008 (though, 62 percent described it as too negative in 2004).[28]

Why did campaign ads become more negative? One possibility is simply because political strategists have long believed that negative ads work. They point to evidence such as the 1988 presidential campaign, where George H.W. Bush made up a ten-point disadvantage after a Bush-backed group ran the now famous "Willie Horton" attack ad against his opponent, Michael Dukakis. The ad accused the former Massachusetts governor of giving Horton—a convicted murderer—a weekend pass from prison. Horton had committed rape and assault while furloughed from prison, though the furlough program was started by Dukakis' predecessor, a Republican.

On the one hand, the negative ad was largely credited, in media circles, for Bush's come-from-behind win. One the other hand, economic growth in terms of the nation's Gross Domestic Product, was over 3.5 percent in 1988. Political scientists estimate that, regardless of who is running, what they say, and what they do, the candidate in the incumbent party (Bush, who was vice president to term-limited Ronald Reagan) with an economy as strong as it was in 1988 would get 53 percent of the vote. Bush got 53.4 percent.[29]

Another reason that negative ads dominate today is because outside groups are airing more ads than ever before. In the 2012 federal races, for example, 83 percent of ads runs by interest groups were negative, while only 39 percent of the ads run by candidates were. The risk of backlash—meaning the ad's sponsor also suffers a decline in favorability for airing a negative ad—gives candidates pause when thinking about going negative. Outside groups aren't as concerned about backlash effects, and thus are more likely to go on the offensive.

Some scholars have noted the distinction between outright negative ads and cynical ads. Cynical ads tend to accuse opponents, the other party, or the government in general of being dishonest, distrustful, immoral, incompetent, self-interested, or out of touch. In one study where researchers examined over six hundred ads from the 2008 Senate races, they found that over 40 percent featured a cynicism appeal.[30]

Emotions and Information

Regardless of the tone of a campaign ad, its ultimate goal is to increase support for the sponsoring candidate or decrease support for the opposing candidate(s). In order to do this, it either needs to provide voters with information to help them see that the sponsoring candidate is the right choice for them, give voters reasons to the opposing candidate is the wrong choice, or provide an emotional experience that leaves the voter feeling positive about the candidate (or, in the case of negative ads, fearful about the alternative).

When it comes to political messaging, it's not just what you say but how you say it. Words that are wrapped in an emotional appeal simply have more *oomph*. Two of the more common emotional appeals in campaign ads are fear and enthusiasm. Researchers have found that enthusiasm-triggering ads tend to encourage voters to feel positive about their prior beliefs while fear appeals are more likely to make voters feel unsettled about their choice.[31]

Nonverbal cues in the ad do the lion's share of the work eliciting these emotions. Music, colors, styles of camera movement, imagery, and narrator tone can all be manipulated to try and trigger a particular emotional response from viewers. Campaigns have to think about things like whether they'll have a man or woman doing the voice-over. An analysis of ads from the 2010 and 2012 elections shows that only 20 percent of ads feature only women's voices, and ads focused on issues viewed as *feminine* or *nongendered* tended to be seen as more credible when voiced by a woman.[32]

Campaign Issues

One major thing that campaigns do is try and define what the election is about. In other words, which issue do they want to run on? In some elections, the political environment doesn't leave candidates much of a choice. In the 2010 midterm elections, for example, the United States was fresh off the heels of the 2008 economic recession. Since it was what was on the minds of most Americans, ads for both Democratic and Republican candidates tended to focus on the issue. Recall that Lynn Vavreck has shown that *how* candidates choose to focus on the economy—based upon whether their party is shouldering the blame for a poor economy or reaping the benefits of an economic boom—is crucially important to candidates' electoral fortunes.[33] Some research suggests that as the volume of ads increases in competitive races, competitors tend to focus on the same issues.

But when there's a chance to get people to think about a particular issue that plays particularly well for one candidate, campaigns will try and make that issue salient in their ads. Think of it as a way of trying to create a theme or frame for the election. When candidates are hoping to make the election about different issues, you can see the differences by looking at which issues are emphasized in ads. Political scientist John Petrocik's theory of issue ownership argues that the public tends to think that each political party in the United States is better than the other at handling particular issues. For example, Republicans tend to get higher marks on taxes and national security while Democrats are more favorably evaluated on issues like health care and education. If candidates can get people to focus on the issues their party *owns*, they tend to perform better at the ballot box.[34] However, candidates do not always seek to highlight issues their party owns.[35] Parties might be more likely to *lease* issues than own them, as their performance while in office can affect what the public thinks about who owns what.[36] And, parties tend to *trespass* on the other side's issues more than was previously appreciated. In 2014, for example, Democratic ads mentioned taxes more often than Republicans, and Republicans mentioned Obamacare more often than did Democrats. In 2018, we had a swap: nearly half of Democrats' ads in federal and gubernatorial races mentioned healthcare, while the top issue for Republicans was taxes. The difference was not just in which issues were mentioned, but also in how the issues were framed (recall Chapter 6).

Beyond TV Ads

Television ads are far and away the most studied form of political advertising, but scholars have recently turned their attention to the content of digital advertising.

Twitter

Twitter is an increasingly important tool used for campaigning, but it doesn't attract a lot of political advertising. For example, in the run-up to the 2018 midterms (June to November), Twitter reported about $2 million spent on political advertising. In the same time period, Facebook took in nearly $300 million from eighty-five thousand campaign ads.[37] The lack of spending may be due to Twitter's audience which, while highly engaged, isn't very broad. A little over 20 percent of US adults use Twitter, and users tend to be younger, more educated, and urban.[38] Of course, a campaign's tweets are also guaranteed to appear in their followers' feed, so there's less incentive to pay up for actual advertisements that reach nonfollowers as sponsored posts.

One interesting question that researchers have asked about how Twitter fits with an overall advertising strategy is whether there is cohesion between a campaign's TV messaging and its campaign tweets. One study found both similarities and differences. On the one hand, there wasn't a lot of consistency between TV ads and tweets in terms of which issues were being discussed, and tweets were overall more positive in tone whereas TV ads tended to fall into the contrast or negative category. On the other hand, when a candidate's TV ads got more negative, so did their tweets.[39] As is the case with TV advertising, the volume of campaign tweets tended to increase as Election Day neared.

The more competitive the race, the more likely candidates attacked each other on Twitter.[40] Third-party candidates are increasingly using Twitter as well to advertise their issue positions. Minor-party candidates are far more likely to tweet about their issue positions than major-party candidates.[41]

YouTube

If you see a campaign ad on TV, you can probably also find it on YouTube. The platform started to gain steam in the political world in 2008 when the Obama campaign heavily used the video-streaming service—posting nearly two thousand ads over the course of the election. Today, nearly every major candidate hosts a YouTube channel. From the time candidates started announcing their candidacy for the 2016 election in 2015 to Super Tuesday, YouTube users watched 110 million hours of candidate and issue-related videos.[42]

The appeal of the platform is obvious: over 70 percent of Americans use YouTube, and like most social media, posting is free.[43] Theoretically, the no-cost nature of YouTube would allow nontraditional voices (e.g., smaller interest groups or politically active citizens) to join the political advertising fray, but at least one study has shown that YouTube videos sponsored by candidates tend to be viewed much more frequently than videos sponsored by parties, groups, or other individuals. That same study also found that negative YouTube candidate videos were viewed more heavily than positive ones.[44] While some of the content on a candidate's YouTube channel is just a copy of their broadcast TV ads, there's growing interest in developing content specifically for online. YouTube even encourages campaigns to design videos that will play well on the streaming giant; they have two advertising teams that work directly with campaigns.

Besides having a YouTube channel where campaigns post their video ads, they can also pay YouTube to advertise during other videos. Because of its overall cheaper rates (relative to TV) and access to a different audience (YouTube's demographics skew younger), many candidates have embraced ad-buys on the video-hosting giant. In 2016, three political ads broke onto YouTube's top-ten ad leaderboard. In the weeks before the 2016 primaries, YouTube ad time sold out in early caucus states.[45]

Facebook

About 70 percent of Americans use Facebook. That's over 170 million people. Globally, over one billion people use the social networking giant's site. No matter how you slice it, that's a lot of eyeballs scrolling through newsfeeds. And with affordable ad rates, the social media behemoth is becoming increasingly popular for campaign ads.

In the 2016 presidential election, Donald Trump and Hillary Clinton spent a combined $81 million on Facebook ads, with Trump's campaign saying it spent as much as 80 percent of its digital advertising budget on the platform.[46] And it's not just presidential races drawing in the dollars. In the months before the 2018 midterms, Texas Senate hopeful Beto O'Rourke spent over $5 million on six thousand ads on the platform (edging out the Trump-supporting Make America Great Again committee, which is consistently a top spender on Facebook).

One thing that appeals to campaigns about advertising via Facebook is the ability to test and tailor ads. Because they can measure real-time engagement with their ads, campaigns can run multiple versions of an ad to see which version is most effective. And because Facebook allows users to target ads to certain demographics, interests, and other social markers, campaigns are able to see which ad plays best with very specific audiences.

How do campaigns know if an ad is effective? They may look at internal polling data to see if their numbers budge, but that would be a pretty large effect for an ad campaign. A more common way of judging ad success is to look at click-through rates. An ad may catch someone's attention enough for them to visit the sponsor's website—or, even better, make a campaign donation. In an internal Facebook memo obtained by Bloomberg, Facebook's data scientists say that 84 percent of Donald Trump's 2016 election ads on the social media outlet asked people to make a donation to his campaign.[47]

Fake and Foreign-Backed Ads

With social media making political advertising more accessible than ever before, groups with ulterior motives have capitalized on the opportunity to sow seeds of confusion, misinformation, and divisiveness. The 2016

Photo 8.2 Democrats on the House Intelligence Committee released 3,500 Facebook ads purchased before the 2016 presidential election by the online troll farm Internet Research Agency. Many of the ads aimed to stoke racial and religious tensions, like this ad linking Hillary Clinton to the Islamic faith.

election, in particular, was plagued by paid advertising backed by radical groups and foreign powers. According to a report from the House Intelligence Committee, there were at least 3,500 Facebook ads financed by the Russian government designed to stir up racial tensions, emphasize anti-immigration stances, or reinforce negative sentiment about Democratic candidate Hillary Clinton. Notably, most efforts to influence the election were not done through ads, but rather through organic activity (posting via pages, commenting on posts or news articles, creating fabricated accounts).

Facebook has recently tightened up its political advertising policy. Anyone wanting to run political ads (defined rather broadly) must now go through a verification process that confirms their identity and location. Paid content also now has a *paid for* disclosure so users can easily identify the sponsor, and users can find out which demographic groups are targeted by the ad. All political ads that run on the platform are archived in an online library that is publicly accessible. In the run-up to elections, Facebook has started limiting political ads to in-country sponsors.

Twitter has also taken steps to improve political ad quality. The platform now requires anyone buying political ads to go through a certification process that asks them to prove they are located in the United States and that they have a profile that clearly communicates who they are and how to contact them.

Does Political Advertising Work?

For all the money that campaigns spend on ads, you'd assume they get a huge payoff in terms of increased support. Surely those hundreds-of-thousands-of-dollars TV ads are buying votes! This is easy enough to test: just take a look at the poll numbers after a new ad is released.

In the 2008 Democratic primary race, Hillary Clinton released her "3 a.m. phone call" ad, which was meant to highlight the difference in the level of preparedness between her and her opponent, Barack Obama. The ad featured a ringing phone at the White House juxtaposed over video of children sleeping in their beds. The ad's purpose was to raise questions of Democratic primary voters regarding whether Barack Obama was as prepared as Hillary Clinton to take on the job as commander in chief. Pundits gushed over the ad, with consensus building that it would return her momentum as Obama edged upward in the polls. So did it? Did the ad give Clinton back her edge? Considering Obama won the primary, the ad couldn't have accomplished all that much. But what's more, the polling numbers before and after the ad show that this widely praised ad had negligible effects on voters' preferences.[48]

This comes as no surprise to those who study the efficacy of political advertising. An ad can be the greatest ad there ever was and still not sway

| Photo 8.3 Hillary Clinton's 3 a.m. Phone Call Ad From the 2008 Primaries

many voters. A candidate can spend three times as much money as an opponent on advertising—as Hillary Clinton did in the 2016 election—and still lose. The twelfth richest person in the world can spend over half a billion dollars of his own fortune on ads and still not win a party's nomination.[49]

Campaign ads have a limited impact on voters, something researchers refer to as a *conditional* effect. This means that ads do not impact each person in the same way. In fact, studies indicate that most people aren't very influenced by ads at all.

Who Is Persuadable?

We sometimes think of our fellow citizens as hapless sheep, completely at the mercy of a campaign's snazzy, persuasive messages. This idea that audiences are easily swayed is known as the hypodermic needle or magic bullet theory (you can read more about it in Chapter 7). Scholars have known for decades now that this isn't how messaging works. Audience members' reactions to messages depend on message features, timing, context, and characteristics of the individual interpreting the message. Imagine you're running a campaign and your team comes up with (what you think is) the greatest TV ad that's ever been made. You run it . . . you wait . . . and . . . nothing. No rise in the polls. What happened? Maybe few people saw your ad because you ran it during a show that 90 percent of viewers DVR so they can skip commercials. Maybe you ran it during a week where major breaking news stole all the focus away from the campaign. Maybe the content of the ad wasn't appealing to the demographic you were trying to reach, or maybe the people you tried to target are simply never going to be willing to consider your candidate. The point is, ads fail to persuade for all sorts of reasons: the main one being that not that many people are persuadable in an election context to begin with.

If the main purpose of a campaign ad is to garner votes, then the ideal target is someone who is open to consideration. Strong partisans, or those who have already made up their minds, aren't likely to change their minds based on your ad (or anything else, for that matter).

On the one hand, there's reason to assume the percentage of these persuadable voters is increasing. Today, the largest political identification today is Independent (42 percent of Americans claimed this political ID in 2017).[50] People often assume the label of Independent indicates a willingness to swing between the two major parties or back a third-party candidate. On the contrary, the vast majority of Independents demonstrate a consistent preference for one party. Political scientists point out that when it comes to partisan beliefs, most Independents are generally indistinguishable from their Democrat or Republican counterparts.[51] An Independent voter is not synonymous with *moderate voter*, nor does it indicate that a voter is sincerely considering candidates on either side of the aisle. Those voters—the ones who might be persuadable—are called *swing* voters or *undecided* voters.[52]

There were an unusually high number of undecided voters in the 2016 election. According to one study, about 10 percent of likely voters hadn't chosen between Trump and Clinton three months before the election.[53] By election day, that number was still over 5 percent. When you lump together undecided voters with those who said they were voting third-party, data journalism site FiveThirtyEight estimates 12.5 percent of voters were not firmly on Team Trump or Team Clinton by Election Day.[54] Similarly, when pollsters started measuring support for Brexit—whether the United Kingdom should exit the European Union—15 percent were initially undecided. The day before the referendum, 9 percent still said they were undecided.[55]

On the other hand, the two main US political parties are increasingly different from one another, and there is little ideological overlap between the two.[56] Think about it this way: while it was once easy to find a conservative Democrat or a liberal Republican, the average Democrat today is fairly liberal and the average Republican is fairly conservative. The parties are more distinct than they once were. This could mean that voters aren't easily able to swing between the two, resulting in a smaller pool of persuadable advertising targets. Research has shown that political advertising is more effective when partisan cues are missing, such as in primary races.[57]

Political scientists Sunshine Hillygus and Todd Shields' research shows that the most persuadable voters are those who hold issue positions that are different than their party's position. Politicians try to exploit these *wedge issues* in their messaging to voters they are trying to persuade. Democrats who favor wide-ranging gun rights, for example, might be persuaded to vote for Republicans while pro-choice Republicans might favor Democrats in some elections.[58] Edward Carmines, Michael Ensley, and one of this book's authors have shown that people with heterodox preferences (liberal on one major set of issues but conservative on another) have weaker partisan preferences, split their tickets more often when they vote and participate less than voters with orthodox partisan views.[59]

Ads Can Help Familiarize Voters With Candidates

Campaign ads tend to work best when candidates are unfamiliar to voters. When voters do not already have an opinion on a candidate, ads can provide valuable knowledge, an initial impression or *vibe* of a candidate, or simply help ensure name recognition. The first hurdle to gaining support is making sure that voters know you're an option, and advertising can go a long way in establishing familiarity for lesser-known candidates.

Because ads are most effective for people who do not already have opinions about the candidates, researchers have found that down-ballot races and challenger candidates benefit the most from advertising. People are less likely to know the people running for their House district than they are to know about the folks running for president, creating an opportunity for political strategists a chance to familiarize voters with a candidate on the campaign's terms. Researchers from the WMP used a predictive model to see how increasing ad volume for the Democratic candidate in the 2000, 2004, 2008, and 2012 presidential contests would have impacted the vote. They found a modest increase in ads would have gained the Democrat less than an additional 1 percent of voters. For a Senate race, however, the researchers found that running more ads could have earned the Democratic candidate an additional vote share ranging 1.5 percent (in 2014) to over 4 percent (in 2006).

Ads Work Better When the Other Candidate Doesn't Air as Many

An avalanche of ads may help tip the polls in your favor, especially if your opponent skimps on the ad budget. One study of advertising in the 2008 presidential election found that when Obama aired one thousand more ads than his opponent John McCain in a given county, he did 0.5 percentage points better than John Kerry did in that county in 2004.[60] That's a whole lot of ads for half of a percentage point, but it suggests that wildly outspending your opponent on ads could pay off. The value of out-advertising your opponent is one reason that election advertising is often referred to as an *arms race*.

Even if out-advertising an opponent doesn't lead to electoral success, it may at least help stave off a more crushing defeat. In the 2014 midterm election, for example, Democrats ran more ads than Republicans in nearly every media market. They still lost—Republicans picked up twelve House seats—but without the ad blitz, it could have been worse.

Ad Effects Are Short-Lived

Whatever effects campaign ads have, the evidence suggests they don't last long. Researchers who conduct lab experiments to test ad effects—that is, they show subjects an advertisement in an artificial setting and then ask about their vote choice or attitudes toward the candidate—do tend to find short-term changes in preferences and attitude. But longitudinal studies, where researchers follow up with voters throughout a campaign to ask them about their preferences, generally find that ads do little to persuade voters long term.

There are exceptions. Some studies have documented longer term ad effects. For example, one study of the 2000 presidential election found that advertising effects were small but traces could still be found as many as six weeks later.[61] Another study found that an Obama campaign ad did have a measurable short-term effect on 2012 voters. While that effect decayed among most viewers, it seems to have persisted among those who hadn't already committed to a candidate when they first encountered the ad.[62] Overall, a study that looked at the results of lots of different studies concluded that ads can have some impact early, but not later, in a race . . . and that those small effects didn't last until Election Day.[63]

The short-lived influence of political ads has also been documented in field experiments, meaning, experiments in a real-life setting. In one particularly cool study, a team of political scientists teamed up with Rick Perry's Texas gubernatorial campaign.[64] The group randomly assigned ads to different Texas media markets and tracked Perry's support in markets where the ads aired to compare with markets where they did not air. They found that Perry's numbers jumped 5 percent! But alas, the effect only lasted a week.

What About Negative Advertising? Does It Work?

A quick Google search about negative political ads would leave you confused about whether negative advertising sways voters. One top-level search result is a newspaper headline that declares negative ads are successful because "mud sticks." But two results down, you get: "Think negative

| **Photo 8.4 George H.W. Bush's "Willie Horton" Attack Ad**

ads work? Think again." The nuance of negative advertising effects doesn't lend itself to catchy headlines. The article titled, "Do negative ads work? The answer is complicated" probably gets fewer clicks.

First, a few things scholars do agree on. There is some evidence that negative advertising is more effective than positive ads at commanding attention.[65] Researchers who have given one group of subjects a positive ad (with upbeat music and lots of smiles) and another group a negative ad (with dark images and ominous music) have found that negative ads trigger a sense of fear, which may increase interest in learning more about the candidate. Positive ads, on the other hand, increase enthusiasm about a preferred candidate and provide affirmation. This would explain why leading candidates tend to focus on ads with positive emotional appeals and trailing candidates are more likely to use fear appeals.[66]

But a campaign's primary goal in crafting a negative ad isn't to encourage information seeking; the ad's main mission is to take down the opponent! How successful are negative ads in this endeavor?

In a 2007 meta-analysis (a study of studies), researchers analyzed 111 studies examining the effects of negative advertising.[67] They looked at whether other researchers have found that negative campaign ads 1) increase dislike of the attacked candidate; 2) increase dislike of the attacking candidate—in other words, a backlash effect; 3) decrease voter turnout. They found a small overall effect of attack ads on the attacked candidate. In around two-thirds of the studies they looked at, researchers had found that ads attacking a candidate tended to make people slightly more apprehensive about that candidate. On the flip side, they also found that in thirty-three out of forty studies, researchers noted a backlash effect: running an attack ad seems to also increase dislike of the attacking candidate. So what is the net effect? That is, is it worth taking a little bit of a backlash effect in order to tear down your opponent? The research team notes that there isn't enough evidence to conclude whether the attack results in a net gain for a candidate. Their conclusion:

> Negative campaigning is no more effective than positive campaigning holds even though negative campaigns appear to be somewhat more memorable and to generate somewhat greater campaign-relevant knowledge.[68]

Many political scientists have also considered whether negative campaign ads might decrease voter turnout. You can see why this might happen, as all the negativity in politics can easily turn people off to the process. One thing that can result from this sort of political apathy is called demobilization—basically, making people less likely to vote. The meta-analysis reviewed fifty-seven studies, some of which found that negative ads seem to increase people's intentions to go vote, while others found that negative ads make people less likely to say they're going to the polls. The inconsistencies led the study's authors to conclude that there isn't enough consistent evidence to say that negative ads decrease (or increase) voter turnout. However, the evidence does suggest that such ads have a small but consistently negative impact on public sentiment toward the political system. Increased exposure to negative ads makes people less trusting of and favorable toward the government.

Subliminal Messaging?

When you think of subliminal messaging, you probably think of the popular theory that Disney hid secret messages in its classic movies—such as when floating flower petals appear to spell a dirty word in the Lion King. That one falls into more into the realm of conspiracy theories, but *hidden* or subtle messaging isn't uncommon in advertising. Remember the Coca-Cola cups that were strategically placed on the American Idol judging table? The show's green room was even colored a Coca-Cola red.

The idea behind this type of messaging is that it can circumvent normal information processing. It *sneaks in*, so to speak. But while subtle product placement and good branding might be an effective strategy, there's little research that creating hidden content or inserting secret words into commercials actually affects viewers. It's also unclear whether any campaigns have even tried such a strategy. During the 2000 presidential election, the George W. Bush campaign was accused of inserting a subliminal message in an ad where the word *bureaucrats* flashed on screen but one frame showed only the letters *rats*. The campaign said the flash frame was only meant to call more attention to the word bureaucrats.

One study tried to see whether subliminal political messaging works.[69] The researchers showed participants images with hidden messages. The subjects who saw the message *rats* later had less positive evaluations of fictional political candidates, compared to those who saw other subliminal messages. There isn't much additional research to support the efficacy of subliminal messaging, but it's a finding that merits some replication from other researchers nonetheless.

But it isn't that out-there to assume that subtle messages can sway voters. Studies have shown that people tend to report more conservative political views when a bottle of hand sanitizer is placed in the room[70]—or report colder feelings toward gay men when in a room with a bad smell.[71] The authors of those studies reason that reminders of physical purity and feelings of disgust can trigger thoughts about moral purity.

Is Advertising Worth It?

Donald Trump won the 2016 election by eking out eighty thousand votes in battleground states, so theoretically, even tiny effects from advertising could potentially change the outcome of a race. Some scholars have gone so far as declaring that an advertising advantage is what won George W. Bush the 2000 election.[72]

And even if advertising does not necessarily recruit additional voters, the effects of positive advertising demonstrate that ads may be able to help keep voters who are already on board. Additionally, if one side engaged in heavy advertising and the other side did none, we would be far more likely to uncover major advertising effects. Until a candidate is willing to completely forego advertising for the sake of an interesting experiment, we can't be sure what the effect of zero advertising would be. In the real world setting we investigate advertising effects in, it's difficult to isolate cause and effect during a political campaign, making it difficult to know whether advertising pushes you across the finish line (or just short of it). The payoff for advertisement may be uncertain, but it's something that *could* help, and that's enough for most political strategists.

Mobilization

One theory of political advertising is that it may not get people to change their mind (persuasion) but it may convince them to go to the polls (mobilization). Researchers have found very little evidence that TV advertising encourages people to vote. In a field experiment, one team showed that the volume of advertising in a given media market had no bearing on turnout rates. That's consistent with individual studies[73] and a meta-analysis[74] (a study of other studies) that have all shown that political advertisements do not have a mobilizing effect.

Nonpartisan get-out-the-vote efforts have been more successful at mobilization. One field experiment showed that TV public service announcements could increase voting among young voters by as much as 3 percent.[75] Similar results have been found for online get-out-the-vote efforts. In the 2010 elections, for example, Facebook experimented by offering some users a digital "I Voted" sticker that included information about whether or not their friends had voted. They found that those who received the sticker with info about their friends' voting habits were slightly more likely to vote—a small but measurable increase of about 340,000 extra votes overall.[76]

If not TV advertising, what does get people out to the polls? Good old face-to-face communication. A series of field experiments from Alan Gerber and Donald Green show that a single in-person conversation with a canvasser can boost turnout by as much as 20 percent.[77]

Effectiveness of Online Ads

Scholars have spent substantially less time testing the effectiveness of online advertisements. On the one hand, there's no compelling reason to think digital advertising would have significantly different impacts than TV advertisements. That is, why should digital ads persuade voters when television ads so rarely do? On the other hand, the ability to target specific audiences online—especially via social media—may pave the way for limited effect on specific groups.

So far, studies that have looked at the effects of online campaign ads have been largely consistent with the effects (or lack thereof) found for TV advertising. For example, one experimental study focused on repeated exposure to ads on Facebook. After exposing participants to nearly forty ads for a candidate over the course of several days, they concluded that each ad results in 1 in every 1,700 people will learn a candidate's name or gain a favorable impression of them.[78] So, not a large effect.

News Media and Political Ads

"I'm not a witch," 2010 Senate Republican candidate Christine O'Donnell declared on TV screens across America. The ad was crafted in response to O'Donnell's assertion she had dabbled in witchcraft—something the Tea Party candidate had admitted to in a decade-old interview with Bill Maher that had resurfaced during her campaign. Some analysts loved the ad, saying it highlighted the ridiculousness of the witchcraft claims. Others hated it, saying the ad came off so creepy and absurd that it managed to reinforce the witch angle. Either way, the ad generated buzz—enough that the ad itself became the subject of media coverage.

Ad amplification happens when paid-for advertising gets free air time in the form of news coverage. It's sometimes referred to as free advertising or earned media—and it's not uncommon. One study looked at over 1,600 news stories about gubernatorial elections in 2006 and found that 6 percent of the stories were about campaign ads.[79] The percentage was even higher for Senate elections—almost 13 percent. It doesn't necessarily take an ad defending yourself from claims of witchcraft to make news headlines! With today's focus on social media, ads may make headlines not necessarily because they intrigued pundits or journalists, but because they went viral: attracting a lot of attention online. If everyone is talking about it, it's much more likely to make it onto the news.[80]

The "Not a Witch" ad got people talking. So did Carly Fiorina's 2010 "Demon Sheep" ad (someone actually crawled around a field in a sheep costume).[81] Or the famous 1984 "Daisy Girl" ad, which was pulled off air but still got extensive media coverage.

It's controversy-steeped ads like these that are most likely to make it into headlines. One study shows that negative and comparative ads get twice as much play in news coverage than positive ads.[82] This is likely because these types of ads tap into the news value of *conflict*; journalists are drawn to stories that feature multiple perspectives facing off against one another. So, a series of attack ads and a rebuttal would be an appealing news story to tell (and to hear! Recall Chapters 5 and 6 for more on why audiences are attracted to negative news). TV journalists seem to be especially prone to this, with one study finding that as campaigns become more negative, TV news mentions ads at a higher rate than newspapers.

Other reasons why journalists might focus on a campaign ad in news coverage include: to evaluate the success of the ad; to fact-check it; or to illustrate a point about the tone of the race, strategy and campaign tactics, or a policy issue.[83] Whether news coverage of a campaign ad has a good or bad effect on the ultimate outcome (to get votes) is a matter of debate. On the one hand, free media is free media. On the other hand, the media attention could exacerbate whatever effect the ad had in the first place, which may have been undesirable.

Beyond trying to make news headlines, campaign ads may also attempt to *shape* news headlines. News media coverage tends to direct the public's attention toward certain issues, a phenomenon known as *agenda-setting*. As Bernard Cohen once mused, the press "may not be successful much of the time in telling people what to think, but it is stunningly successful in telling its readers what to think about."[84] Recognizing this, part of a campaign's ad strategy may include talking about issues they want the public to think about, or talking about issues in the way they want the issue covered in the news. You'll remember from Chapter 6 that the latter is called framing, and, more specifically, frame building, where political figures try to construct a narrative in the news media. Does it work? Do journalists use the framing that campaigns use in their ads? Research shows varying levels of success.

From Research to Real Life

Next time campaign ad season rolls around, take some time to evaluate what you're seeing. Are you noticing attack, positive, or contrast ads? Are the campaigns in the race using repetitive messaging, ominous music, dark imagery, or unflattering photos? Who paid for the ad and is that sponsor able to accept dark money contributions? Which issues are the candidates focusing on—are the competitors honing in on the same key topics or are they each trying to emphasize different things?

But also remember that no matter how compelling (or absurd) a political ad might be, its effects are limited. Voters are not plastic bags floating in the wind. Most of the people seeing campaign ads already know who they're voting for—or have decided not to vote at all. Persuasion via political advertising is effective on the margins; that is, in contests that come down to a few percentage points, a solid ad campaign *could* be a deciding factor.

Next time you see an ad and think, "How could this possibly change someone's mind?" remember that the intent of the ad might not be so obvious. It may be designed to mobilize the base, encourage journalists to talk about issues the candidate wants to talk about, introduce new information about a candidate, or simply sow confusion. A single ad is rarely a *game changer*, but in a contest where every vote counts, you can understand how there are entire careers dedicated to identifying pockets of persuadable voters and figuring out how to reach them.

DIY Research

Erika Franklin Fowler, Wesleyan Media Project, Wesleyan University

Fowler, E. F., Ridout, T. N., & Franz, M. M. (2016, December). Political advertising in 2016: The presidential election as outlier? *The Forum, 14*(4), pp. 445–469.

Erika Franklin Fowler is an associate professor of government at Wesleyan University and is director of the Wesleyan Media Project—which tracks,

(Continued)

(Continued)

codes, and analyzes the content and effects of political ads in real-time during elections in the United States. As you have no doubt noticed, we rely heavily on the WMP's data and research in this chapter. Fowler is coauthor of *Political Advertising in the U.S.* and has published more than forty articles and book chapters on political advertising, public opinion, political communication, and health communication. Her coauthored article that we feature here is focused upon the unusual advertising strategies undertaken by the 2016 presidential candidates. Our conversation, which took place over email, is below.

Wagner and Perryman: You and your coauthors find that Hillary Clinton's advertising was unconventional in terms of the overall message strategy. How might that have affected the 2016 election?

Fowler: Yes, presidential campaigns, even when they go negative, tend to focus on substantive policy issues. Unlike any other presidential candidate for whom we have data (2000–2016), Hillary Clinton's advertising was overwhelmingly focused on the personal characteristics of Donald Trump rather than on policy considerations. This focus took away a prime and controlled opportunity to make the case to citizens for why they should vote for her, which combined with media coverage of her emails left very few citizens getting messages about her policy proposals.

Wagner and Perryman: What is the most important decision you and your collaborators make in the design phase of the Wesleyan Media Project's collection and coding of campaign ads in each election cycle? How did that decision affect what you discovered in the *Forum* article?

Fowler: Because we have been tracking advertising for so long, we have to think very carefully about our legacy variables and any changes we want to make to avoid issues with the comparability of the time series. New issues arise (like opioids) and new laws are passed (like the ACA or the tax bill), and when they do, we have to make choices about how to include them. In the case of the 2016 *Forum* article, we relied primarily on a legacy variable (for which we were fortunate to have comparable data dating back to 2000) asking our coders to distinguish between ads that focus on personal characteristics, ads that focus on substantive policy, or ads that feature some of both.

Wagner and Perryman: If a student reading this book wanted to conduct a campaign advertising research project for their class, how might the WMP help them get started?

Fowler: There is a lot of information on the Wesleyan Media Project website that could be helpful. I would especially recommend taking a look at our data access page (mediaproject.wesleyan.edu/dataaccess) that has the codebooks we use for each cycle along with our variable matrix, from which you can see when variables were added, changed, or deleted. At the end of the codebook, you will also find intercoder reliability statistics, which are a good indication of how challenging some of the variables are to code. Some variables that might seem easy are not always easy in practice; for example, if you want to code for Congress, you need to make a lot of decisions about whether a picture of the building counts, whether a reference in the paid-for byline (e.g., "John Smith for Congress") counts, whether that same reference if only shown in a picture on screen counts, etc.

Wagner and Perryman: What kinds of research opportunities are out there for students who want to study political advertising in their communities?

Fowler: There are so many opportunities to study political advertising! You can watch local TV in your area and capture the ads. If you don't have TV, there are the platform advertising libraries from Facebook and Google that are accessible online where you can go and search for an issue or candidate you want to analyze and you can access the ads right there on your computer screen. There are also direct mail flyers delivered by the postal service, and political scientists have sometimes asked residents to keep all of the political mail they get to turn over to researchers to study.

How Can I Help?

Katie Harbath, Facebook

Katie Harbath is public policy director for global elections at Facebook. She and her team are responsible for managing and coordinating the company's election efforts across over forty teams and five hundred people at Facebook, Instagram, WhatsApp, and Messenger as well as providing customer support for candidates, political parties, elected officials, and governments on how to best use these tools to connect and engage with people. A graduate of the University of Wisconsin-Madison's School of Journalism and Mass Communication, Harbath has been featured in academic research about Facebook and in *The Washington Post's* coverage of government and social media. She was a digital strategy leader for the Rudy Giuliani for President campaign and the Republican National Committee. In 2009, she was named a Rising Star by *Campaigns and Elections* magazine. We spoke to her over email.

(Continued)

(Continued)

Wagner and Perryman: Thinking back to when you first started working with politicians, what are some of the things that they did not understand, in general, about social media that they do seem to understand now? What do they still need the most help with?

Harbath: At first the biggest things they didn't understand was how to even use the tools and post content that wasn't press releases. The content from many politicians has gotten much better and more personal but engaging on a large scale continues to be a challenge. There's also just more content on social media platforms so it is more difficult to gain attention and engagement.

Wagner and Perryman: What are you doing at Facebook to help work on issues of election integrity? What have been your biggest successes? What are the major challenges that have your attention?

Harbath: There are five main areas we are focused on to protect the integrity of elections on Facebook. That includes removing fake accounts, reducing false news, bringing more transparency to political advertising, disrupting bad actors and supporting an informed and engaged electorate. We've made a lot of changes and improvements in recent elections such as the US midterms, Brazil, India, Indonesia, and the European Parliament elections. One of the biggest successes has been bringing more transparency to political ads. All of these issues continue to be challenging as we are just at the beginning of learning how to best manage them. This is also an arms race where bad actors will keep getting more sophisticated and we will need to keep trying to be one step ahead.

Wagner and Perryman: You note you are trying to stay one step ahead. How, if at all, can scholars who study social media, political communication, and the like help you do that?

Harbath: We work really closely with researchers regarding elections through our Election Research Commission Social Science One (https://socialscience .one/). These researchers will be able to help us both understand trends that did happen and what might be coming. They can also help us to think about the policies we should put into place such as around political ads, fact checking, etc.

Wagner and Perryman: What skills are the most prized at Facebook when it comes to hiring people to work on the issues you work on?

Harbath: Experience. We look for people who have worked on campaign or these issues in the real world and understand the threats that we might be facing. We also need people who can work in a very fast paced and regularly changing environment.

Wagner and Perryman: What is your advice to young people looking to work in social media and politics?

Harbath: Get experience. Volunteer for a local candidate to help them with their social media presence. Be willing to move and do a lot of jobs early on to gain experience across a spectrum of campaigns and in government life.

Mediated Elections

DEMOCRACIES REQUIRE FREE AND FAIR ELECTIONS in which voters select their representatives from a list of alternatives. Ideally, voters make informed choices based upon what they learned from the free flow of information in their society during the election season.[1] Since most voters do not meet the candidates or choose to spend a great deal of time on their own investigating candidates' issue positions, records of experience, and personal qualities, they need to learn about the candidates from somewhere. Traditionally, citizens use the news media and conversations with others to follow and learn about elections. Increasingly, social media and satirical media programming are becoming sources of campaign information as well.

How well do these various tools perform with respect to informing the public about elections? The evidence is mixed, at best. In order to understand how elections operate in a mediated society, this chapter begins with a discussion of election fundamentals in the United States. With that baseline in mind, we turn to a description of the roles the news media play in elections and types of election coverage. After examining how debates and campaign advertising flow through the information ecology, we review recent research on gender, race, and elections; media effects in elections; and a discussion of social media in electoral contexts.

Fundamentals of Elections

It is not hard to find someone who will tell you with absolute certainty that *the media* elected Donald Trump. It is just as easy to find a person to tell you, with the same level of confidence, that *the media* wanted Hillary Clinton to win the presidency in 2016. Before we get into how news coverage, political conversation, and social media use affect elections, we need to ask, "Affect them compared to what?" That is, we need a baseline understanding of the major factors that are largely independent of political communication that influence election results. Five historically and empirically important factors are the state of the economy, presidential approval, electoral structures, incumbency, and candidate quality.

Elections and the State of the Economy

In a world of instantaneous news and social media reaction to campaign rallies, debates, gaffes and scandals, billions of dollars of candidate television advertising, millions more of special interest spending, and messaging, how can a few fundamental elements correctly predict the winner of almost every election of the past sixty years months before any ballots are counted, and indeed, before many of the candidates are even known?

First, a growing economy is good news for the incumbent or the incumbent's political party in American elections. Historically, the American people have responded to strong growth in the country's Gross Domestic Product by rewarding the incumbent or incumbent's political party with another term in the White House. For the past sixty years, we can observe an obvious relationship between the growth in the nation's GDP (and the real disposable income per capita, RDI) and the percentage of the two-party vote earned by the presidential candidate representing the incumbent's party. Interestingly, the state of the economy *on Election Day* is typically less consequential than how the economy was doing the summer before the second Tuesday in November. Figure 9.1 reveals the linear relationship between a growing GDP from January to June of the election year and an increase in the incumbent party's share of the two-party presidential vote. Looking at 1956, 1964, 1972, 1980, 1984, 1992, 1996, 2004, and 2012 (the years the incumbent president himself was seeking reelection), the relationship is even stronger than it is for years when a presidential candidate from the same party is running for president after the current president was either term-limited or not seeking reelection (1968).

The relationship between the economy and vote choice is a general one and there are certainly exceptions to this rule. Figure 9.1 shows that the economy was growing in 1976 when President Gerald Ford lost to Democrat Jimmy Carter. The economy was overshadowed by the Watergate scandal which resulted in President Richard Nixon resigning from office in 1974 and Ford controversially pardoning him shortly thereafter. In 1992, the economy was actually steadily climbing out of the recession that doomed President George H. W. Bush's reelection bid in 1992. As we will see below, campaign messaging on the economy is important. Bill Clinton rode his "it's the economy, stupid" campaign strategy into the Oval Office in 1992. But in general, a growing economy is good for the president seeking reelection. Of the seventeen presidential elections displayed in Figure 9.1, only five saw the incumbent or incumbent's party earn less than 50 percent

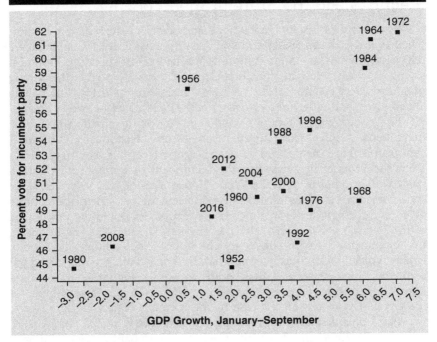

Figure 9.1 GDP Growth and the Popular Vote for Presidential Candidates of the Incumbent's Party, 1952–2016

Source: GDP data from US Department of Commerce Bureau of Economic Analysis, National Economic Accounts, Gross Domestic Product, at http://www.bea.gov/national/; presidential voting data from John Woolley and Gerhard Peters, The American Presidency Project, at http://www.presidency.ucsb.edu/elections.php; Political Behavior of the American Electorate, 14th edition. CQ Press.

of the popular vote if the economy was growing at all, let alone above two percent, a common benchmark for positive growth.

Comparing her performance to candidates running in similar economic circumstances, Figure 9.1 shows that Hillary Clinton, who won the popular vote in 2016, performed better than Democrat Adlai Stevenson in 1952, who lost an open seat presidential election to Dwight Eisenhower while seeking to replace fellow Democrat Harry Truman, who was president, and worse than President Eisenhower in 1956, who cruised to victory despite an economy that was growing at a slower rate than the 2016 economy.

Despite news coverage that reports the unemployment rate with more intensity than the economic growth rate, not all economic indicators are created equal when it comes to understanding election results. GDP and RDI generally help us predict election results. Even so, hundreds of stories were written about how the nation's high unemployment in 2011 and 2012 spelled disaster for then-President Barack Obama. This, despite the fact that unemployment does not have a consistent relationship with election results. In 1984, when unemployment was relatively high (over 7 percent), President Ronald Reagan thumped Democratic Party nominee Walter Mondale in the general election forty-nine states to one (Mondale's home state of Minnesota and the District of Columbia, which is not a state). The unemployment rate *rose* during the first terms of two-term presidents Dwight Eisenhower, Richard Nixon, and George W. Bush.[2] Unemployment *dropped* during Jimmy Carter's only term before he lost to Ronald Reagan.

Presidential Approval

What makes the 2020 presidential election especially difficult to predict is the disconnect between the state of the economy and the second fundamental factor that affects presidential vote choice—presidential approval. Typically, a growing economy means a presidential approval rate above 50 percent for presidents. President Trump presided over a strongly growing economy at the time we finished our book in the summer of 2019, but his approval rating lagged in the low to mid 40s.[3]

In 2016, Figure 9.1 hinted at trouble ahead for Hillary Clinton. On the other hand, she was running to replace a relatively popular president from her own party, Barack Obama. Obama enjoyed a 53 percent approval rating on Election Day in 2016.[4] Figure 9.2 shows the relationship between presidential approval in an election year and the incumbent party's share of the two-party vote. Thinking back to the elections in which a growing economy was not enough for the incumbent party to earn 50 percent of the popular vote, Figure 9.2 highlights the critical role of presidential approval as an independent indicator of presidential elections. In 1952, Democratic President Truman left office with a dismal 32 percent approval rating. This helped drag down any positive effects of a growing economy, assisting Republican Dwight Eisenhower's bid to win the election. Gerald Ford, who was appointed to be vice president after Spiro Agnew resigned and then ascended into the Oval Office after Richard Nixon resigned in disgrace, presided over a booming growth in GDP, but his pardoning of Nixon and problems with high inflation sank his approval rating and his bid for an electoral victory of his own. President George H. W. Bush lost some support to the unusually strong third-party candidacy of Ross Perot in 1992, but he was also hurt by a lackluster public approval rating.

Presidential approval also matters in congressional elections. The more popular a president, the better the president's party does in congressional elections. This is especially important in midterm elections as the president

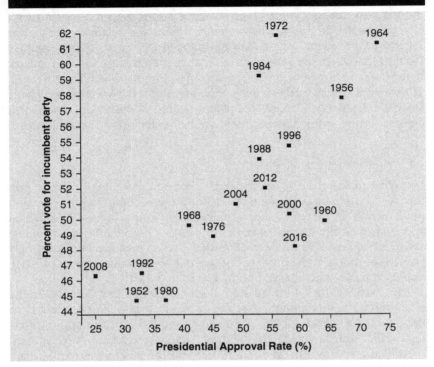

Figure 9.2 Presidential Approval and the Popular Vote for Presidential Candidates of the Incumbent's Party, 1952–2016

Source: Presidential approval and vote share data are from John Woolley and Gerhard Peters, The American Presidency Project, Presidential Job Approval, http://www.presidency .ucsb.edu/data/popularity.php. Political Behavior of the American Electorate, 14th edition. CQ Press.

is not on the ballot. In 2016, President Trump's low approval rate helped Democrats retake the majority in the House of Representatives. Trump's approval rating spent the entirety of the election season underwater. On Labor Day, the time when many election forecasters who ignore factors like news coverage make their predictions, 40 percent of Americans approved of his job performance.[5] Economic growth, measured by Seth Masket, Director of the Center on American Politics and the University of Denver, was just above 2 percent, suggesting something in the way of a twenty-three to twenty-five seat loss in the House. In short, President Trump was unpopular enough and the economy was growing just slowly enough for Democrats to be hopeful and Republicans to be worried. In the end, House Republicans performed worse than the typical midterm losses experienced by the president's party, losing forty-one seats from what they had in the previous Congress, losing their majority in the process.

Electoral Structures

Beyond the state of the economy and the popularity of the president, the rules of the game affect who wins elections. At lower levels of the ballot, some races are nonpartisan. Many city council, school board, and mayoral races consist of candidates who do not have their party affiliations listed on the ballot. In these races, spending being listed first and having a name that people assume to be a man's name have historically advantaged candidates.[6]

Congressional elections expert Gary Jacobson's research shows that nearly 80 percent of any changes in the president's party's number of House seats is due to the economy, presidential approval, and a structural factor: the number of seats the majority has—the more seats the majority has, the more likely they are to lose some.[7]

At the presidential level, winning the popular vote is nice, but winning the Electoral College counts. The Electoral College is the body of electors the Constitution empowers to choose the president. States are given Electoral College votes based upon their population. In 48 states, the candidate who wins the state's popular vote captures all of that state's electoral votes. In Maine and Nebraska, candidates earn two votes for winning the statewide vote and one vote per congressional district they win in each respective state. There are 538 electoral votes. It takes 270 to win. Table 9.1

Table 9.1 Popular Vote Percentage and Electoral Vote Count for the Winning Presidential Candidate, 2000–2016

Year	Popular Vote (%)	Electoral College Votes	Winner
2000	47.9	271	George W. Bush (R)
2004	50.7	286	George W. Bush (R)
2008	52.9	365	Barack Obama (D)
2012	51.1	332	Barack Obama (D)
2016	45.9	306	Donald Trump (R)

Source: John Woolley and Gerhard Peters, The American Presidency Project, available at https://www.presidency.ucsb.edu/.

shows that since 2000, Democrats have won the popular vote four times while Republicans have won it once. However, Republicans won the Electoral College three times to Democrats' two.

Incumbency

If you ever find yourself in a situation where you have to bet on the outcome of an election and the only thing you know is that the incumbent is seeking reelection, bet on the incumbent. You will be right between 80 and 90 percent of the time. Simply knowing whether a congressional district voted for Barack Obama or John McCain in 2008, and nothing else, correctly predicted the results of 85 percent of the races in 2010.[8] Incumbents are also advantaged by the news media, as they get more news coverage than challengers.[9]

Candidate Quality

Not all candidates are created equal. Candidates for office who have previously held another elective office fare better in elections, and election coverage, than political newcomers.[10] This makes sense, thinking back to Chapter 2, given that reporters only have so much time and space to devote to election coverage. When faced with a choice to cover Senator Bernie Sanders or spiritual guru Marianne Williamson on the 2020 Democratic candidate primary trail they are more likely to cover Sanders, who has already demonstrated he can win an election.

Roles of the Media in Elections

Despite the importance of *the fundamentals*, news coverage, political conversation, and social media behavior are also important factors that affect the results of elections. Before unpacking the effects that political communication has on elections, it is important to understand where people choose to get their news from. A 2017 report from the Pew Research Center showed that while a plurality of voters said that they used Fox News as their main source of 2016 election news, it was driven almost entirely by Trump voters. Figure 9.3 shows that 40 percent of Republican voters chose Fox. CNN, Facebook, NBC, local television ABC, CBS, and local radio combined drew a total of 35 percent of Trump voters' main attention. Clinton voters were not as loyal to one source in particular, favoring CNN (18 percent), but using MSNBC, Facebook, local television, and National Public Radio in relatively equal numbers.[11]

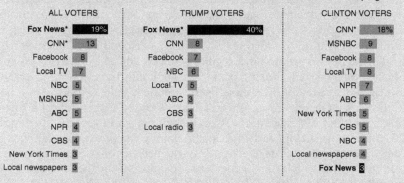

Figure 9.3 Main News Sources for 2016 Voters

Fox News dominated as main campaign news source for Trump voters; no single source as pronounced among Clinton voters

% of voters who named _____ as their "main source" for news about the 2016 campaign

ALL VOTERS		TRUMP VOTERS		CLINTON VOTERS	
Fox News*	19%	Fox News*	40%	CNN*	18%
CNN*	13	CNN	8	MSNBC	9
Facebook	8	Facebook	7	Facebook	8
Local TV	7	NBC	6	Local TV	8
NBC	5	Local TV	5	NPR	7
MSNBC	5	ABC	3	ABC	6
ABC	5	CBS	3	New York Times	5
NPR	4	Local radio	3	CBS	5
CBS	4			NBC	4
New York Times	3			Local newspapers	4
Local newspapers	3			Fox News	3

* Among this group of voters, this source was named at significantly higher rates than the source below it. Significance of any other relationships provided upon request.

Note: Sources shown are only those that were named by at least 3% of each group. Results are based on responses to open-ended questions; respondents could write in any source they chose.

Source: Survey conducted Nov. 29–Dec.12, 2016.

"Trump, Clinton Voters Divided in Their Main Source for Election News"

PEW RESEARCH CENTER

Source: https://www.journalism.org/2017/01/18/trump-clinton-voters-divided-in-their-main -source-for-election-news/

By media platform, television reigned supreme in 2016 across all kinds of elections. Fifty-seven percent of voters used local TV as a campaign news source. Fifty-four percent of voters used cable television as a source of campaign news, as compared to 49 percent who used network news. Just over one-third of voters listed newspapers as a main source of information while 44 percent named some form of radio. Internet or digital news sources were used by 65 percent of voters, an 18 percent jump from the 2012 elections.[12]

Prominence of Election News Coverage

Recall from Chapter 2 that a variety of forces—from journalistic routines to market pressure to audience demands—affect why the news is the way it is. People prefer the simple and dramatic to the wonky and annotated in their news coverage. While democracy requires an informed public making choices between competing alternatives, a host of competing pressures leads journalists to "write breezy infotainment stories that stress the horse race and skim over policy details."[13]

While the average presidential election year's coverage ends up equaling about 13 percent of overall newspaper political coverage, cable news coverage is far different. Figure 9.3's revelation of the prominence of cable news use among Trump and Clinton voters comes as no surprise when we think of it from both structural and market perspectives. Cable news has to fill time. Newspapers have regular sections and smaller news holes to fill each day. As such, getting people to talk about the election, interviewing candidates, taking live shots from campaign rallies, and the like help fill time on cable television. In 2012, more than 40 percent of cable's news hole was filled with election talk. Cable shifted into overdrive during the 2016 election, led, in part, by Donald Trump's ability to get all eyes on him. Five months before Election Day, 60 percent of survey respondents told the Pew Research Center they were "exhausted" by the coverage of the presidential election.[14]

Television stations were laughing all the way to the bank. One network chief said Trump's run was "damn good" for their network.[15] Trump earned far more news coverage in the 2016 primaries than the other candidates seeking either the Republican nomination or the Democratic nomination, earning more than a billion dollars' worth of free attention from the mainstream news media.[16]

While this comes as no surprise to the careful reader of Chapter 2, campaign coverage is notably uniform across platforms. The coverage of campaign events, debates, candidate traits, issues, and the like is remarkably similar. It is also the case that the arc of coverage over the course of the campaign season is similar. There is often more issue coverage earlier in a campaign season. During primary elections, candidates often use competing issue positions to differentiate themselves from members of their same party. As the campaign matures, the issue positions become old news, making way for *game framing* coverage of candidate strategy and the latest polling results. The closer we get to Election Day, the more likely we see stories covered with game frames. Privately owned independent newspapers and small local chains engage in less game-framed coverage as compared to large-chain-owned papers and corporately owned papers. Game-framed coverage is also more likely in papers owned by large diffuse chains than by locally concentrated chains, possibly because they are less likely to invest in local political reporting for races that are not of interest nationally.[17]

Still, the most noteworthy differences are usually related to the breadth of coverage. Newspapers and some digital outlets can provide greater depth to their campaign coverage whereas television news and more click-bait-oriented digital outlets create stereotypes about candidates that help guide their stories. In a study of the 2000 presidential race, Kathleen Hall Jamieson and Paul Waldman found that a great deal of news coverage treated the campaign as Dumbo (George W. Bush) vs. Pinocchio (Al Gore). These stereotypes make candidate behavior that fit the stereotype more likely to receive attention. That is, when George W. Bush said something that made him look unintelligent, it was more likely to receive coverage than when Al Gore did the same. When Gore said something that did not turn out to be true, it garnered more attention than when Bush stretched the truth.[18]

Vetting

Often with the persistent nudging of political campaigns' opposition research teams, news organizations play an important role with respect to the vetting of political candidates. This generally means news attention to a candidate's character and a candidate's potential ability to manage the demands of the office they seek. In terms of character, we mean their general personality traits such as integrity, compassion, communication-style, and personal temperament. Regarding their professional qualifications, coverage usually focuses on their relevant professional background, achievements, and setbacks. Research from Doris Graber and David Weaver revealed that the factors that deserve the most attention as voters face the choice of who to support get little attention in campaign coverage.[19]

King and Queen Maker

With the advent of television, candidates for a party's presidential nomination came into American living rooms, moving them, to some degree, out of the backrooms of the party apparatus. While elite party endorsements remained fundamentally important factors in predicting who would get a nomination, television coverage asserted its importance as well.

In 2008, Hillary Clinton was the frontrunner for the Democratic nomination. However, Barack Obama generated considerable media attention. Did that attention help him win the nomination? Some research found that exposure to news about celebrity endorsements of Obama, such as the one from Oprah Winfrey, did not affect people's feelings of favorability toward Obama, but it did result in people 1) saying they would be more likely to vote for him, and 2) thinking Obama was more likely to be the Democratic nominee.[20] Clinton supporters accused the news media of sexist coverage. Clinton herself said, "It does seem as though the press, at least, is not as bothered by the incredible vitriol that has been engendered by the comments by people who are nothing but misogynists." A content analysis of how television news people addressed the Democratic primary candidates showed that journalists referred to Clinton more informally than Obama and their other major competitors. Importantly, this effect was driven by the gender of the broadcaster. Men showed gender bias when referring to the Democratic presidential candidates.[21]

A study of the overall tone of newspaper, radio, cable television, internet news, and political talk shows found that news coverage toward Clinton and Obama was uniform, with the exception of partisan talk shows. Consistent with studies of previous election cycles, the study found coverage similar for the main contenders. Moreover, they found that the news media tended to focus on Clinton and Obama, paying less attention to the competitive, albeit less hotly contested, Republican primary contest. This *handicapping* of the election gives journalists quite a bit of power to make or break campaigns in the primary season. In the end, king and queen making is "captive to journalistic norms, particularly novelty and preeminence of the horse race frame."[22]

In 2016, an analysis showed that during the year 2015, major news outlets covered Donald Trump in a way that was unusual given how poor his early poll numbers were. The study, led by Thomas Patterson, further found that Trump's improving poll numbers were fueled by a high volume of media coverage during that early period of the campaign known as the *invisible primary*. Trump's coverage at that point was positive in tone, though that changed over the rest of the primary campaign and general election season.[23]

Positive coverage was not necessary to win a primary, however. The same study found Hillary Clinton received the most negative coverage during the invisible primary period. Clinton's biggest rival, Vermont Senator Bernie Sanders (I), did not receive much early coverage. As his media attention grew, his coverage was largely positive in tone, more favorable than coverage of Clinton or Trump.

Structural Biases and Election Coverage

While journalists and news organizations strive to provide balanced coverage of elections, judgments of newsworthiness and other structural biases make it impossible. As described above, imbalances in coverage occur frequently, even if the general behavior of the news media is largely consistent across major candidates. But even that distinction, *major candidates*, is an example of a bias in election coverage. Candidates who poll poorly and, especially, third-party candidates have a very difficult time getting attention from the pack of reporters covering the campaign. Occasionally, a third-party candidate, such as Robert La Follette (Progressive Party, 1924), George Wallace (American Independent Party, 1968), and Ross Perot (Independent, 1992; Reform Party, 1996) get some attention, but it still pales in comparison to what the major party candidates receive.

Another structural bias in presidential races is that about 95 percent of coverage goes to the presidential candidate while five percent goes to each party's vice presidential nominee—even though the VP nominee would become the president in the case of the president's death, resignation or impeachment and conviction. In congressional races, incumbents get more attention than challengers, on average, as they can generate attention via their campaign events *and* by doing their job as a representative (something the challenger usually is not in a position to do).

While newspaper editorials are an example of purposeful bias (after all, editorials are supposed to be expressions of opinion), they are supposed to be independent of the hard news coverage produced by reporters covering the campaign itself. Even so, research has shown that candidates for the US Senate who get endorsed by a newspaper are more likely to receive more positive coverage from that same paper. This could be because the endorsed candidate is simply better—at getting good coverage, campaigning, and so forth. It could also be because reporters understand, even subconsciously, that to get ahead at their paper, they might do well to give better coverage to the editorial side of the paper's preferred candidate. However, research has not been able to tease out the causes to the fact that endorsed candidates get more positive news coverage.

Responding to Social Media

A newer journalistic behavior in election coverage is responding to what happens on social media—both in terms of what candidates do on outlets like Twitter and Facebook and with respect to what citizens express on these same outlets. A study of Donald Trump's Twitter behavior in the 2016 primaries found that news stories and blog posts about Trump were predicted by the volume of retweets of Trump's tweets. Trump tended to tweet more when his coverage lagged. In other words, when the news media began paying attention to other candidates, Trump went on tweet-storms. When his tweets connected with his followers and those followers retweeted Trump, the unconventional candidate received more news coverage (which you will remember absolutely overwhelmed the amount of attention his competitors received).[24]

Beyond being affected by what candidates do on social media, journalists use Twitter as a gauge of public opinion.[25] When they did so during the 2016 election, reporters at thirty-two of thirty-three outlets studied by Josephine Lukito and Chris Wells quoted a tweet in a story that came from the Internet Research Agency (IRA)—a St. Petersburg, Russia-based organization tied to Russian President Vladimir Putin. The ideological orientation of the news organizations did not seem to matter as the liberal Huffington Post and the conservative Daily Caller were the two organizations that quoted the most IRA tweets.[26]

A study of the 2014 Belgium election found that online media outlets affect news organizations that publish less frequently, but newspapers (publishing *only* once a day) often get to issues first, leading the way for other, more supposedly nimble, outlets. Importantly, the study also found that media members who use Twitter have more agenda-setting influence than those who do not.[27]

How Voters Rate Elections Coverage

What do voters think of the coverage they receive during campaigns? The Pew Research Center has asked voters to grade media coverage of the American presidential campaign since 2000. In 2016, voters gave the news media their lowest evaluations yet. In fact, Figure 9.4 shows that when grading Donald Trump, Hillary Clinton, each party pollsters, and voters, the *press* earned the highest percentage of Fs and the lowest percentage of As and Bs combined.

While we presume that voters would certainly benefit from a more policy-oriented election reporting style, it is the case that voters like the horse race.[28]

Figure 9.4   Voter Evaluations of the Parties, the Press, and Pollsters in the 2016 Presidential Race

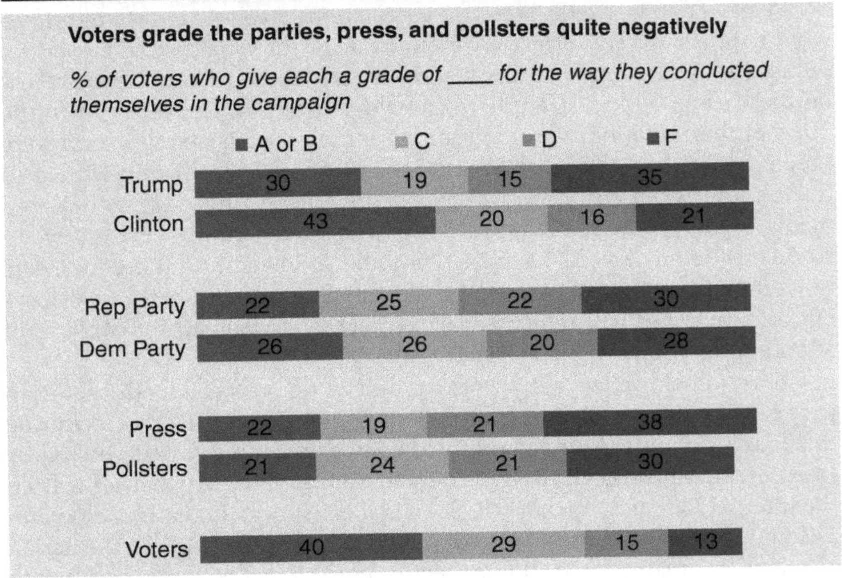

Voters grade the parties, press, and pollsters quite negatively

% of voters who give each a grade of ____ for the way they conducted themselves in the campaign

■ A or B   ▪ C   ▪ D   ▪ F

	A or B	C	D	F
Trump	30	19	15	35
Clinton	43	20	16	21
Rep Party	22	25	22	30
Dem Party	26	26	20	28
Press	22	19	21	38
Pollsters	21	24	21	30
Voters	40	29	15	13

Source: https://www.people-press.org/2016/11/21/voters-evaluations-of-the-campaign/.

Note: "Don't know" responses not shown.

Types of Election Coverage

Horse Race Coverage and Game Frames

What are the different ways that campaigns are covered in the news? Not surprisingly, the most dominant form of reporting is horse race coverage. The Shorenstein Center on Media, Politics, and Public Policy's examination of 2016 campaign coverage revealed that 42 percent of stories focused on issues related to the horse race. Horse race stories focus on who is winning and losing. Many of these stories contain *game frames* related to campaign strategies, conflict, and negative tone (portraying politicians as strategic, untrustworthy miscreants who will do anything to win). Game frames of the horse race are attractive to reporters because using poll data is largely viewed as objective, freeing reporters from accusations of bias.

Coverage of Polls

For years, scholars complained that journalists covered each new election poll in a way that was independent from the polls that came before it. Given that one of every twenty polls is likely to be an outlier (producing results that are not replicated by future polls), researchers worry that uncritical poll reporting makes elections seem more volatile than they typically are. Political communication researchers suggested the journalists report an aggregation of public opinion surveys rather than the results of any single poll. Sites like Real Clear Politics and FiveThirtyEight produce aggregated poll estimates. FiveThirtyEight's Nate Silver makes electoral predictions based upon the aggregated surveys. In 2012, Silver's forecast correctly predicted the Electoral College results in all fifty states and the District of Columbia.

Of course, these predictions were not promises. They were based on probabilities, not certainties. Political scientist Benjamin Toff interviewed forty-one journalists in 2014 and 2015, uncovering what one journalist called a "Nate Silver effect"—a somewhat ironic overreliance on aggregated polls as sacrosanct, rather than a probabilistic prediction. While Silver's prediction was for a Hillary Clinton win in 2016, the percentage chance he gave it was 71.4—a far cry from a sure thing. Silver criticized journalists for not reporting the level of uncertainty that comes with probabilistic predictions. Toff noted that the journalists he interviewed kept close tabs on aggregated poll results as compared to breathlessly reporting dramatic changes in a single poll. However, those same journalists worried about the trade-offs involved with reporting aggregated poll results as compared to other factors they could be covering given their scarce resources. Social science often leaves more questions than it provides answers—something with which contemporary narrative journalism seems less comfortable.[29]

Negative Coverage

If you bring up the topic of *the media* at your family's holiday dinner table, you are sure to hear someone grouse about how the news is so negative. While the evidence we have presented you so far in this book reveals a great many misperceptions people have about news coverage, in the context of political campaigns, this one is right on.

In 2016, a Shorenstein Center report showed that, from January 1, 2015 to Election Day 2016, 77 percent of Donald Trump's news reports were negative and 64 percent of Hillary Clinton's coverage was negative. Does this indicate a bias in favor of Clinton? Upon inspection, no. First, most of Clinton's positive stories were horse race stories, showing she was leading in the polls. Second, during the General Election period, from August to Election Day, Trump had a higher percentage of positive stories (44 percent) than Clinton (38 percent).[30]

Stories examining each candidate's fitness for office were negative 87 percent of the time for each major party nominee. Trump earned more coverage than Clinton in every single week of the general campaign; the gap was usually between two and six percent in the Republican's favor. While Fox News provided Trump his most positive coverage, it was still decidedly negative (73 percent). Overall, Trump's most negative stories were about his experience and the controversies he generated on the campaign trail.

By contrast, Fox News gave Clinton her most negative coverage (81 percent) while the *New York Times'* coverage was negative 61 percent of the time. Clinton's stories coming out of the debates with Trump were positive as well.

Negativity in election coverage is not simply an American news phenomenon. An in-depth study of news coverage in the European Union parliamentary elections revealed how changes in political structure interact with news coverage. For new countries in the EU, election coverage was not as negative as it was for long-standing members of the EU. Television news was slightly positive, overall, while traditional and tabloid newspapers' coverage edged toward negativity in tone.[31]

Is negative coverage a bad thing? Certainly, there are politicians who are inept, corrupt, or worse and need to be exposed through negative news coverage. Patterson concluded the Shorenstein Center report, writing, "[A] healthy dose of negativity is unquestionably a good thing," but he also noted that negative coverage "erodes trust in political leaders and institutions and undermines confidence in government and policy."[32]

Issue Coverage

Ten percent of stories in the 2016 race were about policy issues, according to the above-cited Shorenstein Center report. When issues are covered, who benefits? One study showed that in the 2006 Texas gubernatorial race, candidates can influence the issues voters find to be salient to them when the media focus on the same issues in news coverage.[33] In presidential races, political scientist Danny Hayes content analyzed newspaper coverage of the 1992, 1996, and 2000 elections, finding that candidates get more positive coverage when the news media cover issues that their party "owns."[34] The *issue ownership hypothesis* begins with the notion that the public, rightly or wrongly, believes that one political party is better at handling a particular political issue as compared to the other major party. If people are thinking more about the issue a party owns when they go to vote, it benefits the party that owns the issue. Hayes found that across the three election cycles, stories about issues like crime, national security, and taxes, which the public tends to conclude that Republicans own, were more positive for Republican candidates while stories about like education, health care, and social security, which Democrats tend to own, favored Democratic candidates. This means that candidates have incentives to focus on the issues their party owns when talking substance on the campaign trail, hoping to generate issue stories that are more likely to favor their candidacy.

Issue Coverage and Political Conversation

Another study used a lengthy newspaper strike in Pittsburgh to estimate how the lack of newspaper coverage of congressional campaigns affected political discussion. During the times that striking reporters prevented newspapers from covering the elections, research showed that people talked about politics less.[35]

It is not just the absence of issue coverage that can affect political talk among friends and family. Issue coverage can get so heated and polarizing that it can lead to people avoiding political talk altogether. A study of the controversial recall election of Governor Scott Walker in Wisconsin found that a third of Wisconsinites reported that they stopped talking to someone about politics because of their views about the recall.[36] A follow-up study in 2018 found that Wisconsin politics was further polarizing as more than 50 percent of Wisconsinites had stopped to talking to someone about politics and 10 percent of people had ended a friendship over political differences. Indeed, Jamie Settle and Taylor Carlson used a series of inventive experiments to demonstrate that people demand more compensation to engage in political discussion with people in a different political party, for both political *and* nonpolitical topics.[37]

Scandal Coverage

Scandals are a part of many election cycles. In 2016, Democratic nominee Hillary Clinton dealt with the scandal about her use of a private

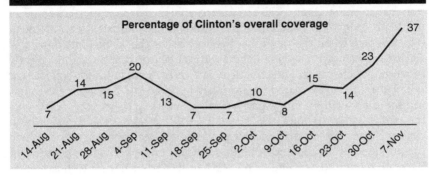

Figure 9.5 Hillary Clinton's "Scandal" Coverage During the 2016 General Election

Source: Harvard Kennedy School Shorenstein Center of Media, Politics, and Public Policy
https://shorensteincenter.org/news-coverage-2016-general-election/.

email server while she was Secretary of State and Donald Trump dealt with a host of scandals—from claiming he could shoot someone on 5th Avenue in New York and improve his standing in the polls to dealing with the fallout of a leaked conversation with *Access Hollywood* about how Trump believed his celebrity status made it permissible for him to sexually assault women.

While Trump's *Access Hollywood* scandal was an example of a media feeding frenzy (see Chapter 2), Clinton's scandal coverage was a regular part of her coverage every week. Figure 9.5's Shorenstein Center and Media Tenor data reveals that Clinton's scandal coverage nearly tripled in the last three weeks of the campaign—a time when coverage typically becomes more neutral. Clinton blamed the outsized attention on her emails for her Electoral College loss to Trump.

In the 2006 congressional elections, the Republican Party dealt with a set of scandals, most notably from Florida Congressman Mark Foley's inappropriate behavior with congressional pages. However, public views about scandals and about the institution of Congress consistently led to negative evaluations of Republicans *and* Democrats. As is typical in midterms, the approval of the president, in this case, the sizable unpopularity of President Bush was consistently associated with negative views of Republicans and positive views of Democratic office seekers. Still, news organizations covered parts of the campaign season differently. NBC and FOX treated congressional scandals in different ways. FOX paid less attention to them, choosing to cover them in ways that were more negative about Democrats than Republicans. NBC's coverage focused on the more explicit nature of the scandals and prominent Republicans involved in the stories, such as Foley. Both television news outlets covered congressional news in a more neutral manner as Election Day drew near.[38]

Satirical Coverage and Outrage in Elections

Satirical late-night television has an expanding role in elections while host-driven *outrage* programming is louder than ever. Candidates regularly appear on network late programs like *The Late Show with Stephen Colbert* and *Late Night with Seth Meyers* to kick off their candidacy for higher office. *Full Frontal with Samantha Bee*'s host invited the nearly two dozen Democrats seeking the presidency in 2020 to come and drop out of the race on her show. Jimmy Fallon received criticism for going too easy on Donald Trump during his visit to the *Tonight Show* before the 2016 election. On the outrage side, *Hannity* host Sean Hannity appeared at rallies with President Trump. *Info Wars* conspiracy monger Alex Jones blamed liberal anger after Hillary Clinton's election loss for getting sued for making up hurtful stories about the horrific Sandy Hook school shooting.[39]

Political communication scholar and satire expert Dannagal Young pairs the ironic programming of late-night liberal satire with the outrage programming of conservative cable and web-based programming. Liberal political satire and conservative outrage programming serve similar needs for their audience and have parallel effects on their audiences. What is most compelling about Young's argument is that these types of programming seem to be different from each other because of the different psychological frameworks that animate liberalism and conservatism. Liberals are simply more comfortable with ambiguity, rumination, experimentation, and hybridity, which nudge them toward Stephen Colbert, John Oliver, Samantha Bee, and others who stew in those ideas. Conservatives, especially social and cultural conservatives, are different. They have a strong desire for certainty. They prefer realistic art to the liberal's abstract art and stories with a clear ending as compared to stories with ambiguous ones. Rush Limbaugh, Sean Hannity, and the like provide that coverage for them.

Debate Coverage

Some of the most-watched, and discussed, aspects of elections are debates. These are high-stakes events where candidates have far less control over their message than they do when they are advertising or giving their typical stump speech. Even so, candidates often answer the question they wished they were asked as compared to the question they were asked in debates, especially when they are asked about something that is not good for their campaign such as a scandal or an issue like the state of the economy when the economy is not growing and the president is in the candidate's party.[40]

Typically, debates are not thought to affect vote choice very much. A study of the 1980 debates between Ronald Reagan and Jimmy Carter found that knowing who debate-watchers favored going into the debate was by far the best predictor of who people thought won the debate.[41]

In terms of learning about candidates, debates tend to teach people about challengers, but not incumbents. They can change how people think about the character of candidates but usually only affect vote choice by strengthening preferences that the debate-watcher already had as compared to changing the mind of a voter.[42] Debate viewing can serve as a mediator between television news viewing and vote choice, but it still tends to act as a partisan-reinforcing mechanism when it comes to casting a ballot.[43]

Of course, most people do not watch debates. They are, however, likely to encounter discussion of who won the debate. Research led by Kim Fridkin analyzed media coverage (online, newspapers, and television) about the final 2004 presidential debate and compared the reactions about who won to those who saw the debate and those who did not. They found that those who did not see the debate were significantly affected by the post-game media coverage concerning who won.[44]

Increasingly, fact-checking journalism is inserting itself into presidential debates. The Washington Post's fact checkers Glenn Kessler and Michelle Ye Hee Lee minced no words after the first general election row between Donald Trump and Hillary Clinton:

> In the first debate between presidential contenders Donald Trump and Hillary Clinton, Trump repeatedly relied on troublesome and false facts that have been debunked throughout the campaign. Clinton stretched the truth on occasion, such as when she tried to wiggle out of her 2012 praise of the Trans Pacific Partnership as a "gold standard." But her misstatements paled in comparison to the list of Trump's exaggerations and falsehoods.[45]

Research in a New Jersey gubernatorial debate showed evaluations of the candidate's debate performance and evaluations of the debate winner are improved when they saw a fact-check that confirmed the accuracy of a candidate's statement. People were even more likely to want to vote for a person who had a positive result from a fact-check. On the other hand, their evaluations of the debate were negatively affected by fact-checks revealing that a candidate was being dishonest.[46]

Not only are fact-checks changing how we view debates, we are literally changing how we view debates via our use of a second screen (watching the debate while also reading and commenting on social media). One study chronicled the first and third 2012 presidential debates to evaluate the impact of candidates' verbal and nonverbal behaviors on viewers' second screen behaviors. They found that the nonverbal communication behaviors of candidates, such as their facial expressions and gestures, affected the amount and tone of people's public expression on social media during debates.[47]

Gender, Race, and Election Coverage

Beyond structural and content features of election coverage, scholars have spent considerable time and effort investigating how the gender and racial identities of candidates are related to the coverage they get. The evidence generally lies between examples of how women and candidates who are not white get comparatively worse coverage in elections and examples of when there are fewer, if any, major differences in how campaigns in the United States treat women and members of racial minority groups. When campaigns, regardless of who is running, focus on issues women find important, women became more likely to vote Democratic. Men's vote choices were unaffected.[48]

Congressional Races

Regarding gender and running for office, women are less likely to run for office than men even though they are as likely to win as men are when they run. Women, no matter how personally successful they have been, are far less likely to have ambitions for higher office as they are less likely than men to be recruited to run, less likely than men to think that they are qualified to run (even when their qualifications are the same as men's).[49] Moreover, in races in which women run, news coverage tends to focus more on the coverage of traits as compared to qualifications. This is especially true for executive offices, like governor, where women candidates are more likely to get trait coverage and less likely to receive issue coverage.[50]

However, Jennifer Lawless and Danny Hayes conducted a detailed content analysis of local newspaper coverage from almost 350 US House districts and nationally representative survey data from the 2010, finding that a candidate's gender was unrelated to journalists' coverage of, or voters' attitudes toward, the women and men running for Congress. The authors found that understanding how gender affects congressional campaigns is best understood by examining what affects campaigns even more generally: partisanship, ideology, and incumbency.[51]

What happens when women run against each other? An experimental analysis varied whether women running against each other were covered by the news media as touting stereotypically masculine or feminine issues and traits. The results indicated that Democrats and Republicans preferred a partisan who created a gender balance between masculinity and femininity.[52]

A content analysis of newspaper news coverage of candidates during election campaigns in Australia, Canada, and the United States revealed that higher numbers of women in office in Australia and Canada did not translate into more gender-neutral coverage. All three countries had similar patterns of gender stereotypes linked to candidates' traits and issues.[53]

With respect to news coverage of race in elections, research has not shown that coverage has a direct impact on the outcome of elections, but it has revealed that journalists in the 1980s and 1990s used a different set of norms to guide their reporting in elections that include a minority candidate than they have used when only white men are running. During Douglas Wilder's historic win as the first black governor of Virginia in 1989, few news stories about the Wilder campaign were explicitly about race. Instead, reporters made a variety of indirect references to race, referring to Wilder as *making history*. This is consistent with Nayda Terklidsen and David Damore's racial dualism in news coverage hypothesis—the news media play the role of racial arbitrators by limiting racial emphases and the news media bring race front and center by highlighting candidate race. These styles of coverage can occur simultaneously. Coverage of elections with black candidates suppresses the use of race among the candidates themselves, but highlights the race of black candidates and their constituents.[54]

Using panel data in 2008, research showed that the image of Barack Obama present in news coverage contradicted negative racial stereotypes. Supporters of Obama's Republican opponent, John McCain, exhibited the largest drops in negative racial stereotypes when they were exposed to coverage of Obama. Even stories that portrayed Obama negatively resulted in conservative viewers expressing fewer racial stereotypes as the negative portrayals did not use racial stereotypes.[55]

State and Local Races

Local news media play a similar role to national media in campaigns. In some respects, local and state media are increasingly important to elections, especially as candidates begin spending more on advertising. Current research suggests that local stations do not provide much information to citizens about the qualifications of candidates seeking state and local offices. Coverage of senate and gubernatorial races in 2004, 2006, and

2008 revealed negative news coverage that was not very substantive. This was particularly true for local news organizations that were owned by public shareholders and were thus less insulated from market pressures.[56]

Social Media and Elections: The New Frontier

Social media use is neither poison nor antidote for the current state of political elections (see Chapter 3). Most effect sizes of social and mobile media use are small, but the rate at which technology and its use are changing require scholars, activists, and citizens to keep up as best we can to help us, to borrow Doris Graber's phrase, "tame the information tide." Research shows that campaigns use the interactive affordances of social media and digital media more generally when they help the strategic goals of campaigns.[57] That is, they tend to try and control their message on social media rather than use the potential for interactivity from citizen input on social media. Much of the early use of the web by campaigns was as a conduit to raise money. Visit any 2020 presidential or congressional candidate's website and you will find a prominent "DONATE!" button.

Even so, the number of people using social media to follow politics and politicians is on the rise. One study of the 2016 election found social media use for politics was actually related to less *support* for Republican populists, such as Donald Trump, but that different kinds of social media use were linked to an increase in the likelihood of support to a level close to that of the traditional television viewing. Notably, the patterns were almost the inverse of support for Democratic populists, in this case namely Bernie Sanders.[58]

An ambitious 2016 study that tracked the digital ads people encountered during the US presidential campaign found that of several unidentifiable suspicious groups, those that were foreign entities seeking to influence the American election ran the most divisive digital issue ads. The study, led by political communication scholar Young Mie Kim, found that one in six of these groups were from Russia and that their ads were targeted to battleground states, much in the same way that traditional television advertising is in presidential campaigns. Thousands of ads were purchased by Russian-linked groups trying to affect the election. How consequential were these ads and other fake news articles pushed by Russia in 2016? A study found that while one in four Americans visited a fake news website in 2016, about 60 percent of the total number of fake news visits came from a sliver of Trump supporters.[59] On Twitter, another study found that one percent of individuals accounted for *80* percent of fake news clicks and only 0.1 percent accounted for 80 percent of the fake news that was shared on Twitter.[60] Brazen misinformation is easy to find, but most of us do not encounter it very often or in much depth.

Effects of Mediated Campaigns

After months of campaigning, scores of stories, and a set of debates, what do people learn from campaign news coverage? As with most questions in this book, the answer is that it depends. Most often, the factors that the answer depends upon include political knowledge, partisanship, information sources, and political interest.

Coverage and Learning

Despite numerous content analyses examining campaign coverage at various levels of government, studies that are able to integrate content analysis with public opinion data that measures people's attitudes before, during, and after the election season are rarely done. Too often, researchers were willing to assume that if the news coverage existed, people must have seen it. However, we know now that this is not so. As such, causal answers to the question of what campaigns teach citizens remain somewhat elusive. Research over the decades allows us to draw some general conclusions.

Perhaps not surprisingly, most voters do not recall much specific issue information they learned over the course of a campaign. If what they learn is consistent with the worldview they had when the election season began, they are likely to have processed that news in such a way as to store in their memory the general impression of what they learned. If the information was discordant with their preexisting views, they often reject it.

Coverage and Vote Choice

For media messages to change votes, people need to be open to messages suggesting change. As with framing effects, they need to find campaign messages applicable, available, and accessible. Campaign messages are most effective when they build off of reality—such as when incumbents talk about their economic plans in a time of economic growth. When candidates achieve convergence between their own agendas and the news media's agenda, they are more likely to influence vote choice as well. Further, the more positive the tone of coverage toward a party, the more likely people are to vote for that party.[61] The editorial slant of newspapers affects voting decisions as well.[62]

Coverage and Turnout

Just having information affects voter turnout. In 2005, a group of scholars randomly assigned participants in a study in Virginia to receive a free subscription to *The Washington Post* (with a liberal editorial page), *The Washington Times* (with a conservative editorial page), or nothing. They found that voter turnout increased for those who received a newspaper as compared to those who did not.[63]

Specific source use can matter as well. Research examining what happens when Fox News became part of a media market's cable package found that Fox News affected voter turnout and the Republican vote share in the Senate.[64] Research examining Spanish language news in the United States found that Hispanic voter turnout increased by 5 to 10 percentage points in media markets where Spanish-language local television news was available.[65]

More traditional communication that occurs outside of media coverage affects turnout as well. The ground campaign, often involving door-to-door conversations between voters and volunteers, might have increased turnout in swing states by seven to eight percentage points in 2012.[66]

From Research to Real Life

Sometimes, it feels like we live in a 24-hour election cycle. The minute an election ends, someone who is talking on television or posting on Twitter will ask about what is going to happen in the next election. Just knowing that there is more to democracy than the next horse race or game frame can make your life a heckuva lot more enjoyable.

Knowing how structural factors (like the state of the economy) affect election results can also help keep you from stressing about the result of each and every poll that pits your candidate against those you hope are not chosen to represent you. You do not have to live and die with every poll. If the economy is strong and you favor the incumbent, you now know that things are more likely to go your way on Election Day, especially if the incumbent makes that economic growth a major part of the public argument they make to get reelected.

One thing that is especially nice about the era in which we are all living is that the modern communication ecology lets us talk back to those providing us election coverage. We can chide reporters for only giving us the latest strategy in the horse race. We can push for more substantive information about candidates. We can demand more extensive fact checking to hold politicians accountable for the claims they make about what is true. We can monitor whether the question a woman gets about running for office while raising a family gets asked in the same way—with the same assumptions underlying the question—for men seeking higher office.

Joshua Darr, Louisiana State University

Darr, J. P., Hitt, M. P., & Dunaway, J. L. (2018). Newspaper closures polarize voting behavior, *Journal of Communication, 68*(6), 1007–1028.

Joshua Darr is an assistant professor of political communication and D. Jensen Holliday Professor in the Manship School of Mass Communication at Louisiana State University. He has published more than a dozen articles about newspaper coverage of elections, news deserts, elections, and public attitudes about government. His work has been featured for wider audiences in *Scientific American*, Vox, *The Washington Post*, Axios, and FiveThirtyEight. His article, coauthored with Matthew Hitt and Johanna Dunaway, won the Association for Education in Journalism and Mass Communication's Lynda Lee Kaid Award, awarded to the best published article in political communication in 2018. Darr and his collaborators argue that newspaper closings contribute to the nationalization of politics, fostering greater polarization in the public. The article uses an exciting, smart, and forward-thinking design to cast a revealing light upon how the availability of local news matters when it is gone. Our Q&A with Darr, conducted over email, is below.

Wagner and Perryman: Your article shows that newspaper closures cause a decrease in split-ticket voting. Why does a decrease in split-ticket voting stem from a newspaper closing?

Darr: We argue that when a newspaper closes, people are more likely to vote for their party up and down the ballot because they replace that local option with a national news outlet. National political news is focused on the president, Congress, and partisan competition, which makes partisan considerations seem more important. Our findings aren't about the local information supplied by local newspapers; instead, we argue that polarization comes from the sources people replace local newspapers with once they are gone.

Wagner and Perryman: What was the most important decision you and your coauthors made in the course of working on this article? How did that decision influence what you were able to discover?

Darr: We chose to include weekly newspapers and newspaper mergers in our study, unlike some other studies of newspaper closures. Weekly newspapers likely don't include much political content, so they are easy to overlook. By including weeklies, we were able to discover that polarization is likely explained by replacement, not loss of information. A media outlet doesn't have to contain political information to have political effects!

Wagner and Perryman: If a student reading this book wanted to conduct research for a term paper, on an admittedly smaller scale, about newspaper closures or news deserts more generally, where would you suggest they start?

Darr: The best place to find recent newspaper closures is run by the Center for Innovation and Sustainability in Local Media (www.cislm.org) at the University of North Carolina-Chapel Hill. You can see recent newspaper closures by state and county, though they don't come with dates of closure. A great project would be a state-level case study of the effects newspaper closures, starting with the UNC database and finding the closure dates for the newspapers and examining mayoral or state legislative elections in those areas.

Wagner and Perryman: What kinds of skills do people develop in the political communication research process that would serve them well no matter what they end up doing?

Darr: Political communication research requires collecting original data from news organizations, from the government, and from voters and media consumers, and combining them in new and creative ways. I have learned so much about survey design, data management, content analysis, and qualitative interviewing from my research into the political communication questions that I want to answer. A sophisticated understanding of media, politics, and data will be valuable no matter what in today's data-driven, media-saturated world.

How Can I Help?

Brian Reisinger, Platform Communications

The vice president of Platform Communications, Reisinger has been at the epicenter of some the closest statewide elections in the hotly contested swing state of Wisconsin. Recently, he has been in charge of campaign communications for Senator Ron Johnson's (R) successful reelection campaign in Wisconsin in 2016 and Governor Scott Walker's (R) unsuccessful reelection bid by a razor-thin margin in 2018. Johnson's win was especially notable as the senator had been behind in nearly every major poll for months heading into Election Day. Reisinger likens a political campaign to a house fire, saying that the things he can't remember about his life from before the campaign began were "lost in the fire." Reisinger and Wagner spoke over the phone.

(Continued)

(Continued)

Wagner: What do you think are the most important ways that communication affects political campaigns (inside the campaign itself, with the news media, with donors and supporters and with the general voting public)?

Reisinger: Political campaigns are an incredible place for communications professionals to learn because in a campaign, the message is literally at the core of everything you do. You might be creating a message for a company, but in the campaign the message is around literally who they (the candidates) are. It informs the message, how the campaign operates, literally everything. If a campaign is a good one, it will reflect who the candidate is. With the news media, the major themes of a stump speech are tested in the media. Journalism, they say, is the rough draft of history. In a campaign it is on overdrive.

With donors, you have to be able to take the message, and tailor it to specific audiences.

Finally, being able to motivate grassroots is one of the most important and most overlooked campaigns do. You have to engage supporters and motivate them. Sometimes, you might be running about what's going on in Washington. Other times, the campaign centers on a specific issue like life or the 2nd amendment. When political professionals say the public is not informed—that's wrong—what they are really saying is that their message hasn't connected with the voters.

Wagner: From a communications perspective, how were the campaigns you worked on similar and how were they different?

Reisinger: There are a lot of similarities between Governor Walker and Senator Johnson. Both are good men who shared core principles. Working for them was deliberate on my part. One of the most important things you can do is pick a boss you can believe in. These are hard jobs and you want to wake up working for a man or woman you can believe in.

Every candidate is unique. Senator Johnson is well-known for his high level of candor—whether it is helpful or not or people want to hear it or not. It has served him well in Washington and on the campaign trail. It also makes for a fun, interesting and challenging campaign environment. He's going to say what he wants and you go along for the ride. The challenge to that is that a guy who answers anything honestly can involve a lot of really interesting challenges and problems to solve.

Governor Walker—core to his personality is that he would do what he said he was going to do and keep his promises. Everything with the governor focused on what we told the people of Wisconsin we were going to do this and how we were going to do it. It guided everything we did.

Wagner: What skills are the most valuable for young staffers to have when working on statewide political campaigns like the ones you have worked on for people like Senator Ron Johnson and Governor Scott Walker?

Reisinger: The number one ingredient by far is work ethic. It isn't fun to hear, you'd rather hear magic bullets, but the reality is if you show up and work hard it gets you far down the road. A campaign is a meritocracy. You have to fight every day for your candidate and help them win. That's very challenging.

The next thing is being adaptable and rolling with the punches. Every day is different, you have to accept that and adapt.

Another layer—communications skills—good writing, good verbal communication and the ability to represent and understand a message. It is also about being organized and having a plan in a state of chaos is a difficult thing to do.

Wagner: What are some ways young people seeking to make a difference in their community, state, or nation can get a foot in the door on political campaigns?

Reisinger: One of the quickest portals is to intern for a campaign. Campaigns are constantly in need for people who are willing to work hard and let campaigns use their resources well. People who do whatever's asked of them climb really quickly. Each move up will be more interesting and closer to the action.

10

Governing, Policymaking, and the Media

THE NEWS MEDIA ARE OFTEN referred to as the *fourth branch* of government in the United States. But what role, if any, do the media play in policymaking? It may seem strange to think of the news media as policymakers. After all, they are unelected and the Constitution does not list them as one of the key players in the governing process. Sean Hannity, Rachel Maddow, and the editorial pages at the *New York Times* or *Wall Street Journal* do not cast roll-call votes on legislation. However, political parties and interest groups are not mentioned as policymakers in the Constitution either, but they play crucial roles in governing. Some scholars refer to the media as a political institution, critical to governing in the United States.

Clarifying how the news media affect governing and policymaking is a major challenge of social science research. Policy scholars tend to underplay the importance of the news media in their research while political communication scholars tend to focus on media effects on the public as compared to effects on public policy. Even so, scholars have shed some light upon ways in which the media contribute to governing.

The News Media as a Political Institution

For decades, public policymaking had been thought of as an insider activity. Political communication scholar Timothy Cook argued that during the 1970s and 1980s, media coverage became a strategic weapon of lawmakers.[1] Political events get staged with journalists' responses in mind. This is an example of the mediatization of politics that draws criticism since the news media are not accountable to the public in the same way that democratically elected lawmakers are.[2]

Cook argued that the news media were not merely a part of politics, but that they were a part of government. This characterization is one that journalists bristle at, as it seems antithetical to the job of reporting the verifiable truth. But news organizations have almost always been deeply intertwined with politics. In the nineteenth century, political parties exhibited considerable control over the press. Newspapers often acted as the voice of a party while simultaneously relying for survival upon government printing from various levels of government.

One thing that makes the news media a political institution in the eyes of Cook and others who shared the institutionalist perspective was that, as discussed in Chapter 2, despite the variety of potential viewpoints available to the news media, the actual range of discussion present in news reporting is fairly narrow. If the news sought to promote a wide, diverse range of political alternatives, it would be difficult for the media to have major independent effects on society. The more homogenous media coverage, the more power that coverage exerts as a political institution and potential policymaker. This is because ambitious, astute politicians should be able to understand how the news media determine what is newsworthy. Once they do, they can use that knowledge to behave in ways to make it more likely that they will obtain more and positive coverage in the news. If politicians do not play by the media's rules, they might be shut out from coverage.[3] The homogeneity hypothesis also implies that the news media will be a less influential policymaker in times of low homogeneity or in times of an increasingly fragmented media ecology. Beyond the news side of the news media, Benjamin Page has suggested that the editorial side of newspapers influences the key players in public deliberation about important issues.[4]

In her book *The Power of Communication: Managing Information in Public Organizations*, political communication pioneer Doris Graber finds that government officials view effective communication as a strategy for effective policymaking. The news is a cheap, authoritative, and clear way to communicate to the public, as well as to people in the government itself.[5]

Cook argues that newsmaking and policymaking are essentially indistinguishable.[6] Modern presidents *go public*—take their show on the road to persuade the people to pressure Congress to adopt the president's program—with regularity. While these efforts may not move public opinion, they can affect how the news covers an issue or how members of Congress perceive it.[7]

Agenda-Setting and Public Policy

A major reason that governments create the policies they do is that a policy proposal got onto the public's or lawmakers' agenda.[8] Deciding what to cover is critically important to any political system.[9] Scholars focusing on political communication and researchers focusing on public policy both agree that what issues animate the agenda affect what policies get enacted.

In an influential article, Michelle Wolfe and colleagues argue that the factors that make up the public's agenda cannot be understood without understating how the policymaking process affects both lawmakers' and the public's agendas.[10] Understanding how newsmaking works helped government officials concerned with issues like terrorism and missing children construct public social policies.[11] Journalists and public officials can also collaborate to affect policy. One study found that investigative journalism on toxic waste issues led to the issue finding its way onto the public agenda, preceding changes in public policy.[12] Another, led by Fay Lomax Cook, found that while media coverage influenced the public agenda of an issue, policy change came from collaboration between journalists and people working for the government.[13]

Overall, though, most research has not examined how the policymaking agenda affects the public agenda. Policy researchers tend to want to know what causes the policy agenda to change. In the policy world, as in the contemporary communications ecology, information flows in multiple directions (recall Chapter 3).

As we described in Chapter 5, attention is a very valuable commodity in the communication ecology. The same is true in the policy world. Since the news media are influential in determining who or what gets attention, policy scholars Frank Baumgartner and Bryan Jones claim the media are fundamental to an information-processing approach to policymaking.[14] Other approaches threw cold water on the media's role in public policymaking because media were limited in being able to gain the attention of people in the policy world who were doing the hard work of generating policy proposals.[15] Jones and Wolfe argued that Kingdon was ignoring how the media can amplify agendas as much as it can set them.[16] That is, the gatekeeping process signals to others what policy proposals are important and require attention. This effect, however, can also free policymakers who are not getting media attention to move quickly and out of public view. The news media also prime the public to be ready for policy action and can quickly become ensconced in policymaking activities themselves, as Cook and others argued above. Indeed, media attention can actually slow down the speed at which policies get made.

Analyzing the issue of drunk driving between 1978 and 1995, a study found that heightened media attention to the drunk-driving problem at the beginning of the issue's life attracted greater policy attention to this issue. It also had the effect of pressuring policy makers to generate immediate, short-term solutions to the problem. However, as the volume of media attention to this issue started to wane in the late 1980s forward, policy preferences gradually shifted to long-term solutions to solve the problem of drunk driving.[17]

Policy change attempts are often spurred by a focusing event, such as an oil spill, earthquake, or mass shooting. Media coverage of the event can bring about enthusiasm for change in the early days of the reporting.[18] Of course, not all coverage is the same. Fleeting coverage makes sustained interest unlikely by the public, and possibly by the government. Explosive coverage (recall the alarm/patrol hybrid model discussion in Chapter 1) can turn into patrol coverage, sustaining public interest long after the focusing event explosion has dissipated. These events provide narrow windows of opportunity for strategic politicians and government officials to reframe an issue. When an issue leaps onto the agenda and people look to the news media's interpretation function to help make sense of it (see Chapter 1), the chance to reframe an issue is a chance to set policy change in motion.

Wolfe and colleagues point out that crime is a good example of this process. In the 1960s, the violent crime rate grew quickly. Media coverage, not surprisingly, did as well. Even though the public started to worry more about economic issues by the mid-1970s (causing concern about crime to drop) media and congressional actors remained interested in crime. Federal spending to address violent crime increased in the 1960s and after stagnating for a bit began to rise quickly in the 1980s. As Wolfe et al. point out,

> Media coverage was an important component of this "crime policy ratchet," but it neither constructed the crime wave nor caused the policymaking agenda to shift . . . (it became) a cause of policy itself, as it feeds back into the cycle of coverage, public attention, elite focus and policymaking commitment.[19]

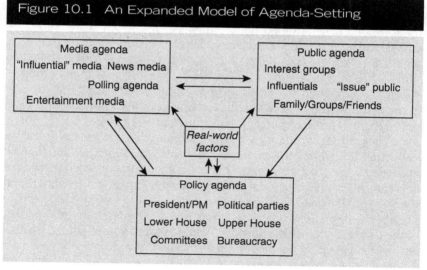

Figure 10.1 An Expanded Model of Agenda-Setting

Source: Stuart N. Soroka. (2002). "Issue Attributes and Agenda-Setting by Media, the Public and Policymakers in Canada," *International Journal of Public Opinion Research* 14(3): 264-285.

Political communication scholar Stuart Soroka's expanded model of the agenda-setting process considers the media, public, and policy agendas as influencing each other, all while being affected by real-world factors (see Figure 10.1).[20]

This model is useful to understand how a variety of factors relevant to media attention dynamics affect public policy. These include venue shopping, attribute intrusion, and framing.[21]

Venue Shopping

Political scientist E.E. Schattschneider famously argued that whoever is able to define the scope of conflict has the advantage in any political situation. With respect to public policy, most work is done in what are referred to as policy subsystems (the stakeholders, lawmakers, interest groups, and other actors who are dealing with a policy problem). Sometimes, it is to the advantage of someone who has a policy goal to, as Schattschneider would say, expand the scope of conflict.

For example, if your neighbors host loud parties on their deck every Thursday night—parties that keep you from being able to get a good night's sleep before your classes or work on Friday morning—you might begin by appealing to their good nature and asking them to quiet down. If that does not work, you expand the scope of conflict to see if other neighbors have the same complaint. If they do, but those complaints do not move your noisy neighbors to quiet down, you might expand the scope of conflict to your city government or state legislature to advocate for a policy remedy in the form of a neighborhood noise ordinance. You might share your story with a local reporter who could chronicle your ongoing battle for a peaceful night's sleep and tie your quest to a larger set of issues. With each expansion of the scope of conflict, more actors become involved in the problem. When that happens, there are more opportunities to change the status quo. In the policy world, the news media can often galvanize public interest and define the problem as a public problem instead of a private one.

Policy can get made in a variety of venues. At the federal level, we know that Congress, the executive branch, and the Supreme Court can all make decisions that can affect the lives of millions. In our federal system of government, venues also exist at the state, municipal, and neighborhood levels. Typically, policy advocates shop around for the venue that looks to provide the best chance for victory. You would not start with the President of the United States with your noise complaint, but you might start with a city councilperson or neighborhood association president.

At higher levels of government problems are often defined by symbols.[22] Sometimes, these symbols come in the form of people who are exemplars of a policy problem. You might have noticed that presidents tend to invite a small number of people to the State of the Union address each year. There, the president tells the person's story and ties it to a larger issue that is part of a policy proposal the president wants Congress to consider in the upcoming term. Of course, getting mentioned in the State of the Union address is something that only happens to precious few policy ideas. More often, the policy community conducts systematic analyses to generate a recommendation about what to do to solve a problem. The news media can motivate various policy communities to get involved, expanding the scope of conflict. One example of this is the issue of child abuse, which, with academic research and the news media's help, redefined the issue to be a public problem rather than a private one. Once it was a public problem, a public remedy from the government became possible.[23]

Attribute Intrusion

One strategy policy entrepreneurs seek to use the media for is to redefine problems.[24] Policy scholars often think about a choice space—made up of the issues facing a legislature. A second space is called an attribute space. This space is one in which there can be multiple definitions of the same issue (recall Chapter 7's discussion of framing).[25] For example, in Wisconsin in 2019, Republicans in the state legislature attempted to redefine the abortion issue in a way that required a policy protecting newborns who were born in a failed abortion attempt. Doctors noted that first, this is incredibly rare, and second, there are already laws in place that provide protections to newborns and levy penalties on doctors who do not give appropriate medical care to such babies.[26] What matters, as was the case with framing effects, is the weights people place on the various attributes of an issue—weights that can change quickly during a public policy debate occurring in the news media.

One area of disconnect between policy entrepreneurs and the news media in the problem definition phase of a policy is that the policy people are looking for a problem defined by government sources and the news media are looking for the most newsworthy definitions of a problem, regardless of their policy relevance.[27] As Wolfe and colleagues argued,

> The policy process tradition underscores the importance of *changes* in issues—their corresponding images and ideas—to explain how the policy agenda is set and how it evolves. How do the media matter in changing or transforming policies? Changes in policy images, especially from positive to negative, can lead to policy change. Nuclear power is a classic example. At first, policies in this issue area were made in subsystems, as the idea of nuclear power was imbued with positive images of economic growth and prosperity. Nuclear power appeared on the macropolitical agenda

and was severely limited when concern over health risks and environmental disasters transformed the issue into one with a negative image.[28]

As issues get understood in a different way, the weights people apply to different definitions of the policy problem change.[29] This is not to say that news coverage changes what congresspeople, state legislators, presidents, or governors think. It is, however, to note that the news media can affect what lawmakers choose to pay attention to and how they pay attention to it.

Framing and Policy Change

At first, framing seems like a peculiar way for a public policy to be affected by the news media. Classic policy research has tended to find that news coverage had little effect on what lawmakers and government staffers chose to prioritize.[30] However, if the news media devoted no attention to an issue, it is difficult to imagine a large group of citizens getting mobilized around it for a sustained period of time. Just as framing effects are not present in all contexts, policy-framing effects should only be expected in particular circumstances. Major shifts in media attention are often associated with changes in policy frames—a crucial factor in the policy change process that considers an issue's salience and definition, agenda-setting, negotiation, and policy change.

Policy experts tend to enter into conversations about policy change believing that they understand how people think about the issue already.[31] This makes the job of issue redefinition harder. Sometimes, that redefinition can come by changing how different partisan actors choose to think about the issue. When interest groups began pushing partisans to take clear positions on the abortion issue in the 1970s and 1980s, the parties initially resisted. Both parties had large numbers of pro-life and pro-choice voters. Media coverage of the issue, activist pressure on partisans, and leadership from the parties' presidential candidates led to a different public conversation on abortion. It was not that people's attitudes changed about the issue, it was that the parties now offered competing positions on the issue, making it easier for people who cared deeply about abortion to find the party that was right for them.[32]

That said, issues can get redefined over time via framing. In their comprehensive analysis of fifty years of issue frames covered with respect to the death penalty, a group of researchers found that a new frame, focusing on the innocence of some death row inmates, rose during the 1990s. They found that the *salience*, *resonance*, and *persistence* of different frames were important factors that affected public opinion and policy change. Their unique analytic strategy allowed them to identify *clusters of arguments*

| Photo 10.1 Death Penalty Opposition Grows in Unlikely Places

about the death penalty within a large database of newspaper stories. This allowed them to see when the innocence theme began to rise, but also how that frame was reported on in concert with other arguments about capital punishment, like racial injustice and inadequate legal representation. Of course, several other frames would enter into and fall out of conversation over the decades. When the innocence frame gained traction, however, it spurred clear policy changes. States introduced moratoriums on the death penalty. States executed fewer people. States sentenced fewer people to capital punishment.[33]

Framing efforts do not end after legislation has been enacted or policy changed. Policy advocates who were unsuccessful in achieving their policy aims continue to advocate for their preferred outcomes. They do so by altering their framing strategies. An example of this was studied by analyzing ten congressional committee hearings held between 1957 and 2006 pertaining to federal funding regarding water policy in North Dakota. The initial frames emphasized the benefits to be derived from water diversion, while subsequent frames redefined the issue via a more defensive posture that emphasized the limited harm that water policy would cause.[34] This is not to say that problem redefinition results in grounding issues in greater scientific depth. An analysis of North Dakota state legislative and US congressional committee hearings preceding the authorization of a water policy involving the popular Devils Lake revealed that state and federal legislators were each equally likely to invoke constituents' localized concerns in framing arguments, and scientific evidence was not persuasive in either state or federal hearings.[35]

Who Leads Whom?

Relationships between mass media, the public, and policymakers are at the center of political life. These interactions affect a wide range of research interests, including the media's role in opinion formation and public policy, and the degree to which public policy follows or leads public opinion. In a study of Canadian policymaking, the factor that affected who led whom was *issue attributes*. Political communication scholar Stuart Soroka found that agenda-setting is systematically linked to issue attributes. A study of inflation, the environment, and the debt/deficit showed that the news media leads for the latter two issues only. Media influence's real potential appears restricted for issues that the public experiences directly.

That is, the news media's policymaking role was stronger for environmental and debt/deficit issues. Regarding the environment, effects between media, public, and policy agendas moved in multiple directions. The debt/deficit issue, on the other hand, displayed very strong media effects on the public. For this issue, policymakers initiated the rise in issue salience—an important finding, since there has not been much research on public agenda-setting that has sought to empirically connect the policy, media, *and* public agendas.

An analysis of policymaking in Denmark over a two-decade time frame found that the news media could affect the agendas of political parties when it was in the parties' interests. That is, news coverage to an issue a party owned (see Chapter 9) was an issue that parties expressed willingness to continue raising publicly. An understanding of party politics is essential to unpacking when the news media are likely to lead a policy change process.[36]

In a study from Nayla Fawzi, media coverage was shown to strongly influence the political agenda. However, the subsequent formulation, evaluation, and termination of policy stages were also affected by the news media. Only the implementation stage of the policy process was less susceptible to media influence. The different groups of political actors and journalists surveyed in Fawzi's study generally agreed upon the estimations of the strength of the media effects as well.[37]

The Media Ecology and Foreign Policy

It is well known that the digital revolution puts more information into the hands of typical individuals than ever before in human history. One surprising consequence of this fact has been the emergence of a number of serious challenges to the capacities of individuals to learn what they need to know to be good democratic citizens. Despite relatively easy access to virtually limitless access to the entire universe of human knowledge, most contemporary Americans know *less* about public affairs than at any time since it has been fairly accurately measured (around World War II).[38]

Elites historically enjoyed a great deal of latitude on foreign policy issues, especially in the early stages of foreign policy events. The changing media environment (see Chapters 2 and 3) appears to have altered the relationships between the three key actors—citizens, elites, and the media—with important implications for how well citizens can constrain their leaders in foreign policy. The media changes appear to erode democratic constraint on foreign policy. This means that democracies are less democratic when it comes to foreign affairs.

Shana Gadarian found that foreign policy views among the public change dramatically when the information environment is emotionally powerful as compared to being free from emotional language. Citizens who were concerned about terrorism became more likely to adopt hawkish foreign policy views they saw communicated in threatening news stories when that policy was matched with fear-inducing cues. This reveals that the role of the media is broader than simply providing a conduit for elites to speak to the public on foreign policy matters; the news media influences the public through their own means of storytelling as well.[39]

Journalistic Methods That Contribute to Policy Action

Since the news media play a large role in constructing political reality for the citizenry, the way they engage in investigative reporting and other kinds of news coverage that can affect public policy is important.

A classic example of improper behavior took place in 2004. *60 Minutes* broke a story about President George W. Bush's service in the National Guard. Mired in a tough reelection fight, the story did Bush no favors, claiming that his status as the son of George H.W. Bush helped him get a national guard commission during the 1970s—a commission that the story alleged he did not even appropriately fulfill.

It turned out that the key source in the story was flawed. Upon learning this, CBS began an investigation that resulted in them retracting their story. CBS news anchor Dan Rather resigned shortly thereafter as did other people working high up at CBS. It turned out that CBS did not make any effort to investigate the background of the source who had *leaked* documents that appeared damning to Bush. The documents were fakes.

Even media behavior that ends up revealing actual uncomfortable truths about people can be problematic. NBC's popular "To Catch a Predator" segment on *Dateline NBC* would lure men to come to a location where the man thought he would be meeting up with a young girl. Sometimes, the men would show up and be *caught* on camera as a sexual predator. While sexual predators are undeniably awful, one of the men on the show committed suicide after it was clear that his identity could become known. The network argued it had done nothing wrong though a judge told NBC they had crossed a line by engaging in a reckless foray into law enforcement.

From Research to Real Life

The news media's role in public policy affects US politics in ways that influence lawmakers, institutions, and the people more generally. Given the real limits on how news gets produced, this is a serious issue for our collective democratic health. Graber and Dunaway posit that "at the heart of many instances that actively engage newspeople in politics lies the desire to produce exciting news stories" (p. 218).[40] Good journalism, of course, requires good storytelling to bring in an audience. Some scholars advocate for an adaptation of a more narrative framework in journalism to use storytelling to frame public policy issues.[41] Whether journalists' own ethical standards make it more or less likely that they will be good at governing with the news is an open question.

How can you use the information in this chapter to advance your own political and social goals? Thinking about the news media as a governing institution alerts you to the value that getting your perspective covered in the news can bring to your policy agenda. For example, you know that journalists use Twitter to troll for examples of public opinion, including tweets in their stories to highlight a modern *person on the street* perspective. So tweet. Tag the journalists covering the beat that matters to you. Write letters to the editor—the evidence continues to show that these efforts to include yourself in the public conversation are important. Respond to candidates social media feeds to have the chance to shape how they interpret whether their messaging is landing in the way that they had hoped. Think about which venue is most appropriate for your message and then spend some time crafting a message for that venue. Show up to local government meetings and consider running for a local office or volunteering for a local board, activist group, or political party. Using your political communication skills to advocate for what you believe is right is a high calling.

Sue Robinson, University of Wisconsin-Madison

Robinson, S. (2017). *Networked news, racial divides: How power and privilege shape public discourse in progressive communities.* New York, NY: Cambridge University Press.

Sue Robinson is Helen Firstbrook Franklin Professor of Journalism at the University of Wisconsin-Madison. Robinson is author of more than thirty books, articles, and chapters examining how journalists and news organizations use new technologies to conduct public affairs reporting and how audiences can use these new technologies for civic engagement. Her book won the James Tankard Award from the Association for Education in Journalism and Mass Communication in 2019. She is past winner of the AEJMC Krieghbaum Under-40 Award. She teaches courses in journalism studies, qualitative research methods, reporting, multimedia and social media, and social justice. She advises The Black Voice and the National Association for Black Journalists at UW-Madison. Our conversation, conducted over email, is below:

Wagner and Perryman: What are some of the ways that privilege shaped discourse in the communities you studied?

Robinson: When you have a public discourse shaped by a dominant ideology that has been in place for a very long time, privilege manifested:

- when those schooled in the evidence, discourse protocols and ways of speaking that the policymakers most valued could effectively dominate the public conversation;

- for those who were networked online and offline with those in power via the same kind of communication channels;

- when those in charge of major communication vehicles (like journalists or public information officers) had their own routines, norms and constraints that tended to amplify voices of the status quo while not always being inclusive of marginalized people who didn't follow their rules of participation.

Wagner and Perryman: As a white woman, how did you build trust with the various communities that were the focus of your research?

Robinson: Very, very slowly and poorly at first. It took me a year to even realize I needed to build trust in ways that were different than how I had been taught to do so as a white reporter and white researcher. Then it took me more time to actually do the work I needed to do on myself, to identify how my own

(Continued)

privileges and biases were shaping the research and the way I asked questions and understood the answers. I went to social justice conferences, audited classes, read books, and mostly just listened to understand that Whiteness was indeed something that was interfering with my own work—not to mention my personal life. Then I started volunteering around town, expanding my social circle, and immersing myself in different communities to build trust.

Wagner and Perryman: What did your book teach you about what it is we should be doing to amplify the voices of all people, build trust and tackle the major problems you chronicled in your book?

Robinson: It taught me first that we white people who have power need to listen to people who do not look or think like us with an open mind, to try out suggestions that we would otherwise dismiss immediately, and to step aside so that our own voice does not drown out someone else's. The process of doing this book, for example, forced me to rethink how I was training journalists as a professor and that I needed to teach them how to help marginalized folks to amplify their perspectives using mainstream, public communication channels while giving up some control over the story. This—as you can imagine—is very controversial idea in mainstream journalism circles.

Wagner and Perryman: For students interested in doing their own research projects examining public dialogues about racial inequality and opportunities for better discourse in their communities, where do you recommend they start? What about students looking to cover these issues for their school paper?

Robinson: First, the student needs to be introspective and explore their own identities, privileges and biases so they do not fall into the trap of thinking they understand race in discourse without truly getting it. If they identify as white, I recommend they check out their local YWCA chapter or Urban League for racial justice courses and begin reading books like the New Jim Crow or Warmth of Other Suns, or White Fragility or any of the excellent scholarship around race and public discourse. If they are of a different race other than white, it is still important to recognize how "other" they might appear to people not in academia, not of their particular education level or race or gender or politics or religion or able-bodiedness etc. That beginning work is priority for both academics and journalists, in my opinion. Then I would start listening to people who have been doing the work for a while. Ask them for introductions. Show up to their functions (and not just to the interview you scheduled). Offer to show them their words before publication. Follow-up with them after the project is done to let them know what happened to their efforts. Offer to pitch in with whatever they are working on. Check the inevitable defensiveness. Be authentic. And be willing to stay in the room even when it might get uncomfortable.

How Can I Help?

The Honorable Adam Morfeld, Nebraska State Senator and Executive Director of Civic Nebraska

Adam Morfeld is a two-term state senator in Nebraska. He also runs the successful nonprofit organization Civic Nebraska, which he founded as an undergraduate student at the University of Nebraska-Lincoln (and wrote a senior honor's thesis coadvised by one of the authors of this book). Civic Nebraska employs more than eighty Nebraskans who work to build civic leadership skills, improve civic life in communities, and pursue nonpartisan and modern elections. Even as a successful, highly experienced veteran of politics, Morfeld is only 34. We talked with him about both of his jobs over email.

Wagner and Perryman: What motivated your civic engagement at such a young age?

Morfeld: Compared to many of younger elected colleagues, I actually feel as though I was behind the curve in getting involved in politics and civic engagement only until after I was twenty—many of them had been volunteering for candidates and non-profits since their early teens. What sparked it for me was coming to college at the University of Nebraska-Lincoln after working a few years full-time as a grocery manager. I arrived at UNL and everyone around me was involved politically, involved in student government, and generally excited about advocating for something. So I ran for student government, interned for a political party, and realized that issue based advocacy was what excited me, which is what led me to run for the Legislature and start my non-profit, Civic Nebraska.

Wagner and Perryman: You are an active social media user, conversing with your constituents—whether they agree with you or not. How do you approach using social media and do you think other public servants should do more engaging with the "other side" on social media platforms?

Morfeld: For elected officials who use it, social media *can* be a powerful tool for constituent engagement and advocacy. Like any tool, it must be used responsibly, and it cannot be given outsized consideration in terms of gauging public opinion in your district without context. In terms of my approach with social media, I use it more broadly disseminate my yearly constituent updates and newsletters, while also providing daily and breaking updates on legislation that I believe is important to my district. It also allows me to

(Continued)

(Continued)

discuss issues with constituents either publicly or privately through direct messaging. In terms of debating my legislative colleagues, there is an unwritten rule that we save the debates for the floor of the legislature, but for executive branch officials that I do not have the opportunity to confront in legislative debate I will express my support or opposition to their actions via social media, just as I do in a press release or comments to the media. It's an important part of communicating ideas and policy positions. I think elected officials who do not use social media at all are really doing a disservice to their constituency—especially their young voters who often do not consume news the same ways as older constituents.

Wagner and Perryman: What skills have been the most useful to you when it comes to 1) campaigning for office and 2) when it comes to governing?

Morfeld: The skills most important when campaigning for office are the ability to briefly tailor and communicate what you stand for and your ideas in a way that resonates with your voters, but most importantly, doing more listening than talking. When you knock on a door or make a phone call to a voter, you should spend 10 percent of your time talking about who you are and what you want to do, and 90 percent of the time listening to the concerns, dreams, and hopes of the voter. All too often people both young and old running for office think that it is all about big speeches, radio ads, and fancy fundraisers. Unless you are running for US Congress, US Senate, or a statewide office, most of the time during a campaign is about door to door interactions, phone banking, and just talking to people. If you are not willing to connect directly with voters, then go find a different passion or line of work.

When it comes to governing, the most important skills are your ability to listen to other elected officials and key stakeholders values and goals, and then connect their values with your values—even when it seems as though you are worlds apart. That ability to connect your values with others values will allow you to find common ground, forge consensus, and in the end advance public policy. Those are the successful policymakers—the ones that do more listening than talking and bring people together. It happens more often than not on the state, local, and even federal level—we just don't hear a lot about it because it is not sexy.

Wagner and Perryman: What are the similarities and differences regarding your communication goals and behaviors when it comes to your day job at Civic Nebraska and regarding your public service as Senator Morfeld?

Morfeld: I keep my personal non-profit capacity and my official legislative capacity strictly separate since I was elected to the legislature. I think it is important to keep them separate—as I take positions as a state senator that have nothing to do with my non-profit and quite frankly are issues that my non-profit likely would not take a position on. Being the executive director of a civic leadership and civic health non-profit often involves a lot less taking positions on issues, and more building consensus, asset mapping, and empowering others to identify their passions and goals for their community. Whereas, in my role as a state senator, I am more focused on representing my community, taking positions on issues that I feel are important to them, and then building consensus internally among my colleagues. It is a different goal and different mission.

Wagner and Perryman: What skills are most important for your staff members in the legislature to have? What about those who work with you at Civic Nebraska?

Morfeld: Some of the most successful staff members in the legislature are those who deeply understand the process and can anticipate their senator's needs based on the process and the issue their legislator advocating for. Often times being in the legislature is like drinking out of a fire hose—so many complex issues coming at a legislator in one day, and the legislator is focused on understanding the issues, keeping track of votes, and finding consensus. So having someone who understands the legislative process, keeping track of that process, and anticipating your needs based on that is critical. This requires someone who has strong analytical, detail, and research skills. I would say a person that works at Civic Nebraska must possess those three skills as well, but given that we do civic leadership and civic health work, they must also be a really good listener and consensus builder.

The Future of Mediated Politics

THE YEAR IS 2040. What social media platform is all the rage? Is social media even a thing anymore, or are we all communicating via hologram? How do people get news? Is *The New York Times* still in business? Has Google Glass made a comeback? How does the president communicate with voters? Do we still elect the president with the Electoral College? How has our system of government changed?

Many of us like to think the future offers an abundance of opportunity for political communication to help set us upon a productive, positive path for the future. Others of us prefer to worry about the swamps and chasms that might thwart our trip along the path of changes in political communication.[1] No one can predict our future political culture or what technology will bring, but one goal of research is to understand how human nature, context, culture, and the structure of media and political institutions produce observable effects—that is, researchers hope that by understanding the way things are, we can apply those lessons to how things *will be*. There are reasons to suspect that some of the phenomena we see in today's political communication will prevail and others might adapt to new environments. Entirely new effects may emerge, or new technology or major shifts in our political system could make some effects obsolete. In this chapter, we will discuss major questions and issues facing elected officials, citizens, and journalists in the arena of political communication today—and reflect on a small range of changes we might see in the years to come.

New Technology

We're always finding new ways to communicate. Before 2004, no one (well, perhaps aside from Mark Zuckerberg) could have imagined a website that would give you the chance to watch your high school classmates, colleagues, and grandma all interact on a single post. In fact, people might have wondered what a post was. And it wasn't so long ago where you wouldn't have learned about breaking news from your smartphone buzzing in your pocket, but instead would have found out hours later when you turned on the nightly news. Communication technology changes are rapid and relentless.

Some of the questions we'll be asking in the field of media and politics in the next decade will center on how lawmakers, journalists, and citizens adapt to new technology. In journalism, researchers are looking into how reporters can use virtual reality, drones, and 360 cameras to enhance their reporting. In politics, microtargeting technologies make it easier to identify pockets of persuadable voters and design messages especially for them. Online, emerging social media platforms will give voters new ways to engage in, or avoid, political discussions.

As you learned in Chapter 5, scholarship provides mixed results as to whether social media has been a positive thing for political participation and deliberative political talk. Research will continue to look at how social media impacts politics, digging deeper into *when* it has positive effects and *why*. It will also continue unpacking *for whom* it has positive and negative effects and why. Understanding the likelihood of whether people participate in politics online requires understanding a user's motivations for being on social media (e.g., the uses and gratifications approach), the makeup of their online network, their interest in and knowledge of politics, their personality, and their perception of whether it's normal and acceptable to talk politics. Ultimately, scholars want to know what sorts of online political actions could increase offline political participation, encourage civility, and foster deliberative discussions that bridge divisions rather than exacerbate them. Fresh platforms and features could bring new opportunities to improve the political discussion environment online.

Social media outlets will also continue to play a role in political campaigns and in day-to-day news coverage. News outlets will still need to direct clicks to their websites via social media, though they face an uphill battle as users continue to read only the headlines.[2] Some changes for the social media-news media relationship are already underfoot. For example, Facebook has made changes to try and get more local news in users' feeds. In 2018, it launched the "Today In" feature, which pulls in local news and events to a specific page tailored to a user's geographic location. That feature inadvertently cast a revealing look at news deserts, as the company had trouble finding local news stories to populate the feature for one of every three US users.[3] Facebook is also attempting to bring users more local news by investing $300 million in local news initiatives and organizations (Google also pledged $300 million in news initiatives in 2018).[4] While more local news in the newsfeed is a good thing—there's also reason to be cautious. Recent research shows that 22 percent of the comments sampled from local news outlets' posts on Facebook featured extreme incivility and 19 percent featured rudeness. Over 40 percent of those rude and uncivil comments were personal rather than impersonal.[5] Some news organizations have nixed comment sections on their websites out of consideration for how uncivil discussions can impact perceptions of the content, the news source, or other citizens—but without such an option on Facebook, media outlets may have to invest in moderation or messaging strategies that encourage civil discussion.

As for advertising, Facebook, in particular, will likely be an important avenue for ad dollars in future elections. From April to June 2019, 2020 presidential candidates spent $14 million just on Facebook ads, and we can expect that the A/B message testing executed so successfully by the Trump campaign in 2016 will be used again in future elections, meaning users can expect to see campaign ads tailored to them on their newsfeeds. That personalization of ads will be a trend to watch, as you learned in Chapter 8 that people express discomfort with over-personalized ads. You might also notice more ads from outside groups, not necessarily because there will be more, but because they are more likely to be properly labeled. Facebook and Twitter are now verifying the sponsors of political ads and requiring disclaimers. The change could force nefarious or dark-money groups looking to influence the election to try other tactics, such as using bots to spread their messages on Twitter, or creating pages or groups to reach people on Facebook. Now that Facebook is keeping a library of its approved political ads, content analyses will be able to shed light on whether the new policies helped increase ad transparency. It is our hope that social media giants follow the advice of Rebekah Tromble and Shannon McGregor and work to systematically involve political communication scholars in the decisions the companies make about how they operate in the future.[6]

Elected officials will continue using social media to communicate directly with citizens. Recalling Chapter 5, you know that communication has largely been top-down. Campaigns may benefit from increasing engagement on social media and interacting with users. We may see increasing displays of personality on social media, as the tactic has been successful for Trump. As freshman House member Alexandria Ocasio-Cortez has recently demonstrated, Trump is not unique in being able to command attention through spirited social media activity. One thing to watch for is how changing platform rules impact how elected officials speak to the masses. For example, Twitter rolled out a change in June 2019 to mark tweets from public figures that violate the platform's rules. The tweets will remain on the site, assuming they're determined by Twitter staffers to be in the public's interest, but they'll be hidden from searches and trending topics. This may dull the reach of bombastic and controversial tweets, or it may ultimately draw more attention to them.

Eventually, we may not even be talking about Facebook or Twitter. We already recognize that it is mainly our older former students who we are keeping in touch with on Facebook. Some new social media platform may arrive on the scene, or a major and unforeseen tide will shift and we'll all log off entirely. That seems unlikely, as only 10 percent of Americans currently do not go online.[7]

But one technology we will likely see less of is cable television. According to a report from *Variety*, 34 percent of US households won't have a traditional TV subscription in 2020. The pay TV industry saw a 4 percent decline in 2018 and is looking at a 5 percent dip in 2019 as consumers move toward streaming services like Netflix, Hulu, and Amazon Prime.[8] Cord cutting has yet-to-be-realized consequences for political communication. First, the reach for traditional TV political ads may shrink. You can still get network TV without a cable subscription, but if people are using their TV time to watch Netflix instead of *Nightly News,* campaigns will have to reach those voters some other way (of course, as we discussed in Chapter 8, the ability of those ads to make a difference is uncertain to begin with). Second, TV news, especially local TV news, will eventually have to adapt. Young people aren't consuming local TV news, and they're the most likely group to ditch the cable subscription. Will local TV stations evolve, or will they continue producing a news product that's attractive only to an aging audience? The formula that has worked for TV news for so long may be fundamentally unappealing to younger audiences who may want a new type of news delivered in a new way (e.g., on-demand mini newscasts available via smartphone, local news apps for smart TVs). These seismic shifts in technology preferences and audience profiles will be an immense challenge for the broadcast TV industry over the next few decades.

The Public–News Media Relationship

Expanding News Options

The digital revolution led to an explosion of online news sources. Not only do traditional outlets (e.g., CNN, NBC News) maintain websites, social media pages, and apps, digital-native news sources have aggressively staked out online territory. These outlets (e.g., The Huffington Post, Vox, Politico, and Buzzfeed) aren't associated with a traditional newspaper, radio station, or TV channel. While television is still the most popular way to get news (49 percent of Americans *often* get news via TV), news websites (33 percent *often* get news this way) and social media (20 percent use it *often* to get news) are catching up.[9] During the 2016 election, 14 percent of Americans said social media was their most helpful election information source—on par with the number of people who named local TV news as their main source of information.[10] Communication scholars will be keeping an eye on whether the trend toward getting political information online, through social media, or via smartphone apps will eventually overpower traditional media channels.

The growing buffet of news sources hasn't necessarily made it easier for people to stay up to date on the news. In fact, a 2018 report from the Knight Foundation and Gallup found that 58 percent of Americans say that the plethora of information sources available makes it harder to stay informed.[11] Another study showed that 68 percent of Americans feel worn out by the amount of news available.[12] Some scholars worry that the ubiquity of today's media environment will lead to *news avoidance*, where citizens actively dodge news media. Some polls show that's already happening: the Reuters Institute found that nearly 40 percent of Americans *often* or *sometimes* avoid the news.[13] Researchers Ruth Palmer and Benjamin Toff argue that increasing political polarization could make news avoidance more common, asking, "How does one strike the right balance between staying informed and tending to the intellectual and emotional burdens that increasingly accompany it?"[14]

And with the increasing number of news sources overall . . . comes an increasing number of partisan news sources. An analysis from *Axios* shows an uptick in the number of left-leaning partisan sites around the time of George W. Bush's presidency, and a similar rise of right-leaning sites during Barack Obama's presidency.[15] Why is partisan news reemerging? The most obvious explanation is access and opportunity; the digital frontier has provided a chance for any budding publication—including partisan ones—to stake out a piece of online real estate. There's also the economic argument. *Fox News*, the long-time ratings leader in cable news, has shown that there's an appetite for partisan news. Demand for partisan content could increase as Americans become increasingly polarized.

One problem researchers need to sort out when exploring the emergence and effects of partisan media is defining it. As we discussed in Chapter 4, defining bias is not straightforward. Researchers are using various methods to identify news outlets as left- or right-leaning. Does *The New York Times* favor Democrats? How do you determine that? If it reports more news that reflects poorly on conservatives, is that bias—or is it merely a reflection of the current political environment? As you continue to hear about how partisan media operate and impact their audiences, it's important to ask yourself: who decided this outlet was partisan and how did they figure that out?

There is, to be sure, a subset of news outlets that we can comfortably label *partisan*. What happens when citizens are exposed to news from places like *Brietbart* or *U.S. Uncut*? Remember, most people tend to get their news from mainstream, nonpartisan sources; so, is it really a problem if the partisan media industry continues to grow, or if it becomes a part of the average Americans' news diet? Markus Prior's research on media habits and political polarization concluded that partisan media do not necessarily cause citizens to support more partisan lawmakers and policies.[16] Other scholars argue that access to partisan media *is* a likely cause of political polarization.[17] Some note that regardless of how partisan media impact those who consume it, the audience for the content is relatively small and consists mainly of strong partisans. And yet, one recent study shows that partisan media can impact those who don't consume it because those who do watch and listen to partisan media tend to spread its message.[18] Additional studies that track media habits and attitudes over time would help us understand the effects of exposure to partisan media.

Fake News and Media Trust

Americans place *made-up news* among the big problems the United States is facing—about the same percentage who call *violent crime* (49 percent) and *the gap between the rich and poor* (51 percent) "big" problems.[19] As we discussed in Chapter 4, truly fake news stories (fabricated information packaged as a news story and intended to deceive) make up a small portion of the news environment. Recall from Chapter 9 the study that found that voters in the 2016 presidential election were exposed to only a handful of fake news stories in the months leading up to the vote,[20] while another study shows fake news consumption was limited to certain subgroups (e.g., 10 percent of the people with the most conservative media diets made up the lion's share of the visits to fake news websites during the election).[21]

But fake news is seen as a problem, and that may present problems of its own. First, in an effort to fix this *big problem*, solutions may have unintended consequences. On the one hand, the rise of fake news has inspired tools like bot detection software that could not only stop the spread of fake news but could also improve the quality of online discussion. On the other hand, concern about fake news could also lead to regulations that might hinder the free flow of information online. Should the government get to decide what counts as *fake*? You can imagine how easily fake news regulation could turn into a tactic to control political speech. Still, it's reasonable to ask what sorts of responsibilities social media companies have in stopping the spread of damaging information. Though social media giants like Facebook and Google have already taken steps to address the spread of damaging information on their platforms, it will be interesting to see whether additional fake-news-fighting measures will be the result of self- or government-ordered regulation.

Of course, scholars will continue to investigate why people fall for false news stories and how fake news impacts the broader media environment (e.g., recall from Chapter 5 that fake news can help define the agenda for partisan news outlets). But researchers will also need to look at how the popularization of the term *fake news* may be impacting perceptions of media in a general sense. Trust in media is still historically low, though it has rebounded a bit, mostly due to attitudes among Democrats.[22] Trump's use of *fake news* as a general insult for the press provides a new way of casting doubt on the accuracy of news stories. Forty percent of Republicans say that news stories that cast a politician or political group in a negative light are *always* fake news.[23]

The term has certainly strayed from its original meaning and is so politically loaded that many pundits and analysts have stopped using it. Still, research into the spread and effects of disinformation will continue, and hopefully, public discussions about the importance of verifying information and sources will continue as well.

Reconsidering Objectivity

The culmination of several current trends in journalism—accusations of media bias, the Trump administration's frequent dishonesty, the popularity of partisan sources, increasing concern about fake news, the shock of the 2016 election results—has prompted a lot of introspection about today's journalism. If the president lies, should journalists call it a lie? If journalists air a negative story about Donald Trump, must they then pursue a negative story about Hillary Clinton? If a journalist seeks out a quote on climate change from a scientist, must they also reach out to a climate change denier for an alternative perspective? Should journalists tell both sides of a story when one of the sides consists of white nationalists, or homophobic groups, or people who falsely believe the Sandy Hook Elementary School shooting was a hoax?

Today's journalists are wrestling with the notions of balance and objectivity. To some, objectivity is a state of being, describing a truly disinterested observer who dutifully reports on whatever is being said with no regard for partisanship. To others, objectivity describes the reporting process, a value-free way of evaluating evidence and presenting it fairly. As Brent Cunningham of the *Columbia Journalism Review* put it, the quest to remain objective can lead to lazy *just the facts* or *both sides* reporting. Instead, he argues that reporters should "develop expertise and to use it to sort through competing claims, identify and explain the underlying assumptions of those claims, and make judgments about what readers and viewers need to know to understand what is happening."[24]

Media ethicist Stephen J.A. Ward argues that journalism should reimagine objectivity. His *pragmatic objectivity* recognizes that journalists are inherently subjective humans who choose which angle to take, which facts to report, which quotes to use, and so on. Like Cunningham, Ward argues that it is the reporting process, not the journalist, which should be objective, likening a journalist to other professions with objective decision-making processes (e.g., scientists, judges). Ward argues that pragmatically objective journalists are impartial only in that "they do not let their partialities or interests undermine objective judgment and inquiry. They do not prejudge the story before fairly weighing all relevant evidence. But after such inquiry, journalists are free to draw an informed conclusion. Such is the method of investigative journalism."[25]

Ask ten journalists how they define objectivity, and you'll likely receive ten different definitions. Journalists may share a dedication to truth finding, fair reporting, and holding the government accountable, but those abstract principles can take on many forms when put into practice. One positive thing that has emerged from the conversation about fake news, media trust, and the difficulties of reporting on the Trump administration is that the conversation is happening in the first place. Journalists, alongside the public, need to think critically about the role of news media in democracy. We should question traditional practices, hold journalists accountable when they fall short—and at the same time—recognize and support the important role than journalists fill. The conversation about the evolution of the modern journalist is far from over.

A Changing News Industry

Aside from philosophical dilemmas, the news media industry also continues to wade through a sea of institutional and structural changes. Revenue continues to be pressing problem, especially for newspapers. Advertising dollars in the newspaper industry were $16.5 billion in 2017—that's down from $49.4 billion in 2005. About 31 percent of newspapers' advertising revenue now comes from digital ads. [26]

News Deserts

According to the Associated Press, 1,400 cities and towns across the United States have lost a local newspaper in the past fifteen years.[27] These are cities like Waynesville, Missouri, and Youngstown, Ohio. Over 170 US counties do not have a local newspaper, and nearly half of all counties have only one newspaper.[28] Countless others have what the University of North Carolina professor Penelope Muse Abernathy calls *ghost papers*: newspapers that still technically exist but lack the resources necessary to actually report the news.[29] Meanwhile, growth in the news industry is mostly in the digital sphere—jobs that are concentrated in urban areas.[30]

What happens to a place when it becomes a news desert? Local news consumption is associated with many positive democratic outcomes, including voter turnout[31] and feeling a connection with one's community.[32] One study found that without newspapers acting as watchdogs on the local government, individual taxpayer bills rose an average of $85.[33] Local TV stations may step up to fill some of the news void, but broadcast media markets typically stretch across multiple cities or counties, and coverage tends to be surface-level, or intensely focused on crime.[34]

Local newspapers appear to be irreplaceable—and preserving those that have survived so far is an uphill battle. As online ad revenue has failed to provide the support that print ads once did, newspapers have tried various ways to bring in dollars. A report from the Tow Center for Digital Journalism outlines seven ways local papers are bringing in money: 1) subscriptions and single copy sales; 2) paywalls and digital subscriptions; 3) event hosting; 4) media services (e.g., building apps and websites); 5) newsletter sponsorship and embedded advertising; 6) paid obituaries; and 7) turning to nonprofits or crowdfunding for support.[35]

While the death of local newspapers in not a new trend, only a quarter of Americans realize that their local news outlets are *not doing well* financially. Only 14 percent say they've paid for local news.[36] Future research will focus on how local news organizations make the case for their own survival and the repercussions for communities living in news deserts.

Mega-Owners

News ownership is increasingly concentrated (see Chapter 2). As of 2016, five companies owned over one-third of local TV news stations.[37] The three largest newspaper chains owned nearly nine hundred newspapers—that's nearly twice as many as the two largest chains held in 2004.[38]

The future of media ownership concentration may rest on how the FCC handles mergers going forward. In 2017, the FCC eased rules on how many stations a broadcaster could own and relaxed restrictions on revenue and resources that stations in a given market could share. The change was widely perceived to be beneficial to Sinclair Broadcasting Company, a conservative ownership group that, at the time, was trying to buy Tribune Media. In a reverse course, the FCC chairman said he had concerns about the merger, and the deal fell through. The merger would have given Sinclair a TV presence in over 70 percent of US households.

That particular deal is off the table, but the relaxed FCC rules regarding media ownership have left the door open for future deals. One FCC change now allows owners to operate stations without a physical, local space—that is, someone can own a station in Missouri but run it from New York. Another change relaxed a rule that prevented TV station owners from owning more than one of the top four stations in a market. Whether the mega-owner is Sinclair or some other group, the idea of a small group of large corporations owning a majority of news outlets is a concerning trend. As you learned in Chapters 5 and 6, mass media can impact which issues people think are important and how they think about those issues. The idea

Hi, I'm [anchor] and I'm [anchor].

Our greatest responsibility is to serve our [local] communities. We are extremely proud of the quality, balanced journalism that [station] produces.

But we're concerned about the troubling trend of irresponsible, one sided news stories plaguing our country. The sharing of biased and false news has become all too common on social media.

More alarming, some media outlets publish these same fake stories . . . stories that just aren't true, without checking facts first.

Unfortunately, some members of the media use their platforms to push their own personal bias and agenda to control 'exactly what people think' . . . This is extremely dangerous to a democracy.

At [station] it's our responsibility to pursue and report the truth. We understand Truth is neither politically 'left nor right.' Our commitment to factual reporting is the foundation of our credibility, now more than ever.

But we are human and sometimes our reporting might fall short. If you believe our coverage is unfair please reach out to us by going to [contact info]. We value your comments. We will respond back to you.

We work very hard to seek the truth and strive to be fair, balanced and factual . . . We consider it our honor, our privilege to responsibly deliver the news every day.

Thank you for watching and we appreciate your feedback.

Source: http://nymag.com/intelligencer/2018/04/anchors-reciting-sinclair-propaganda-is-terrifying-in-unison.html

behind the original FCC rules was to ensure that one person—or company—didn't have a monopoly on the information that a community receives. The Sinclair-Tribune deal may be dead, but watch out for the next one.

Appealing to Audiences

The days where the family gathered around the television to watch the evening news are long gone. Today, audiences get news from their social media newsfeeds, smartphone apps, podcasts, and still for many, through traditional channels like newspapers and local TV stations. The audience is changing. The industry is changing. And finding new ways to connect with increasingly time-stretched consumers in a crowded news environment is a huge challenge facing the journalism industry.

Millennial news habits—or more generally, how younger people get news—are something that elected leaders, researchers, and journalists are very interested in. Younger Americans are more likely than their older counterparts to get news online and via social media. They're far less likely than older news consumers to use newspapers or local, network, and cable news.[39] Will these tendencies change as they age? If they don't, it could certainly spell trouble for traditional news formats, which will either fold or adapt to attract these young news consumers as they age.

Younger news consumers aren't necessarily less interested in news. Some polling shows that only a quarter of those 18 to 29 follow news *most* or *all* the time,[40] while other polling shows nearly 60 percent of that same age group follow news at least once a day.[41] They may also have higher levels of media literacy, demonstrating that they're better than older news consumers at distinguishing fact from opinion,[42] though one study on youth media literacy shows that 82 percent of teens couldn't tell the difference between *sponsored content* and a real news story.[43] Education initiatives that target young news consumers will be increasingly important as technology continues to enable disinformation and misinformation online.

But the major question for the news industry and elected officials will be how to adjust to this new audience. Campaign ads and candidate appearances on network and local TV won't have the same reach. Messaging strategies that work on traditional channels might not be as effective when applied to new media. Issues that do not currently receive much attention in politics or news—student loan debt, stagnant wages, climate change, wealth inequality, and social justice—are important to younger generations. New news organizations will have to prove themselves to be credible to their intended audience.[44] Will media and political priorities evolve to reflect younger generations' interests? As young people filter into newsrooms and crack their way into the political arena, expect changes.

The Great Divide

Americans are divided. Many Democrats and Republicans do not like each other.[45] The two major parties have little overlap when it comes to policy preferences.[46] Members of Congress are increasingly ideological, a trend that doesn't appear likely to reverse course any time soon.[47] What implications will the great divide have for media and politics moving forward?

First, we can expect amplification of two psychological effects: hostile media perception and motivated reasoning. Both could have major impacts on how people choose and respond to political media messages. As you remember from Chapter 7, hostile media perception is a phenomenon where people tend to see mediated information as being hostile to their views. It happens far less often when people evaluate messages from their preferred media sources, but even then, it can still be an issue when audiences evaluate media at large. In other words, people might say, "My media isn't biased against my candidate, but *the media* is."[48] The reason we might expect to see these perceptions become more common is because 1) the perception is more common in heightened *us versus them* scenarios, for which polarization certainly qualifies; and 2) the perception is triggered when people believe others are being negatively impacted by media. Because people sense that the public is divided (in fact, they tend to overestimate polarization) and they know that partisan media exist, they tend to believe others are attracted to news that fits their views.[49] As you can see from Figure 11.1, people are convinced that media coverage has undesirable effects on others. It's a cycle that is hard to break; people see media as biased partly because they're concerned that it has negative effects on others, and simultaneously, the sense that news outlets are a negative influence reinforces the notion that media are biased.

Second, we might expect increasing loyalty to partisan perspectives to amplify motivated reasoning effects. As we discussed in Chapter 7, there are several explanations for partisan motivated reasoning. Some scholars argue that it's an emotions-based phenomenon of biased information processing where the motivation to maintain partisanship overrides the desire

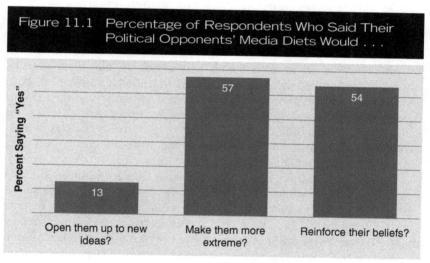

Figure 11.1   Percentage of Respondents Who Said Their Political Opponents' Media Diets Would . . .

Source: Perryman, M. R. (2019). Where the other side gets news: Audience perceptions of selective exposure in the 2016 election. Forthcoming at International Journal of Public Opinion Research.

Note: N = 647[50]

to be accurate or objective. Others show that motivated reasoning is most common among those who demonstrate low levels of analytical thinking—in other words, they argue it is a result of lazy processing.

Either way, we would expect a polarized political environment to exacerbate the tendency to accept only attitude-confirming information. Increasing identification with *your side* and not *the other side* would only make you more motivated to maintain your partisan beliefs at all costs. When emotions are high, emotional processing is expected. Similarly, partisanship is quite salient in a divided political environment. That is, partisanship cues are always around, making it easy to invoke tribalism when interpreting political information. A simple cue of "this is what my side believes" can absolve you from having to analyze incoming information: it either fits, or it doesn't—an ideal context for lazy processing. Political psychologists will continue to explore how the parties and partisanship influence the processing of political information with findings that could have major implications for how politicians and journalists share facts and attempt to correct misinformation.

Media and Politics Post-Trump

2016 Election Lessons for Journalists

Donald Trump's electoral victory has prompted reflection among reporters about how they cover elections. Besides all the traditional problems with coverage (e.g., overwhelmingly negative coverage, horse race coverage), candidate Trump received a huge amount of free (i.e., *earned*) media. By some accounts—as much as $5 billion of it. He was, after all, an unusual candidate, one skilled at commanding attention. As an opinion writer in *The Hill* described it, "For its part, the media, particularly television, has been unable to resist the temptation to cover Trump as a sensational spectacle. The press sees fit to chase every shiny object Trump dangles in front of it."[51] Or as the American Press Institute's Tom Rosenstiel put it, "We need journalists to cover what is important, not bark at every car."[52]

Meanwhile, reporters doggedly reported on Hillary Clinton's use of a private email server while serving as secretary of state. One analysis shows her email scandal received twice as much media attention as all of Trump's scandals combined.[53] As scholar Thomas Patterson concluded in his report on 2016 coverage for the Shorenstein Center (which we dealt with in detail in Chapter 9), Clinton's negative coverage amounted to false equivalency:

> When journalists can't, or won't, distinguish between allegations directed at the Trump Foundation and those directed at the Clinton Foundation, there's something seriously amiss. And false

equivalencies are developing on a grand scale as a result of relentlessly negative news. If everything and everyone is portrayed negatively, there's a leveling effect that opens the door to charlatans. The press historically has helped citizens recognize the difference between the earnest politician and the pretender. Today's news coverage blurs the distinction.[54]

One reason reporters were tough on Clinton was because she was widely considered to be the front-runner, consistently leading in national polls. As we know now, the regular margin of error combined with some pollster errors in several state-level polls was enough to give Trump the win in the Electoral College. Polls are useful tools but also imperfect ones. They provide only a snapshot of voter preferences at a moment in time and are unable to fully account for undecided and reluctant voters. They're also probabilistic, meaning, a Trump win was unlikely, not impossible. To be sure, there was some bad polling in the 2016 election. But as FiveThirtyEight's Nate Silver argues, journalists adopted the Clinton-will-win narrative when polls actually gave her about a 70 percent chance of winning. He chalks some of that up to simple deadline writing—journalists have to write quickly, so adopting a cohesive narrative to frame stories is a matter of convenience. But he also blames confirmation bias, with a lot of journalists simply believing that a candidate like Trump wouldn't prevail: "Presented with a complicated set of facts, it takes a lot of work for most of us not to connect the dots in a way that confirms our prejudices. An editorial culture that emphasizes 'the narrative' indulges these bad habits rather than resists them."[55]

Polls and polling aggregators will continue to play a role in future elections, and reporters will again be in the position where they have to communicate or interpret statistical concepts to the audience. This coverage often falls short. For example, one study found that only about half of analyzed coverage of polls provided the margin of error and of the news stories that did include it, nearly half interpreted it incorrectly.[56] Future reporting should not disregard polls—they are useful tools to understand public opinion—but it should understand their meaning (and limitations). As technology makes polling more accessible than ever before, how polls are reported via news media and the effects of that coverage will continue to be important areas for research.

Some media experts have pushed back on the notion that media coverage failed the voters in the 2016 election. As Susan B. Glasser, who served as *Politico's* editor during the election, argues, "The media scandal of 2016 isn't so much about what reporters failed to tell the American public; it's about what they did report on, and the fact that it didn't seem to matter. Stories that would have killed any other politician . . . did not stop Trump from thriving in this election year."[57]

A Post-Truth Era?

One of the loudest conversations to emerge in the political reporting sphere after the 2016 election was a debate over the notion of a post-truth era. The term refers to a political culture where emotions and partisanship guide what people believe and facts are facts only if they benefit your side (you might notice this sounds a lot like *motivated reasoning*, which you learned about in Chapter 7). Post truth describes a political environment where a shared reality based on evidence-based facts has frayed, replaced by ideologically driven *alternative facts*.

Does that describe our modern political system? To many, the Trump administration's ability to lie without paying a political price is a signal that facts have lost their luster. The argument is not that Trump ushered in an era of freedom from facts, but that he is a product of cultural and political change that has been brewing for years. Author Michiko Kakutani argues that *truth decay* has been happening for decades, and that what we're seeing with modern political Right is a hijacking of postmodern thinking. Postmodernism describes a way of thinking that accepts that there are multiple legitimate ways to understand an event or issue—that is, truth is relative. This way of thinking gave minorities and disenfranchised voices a chance to challenge the status quo, but "it has also been exploited by those who want to make the case for offensive or debunked theories, or who want to equate things that cannot be equated." Kakutani notes that news media have helped this way of thinking along by adhering to the notion of *balance* even when competing perspectives do not offer the same weight of evidence.[58]

At the same time, the birth of the internet gave rise to an abundance of sources, "too many sources, too many methods, with varying levels of credibility, depending on who funded a given study and how the eye-catching number was selected."[59] If they look hard enough (or sometimes not hard at all), people can seemingly find a source to back any view. And if that source conflicts with what the *experts* are saying, that won't be a deal-breaker. As Tom Nichols argues in his book *The Death of Expertise*, Americans have become increasingly uncomfortable with the idea that some opinions are superior to others: "Democracy does not denote a state of actual equality among all human beings, it is a state of political equality. At some point we got it in our heads that every opinion is worth the same."[60]

Another perspective is that Trump's ability to lie with impunity is a symptom of a growing complacency with authoritarianism. Why continue to say things that are not true when you know that someone is going to call you out for it? Many argue it's a show of power: "Every time [Trump] lies, especially when he lies about something really obvious—like the size of the Inauguration—he's saying 'I can say whatever I want, whenever I want to, and there's nothing you can do about it.'"[61] Lee McIntyre, author of *Post-Truth*, says Trump is following an authoritarian playbook, characterized by "leaders lying, the erosion of public institutions and the consolidation of power."[62]

But why, if these forces have been at work for some time, are we just now experiencing a politician who is willing and able to lie so freely? The culprit, Andrew Sullivan writes in *The Intelligencer,* is political tribalism. Not political parties or the Left and Right divide, but

> two tribes where one contains most racial minorities and the other is disproportionately white; where one tribe lives on the coasts and in the cities and the other is scattered across a rural and exurban expanse; where one tribe holds on to traditional faith and the other is increasingly contemptuous of religion altogether; where one is viscerally nationalist and the other's outlook is increasingly global; where each dominates a major political party; and, most dangerously, where both are growing in intensity as they move further apart.[63]

Is there a path forward that restores our faith in facts? Stephan Lewandosky writes that ultimately the post-truth era will end "only when there is sufficient motivation among politicians and the public alike to be well-informed" and "when there are political, social, and professional incentives to adequately inform."[64] That sounds like a tall order. As does any attempt to restore trust in institutions such as the press and Congress that have deteriorated in stature over the decades. Pundits and scholars instead point to information diets, suggesting internet users and social media platforms take steps to pop the filter bubble. But as you learned in Chapter 7, concerns that people are only—or even primarily—interacting with *news that fits their views* may be overblown. Some suggest creating more opportunities for discussion with politically dissimilar others or promoting fact-checks that can adjust misinformed beliefs. But as you learned throughout this book, attempts to broaden others' political perspectives or correct misinformation can be difficult, and sometimes even backfire.

But that doesn't mean that we stop trying. Researchers will continue to explore how to break the bonds of political partisanship over all else, encourage civility, and communicate facts effectively. The answers are complicated and difficult to find, but curiosity will always fuel discovery. Journalists will continue to uncover wrongdoing, relay important issues to the public, and record the first version of history. They'll make mistakes as they adapt to a rapidly changing industry, but hopefully what emerges is a press with a renewed passion for truth. Elected officials will continue fighting for their vision for the country. Some of their efforts won't be in good faith, but those bad actors can be outnumbered by those who truly want a better world.

But the most important players in the future of political communication are the citizens. We must challenge our own ideas, where they come from, and why we think the way we do. We must thirst for information and evaluate incoming messages carefully. And we must continue holding those with the microphone accountable. Citizens should @ their senators, and proudly display Facebook's virtual *I voted* sticker, and push back when they think journalists have missed the mark. Our political system may be currently tainted by negative partisanship, misinformation, and fierce division, but beneath all that, the American experiment has been—and always will be—defined by the engagement of its citizens. Politics may happen in a noisy room, but with a solid understanding of modern communication practices, you can make yourself heard.

Notes

Preface

1. Prior, M. (2007). *Post-broadcast democracy*. New York, NY: Cambridge University Press.

2. Edgerly, S. (2015). "Red media, blue media, and purple media: News repertoires in the colorful media landscape," *Journal of Broadcasting & Electronic Media*, 59(1), 1–21.

3. Converse, P. (1964). The nature of belief systems in mass publics. In D. Apter, (Ed.), *Ideology and Discontent*. New York, NY: The Free Press.

4. Delli Carpini, M. X., & Keeter, S. (1996). *What Americans know about politics and why it matters*. New Haven, CT: Yale University Press; Ferrin, M., Fraile, M., & Garcia-Albacete, G. M. (2019). Adult roles and the gender gap in political knowledge: A comparative study. *West European Politics*.

Chapter 1

1. Strömbäck, J. (2008). Four phases of mediatization: An analysis of the mediatization of politics. *Press/Politics*, 13(3), 228–246.

2. Graber, D. A., & Dunaway, J. (2017). *Mass media and American politics*, 10th ed. Washington, DC: CQ Press.

3. Wagner, M. W., & Gruszczynski, M. (2016). When framing matters: How partisan and journalistic frames affect individual opinions and party identification. *Journalism & Communication Monographs*, 18(1), 5–48.

4. Mutz, D. C. (2006). *Hearing the other side: Deliberative versus participatory democracy*. New York, NY: Cambridge University Press.

5. Graber, D. A., & Dunaway, J. (2017).

6. Patterson, T. E. (2016). Pre-primary news coverage of the 2016 presidential race: Trump's rise, Sanders' emergence, Clinton's struggle. https://shorensteincenter.org/pre-primary-news-coverage-2016-trump-clinton-sanders/

7. Bruni, F. (2019). Will the media be Trump's accomplice in 2020? *The New York Times*. https://www.nytimes.com/2019/01/11/opinion/trump-2020-media.html

8. https://www.theatlantic.com/politics/archive/2016/06/trump-media/487202/

9. https://www.theatlantic.com/ideas/archive/2019/06/bill-barr-calls-intelligence-investigation-spying/591223/

10. https://www.nytimes.com/2018/11/07/upshot/2018-midterms-blue-wave-democrats.html

11. Hughes, C. (2016). It's not easy (not) being green: Agenda dissonance of Green Party press relations and newspaper coverage. *European Journal of Communication*, 31(6), 625–641.

12. Wagner, M. W. (2007). The utility of staying on message: Competing partisan frames and public awareness of elite differences on issues. *The Forum*, 5, 1–18.

13. https://www.nytimes.com/2016/10/20/us/politics/presidential-debate.html

14. https://thehill.com/blogs/ballot-box/presidential-races/302002-trump-jokes-ill-accept-election-results-if-i-win

15. Downs, A. (1957). *An economic theory of democracy*. New York, NY: Harper.

16. Popkin, S. L. (1991). *The reasoning voter: Communication and persuasion in presidential campaigns*. Chicago, IL: University of Chicago Press.

17. Schudson, M. (1999). *The good citizen: A history of American civic life*. Cambridge, MA: Harvard University Press.

18. Zaller, J. (2003). A new standard of news quality: Burglar alarms for the monitorial citizen. *Political Communication, 20*(2), 109–130.

19. Boydstun, A. E. (2013). *Making the news: Politics, the media, and agenda setting*. Chicago, IL: University of Chicago Press.

20. https://www.washingtonpost.com/graphics/2018/politics/kavanaugh-ford-hearing-chyrons/?utm_term=.277a4fd28586

21. https://www.npr.org/2018/10/03/654054108/poll-more-believe-ford-than-kavanaugh-a-cultural-shift-from-1991

22. Theiss-Morse, E. A., Wagner, M. W., Flanigan, W. H., & Zingale, N. H. (2018). *Political behavior of the American electorate*, 14th ed. Washington, DC: CQ Press.

23. Vavreck, L. (2009). *The message matters: The economy and presidential campaigns*. Princeton, NJ: Princeton University Press.

24. Freedman, P., Franz, M., & Goldstein, K. (2004). Campaign advertising and democratic citizenship. *American Journal of Political Science, 48*(4), 723–741.

25. Strach, P., Zuber, K., Fowler, E. F., Ridout, T. N., & Searles, K. (2015). In a different voice? Explaining the use of men and women as voice-over announcers in political advertising. *Political Communication, 32*(2), 183–205.

26. Eveland Jr, W. P., Hayes, A. F., Shah, D. V., & Kwak, N. (2005). Understanding the relationship between communication and political knowledge: A model comparison approach using panel data. *Political Communication, 22*(4), 423–446.

27. Kim, S. H. (2008). Testing the knowledge gap hypothesis in South Korea: Traditional news media, the internet, and political learning. *International Journal of Public Opinion Research, 20*(2), 193–210.

28. Jerit, J. (2009). Understanding the knowledge gap: The role of experts and journalists. *The Journal of Politics, 71*(2), 442–456.

29. Stroud, N. J. (2017). Attention as a valuable resource. *Political Communication, 34*(3), 479–489.

30. Gruszczynski, M., & Wagner, M. W. (2017). Information flow in the 21st century: The dynamics of agenda-uptake. *Mass Communication and Society, 20*(3), 378–402.

31. Druckman, J. N. (2004). Political preference formation: Competition, deliberation, and the (ir) relevance of framing effects. *American Political Science Review, 98*(4), 671–686.

32. Wagner, M. W., & Gruszczynski, M. (2016). When framing matters: How partisan and journalistic frames affect individual opinions and party identification. *Journalism & Communication Monographs, 18*(1), 5–48.

33. McLeod, J. M., Scheufele, D. A., & Moy, P. (1999). Community, communication, and participation: The role of mass media and interpersonal discussion in local political participation. *Political Communication, 16*(3), 315–336.

34. Wolfsfeld, G., Yarchi, M., & Samuel-Azran, T. (2016). Political information repertoires and political participation. *New Media & Society, 18*(9), 2096–2115.

35. Schudson, M. (1999).

36. https://www.psychologytoday.com/us/blog/home-base/201606/in-defense-Millennials

37. Chu, Y. H., & Welsh, B. (2015). Millennials and East Asia's democratic future. *Journal of Democracy, 26*(2), 151–164.

38. https://www.pewresearch.org/fact-tank/2019/05/29/gen-z-Millennials-and-gen-x-outvoted-older-generations-in-2018-midterms/

39. https://www.theatlantic.com/sponsored/allstate/when-it-comes-to-politics-do-Millennials-care-about-anything/255/; Milkman, R. (2017). A new political generation: Millennials and the post-2008 wave of protest. *American Sociological Review, 82*(1), 1–31.

40. Shah, D. V., McLeod, J. M., & Lee, N. J. (2009). Communication competence as a foundation for civic competence: Processes of socialization into citizenship. *Political Communication, 26*(1), 102–117.

41. Kahne, J., & Westheimer, J. (2003). Teaching democracy: What schools need to do. *Phi Delta Kappan, 85*(1), 34–66.

42. Edgerly, S. (2017). Seeking out and avoiding the news media: Young adults' proposed strategies for obtaining current events information. *Mass Communication and Society, 20*(3), 358–377. doi: 10.1080/15205436.2016.1262424

43. Wells, C. (2015). *The civic organization and the digital citizen: Communicating engagement in a networked age.* New York, NY: Oxford University Press.

Chapter 2

1. Graber, D. A., & Dunaway, J. (2017). *Mass media and American politics,* 10th ed., Washington, DC: CQ Press.

2. Bennett, W. L. (2009). *News: The politics of illusion.* New York, NY: Pearson Longman.

3. Epstein, E. J. (1973). *News from nowhere.* New York, NY: Vintage.

4. https://www.pbs.org/newshour/show/viral-video-raises-worry-over-sinclairs-political-messaging-inside-local-news; https://www.nbcnews.com/nightly-news/video/tv-anchors-decrying-fake-news-puts-spotlight-on-sinclair-broadcast-group-1200738371824

5. https://www.newsweek.com/democratic-debate-full-transcript-miami-435555

6. https://www.pbs.org/newshour/politics/trump-asked-russia-to-find-clintons-emails-on-or-around-the-same-day-russians-targeted-her-accounts

7. Bennett, W. L. (1990). Toward a theory of press-state relations in the United States. *Journal of Communication, 40*(2), 103–127; Bennett, W. L. (1996). An introduction to journalism norms and representations

of politics. *Political Communication,* 13(4), 373–384.

8. Althaus, S. L., Edy, J. A., Entman, R. M., & Phalen, P. (1996). Revising the indexing hypothesis: Officials, media, and the Libya crisis. *Political Communication,* 13(4), 407–421; Hayes, D., & Guardino, M. (2010). Whose views made the news? Media coverage and the march to war in Iraq. *Political Communication,* 27(1), 59–87.

9. Patterson, T. E. (1994). *Out of order.* New York, NY: Vintage.

10. Groeling, T. (2010). *When politicians attack: Party cohesion in the media.* Cambridge, UK: Cambridge University Press; Groeling, T., & Baum, M. A. (2009). Journalists' incentives and media coverage of elite foreign policy evaluations. *Conflict Management and Peace Science,* 26(5), 437–470.

11. Entman, R. M. (2003). Cascading activation: Contesting the White House's frame after 9/11. *Political Communication,* 20(4), 415–432; Hayes, D., & Guardino, M. (2013). *Influence from abroad: Foreign voices, the media, and US public opinion.* Cambridge, UK: Cambridge University Press.

12. Barnhurst, K. G., & Mutz, D. (1997). American journalism and the decline in event-centered reporting. *Journal of Communication,* 47(4), 27–53.

13. de Vreese, C. H. (2014). Mediatization of news: The role of journalistic framing. In *Mediatization of politics* (pp. 137–155). London, UK: Palgrave Macmillan.

14. Bennet, W. L. (2009). *News: The politics of illusion.* New York, NY: Pearson Longman.

15. https://www.journalism.org/fact-sheet/newspapers/

16. Weaver, D. H., Willnat, L., & Wilhoit, G. C. (2019). The American journalist in the digital age: Another look at US news people. *Journalism & Mass Communication Quarterly,* 96(1), 101–130.

17. Graham, J., Haidt, J., & Nosek, B. A. (2009). Liberals and conservatives rely on different sets of moral foundations. *Journal of Personality and Social Psychology,* 96(5), 1029.

18. https://www.washingtonpost.com/blogs/erik-wemple/wp/2017/01/27/dear-mainstream-media-why-so-liberal/?utm_term=.71b8e6101914 https://www.cjr.org/first_person/republicans-media.php

19. McGregor, S. C., & Molyneux, L. (2018). Twitter's influence on news judgment: An experiment among journalists. *Journalism.* https://doi.org/10.1177/1464884918802975

20. https://www.cjr.org/tow_center_reports/how-journalists-imagine-their-readers.php

21. https://www.cjr.org/tow_center_reports/how-journalists-imagine-their-readers.php#acknowledgements

22. DeWerth-Pallmeyer, D. (2013). *The audience in the news.* New York, NY: Routledge.

23. Usher, N., Holcomb, J., & Littman, J. (2018). Twitter makes it worse: Political journalists, gendered echo chambers, and the amplification of gender bias. *The International Journal of Press/Politics,* 23(3), 324–344.

24. https://deadline.com/2015/08/virginia-tv-newswoman-and-camerman-killed-in-on-air-attack-1201506687/

25. https://www.nytimes.com/2018/06/28/us/capital-gazette-annapolis-shooting.html

26. Dunaway, J. (2008). Markets, ownership, and the quality of campaign news coverage. *The Journal of Politics*, 70(4), 1193–1202; Dunaway, J. (2013). Media ownership and story tone in campaign news. *American Politics Research*, 41(1), 24–53.

27. Demers, D. (1996). Corporate newspaper structure, editorial page vigor, and social change. *Journalism & Mass Communication Quarterly*, 73(4), 857–877.

28. McChesney, R. W. (1999). *Rich media, poor democracy: Communication politics in dubious times*. Champaign: University of Illinois Press; McChesney, R. W. (2004). *The problem of the media: U.S. communication politics in the twenty-first century*. New York, NY: Monthly Review Press.

29. Cappella, J. N., & Jamieson, K. H. (1996). News frames, political cynicism, and media cynicism. *The Annals of the American Academy of Political and Social Science*, 546(1), 71–84; Iyengar, S., Norpoth, H., & Hahn, K. S. (2004). Consumer demand for election news: The horserace sells. *The Journal of Politics*, 66(1), 157–175.

30. Lawrence, R. G. (2000). Game-framing the issues: Tracking the strategy frame in public policy news. *Political Communication*, 17(2), 93–114.

31. Meltzer, K. (2007). Newspaper editorial boards and the practice of endorsing candidates for political office in the United States. *Journalism*, 8(1), 83–103; Dunaway, J. (2008). Markets, ownership, and the quality of campaign news coverage. *The Journal of*

Politics, 70(4), 1193–1202; Dunaway, J. (2013). Media ownership and story tone in campaign news. *American Politics Research*, 41(1), 24–53.

32. https://www.newyorker.com/magazine/2019/01/28/does-journalism-have-a-future?

33. Wells, C., Shah, D. V., Pevehouse, J. C., Yang, J., Pelled, A., Boehm, F., ... & Schmidt, J. L. (2016). How Trump drove coverage to the nomination: Hybrid media campaigning. *Political Communication*, 33(4), 669–676.

34. https://fox11online.com/news/election/both-parties-react-to-spring-election-results

35. https://www.niemanlab.org/2018/12/government-funds-local-news-and-thats-a-good-thing/

36. https://www.thenation.com/article/how-save-journalism-0/

37. https://academic.oup.com/jcmc/advance-article/doi/10.1093/jcmc/zmz009/5489530

38. https://doi.org/10.1093/joc/jqy051

39. https://www.tandfonline.com/doi/full/10.1080/08838151.2017.1309418?casa_token=vW_PnRB4TswAAAAA:-9X_bECEsf56YrsEIwDc9h6SvFM-D31c1h-Cklyvq3eJcMrxsgKXk-dGHexkqORcsSOR6IeTuP3P6Jxg

40. https://www.researchgate.net/profile/Dhavan_Shah/publication/303710544_Coproduction_or_cooptation_Realtime_spin_and_social_media_response_during_the_2012_French_and_US_presidential_debates/links/57a0419108aec29aed215360/Coproduction-or-cooptation-Real-time-spin-and-social-media-response-during-the-2012-French-and-US-presidential-debates.pdf

Chapter 3

1. Shah, D. V., McLeod, D. M., Rojas, H., Cho, J., Wagner, M. W., & Friedland, L. A. (2017). Revising the communication mediation model for a new political communication ecology. *Human Communication Research*, 43(4), 491–504.

2. Chaffee, S. H., & Metzger, M. J. (2001). The end of mass communication? *Mass Communication and Society*, 4(4), 365–379.

3. Graber, D. A., & Dunaway, J. (2015) *Mass media and American politics*, 9th ed. Washington, DC: CQ Press.

4. Beam, R., Weaver, D. H., & Brownlee, B. (2009). Changes in professionalism of U.S. journalists in the turbulent twenty-first century. *Journalism and Mass Communication Quarterly*, 86(2), 277–298.

5. Stroud, N. J. (2011). *Niche news: The politics of news choice*. New York, NY: Oxford University Press.

6. Mutz, D. (2015). *In-your-face politics: The consequences of uncivil media.* Princeton, NJ: Princeton University Press.

7. Mutz, D., & Reeves, B. (2005). The new videomalaise: Effects of televised incivility on political trust. *American Political Science Review*, 1, 1–15. doi:10.1017/S0003055405051452

8. Pingree, R. J., Brossard, D., & McLeod, D. M. (2014). Effects of journalistic adjudication on factual beliefs, news evaluations, information seeking, and epistemic political efficacy. *Mass Communication and Society*, 17, 615–638. doi:10.1080/1 5205436.2013.821491

9. Gruszczynski, M., & Wagner, M. W. (2016). Information flow in the 21st century: The dynamics of agenda-uptake. *Mass Communication and Society*.

10. Bennett, W. L., & Iyengar, S. (2008). A new era of minimal effects? The changing foundations of political communication. *Journal of Communication*, 58, 707–731; Fletcher, R., & Nielsen, R. K. (2018). Are people incidentally exposed to news on social media? A comparative analysis. *New Media & Society*, 20(7), 2450–2468.

11. Wells, C., Shah, D. V., Pevehouse, J. C., Yang, J. Pelled, A., Boehm, F., ... & Schmidt, J. L. (2016). How Trump drove coverage to the nomination: Hybrid media campaigning. *Political Communication*, 33, 669–676.

12. https://www.vox.com/mischiefs-of-faction/2019/3/29/18286836/wisconsin-swing-vote-democratic-primary

13. Edgerly, S. (2015). Red media, blue media, and purple media: News repertoires in the colorful media landscape. *Journal of Broadcasting & Electronic Media*, 59, 1–21.

14. McLeod, D. M., Wise, D., & Perryman, M. (2017). Thinking about the media: a review of theory and research on media perceptions, media effects perceptions, and their consequences. *Review of Communication Research*, 5, 35–83.

15. Bennett, W. L. (1990). Toward a theory of press-state relations in the United States. *Journal of Communication*, 40(2), 103–127.

16. Stromer-Galley, J. (2000). On-line interaction and why candidates avoid it. *Journal of Communication*, 50(4), 111–132.

17. https://www.journalism.org/fact-sheet/newspapers/

18. https://www.journalism.org/fact-sheet/newspapers/

19. https://www.pewresearch.org/fact-tank/2018/07/30/newsroom-employment-dropped-nearly-a-quarter-in-less-than-10-years-with-greatest-decline-at-newspapers/

20. https://www.usnewsdeserts.com/reports/expanding-news-desert/loss-of-local-news/

21. Barabas, J., & Jerit, J. (2009). Estimating the causal effects of media coverage on policy-specific knowledge. *American Journal of Political Science, 53*(1), 73–89.

22. Eveland Jr, W. P., & Scheufele, D. A. (2000). Connecting news media use with gaps in knowledge and participation. *Political communication, 17*(3), 215–237.

23. Jerit, J., Barabas, J., & Bolsen, T. (2006). Citizens, knowledge, and the information environment. *American Journal of Political Science, 50*(2), 266–282.

24. Friedland, L., Napoli, P., Ognyanova, K., Weil, C., & Wilson III, E. J. (2012). Review of the literature regarding critical information needs of the American public. *Unpublished manuscript submitted to the Federal Communications Commission. http://transition. fcc. gov/bureaus/ocbo/Final_Literature_Review. pdf*, 15–19. https://transition.fcc.gov/bureaus/ocbo/Final_Literature_Review.pdf

25. https://www.journalism.org/fact-sheet/audio-and-podcasting/

26. Sobieraj, S., & Berry, J. M. (2011). From incivility to outrage: Political discourse in blogs, talk radio, and cable news. *Political Communication, 28*(1), 19–41.

27. Hofstetter, C. R., Barker, D., Smith, J. T., Zari, G. M., & Ingrassia, T. A. (1999). Information, misinformation, and political talk radio. *Political Research Quarterly, 52*(2), 353–369.

28. Weeks, B. E., Ksiazek, T. B., & Holbert, R. L. (2016). Partisan enclaves or shared media experiences? A network approach to understanding citizens' political news environments. *Journal of Broadcasting & Electronic Media, 60*(2), 248–268.

29. https://www.journalism.org/fact-sheet/local-tv-news/

30. Individual company Securities and Exchange Commission filings for the full year ending on Dec. 31. Companies included here are: Tribune, Nexstar, Sinclair, Tegna, Gray and Scripps. https://www.journalism.org/fact-sheet/local-tv-news/

31. Wenger, D., & Papper, B. (2018). The state of the industry: Local TV news and the new media landscape. Rep., Knight Found., Miami, FL. https://knightfoundation.org/reports/local-tv-news-and-the-new-media-landscape

32. Arnold, R. D. (2004). *Congress, the press, and political accountability.* New York, NY: Russell Sage.

33. Fridkin Kahn, K., & Kenney, P. J. (1999). *The spectacle of U.S. Senate campaigns.* Princeton, NJ: Princeton University Press.

34. Hayes, D., & Lawless, J. L. (2015). As local news goes, so goes citizen engagement: Media, knowledge, and participation in US House elections. *The Journal of Politics, 77*(2), 447–462.

35. https://www.journalism.org/fact-sheet/network-news/

36. https://www.journalism.org/numbers/network-evening-news-ratings/

37. Robinson, N. W., Zeng, C., & Holbert, R. L. (2018). The stubborn pervasiveness of television news in the digital age and the field's attention to the medium, 2010–2014. *Journal of Broadcasting & Electronic Media, 62*(2), 287–301.

38. Hayes, D., & Lawless, J. L. (2015); Edgerly, S., Vraga, E. K., Bode, L., Thorson, K., & Thorson, E. (2018). New media, new relationship to participation? A closer look at youth news repertoires and political participation. *Journalism & Mass Communication Quarterly, 95*(1), 192–212.

39. https://www.journalism.org/fact-sheet/cable-news/

40. Iyengar, S., & Hahn, K. S. (2009). Red media, blue media: Evidence of ideological selectivity in media use. *Journal of Communication, 59*(1), 19–39.

41. https://www.journalism.org/2014/10/21/political-polarization-media-habits/

42. https://www.journalism.org/fact-sheet/hispanic-and-african-american-news-media/

43. https://www.journalism.org/fact-sheet/hispanic-and-african-american-news-media/

44. Wei, L., & Hindman, D. B. (2011). Does the digital divide matter more? Comparing the effects of new media and old media use on the education-based knowledge gap. *Mass Communication and Society, 14*(2), 216–235.

45. Kenski, K., & Stroud, N. J. (2006). Connections between internet use and political efficacy, knowledge, and participation. *Journal of Broadcasting & Electronic Media, 50*(2), 173–192.

46. https://www.pewinternet.org/2019/04/24/sizing-up-twitter-users/

47. https://www.pewresearch.org/fact-tank/2015/08/19/how-do-americans-use-twitter-for-news/#graphic

48. Settle, J. E., Bond, R. M., Coviello, L., Fariss, C. J., Fowler, J. H., & Jones, J. J. (2016). From posting to voting: The effects of political competition on online political engagement. *Political Science Research and Methods, 4*(2), 361–378.

49. Dunaway, J., Searles, K., Sui, M., & Paul, N. (2018). News attention in a mobile era. *Journal of Computer-Mediated Communication, 23*(2), 107–124.

50. Mutz, D. C. (2002). The consequences of cross-cutting networks for political participation. *American Journal of Political Science*, 838–855.

51. Walsh, K. C., & Cramer, K. J. (2004). *Talking about politics: Informal groups and social identity in American life.* Chicago, IL: University of Chicago Press.

52. Cramer, K. J. (2016). *The politics of resentment.* Chicago, IL: University of Chicago Press.

53. Wells, C., Cramer, K. J., Wagner, M. W., Alvarez, G., Friedland, L. A., Shah, D. V., ... & Franklin, C. (2017). When we stop talking politics: The maintenance and closing of conversation in contentious times.

Journal of Communication, 67(1), 131–157.

54. Gil de Zúñiga, H., Weeks, B., & Ardèvol-Abreu, A. (2017). Effects of the news-finds-me perception in communication: Social media use implications for news seeking and learning about politics. *Journal of Computer-Mediated Communication, 22*(3), 105–123.doi: 10.1111/jcc4.12185; Gil de Zúñiga, H., & Diehl, T. (2018). News finds me perception and democracy: Effects on political knowledge, political interest, and voting. *New Media & Society, 21*(6), 1253–1271. doi: 10.1177/1461444818817548.

55. Foley, J., Wagner, M. W., Lukito, J., Hughes, C., Suk, J., Friedland, L. A., & Shah, D. V. (2019). "Do conspiracy theories find me?": How communication ecologies, information seeking preferences and racial resentment fuel conspiratorial thinking." Unpublished Manuscript.

56. Feezell, J. T. (2018). Agenda setting through social media: The importance of incidental news exposure and social filtering in the digital era. *Political Research Quarterly, 71*(2), 482–494.

57. Chadwick, A. (2011). The political information cycle in a hybrid news system: The British prime minister and the "Bullygate" affair. *The International Journal of Press/Politics, 16*(1), 3–29.

58. Harder, R. A., Paulussen, S., & Van Aelst, P. (2016). Making sense of Twitter buzz: The cross-media construction of news stories in election time. *Digital Journalism, 4*(7), 933–943.

59. Karlsen, R., & Enjolras, B. (2016). Styles of social media campaigning and influence in a hybrid political communication system: Linking candidate survey data with Twitter data. *The International Journal of Press/Politics, 21*(3), 338–357.

60. Wells, C., Shah, D. V., Pevehouse, J. C., Yang, J., Pelled, A., Boehm, F., ... & Schmidt, J. L. (2016). How Trump drove coverage to the nomination: Hybrid media campaigning. *Political Communication, 33*(4), 669–676.

61. Freelon, D., & Karpf, D. (2015). Of big birds and bayonets: Hybrid Twitter interactivity in the 2012 presidential debates. *Information, Communication & Society, 18*(4), 390–406.

62. Bennett, W. L., & Segerberg, A. (2012). The logic of connective action: Digital media and the personalization of contentious politics. *Information, Communication & Society, 15*(5), 739–768.

63. Bigman, C. A., Smith, M. A., Williamson, L. D., Planey, A. M., & McNeil Smith, S. (2019). Selective sharing on social media: Examining the effects of disparate racial impact frames on intentions to retransmit news stories among US college students. *New Media & Society.* Online First.

64. Hermida, A. (2010). Twittering the news: The emergence of ambient journalism. *Journalism practice, 4*(3), 297–308.

65. McGregor, S. C., & Molyneux, L. (2018). Twitter's influence on news judgment: An experiment among journalists. *Journalism.* Online First. https://journals.sagepub.com/doi/full/10.1177/1464884918802975

66. Sk
bergø, E., & Krumsvik, A. H. (2014). Newspapers, Facebook and Twitter. *Journalism Practice, 9*(3), 350–366.

67. https://www.pewresearch.org/fact-tank/2019/03/26/most-americans-especially-republicans-say-local-journalists-shouldnt-express-views-on-local-issues/

68. https://www.pewresearch.org/fact-tank/2019/04/12/for-many-rural-residents-in-u-s-local-news-media-mostly-dont-cover-the-area-where-they-live/

69. https://www.pewresearch.org/fact-tank/2018/09/10/about-a-quarter-of-rural-americans-say-access-to-high-speed-internet-is-a-major-problem/

70. Thorson, K., & Wells, C. (2016). Curated flows: A framework for mapping media exposure in the digital age. *Communication Theory, 26*(3), 309–328.

Chapter 4

1. Knight Foundation. "American Views: Trust, Media and Democracy." Gallup, 2018. https://knightfoundation.org/reports/american-views-trust-media-and-democracy/.

2. Perryman, M. R., & Wagner, M. W. (2019, May). Salient cable, scarce local: Public Perceptions of "the media." International Communication Association (Mass Communication Division), Washington, DC.

3. Grieco, E. (2018). Newsroom employment dropped nearly a quarter in less than 10 years, with greatest decline at newspapers. *Pew Research Center.*

4. Daniller, A., Allen, D., Tallevi, A., & Mutz, D. (2017). Measuring trust in the press in a changing media environment. *Communication Methods and Measures, 11*(1), 76–85.

5. Barthel, M., & Mitchell, A. (2017). Americans' attitudes about the news media deeply divided along partisan lines. *Pew Research Center, 10.*

6. Uslaner, E. M. (1997). John R. Hibbing and Elizabeth Theiss-Morse, Congress as public enemy: Public attitudes toward American political institutions. *Public Opinion Quarterly, 61*(4), 667–668.

7. Daniller et al. (2017).

8. Gottfried, J., & Shearer, E. (2017). Americans' online news use is closing in on TV news use. *Pew Research Center, 7.*

9. Martin, G. J., & Yurukoglu, A. (2017). Bias in cable news: Persuasion and polarization. *American Economic Review, 107*(9), 2565–2599.

10. Weaver, D. H., Willnat, L., & Wilhoit, G. C. (2019). The American journalist in the digital age: Another look at U.S. news people. *Journalism & Mass Communication Quarterly, 96*(1), 101–130.

11. https://ballotpedia.org/Fact_check/Do_97_percent_of_journalist_donations_go_to_Democrats

12. Wagner, M. W., & Gruszczynski, M. (2016). When framing matters: How partisan and journalistic frames affect individual opinions and party identification. *Journalism & Communication Monographs, 18*(1), 5–48. doi: 10.1177/1522637915623965

13. Hayes, D. (2008). Party reputations, journalistic expectations: How issue ownership influences election news. *Political Communication, 25*(4), 377–400.

14. Groseclose, T., & Milyo, J. (2005). A measure of media bias. *The Quarterly Journal of Economics, 120*(4), 1191–1237.

15. Nyhan, B. (2012). Does the US media have a liberal bias?: A

discussion of Tim Groseclose's left turn: How liberal media bias distorts the American mind. *Perspectives on Politics, 10(3),* 767–771; The problems with the Groseclose/Milyo study of media bias, December 22, 2005, http://www.brendan-nyhan .com/blog/2005/12/the_problems _wi.html.

16. Hughes, C. (2016). It's not easy (not) being green: Agenda dissonance of Green Party press relations and newspaper coverage. *European Journal of Communication, 31(6),* 625–641.

17. Lawrence, R. G. (2000). Game-framing the issues: Tracking the strategy frame in public policy news. *Political Communication, 17,* 93–114.

18. Groeling, T. (2008). Who's the fairest of them all? An empirical test for partisan bias on ABC, CBS, NBC, and Fox News. *Presidential Studies Quarterly, 38(4),* 631–657.

19. Leetaru, K. (2011). Culturomics 2.0: Forecasting large-scale human behavior using global news media tone in time and space. *First Monday, 16(9).*

20. Patterson, T. (1994). *Out of order.* New York, NY: Vintage.

21. Kahneman, D., & Tversky, A. (1979). Prospect theory: an analysis of decision under risk. *Econometrica (pre-1986), 47(2),* 263–291.

22. Van der Pligt, J., & Eiser, J. R. (1980). Negativity and descriptive extremity in impression formation. *European Journal of Social Psychology, 10(4),* 415–419.

23. Soroka, S., & McAdams, S. (2015). News, politics, and negativity. *Political Communication, 32(1),* 1–22.

24. Trussler, M., & Soroka, S. (2014). Consumer demand for cynical and negative news frames. *The International Journal of Press/Politics, 19(3),* 360–379.

25. Carter, S., Fico, F., & McCabe, J. A. (2002). Partisan and structural balance in local television election coverage. *Journalism & Mass Communication Quarterly, 79(1),* 41–53.

26. Lott, J., & Hassett, K. (2014). Is newspaper coverage of economic events politically biased? *Public Choice, 160(1/2),* 65–108.

27. Kahn, K. F., & Kenney, P. (2002). The slant of the news: How editorial endorsements influence campaign coverage and citizens' views of candidates. *American Political Science Review, 96(2),* 381–394.

28. Funke, D. (May, 2019). How the Washington Post tallied more than 10,000 Trump falsehoods in less than three years. *Poynter.*

29. Mcginty, E., Webster, D., Jarlenski, M., & Barry, C. (2014). News media framing of serious mental illness and gun violence in the United States, 1997–2012. *American Journal of Public Health, 104(3),* 406–413.

30. Fryberg, Stephanie A., Nicole M. Stephens, Rebecca Covarrubias, Hazel Rose Markus, Erin D. Carter, Giselle A. Laiduc, and Ana J. Salido. "How the Media Frames the Immigration Debate: The Critical Role of Location and Politics." *Analyses of Social Issues and Public Policy* 12, no. 1 (2011): 96–112. https://doi.org/10.1111/ j.1530-2415.2011.01259.x.

31. Gentzkow, M., & Shapiro, J. M. (2010). What drives media slant? Evidence from U.S. daily newspapers. *Econometrica, 78(1),* 35–71.

32. Martin & Yurukoglu. (2017).

33. Federal Communications Commission. (2003). Report and order and notice of proposed rulemaking. Washington, DC: Federal Communications Commission.

34. Wagner, M. W., & Collins, T. P. (2014). Does ownership matter? The case of Rupert Murdoch's purchase of the Wall Street Journal. *Journalism Practice, 8*(6), 758–771.

35. Clay, R., Barber, J., & Shook, N. (2013). Techniques for measuring selective exposure: A critical review. *Communication Methods and Measures, 7*(3), 221–245.

36. Grabe, M., & Bucy, Erik P. (2009). *Image bite politics: News and the visual framing of elections* (Series in political psychology). Oxford, UK; New York, NY: Oxford University Press.

37. Groeling, T. (2008).

38. Kahn & Kenney. (2002).

39. D'Alessio, D. and Allen, M. (2000), Media bias in presidential elections: a meta-analysis. Journal of Communication, 50: 133-156. doi:10.1111/j.1460-2466.2000.tb02866.x

40. https://ethics.journalism.wisc.edu/2011/04/20/the-fall-and-rise-of-partisan-journalism/

41. Shaw, D. L. (1967). News bias and the telegraph: A study of historical change. *Journalism Quarterly, 44*, 3–12.

42. Baldasty, G. J. (1992). *The commercialization of news in the nineteenth century*. Madison: University of Wisconsin Press.

43. Schudson, M. (2001). The objectivity norm in American journalism. *Journalism, 2*(2), 149–170.

44. Prior, M. (2007). *Post-broadcast democracy: How media choice increases inequality in political involvement and polarizes elections*. Cambridge University Press.

45. https://www.adweek.com/tvnewser/evening-news-ratings-week-of-may-27-2/404510/

46. Mullainathan, S., & Shleifer, A. (2005). The market for news. *American Economic Review, 95*(4), 1031–1053.

47. Gal-Or, E., Geylani, T., & Yildirim, T. (2012). The impact of advertising on media bias. *Journal of Marketing Research, 49*(1), 92–99; Hetherington, M., & Weiler, J. (2018). *Prius or pickup?: How the answers to four simple questions explain America's great divide*. Boston, MA: Houghton Mifflin.

48. Klar, S., & Krupnikov, Y. (2016). *Independent politics: How American disdain for parties leads to political inaction*. New York, NY: Cambridge University Press.

49. Mason, L. (2018). *Uncivil agreement: How politics became our identity*. Chicago, IL: The University of Chicago Press; Carmines, E. G., Ensley, M. J., & Wagner, M. W. (2012, October). Political ideology in American politics: one, two, or none? In *The Forum* (Vol. 10, No. 3). De Gruyter; Carmines, E. G., Ensley, M. J., & Wagner, M. W. (2012). Who fits the left-right divide? Partisan polarization in the American electorate, *American Behavioral Scientist, 56* (December), 1631–1653.

50. Pew Research Center. (2014). Where news audiences fit on the political spectrum. https://www.journalism.org/interactives/media-polarization/

51. Gentzkow & Shapiro. (2010).

52. Lord, C., Ross, L., & Lepper, M. (1979). Biased assimilation and attitude polarization: The effects of prior theories on subsequently considered evidence. *Journal of Personality and Social Psychology, 37*(11), 2098–2109; Taber, C., & Lodge, M. (2006). Motivated skepticism in the evaluation of political beliefs. *American Journal of Political Science, 50*(3), 755–769; Nyhan, B., & Reifler, J. (2010). When corrections fail: The persistence of political misperceptions. *Political Behavior, 32*(2), 303–330.

53. American Press Institute. (2018). Confusion about what's news and what's opinion is a big problem, but journalists can help solve it. https://www.americanpressinstitute .org/publications/confusion-about -whats-news-and-whats-opinion-is -a-big-problem-but-journalists-can -help-solve-it/

54. Vraga, E. K., Edgerly, S., Wang, B. M., & Shah, D. V. (2011). Who taught me that? Repurposed news, blog structure, and source identification. *Journal of Communication, 61*, 795–815.

55. McGregor, S.C., & Molyneux, L. (2018). Twitter's influence on news judgment: An experiment among journalists. *Journalism.* (Published online ahead of print: http:// journals.sagepub.com/doi/10.1177 /1464884918802975)

56. Silverman, C. (2017). I helped popularize the term "fake news" and now I cringe every time I hear it. *Buzzfeed News, 31.*

57. Allcott, H., & Gentzkow, M. (2017). Social media and fake news in the 2016 election. *Journal of Economic Perspectives, 31*(2), 211–236; p. 213.

58. Wardle, C. (2017). Fake news. It's complicated. *First Draft News, 16.*

59. Tandoc, E., Lim, Z., & Ling, R. (2017). Defining "fake news": A typology of scholarly definitions. *Digital Journalism,* 1–17.

60. Shao, C., Ciampaglia, G., Varol, O., Yang, K., Flammini, A., & Menczer, F. (2018). The spread of low-credibility content by social bots. *Nature Communications, 9*(1), 4787.

61. Lukito, J., & Wells, C. (2018). Most major outlets have used Russian tweets as sources for partisan opinion: Study. *Columbia Journalism Review, 8.*

62. "Morgue Employee Cremated By Mistake While Taking A Nap." *World News Daily Report,* n.d. https:// worldnewsdailyreport.com/morgue- employee-cremated-by-mistake- while-taking-a-nap/.

63. Gabielkov, M., Ramachandran, A., Chaintreau, A., & Legout, A. (2016, June). Social clicks: What and who gets read on Twitter? In *Proceedings of the 2016 ACM SIGMETRICS international conference on measurement and modeling of computer science* (pp. 179–192).

64. Bronstein, M. V., Pennycook, G., Bear, A., Rand, D. G., & Cannon, T. D. (2019). Belief in fake news is associated with delusionality, dogmatism, religious fundamentalism, and reduced analytic thinking. *Journal of Applied Research in Memory and Cognition, 8*(1), 108–117. http:// doi.org/10.1016/J.JARMAC.2018 .09.005

65. Guess, A., Nyhan, B., & Reifler, J. (2018). Selective exposure to misinformation: Evidence from the consumption of fake news during the 2016 US presidential campaign.

European Research Council, 9. https://www.dartmouth.edu/~nyhan/fake-news-2016.pdf

66. Guess, A., Nagler, J., & Tucker, J. (2019). Less than you think: Prevalence and predictors of fake news dissemination on Facebook. *Science Advances, 5*(1).

67. Guess, Andrew, Lyons, Benjamin, Montgomery, Jacob, Nyhan, Brendan, & Reifler, Jason. (2019). Fake news, Facebook ads, and misperceptions: Assessing information quality in the 2018 U.S. midterm election campaign.

68. Harper, C. A., & Baguley, T. (2019, January 23). "You are fake news": Ideological (a)symmetries in perceptions of media legitimacy. https://doi.org/10.31234/osf.io/ym6t5

69. Sullivan, M. (2017). It's time to retire the tainted term "fake news." *Washington Post, 8.*

70. Van Duyn, E., & Collier, J. (2019). Priming and fake news: The effects of elite discourse on evaluations of news media. *Mass Communication and Society, 22*(1), 29–48.

71. Monmouth University. April, 2018. 'Fake news' threat to media; Editorial decisions, outside actors at fault. https://www.monmouth.edu/polling-institute/reports/monmouthpoll_us_040218/

72. Pew Research Center. (December, 2016). Many Americans believe fake news is sowing confusion. https://www.journalism.org/2016/12/15/many-americans-believe-fake-news-is-sowing-confusion/

73. Silverman, C., & Singer-Vine, J. (2016). Most Americans who see fake news believe it, new survey says. *BuzzFeed News, 6.*

74. Grinberg, N., Joseph, K., Friedland, L., Swire-Thompson, B., & Lazer, D. (2019). Fake news on Twitter during the 2016 U.S. presidential election. *Science, 363*(6425), 374–378.

75. Guess, Nyhan, & Reifler. (2018).

76. Guess, A., Lyons, B., Montgomery, J. M., Nyhan, B., & Reifler, J. (2018). Fake news, Facebook ads, and misperceptions: Assessing information quality in the 2018 U.S. midterm election campaign. http://www-personal.umich.edu/~bnyhan/fake-news-2018.pdf

77. https://osome.iuni.iu.edu/tools/

78. Gentzkow, M., & Yu, C. (2018). Trends in the diffusion of misinformation on social media. *IDEAS Working Paper Series from RePEc,* IDEAS Working Paper Series from RePEc, 2018.

79. Tromble, R., & McGregor, S. C. (2019). You break it, you buy it: The naiveté of social engineering in tech—And how to fix it. *Political Communication, 36*(2), 324–332.

Chapter 5

1. Kam, C., & Zechmeister, E. (2013). Name recognition and candidate support. *American Journal of Political Science, 57*(4), 971–986.

2. Zaller, J. (1992). *The nature and origin of mass opinion.* New York, NY: Cambridge University Press.

3. Clementson, D., & Eveland, W. P. (2016). When politicians dodge questions: An analysis of presidential press conferences and debates. *Mass Communication and Society, 19*(4), 411–429.

4. Rogers, T., & Norton, M. I. (2011). The artful dodger: Answering the wrong question the right way. *Journal of Experimental Psychology: Applied, 17,* 139–147.

5. Taylor, P. W. (January, 2014). Why do politicians prefer old media? *Governing*. https://www.governing.com/columns/dispatch/gov-why-do-politicians-prefer-old-media.html

6. Pew Research Center. State of the news media 2018. https://www.pewresearch.org/topics/state-of-the-news-media/

7. Becker, A. B. (2013). What about those interviews? The impact of exposure to political comedy and cable news on factual recall and anticipated political expression. *International Journal of Public Opinion Research, 25*(3), 344–356.

8. Baum, M. (2005). Talking the vote: Why presidential candidates hit the talk show circuit. *American Journal of Political Science, 49*(2), 213–234.

9. Fowler, J. H. (2008). The Colbert bump: More truthful than truthy. *PS: Political Science and Politics, 41*(3), 531–539.

10. https://www.presidency.ucsb.edu/statistics/data/presidential-news-conferences

11. Duffy, M. J., & Williams, A. E. (2011). Use of unnamed sources drops from peak in 1960s and 1970s. *Newspaper Research Journal, 32*(4), 6–21.

12. https://publiceditor.blogs.nytimes.com/2016/07/15/the-times-gives-an-update-on-anonymous-source-use/

13. Sternadori, M. M., & Thorson, E. (2009). Anonymous sources harm credibility of all stories. *Newspaper Research Journal, 30*(4), 54–66.

14. Green-Pedersen, C., Mortensen, P., & Thesen, G. (2017). The incumbency bonus revisited: Causes and consequences of media dominance. *47*(1), 131–148.

15. Schudson, M. (2003). *The sociology of news.* New York, NY: W.W. Norton

16. Lance Bennett, W. (2016). Indexing Theory. In *The international encyclopedia of political communication,* G. Mazzoleni (Ed.). Wiley Online Library.

17. Amsalem, E., Zoizner, A., Sheafer, T., Walgrave, S., & Loewen, P. J. (2018). The effect of politicians' personality on their media visibility. *Communication Research.* Online First.

18. Pew Research Center. (April, 2018). The public, the political system and American democracy. https://www.people-press.org/2018/04/26/the-public-the-political-system-and-american-democracy/

19. https://www.politico.com/story/2018/08/21/congress-town-halls-gotcha-public-meetings-789430

20. https://www.politico.com/story/2009/08/virtual-town-halls-gaining-popularity-025844

21. https://slate.com/technology/2008/10/forget-robo-calls-obama-s-text-messages-are-this-campaign-s-secret-weapon.html

22. Dale, A., & Strauss, A. (2009). Don't forget to vote: Text message reminders as a mobilization tool. *American Journal of Political Science, 53*, 787–804.

23. Malhotra, N., Michelson, M. R., Rogers, T., & Valenzuela, A. A. (2011). Text messages as mobilization tools: The conditional effect of habitual voting and election salience. *American Politics Research, 39*(4), 664–681.

24. Green, D. P., & Gerber, A. S. (2008). *Get out the vote! How to increase voter turnout* (2nd ed.). Washington, DC: Brookings Institution Press

25. Pew Research Center. (2008). McCain vs. Obama on the Web.

https://www.journalism.org/2008/09/15/mccain-vs-obama-on-the-web/

26. Bernhard, U., Dohle, M., & Vowe, G. (2016). Do presumed online media effects have an influence on the online activities of politicians? *Policy & Internet, 8,* 72–90.

27. Enli, G. S., & Skogerbø, E. (2013). Personalized campaigns in party-centred politics: Twitter and Facebook as arenas for political communication. *Information, Communication & Society, 16*(5), 757–774.

28. Hoffmann, C. P., & Suphan, A. (2017). Stuck with "electronic brochures"? How boundary management strategies shape politicians' social media use. *Information, Communication & Society, 20*(4), 551–569.

29. Messing, S., van Kessel, P., & Hughes, A. (Dec, 2017). Sharing the news in a polarized congress. https://www.people-press.org/2017/12/18/sharing-the-news-in-a-polarized-congress/

30. Pew Research Center. (February 2017). Partisan conflict and congressional outreach. https://www.people-press.org/2017/02/23/partisan-conflict-and-congressional-outreach/

31. van Kessel, P., Hughes, A., & Messing, S. (July 2018). Taking sides on Facebook: How congressional outreach changed under President Trump. https://www.people-press.org/2018/07/18/taking-sides-on-facebook-how-congressional-outreach-changed-under-president-trump/

32. Gerodimos, R., & Justinussen, J. (2015). Obama's 2012 Facebook campaign: Political communication in the age of the like button. *Journal of Information Technology & Politics, 12*(2), 113–132.

33. Duggan, M., & Smith, A. (2016). The Political Environment on Social Media. Pew Research Center. https://www.pewresearch.org/internet/2016/10/25/the-political-environment-on-social-media/

34. Vaccari, C., & Nielsen, R. K. (2013). What drives politicians' online popularity? An analysis of the 2010 U.S. midterm elections. *Journal of Information Technology & Politics, 10*(2), 208–222.

35. Pew Research Center. (August, 2017). Highly ideological members of Congress have more Facebook followers than moderates do. https://www.pewresearch.org/fact-tank/2017/08/21/highly-ideological-members-of-congress-have-more-facebook-followers-than-moderates-do/

36. Gerodimos, R., & Justinussen, J. (2015).

37. Xenos, M. A., Macafee, T., & Pole, A. (2017). Understanding variations in user response to social media campaigns: A study of Facebook posts in the 2010 US elections. *New Media & Society, 19*(6), 826–842.

38. Bene, M. (2017). Go viral on the Facebook! Interactions between candidates and followers on Facebook during the Hungarian general election campaign of 2014. *Information, Communication & Society, 20*(4), 513–529.

39. Pew Research Center. (February, 2017). Partisan conflict and congressional outreach. https://www.people-press.org/2017/02/23/partisan-conflict-and-congressional-outreach/

40. Pew Research Center. (April, 2019). Sizing up Twitter users. https://www

.pewresearch.org/internet/2019/04/24/sizing-up-twitter-users/

41. Tromble, R. (2018). Thanks for (actually) responding! How citizen demand shapes politicians' interactive practices on Twitter. *New Media & Society, 20*(2), 676–697.

42. Ahmadian, S., Azarshahi, S., & Paulhus, D. L. (2017). Explaining Donald Trump via communication style: Grandiosity, informality, and dynamism. *Personality and Individual Differences, 107,* 49–53.

43. Enli, G. (2017). Twitter as arena for the authentic outsider: Exploring the social media campaigns of Trump and Clinton in the 2016 US presidential election. *European Journal of Communication, 32*(1), 50–61.

44. Lee, J., & Xu, W. (2018). The more attacks, the more retweets: Trump's and Clinton's agenda setting on Twitter. *Public Relations Review, 44*(2), 201–213.

45. Kamps, H. J. (2015). Who are Twitter's verified users. *Medium. com.*

46. Wells, C., Shah, D. V., Pevehouse, J. C., Yang, J., Pelled, A., Boehm, F., ... & Schmidt, J. L. (2016). How Trump drove coverage to the nomination: Hybrid media campaigning. *Political Communication, 33*(4), 669–676.

47. Pew Research Center. (April, 2018). The public, the political system and American democracy. https://www.people-press.org/2018/04/26/the-public-the-political-system-and-american-democracy/

48. Propublica. (2018). How to get your lawmakers to listen. https://www.propublica.org/article/users-guide-to-democracy-how-to-get-your-lawmakers-to-listen

49. Butler, D., & Broockman, D. (2011). Do politicians racially discriminate against constituents? A field experiment on state legislators. *American Journal of Political Science, 55*(3), 463–477.

50. Wagner, M. W. (2007). Beyond policy responsiveness in the U.S. House: Do citizens think casework is partisan? *American Politics Research, 35,* 771–89.

51. Congressional Management Foundation. (2016). How mail to congress moves from the back office to the member office. http://www.congressfoundation.org/lc-survey

52. Cluverius, J. (2017). How the flattened costs of grassroots lobbying affect legislator responsiveness. *Political Research Quarterly, 70*(2), 279–290.

53. Bergan, D. E. (2009). Does grassroots lobbying work?: A field experiment measuring the effects of an e-mail lobbying campaign on legislative behavior. *American Politics Research, 37*(2), 327–352.

54. Mazumder, S. (2018). The persistent effect of U.S. civil rights protests on political attitudes. *American Journal of Political Science, 62,* 922–935.

55. Madestam, A., Shoag, D., Veuger, S., & Yanagizawa-Drott, D. (2013). Do political protests matter? Evidence from the tea party movement. *The Quarterly Journal of Economics, 128*(4), 1633–1685.

56. Gillion, D. Q., & Soule, S. A. (2018). The impact of protest on elections in the United States. *Social Science Quarterly, 99,* 1649–1664.

57. Chenoweth, E., & Stephan, Maria J. (2011). *Why civil resistance works:*

The strategic logic of nonviolent conflict (Columbia studies in terrorism and irregular warfare). New York, NY: Columbia University Press.

58. Simpson, B., Willer, R., & Feinberg, M. (2018). Does violent protest backfire? Testing a theory of public reactions to activist violence. *Socius, 4*.

59. Parker, K., Horowitz, J., & Mahl, B. (2016). On views of race and inequality, blacks and whites are worlds apart. Pew Research Center.

60. Shoemaker, P. J., Danielian, L. H., & Brendlinger, D. (1991). Deviant acts, risky business, and U.S. interests: The newsworthiness of world events. *Journalism Quarterly, 68*, 781–795.

61. McLeod, D. M. (1995). Communicating deviance: The effects of television news coverage of social protest. *Journal of Broadcasting & Electronic Media, 39*(1), 4.

62. YouGov. (2014). Public opinion hardens against protesters, softens on police. https://today.yougov.com/topics/politics/articles-reports/2014/08/22/public-opinion-hardens-against-ferguson-residents

63. Pew Research Center. (March, 2017). Large majorities see checks and balances, right to protest as essential for democracy. https://www.people-press.org/2017/03/02/large-majorities-see-checks-and-balances-right-to-protest-as-essential-for-democracy/

64. Skoric, M. M., Zhu, Q., Goh, D., & Pang, N. (2016). Social media and citizen engagement: A meta-analytic review. *New Media & Society, 18*(9), 1817–1839.

65. Theocharis, Y., & Lowe, W. (2016). Does Facebook increase political participation? Evidence from a field experiment. *Information, Communication & Society, 19*(10), 1465–1486.

66. Yamamoto, M., & Kushin, M. J. (2014). More harm than good? Online media use and political disaffection among college students in the 2008 election. *J Computer Mediated Communication, 19*, 430–445.

67. Duggan, M., & Smith, A. (2016).

68. NBC News/Wall Street Journal. (2019). Poll: Americans give social media a clear thumbs-down. https://www.nbcnews.com/politics/meet-the-press/poll-americans-give-social-media-clear-thumbs-down-n991086

69. Prior, M. (2007). *Post-broadcast democracy: How media choice increases inequality in political involvement and polarizes elections*. New York, NY: Cambridge University Press.

70. Bode, L. (2015). Political news in the news feed: Learning politics from social media. *Mass Communication and Society, 19*(1), 24–48.

71. Gil de Zúñiga, H., Jung, N., & Valenzuela, S. (2012). Social media use for news and individuals' social capital, civic engagement and political participation. *Journal of Computer-Mediated Communication, 17*, 319–336.

72. https://www.pewinternet.org/2016/10/25/political-content-on-social-media/

73. Bäck, E. A., Bäck, H., Fredén, A., & Gustafsson, N. (2019). A social safety net? Rejection sensitivity and political opinion sharing among young people in social media. *New Media & Society, 21*(2), 298–316.

74. Vraga, E. K., Thorson, K., Kligler-Vilenchik, N., & Gee, E.

(2015). How individual sensitivities to disagreement shape youth political expression on Facebook. *Computers in Human Behavior, 45,* 281–289.

75. Bode, L. (2016). Pruning the news feed: Unfriending and unfollowing political content on social media. *Research & Politics, 3*(3), 2053168016661873.

76. Gearhart, S., & Zhang, W. (2015). "Was it something I said?" "No, it was something you posted!" A study of the spiral of silence theory in social media contexts. *Cyberpsychology, Behavior, and Social Networking, 18*(4), 28–213.

77. Bialik, K. (2018). 14% of Americans have changed their mind about an issue because of something they saw on social media. *Fact Tank.* https://www.pewresearch.org/fact-tank/2018/08/15/14-of-americans-have-changed-their-mind-about-an-issue-because-of-something-they-saw-on-social-media/

78. Weeks, B. E., Ardèvol-Abreu, A., & Gil de Zúñiga, H. (2017). Online influence? Social media use, opinion leadership, and political persuasion. *International Journal of Public Opinion Research, 29*(2), 214–239.

79. Leetaru, K. (2019). Twitter users mostly retweet politicians and celebrities. That's a big change. *The Washington Post.*

80. Mitchell, A., & Weisel, R. (2014). Political polarization and media habits: From Fox News to Facebook, how liberals and conservatives keep up with politics. Pew Research Center.

81. Bekafigo, M. A., & McBride, A. (2013). Who tweets about politics?: Political participation of Twitter users during the 2011 gubernatorial elections. *Social Science Computer Review, 31*(5), 625–643.

82. Barberá, P., Jost, J. T., Nagler, J., Tucker, J. A., & Bonneau, R. (2015). Tweeting from left to right: Is online political communication more than an echo chamber? *Psychological Science, 26*(10), 1531–1542.

83. Boutyline, A., & Willer, R. (2017). The social structure of political echo chambers: Variation in ideological homophily in online networks. *Political Psychology, 38,* 551–569.

84. Bakshy, E., Messing, S., & Adamic, L. (2015). Political science. Exposure to ideologically diverse news and opinion on Facebook. *Science, 348*(6239), 1130–1132.

85. Duggan, M., & Smith, A. (2016).

86. Duggan, M., & Smith, A. (2016).

87. Bail, C., Argyle, L., Brown, T., Bumpus, J., Chen, H., Hunzaker, M., ... & Volfovsky, A. (2018). Exposure to opposing views on social media can increase political polarization. *Proceedings of the National Academy of Sciences, 115*(37), 9216–9221.

88. Barberá, P., Jost, J. T., Nagler, J., Tucker, J. A., & Bonneau, R. (2015).

89. Goel, S., Mason, W., & Watts, D. (2010). Real and perceived attitude agreement in social networks. *Journal of Personality and Social Psychology, 99*(4), 611–621.

90. Bechmann, A., & Nielbo, K. (2018). Are we exposed to the same "news" in the news feed? *Digital Journalism, 6*(8), 990–1002.

91. Morgan, J., Lampe, C., & Shafiq, M. (2013). Is news sharing on Twitter ideologically biased? *Proceedings of*

the 2013 Conference on Computer Supported Cooperative Work, 887–896.

92. Haim, M., Graefe, A., & Brosius, H. (2018). Burst of the filter bubble? Digital Journalism, 6(3), 330–343; Nechushtai, E., & Lewis, S. C. (2019). What kind of news gatekeepers do we want machines to be? Filter bubbles, fragmentation, and the normative dimensions of algorithmic recommendations. Computers in Human Behavior, 90, 298–307.

93. Hwang, H., Kim, Y., & Huh, C. U. (2014). Seeing is believing: Effects of uncivil online debate on political polarization and expectations of deliberation. Journal of Broadcasting & Electronic Media, 58(4), 621–633.

94. Duggan, M., & Smith, A. (2016).

95. Davis, R. (2009). Typing politics: The role of blogs in American politics. New York, NY: Oxford University Press.

96. Oz, M., Zheng, P., & Chen, G. M. (2018). Twitter versus Facebook: Comparing incivility, impoliteness, and deliberative attributes. New Media & Society, 20(9), 3400–3419.

97. Santana, A. D. (2014). Virtuous or vitriolic. Journalism Practice, 8(1), 18–33.

98. Rowe, I. (2015). Civility 2.0: A comparative analysis of incivility in online political discussion. Information, Communication & Society, 18, 121–138.

99. Koban, K., Stein, J. P., Eckhardt, V., & Ohler, P. (2018). Quid pro quo in Web 2.0. Connecting personality traits and Facebook usage intensity to uncivil commenting intentions in public online discussions. Computers in Human Behavior, 79, 9–18.

100. Gervais, B. T. (2015). Incivility online: Affective and behavioral reactions to uncivil political posts in a web-based experiment. Journal of Information Technology & Politics, 12(2), 167–185.

101. Wang, M., & Silva, D. (2018). A slap or a jab: An experiment on viewing uncivil political discussions on Facebook. Computers in Human Behavior, 81, 73–83.

102. Hwang, H., Kim, Y., & Huh, C. U. (2014).

103. Westfall, J., Van Boven, L., Chambers, J. R., & Judd, C. M. (2015). Perceiving political polarization in the United States: Party identity strength and attitude extremity exacerbate the perceived partisan divide. Perspectives on Psychological Science, 10(2), 145–158.

104. Anderson, A. A., Brossard, D., Scheufele, D. A., Xenos, M. A., & Ladwig, P. (2013). The "nasty effect:" Online incivility and risk perceptions of emerging technologies. Journal of Computer-Mediated Communication, 19, 373–387.

105. Houston, J. B., Hansen, G. J., & Nisbett, G. S. (2011). Influence of user comments on perceptions of media bias and third-person effect in online news. Electronic News, 5, 79–92.

106. https://www.politico.com/magazine /story/2018/10/30/yes-political -rhetoric-can-incite-violence-222019

107. Anderson, M., Toor, S., Rainie, L., & Smith, A. (2018). Activism in the social media age. Pew Research Center, 11. https://www .pewresearch.org/internet/2018/07 /11/public-attitudes-toward-political -engagement-on-social-media/

108. Wolfsfeld, G., Yarchi, M., & Samuel-Azran, T. (2016). Political information repertoires and political

participation. *New Media & Society*, *18*(9), 2096–2115.

109. Anderson, M., Toor, S., Rainie, L., & Smith, A. (2018).

110. Congressional Management Foundation. (2015). Staff survey shows congress following their social media feeds for citizen input. http://www .congressfoundation.org/news/press -releases/1123-new-report-outlines -how-congress-and-citizens-interact -on-social-media

111. Chaffee, S. H., & Metzger, M. J. (2001). The end of mass communication? *Mass Communication and Society*, *4*(4), 365–379.

112. Shehata, A., & Strömbäck, J. (2013). Not (yet) a new era of minimal effects: A study of agenda setting at the aggregate and individual levels. *The International Journal of Press/Politics*, *18*(2), 234–255.

113. Nelson, J., & Webster, J. (2017). The myth of partisan selective exposure: A portrait of the online political news audience. *Social Media+ Society*, *3*(3), 2056305117729314.

114. Lee, J. K. (2007). The effect of the internet on homogeneity of the media agenda: A test of the fragmentation thesis. *Journalism & Mass Communication Quarterly*, *84*(4), 745–760.

115. Rogstad, I. (2016). Is Twitter just rehashing? Intermedia agenda setting between Twitter and mainstream media. *Journal of Information Technology & Politics*, *13*(2), 142–158.

116. Sayre, B., Bode, L., Shah, D., Wilcox, D., & Shah, C. (2010). Agenda setting in a digital age: Tracking attention to California Proposition 8 in social media, online news and conventional news. *Policy & Internet*, *2*(2), 7–32.

117. Feezell, J. T. (2018). Agenda setting through social media: The importance of incidental news exposure and social filtering in the digital era. *Political Research Quarterly*, *71*(2), 482–494.

118. Vargo, C. J., & Guo, L. (2017). Networks, big data, and intermedia agenda setting: An analysis of traditional, partisan, and emerging online U.S. news. *Journalism & Mass Communication Quarterly*, *94*(4), 1031–1055; p. 1048

119. Vargo, C. J., Guo, L., & Amazeen, M. A. (2018). The agenda-setting power of fake news: A big data analysis of the online media landscape from 2014 to 2016. *New Media & Society*, *20*(5), 2028–2049.

120. Kiousis, S., Kim, J. Y., Ragas, M., Wheat, G., Kochhar, S., Svensson, E., & Miles, M. (2015). Exploring new frontiers of agenda building during the 2012 US presidential election pre-convention period. *Journalism Studies*, *16*(3), 363–382.

121. Ku, G., Kaid, L. L., & Pfau, M. (2003). The impact of web site campaigning on traditional news media and public information processing. *Journalism & Mass Communication Quarterly*, *80*(3), 528–547.

122. Boyle, T. P. (2001). Intermedia agenda setting in the 1996 presidential election. *Journalism & Mass Communication Quarterly*, *78*(1), 26–44.

123. Kiousis, S., & Shields, A. (2008). Intercandidate agenda-setting in presidential elections: issue and attribute agendas in the 2004 campaign. *Public Relations Review*, *34*(4), 325–330.

124. Marland, A. (2012) Political photography, journalism, and framing in the digital age. *International Journal of Press-Politics*, *17*(2), 214–233

125. Dunn, S. W. (2009). Candidate and media agenda setting in the 2005

Virginia gubernatorial election. *Journal of Communication, 59*(3), 635–652.

126. Edwards, G. C. III, & Wood, B. D. (1999). Who influences whom? The president, Congress, and the media. *American Political Science Review, 93,* 327–344.

127. Wanta, W., Stephenson, M. A., Turk, J. V., & McCombs, M. E. (1989). How presidents' State of Union talk influenced news media agendas. *Journalism Quarterly, 66,* 537–541.

128. Wells et al. (2016).

129. Conway-Silva, B. A., Filer, C. R., Kenski, K., & Tsetsi, E. (2018). Reassessing Twitter's agenda-building power: An analysis of intermedia agenda-setting effects during the 2016 presidential primary season. *Social Science Computer Review, 36*(4), 469–483.

130. Parmelee, J. H. (2014). The agenda-building function of political tweets. *New Media & Society, 16*(3), 434–450.

131. Metag, J., & Rauchfleisch, A. (2017). Journalists' use of political tweets: Functions for journalistic work and the role of perceived influences. *Digital Journalism, 5*(9), 1155–1172.

132. Van Aelst, P., & Walgrave, S. (2011). Minimal or massive? The political agenda-setting power of the mass media according to different methods. *The International Journal of Press/Politics, 16*(3), 295–313.

133. Olds, C. (2013) Assessing presidential agenda-setting capacity: Dynamic comparisons of presidential, mass media, and public attention to economic issues. *Congress & the Presidency, 40*(3), 255–284,

134. Walgrave, S., & Van Aelst, P. (2016, August 31). Political agenda setting and the mass media. In *Oxford Research Encyclopedia of Politics.*

135. Gruszczynski, M., & Wagner, M. (2017). Information flow in the 21st century: The dynamics of agenda-uptake. *Mass Communication and Society, 20*(3), 378–402; p. 383.

Chapter 6

1. Gamson, W. A., & Modigliani, A. (1994). The changing culture of affirmative action. *Equal employment opportunity: labor market discrimination and public policy, 3,* 373–394; see also Entman, R. M. (1993). Framing: Toward clarification of a fractured paradigm. *Journal of Communication, 43*(4), 51–58; Chong, D., & Druckman, J. N. (2007). A theory of framing and opinion formation in competitive elite environments. *Journal of Communication, 57*(1), 99–118; Chong, D., & Druckman, J. N. (2007). Framing public opinion in competitive democracies. *American Political Science Review, 101*(4), 637–655.

2. Entman, R. M. (1993).

3. Nelson, T. E., Oxley, Z. M., & Clawson R. A. (1997). Toward a psychology of framing effects. *Political Behavior, 19*(3), 221–246.

4. Ajzen, I., & Fishbein, M. (1980). *Understanding attitudes and predicting social behavior.* Englewood Cliffs, NJ: Prentice-Hall.

5. Nelson, T. E., & Oxley, Z. M. (November 01, 1999). Issue framing effects on belief importance and opinion. *The Journal of Politics, 61*(4), 1040–1067.

6. Tversky, A., & Kahneman, D. (1981). The framing of decisions and the psychology of choice. *Science 211*(January), 453–458.

7. O'keefe, D. J., & Jensen, J. D. (2006). The advantages of compliance or the disadvantages of noncompliance? A

meta-analytic review of the relative persuasive effectiveness of gain-framed and loss-framed messages. *Annals of the International Communication Association, 30*(1), 1–43.

8. Druckman, J. N. (2011). "What's it all about?: Framing in political science," in Gideon Keren (Ed.), *Perspectives on Framing.* New York, NY: Psychology Press/Taylor & Francis.

9. Druckman (2011).

10. Chen, S., & Chaiken, S. (1999). The Heuristic-Systematic model in its broader context. In S. Chaiken, and Y. Trope (Eds.), *Dual-Process Theories in Social Psychology.* New York, NY: The Guilford Press; Price, V., & Tewksbury, D. (1997). News values and public opinion: A theoretical account of media priming and framing. *Progress in Communication Sciences,* 173–212.

11. Wagner, M. W. (2007). The utility of staying on message: Competing partisan frames and public awareness of elite differences on issues. *The Forum, 5,* 1–18.

12. Lombardi, W. J., Higgins, E. T., & Bargh, J. A. (1987). The role of consciousness in priming effects on categorization: Assimilation versus contrast as a function of awareness of the priming task. *Personality and Social Psychology Bulletin, 13*(3), 411–429.

13. Shah, D. V., Watts, M. D., Domke, D., & Fan, D. P. (2002). News framing and cueing of issue regimes: Explaining Clinton's public approval in spite of scandal. *Public Opinion Quarterly, 66*(3), 339–370.

14. Lee, N. J., McLeod, D. M., & Shah, D. V. (2008). Framing policy debates: Issue dualism, journalistic frames, and opinions on controversial policy issues. *Communication Research, 35*(5), 695–718.

15. Druckman, J. N. (2001). The implications of framing effects for citizen competence. *Political Behavior, 23*(3), 225–256.

16. Nelson, T. E., Clawson, R. A., & Oxley, Z. M. (1997). Media framing of a civil liberties conflict and its effect on tolerance. *American Political Science Review, 91*(3), 567–583.

17. Druckman (2001).

18. Stanovich, K. E., & West, R. F. (1998). Individual differences in framing and conjunction effects. *Thinking and Reasoning, 4,* 289–317.

19. Levin, I. P., Schneider, S. L., & Gaeth, G. J. (1998). All frames are not created equal: A typology and critical analysis of framing effects. *Organizational Behavior and Human Decision Processes, 76*(2), 149–188.

20. Takemura, K. (1994). Influence of elaboration on the framing of decision. *The Journal of Psychology, 128,* 33–39.

21. Fagley, N. S., & Miller, P. M. (1987). The effects of decision framing on choice of risky vs certain options. *Organizational Behavior and Human Decision Processes, 39*(2), 264–277.

22. Bless, H., Betsch, T., & Franzen, A. (1998). Framing the framing effect: The impact of context cues on solutions to the "Asian disease" problem. *European Journal of Social Psychology, 28*(2), 287–291.

23. Hershey, M. R. (1999). If the party's in decline, then what's filling the news columns? In N. Polsby & R. Wolfinger, (eds.) *On Parties.* Berkeley: University of California.

24. Nelson, T. E., Clawson, R. A., & Oxley, Z. M. (1997).

25. Gross, K. (2000). The limits of framing: how framing effects may be

limited or enhanced by individual level predispositions. Paper presented at the annual meeting of the Midwest Political Science Association, Chicago, IL, April 27–30.

26. Kinder, D. R., & Sanders, L. M. (1990). Mimicking political debate with survey questions: the case of white opinion on affirmative action for blacks. *Social Cognition, 8,* 73–103.

27. Druckman, J. N. (2004). Political preference formation: Competition, deliberation, and the (ir) relevance of framing effects. *American Political Science Review, 98*(4), 671–686.

28. Chong, D., & Druckman, J. N. (2007). Framing public opinion in competitive democracies.

29. Groeling, T. (2010) *When partisans attack.* New York, NY: Cambridge University Press; Chong, D., & Druckman, J. N. (2007). Framing public opinion in competitive democracies; Chong, D., & Druckman, J. N. (2007). A theory of framing and opinion; Druckman, J. N. (2004). Political preference formation; Slothuus, R., More than weighting cognitive importance: A dual-process model of issue framing effects, *Political Psychology, 29*(1), 1–28; Slothuus, R., & De Vreese, C. H. (2010). Political parties, motivated reasoning, and issue framing effects. *The Journal of Politics, 72*(3), 630–645; Wagner, M. W. (2007). Utility of staying on message; Wagner, M. W. (2010). Great communicators? The influence of presidential issue framing on party identification, 1975–2000. In *Winning with Words: The Origins and Impacts of Framing,* B. F. Schaffner & P. J. Sellers (Eds.). New York, NY: Routledge; Brewer, P. R., & Gross, K. (2005). Values, framing, and citizens' thoughts about policy issues: Effects

on content and quantity. *Political Psychology, 26*(6), 929–948.; Hartman, T., & Weber, C. (2009). Who said what? The effects of source cues in issue frames. *Political Behavior, 31*(4), 537–558.

30. Sniderman, P. M., & Theriault, S. M. (2004). The structure of political argument and the logic of issue framing. *Studies in public opinion: Attitudes, nonattitudes, measurement error, and change,* 133–165.

31. Druckman, J. N., Peterson, E., & Slothuus, R. (2013). How elite partisan polarization affects public opinion formation. *American Political Science Review, 107*(1), 57–79.

32. Ibid.

33. Slothuus, R., & De Vreese, C. H. (2010). Political parties, motivated reasoning, and issue framing effects. *The Journal of Politics, 72*(3), 630–645.

34. Aarøe, L. (2012). When citizens go against elite directions: Partisan cues and contrast effects on citizens' attitudes. *Party Politics, 18*(2), 215–233.

35. Turner, J. (2007). The messenger overwhelming the message: Ideological cues and perceptions of bias in television news. *Political Behavior, 29*(4), 441–464.

36. Schemer, C., Wirth, W., & Matthes, J. (2012). Value resonance and value framing effects on voting intentions in direct-democratic campaigns. *American Behavioral Scientist, 56*(3), 334–352.

37. Aarøe, L., & Jensen, C. (2015). Learning to match: how prior frame exposure increases citizens' value matching abilities. *International Journal of Public Opinion Research, 27*(1), 46–70.

38. Lecheler, S., & De Vreese, C. H. (2011). Getting real: The duration of

framing effects. *Journal of Communication, 61*(5), 959–983.

39. Cho, J., Ahmed, S., Park, J. W., & Keum, H. (2016). Value framing effects on the decision-making process: Ethical and material frames and opinions about North Korean nuclear development. *International Journal of Communication, 10,* 21.

40. Lecheler, S., & de Vreese, C. H. (2013). What a difference a day makes? The effects of repetitive and competitive news framing over time. *Communication Research, 40*(2), 147–175.

41. Kellstedt, P. M. (2003). *The mass media and the dynamics of American racial attitudes.* Cambridge, UK: Cambridge University Press.

42. Wagner, M. W., & Gruszczynski, M. (2016). When framing matters: How partisan and journalistic frames affect individual opinions and party identification. *Journalism & Communication Monographs, 18*(1), 5–48.

43. Ellis, C., & Stimson, J. A. (2012). *Ideology in America.* Cambridge, UK: Cambridge University Press.

44. Lecheler, S., Bos, L., & Vliegenthart, R. (2015). The mediating role of emotions: News framing effects on opinions about immigration. *Journalism & Mass Communication Quarterly, 92*(4), 812–838.

45. Schuck, A. R., & De Vreese, C. H. (2006). Between risk and opportunity: News framing and its effects on public support for EU enlargement. *European Journal of Communication, 21*(1), 5–32.

46. Lecheler, S., de Vreese, C., & Slothuus, R. (2009). Issue importance as a moderator of framing effects. *Communication Research, 36*(3), 400–425.

47. Ju, Y. (2006). Policy or politics? A study of the priming of media frames of the South Korean president in the public mind. *International Journal of Public Opinion Research, 18*(1), 49–66.

48. Porto, M. P. (2007). Framing controversies: Television and the 2002 presidential election in Brazil. *Political Communication, 24*(1), 19–36.

49. Jamieson, K. H. (2017). Creating the hybrid field of political communication: A five-decade-long evolution of the concept of effects. In K. Kenski and K. H. Jamieson (Eds.), *Oxford handbook of political communication* (pp. 15–45). New York, NY: Oxford University Press.

50. Cacciatore, M. A., Scheufele, D. A., & Iyengar, S. (2016). The end of framing as we know it… and the future of media effects. *Mass Communication and Society, 19*(1), 7–23.

51. McLeod, D. M., and Shah, D. V. 2014. News Frames and National Security. New York: Cambridge University Press.

52. Chong, D., & Druckman, J. N. (2007). Framing public opinion in competitive democracies. *American Political Science Review, 101*(4), 637–655.

53. Meraz, S., & Papacharissi, Z. (2013). Networked gatekeeping and networked framing on# Egypt. *The International Journal of Press/Politics, 18*(2), 138–166.

Chapter 7

1. Lazarsfeld, P., Berelson, B., & Guadet, H. (1968). *The people's choice; how the voter makes up his mind in a presidential campaign.* New York, NY: Columbia University Press.

2. Stroud, N. (2010). Polarization and partisan selective exposure. *Journal of Communication, 60*(3), 556–576.

3. Knobloch-Westerwick, S., & Meng, J. (2009). Looking the other way: Selective exposure to attitude-consistent and counterattitudinal political information. *Communication Research, 36*(3), 426–448.

4. Garrett, R., & Stroud, N. (2014). Partisan paths to exposure diversity: Differences in pro- and counterattitudinal news consumption. *Journal of Communication, 64*(4), 680–701.

5. Nelson, J., & Webster, J. (2017). The myth of partisan selective exposure: A portrait of the online political news audience. *Social Media Society, 3*(3).

6. Jurkowitz, Mark, Amy Mitchell, Elisa Shearer, and Mason Walkder. "U.S. Media Polarization and the 2020 Election: A Nation Divided." Journalism Project. Pew Research Center, May 30, 2020. https://www.journalism.org/2020/01/24/u-s-media-polarization-and-the-2020-election-a-nation-divided/.

7. Ipsos. (September 2018). Fake news, filter bubbles, and post-truth are other people's problems. https://www.ipsos.com/ipsos-mori/en-uk/fake-news-filter-bubbles-and-post-truth-are-other-peoples-problems

8. Westfall, J., Van Boven, L., Chambers, J., & Judd, C. (2015). Perceiving political polarization in the United States: Party identity strength and attitude extremity exacerbate the perceived partisan divide. *Perspectives on Psychological Science, 10*(2), 145–158.

9. Barthel, M., & Mitchell, A. (2017). Americans' attitudes about the news media deeply divided along partisan lines. *Pew Research Center, 10*.

10. Vallone, R., Ross, L., & Lepper, M. (1985). The hostile media phenomenon: Biased perception and perceptions of media bias in coverage of the Beirut massacre. *Journal of Personality and Social Psychology, 49*(3), 577–585.

11. Hansen, G., & Kim, H. (2011). Is the media biased against me? A meta-analysis of the hostile media effect research. *Communication Research Reports, 28*(2), 169–179.

12. Doherty, C., Kiley, J., & Jameson, B. (2016). Partisanship and political animosity in 2016. *Pew Research Center, 75*.

13. Hoffner, C., & Rehkoff, R. (2011). Young voters' responses to the 2004 U.S. presidential election: Social identity, perceived media influence, and behavioral outcomes. *Journal of Communication, 61*(4), 732–757.

14. Gallup. (November, 2016). Majority of U.S. voters think media favors Clinton. https://news.gallup.com/poll/197090/majority-voters-think-media-favors-clinton.aspx

15. Gallup (2016).

16. Dalton, R., Beck, P., & Huckfeldt, R. (1998). Partisan cues and the media: Information flows in the 1992 presidential election. *The American Political Science Review, 92*(1), 111–126.

17. Gunther, A. C., Christen, C. T., Liebhart, J. L., & Chia, S. C.-Y. (2001). Congenial public, contrary press and biased estimates of the climate of opinion. *Public Opinion Quarterly, 65*, 295–320

18. Perryman, M. R. (2019). Where the other side gets news: Audience perceptions of selective exposure in the 2016 election, *International Journal of Public Opinion Research*, Advance Online Publication.

19. Coe, K., Tewksbury, D., Bond, B. J., Drogos, K. L., Porter, R. W., Yahn, A., & Zhang, Y. (2008). Hostile news: Partisan use and perceptions of cable news programming. *Journal of Communication, 58*(2), 201–219.

20. Perryman, M. R. (2019). Biased gatekeepers? Partisan perceptions of media attention in the 2016 US presidential election. *Journalism Studies, 20*(16), 2404–2421.

21. Gallup/Knight Foundation. (January, 2018). American views: Trust, media, and democracy. https://knightfound ation.org/reports/american-views-trust-media-and-democracy/

22. Domke, D., Watts, M., Shah, D., & Fan, D. (1999). The politics of conservative elites and the 'liberal media' argument. *Journal of Communication, 49*(4), 35–58.

23. https://thehill.com/homenews /administration/437610-trump-calls -press-the-enemy-of-the-people

24. https://www.nytimes.com/2019/05 /14/us/politics/elizabeth-warren-fox -news.html

25. Pennycook, G., & Rand, D. (2019). Fighting misinformation on social media using crowdsourced judgments of news source quality. *Proceedings of the National Academy of Sciences of the United States of America, 116*(7), 2521–2526.

26. Festinger, L. (1957). A theory of cognitive dissonance. Stanford: Stanford University Press.

27. Ableson, R. A. (1963). Computer simulation of "hot" cognition. In Computer simulation of personality: Frontier of psychological theory, ed. Silvan S. Tomkins and Samuel Messick, 277–298. Somerset, NJ: John Wiley and Sons.

28. Taber, C. S., and M. Lodge. 2006. Motivated Skepticism in the Evaluation of Political Beliefs. American Journal of Political Science 50:755–769.

29. Nyhan, B., & Reifler, J. (2010). When corrections fail: The persistence of political misperceptions. *Political Behavior, 32*(2), 303–330.

30. Redlawsk, D., Civettini, A., & Emmerson, K. (2010). The affective tipping point: Do motivated reasoners ever "get it"? *Political Psychology, 31*(4), 563–593.

31. Pennycook, G., & Rand D. (2019). Lazy, not biased: Susceptibility to partisan fake news is better explained by lack of reasoning than by motivated reasoning. *Cognition, 188,* 39–50.

32. Pronin, E., Berger, J., & Molouki, S. (2007). Alone in a crowd of sheep: Asymmetric perceptions of conformity and their roots in an introspection illusion. *Journal of Personality and Social Psychology, 92*(4), 585–595.

33. Meirick, P. C. (2004). Topic-relevant reference groups and dimensions of distance: Political advertising and first- and third-person effects. *Communication Research, 31*(2), 234–255.

34. Jensen, J., & Hurley, R. (2005). Third-person effects and the environment: Social distance, social desirability, and presumed behavior. *Journal of Communication, 55*(2), 242–256.

35. Gunther, A., & Storey, J. (2003). The influence of presumed influence. *Journal of Communication, 53*(2), 199–215.

36. Salwen, M. B. (1998). Perceptions of media influence and support for censorship: The third-person effect in the 1996 presidential election. *Communication Research, 25*(3), 259–285.

37. Salwen, M. B., & Dupagne, M. (1999). The third-person effect:

Perceptions of the media's influence and immoral consequences. *Communication Research, 26*(5), 523–549.

38. Rojas, H. (2010). "Corrective" actions in the public sphere: How perceptions of media and media effects shape political behaviors. *International Journal of Public Opinion Research, 22*(3), 343–363.

39. Barnidge, M., & Rojas, H. (2014). Hostile media perceptions, presumed media influence, and political talk: Expanding the corrective action hypothesis. *International Journal of Public Opinion Research, 26*(2), 135–156.

40. Carlson, T., & Settle, N. (2016). Political chameleons: An exploration of conformity in political discussions. *Political Behavior, 38*(4), 817–859.

41. Van der Meer, T., Hakhverdian, A., & Aaldering, L. (2016). Off the fence, onto the bandwagon? A large-scale survey experiment on effect of real-life poll outcomes on subsequent vote intentions. *International Journal of Public Opinion Research, 28*(1), 46–72.

42. Gunther, A., Bolt, D., Borzekowski, D., Liebhart, J., & Dillard, J. (2006). Presumed influence on peer norms: How mass media indirectly affect adolescent smoking. *Journal of Communication, 56*(1), 52–68.

43. Lang, A., Potter, R., & Bolls, P. (2009). Where psychophysiology meets the media. In J. Bryant, & M.B. Oliver (Eds.), *Media Effects: Advances in Theory and Research.* p. 185–206; p. 186

44. Wise, K., Eckler, P., Kononova, A., & Littau, J. (2009). Exploring the hardwired for news hypothesis: How threat proximity affects the cognitive and emotional processing of health-related print news. *Communication Studies, 60*(3), 268–287.

45. Soroka, S., & McAdams, S. (2015). News, politics, and negativity. *Political Communication, 32*(1), 1–22.

46. Blanton, H., Strauts, E., & Perez, M. (2012). Partisan identification as a predictor of cortisol response to election news. *Political Communication, 29*(4), 447–460.

47. Westen, D., Blagov, P. S., Harenski, K., Kilts, C., & Hamann, S. (2006). Neural bases of motivated reasoning: An fMRI study of emotional constraints on partisan political judgment in the 2004 US presidential election. *Journal of cognitive neuroscience, 18*(11), 1947–1958.

48. Inbar, Y., Pizarro, D., Iyer, R., & Haidt, J. (2012). Disgust sensitivity, political conservatism, and voting. *Social Psychological and Personality Science, 3*(5), 537–544.

49. Ruisch, B., Anderson, R., Inbar, Y., & Pizarro, D. (2017). A matter of taste: Gustatory sensitivity predicts social conservatism. *Paper presented at the annual meeting of the Annual Scientific Meeting of the International Society of Political Psychology, The Royal College of Surgeons Edinburgh, Edinburgh, Scotland, U.K.*

50. Schaller, M. (2011). The behavioural immune system and the psychology of human sociality. *Philosophical Transactions of the Royal Society B, 366*(1583), 3418–3426.

51. Aarøe, L., Petersen, M., & Arceneaux, K. (2017). The behavioral immune system shapes political intuitions: Why and how individual differences in disgust sensitivity underlie opposition to immigration. American Political Science Review, *111*(2), 277–294.

52. Jost, J., Noorbaloochi, S., & Van Bavel, J. (2014). The "chicken-and-egg" problem in political

neuroscience. *Behavioral and Brain Sciences, 37*(3), 317–318.

53. Pronin, E., Lin, D. Y., & Ross, L. (2002). The bias blind spot: Perceptions of bias in self versus others. *Personality and Social Psychology Bulletin, 28*(3), 369–381.

54. Stroud, N. J. (2017). Attention as a valuable resource. *Political Communication, 34*(3): 479–489.

55. Nir, L., McClurg,, S. D. (2015). How Institutions Affect Gender Gaps in Public Opinion Expression, *Public Opinion Quarterly, 79*(2), 544–567.

Chapter 8

1. http://mediaproject.wesleyan.edu/

2. Wesleyan Media Project. (June 2018) TV ad volume nearly doubles over prior midterm cycle. https://mediaproject .wesleyan.edu/june-2018/

3. Berg, R. (August 2018). Meet the man behind some of 2018's most viral campaign videos. *CNN.* https://www .cnn.com/2018/08/03/politics/mark -putnam-viral-ad-maker/index.html

4. Fowler, E. F., Franz, M., Ridout, T. (2016). *Political advertising in the United States.* Boulder, CO: Westview

5. Lapowsky, I. (2016). Here's how Facebook actually won Trump the presidency. *Wired,* November 15.

6. Herrnson, P. S., Panagopoulos, C., & Bailey, K. L. (2019). *Congressional Elections: Campaigning at Home and in Washington.* Washington, DC: CQ Press.

7. Moshary, S. (2014). Price discrimination across pacs and the consequences of political advertising regulation. *mimeographed, MIT.*

8. Eggen, D. (September, 2012). Obama has more control of campaign cash,
and with it an edge in ad rates. *The Washington Post.*

9. Wesleyan Media Project. (September, 2018). Outside group ads up 85% in federal races. http://mediaproject .wesleyan.edu/092018/

10. Ridout, T. N., Fowler, E. F., Branstetter, J., & Borah, P. (2015). Politics as usual? When and why traditional actors often dominate YouTube campaigning. *Journal of Information Technology & Politics, 12*(3), 237–251.

11. Voorhees, J. (November, 2015). Candidates and their super PACs can't legally coordinate. Here's how they do anyway. *Slate.* https://slate.com /news-and-politics/2015/11/how -candidates-and-their-super-pacs -coordinate-through-the-media.html

12. Opensecrets.org. (November, 2016). $1.4 billion and counting in spending by super PACs, dark money groups. Center for Responsive Politics.

13. Wesleyan Media Project. (November, 2018). More dark money ads than any of the past four cycles. https:// mediaproject.wesleyan.edu/110118-tv/

14. Kaye, K. (2017). Data-driven targeting creates huge 2016 political ad shift: Broadcast TV down 20%, cable and digital way up. *Advertising Age.*

15. Nielsen. (July, 2018). Television is still top brass, but viewing differences vary with age. https://www.nielsen.com/us /en/insights/article/2016/television -is-still-top-brass-but-viewing -differences-vary-with-age/

16. Brian Steinberg. (September, 2016). Advertisers flock to Donald Trump-Hillary Clinton presidential debates. *Variety.*

17. Marc Levitt. (November, 2018). The heyday of television ads is over. Political campaigns ought to act like it. *The Washington Post.*

18. Kaye, K. (2012). Digital ad spend gap widens between Obama and Romney. *ClickZ*.

19. Kim, C. (May, 2019). Trump's 2020 campaign is buying a whole lot of Facebook ads. *Vox*. https://www.vox .com/2019/5/21/18634085/trumps -2020-campaign-is-buying-a-whole -lot-of-facebook-ads

20. Fowler, E. F., Franz, M., & Ridout, T. (2016).

21. Turow, J., Delli Carpini, M. X., Draper, N. A., & Howard-Williams, R. (2012). Americans roundly reject tailored political advertising. Annenberg School for Communication.

22. Young, D. [dannagal]. (2018, March 20). PS: reporter asked what Facebook should do to solve this crisis. I replied, "Slow Down and Fix Things." #NotableQuotable. [tweet].

23. Tromble, R., & McGregor, S. C. (2019). You break it, you buy it: The naiveté of social engineering in tech–And how to fix it. *Political Communication*, 36(2), 324–332.

24. Kreiss, D., & McGregor, S. C. (2018). Technology firms shape political communication: The work of Microsoft, Facebook, Twitter, and Google with campaigns during the 2016 US presidential cycle. *Political Communication*, 35(2), 155–177.

25. https://www.youtube.com/watch?v= Zi6v4CYNSIQ

26. https://www.youtube.com/watch?v= mhAavbxpjok

27. Wesleyan Media Project. (October, 2018). 61% increase in volume of negative ads. http://mediaproject .wesleyan.edu/103018/

28. Pew Research Center. (September, 2016). Already-low voter satisfaction with choice of candidates falls even further. https://www.pewresearch .org/fact-tank/2016/09/12/already -low-voter-satisfaction-with-choice -of-candidates-falls-even-further/

29. Theiss-Morse, E. A., Wagner, M. W., Flanigan, W. H., & Zingale, N. H. (2018). *Political Behavior of the American Electorate*, 14th ed. CQ Press.

30. Rijkhoff, S., & Ridout, T. (2019). Your lying, incompetent and selfish member of Congress: Cynical appeals in U.S. Senate advertising. *Social Science Journal, 56*(1), 38–47.

31. Brader, T. (2005). Striking a responsive chord: How political ads motivate and persuade voters by appealing to emotions. *American Journal of Political Science, 49*, 388–405.

32. Strach, P., Zuber, K., Fowler, E. F., Ridout, T. N., & Searles, K. (2015). In a different voice? Explaining the use of men and women as voice-over announcers in political advertising. *Political Communication, 32*(2), 183–205.

33. Vavreck, L. (2009). *The message matters: The economy and presidential campaigns*. Princeton, NJ: Princeton University Press.

34. Petrocik, J. (1996). Issue ownership in presidential elections, with a 1980 case study. *American Journal of Political Science, 40*(3), 825–850.

35. Sides, J. (2007). The consequences of campaign agendas. *American Politics Research, 35*(4), 465–488.

36. Sides, J. (2006). The origins of campaign agendas. *British Journal of Political Science, 36*(3), 407–436.

37. Brustein, J. (November, 2018). Three Democrats are buying almost all the campaign ads on Twitter."

Bloomberg. https://www.bloomberg .com/news/articles/2018-11-02 /three-democrats-are-buying-almost -all-the-campaign-ads-on-twitter

38. Pew Research Center. (June, 2019). State of the news media: Social media fact sheet.

39. Bode, L., Lassen, D., Kim, Y., Shah, D., Fowler, E., Ridout, T., & Franz, M. (2016). Coherent campaigns? Campaign broadcast and social messaging. *Online Information Review, 40*(5), 580–594

40. Evans, H. K., Smith, S., Gonzales, A., & Strouse, K. (2017). Mudslinging on Twitter during the 2014 election. *Social Media+ Society, 3*(2), 2056305117704408.

41. Evans, H., Habib, J., Litzen, D., San Jose, B., & Ziegenbein, A. (2019). Awkward Independents: What are third-party candidates doing on Twitter? *PS: Political Science & Politics, 52*(1), 1–6.

42. Lapowsky, I. (March, 2016). YouTube is the unsung juggernaut of this election season. *Wired.* https:// www.wired.com/2016/03/youtube -unsung-juggernaut-election-season/

43. Pew Research Center. (June, 2019). State of the news media: social media fact sheet.

44. Ridout, T. N., Fowler, E. F., Branstetter, J., & Borah, P. (2015).

45. Harwell, D. (March, 2016). How YouTube is shaping the 2016 presidential election. *The Washington Post.*

46. Bump, P. (October, 2017). "60 Minutes" profiles the genius who won Trump's campaign: Facebook. *The Washington Post.*

47. Frier, S. (April, 2018). Trump's campaign said it was better at Facebook. Facebook agrees. *Bloomberg.*

48. Real Clear Politics. (2008). Democratic presidential nomination polling. https://www.realclearpolitics .com/epolls/2008/president/us /democratic_presidential_nomina- tion-191.html

49. Allison, Bill, and Mark Niquette. "Bloomberg Tops Half a Billion Dollars in Campaign Advertising." Bloomberg.com. Bloomberg, February 24, 2020. https://www.bloom- berg.com/news/articles/2020-02-24/ bloomberg-tops-half-a-billion-dol- lars-in-campaign-advertising.

50. Gallup. (January, 2018). Americans' identification as Independents back up in 2017. https://news.gallup.com /poll/225056/americans-identification -independents-back-2017.aspx

51. Sides, J. (2009). Three myths about political independents. *The Monkey Cage.*; Hawkins, C., & Nosek, B. (2012). Motivated independence? Implicit party identity predicts political judgments among self-proclaimed Independents. *Personality and Social Psychology Bulletin, 38*(11), 1437–1452.

52. Fournier, P., Nadeau, R., Blais, A., Gidengil, E., & Nevitte, N. (2004). Time-of-voting decision and susceptibility to campaign effects. *Electoral Studies, 23*(4), 661–681.

53. Bon, J., Ballard, T., & Baffour, B. (2019). Polling bias and undecided voter allocations: US presidential elections, 2004–2016. *Journal of the Royal Statistical Society. Series A, Statistics in Society, 182*(2), 467–493.

54. Silver, N. (January, 2017). The invisible undecided voter. *FiveThirtyEight.*

55. https://elections.huffingtonpost .com/pollster/uk-european-union -referendum

56. Pew Research Center. (June, 2014). Political polarization in the American public.

57. Kalla, J., & Broockman, D. (2018). The minimal persuasive effects of campaign contact in general elections: Evidence from 49 field experiments, *American Political Science Review*, 112(1), 148–166.

58. Hillygus, D. S., & Shields, T. G. (2008). *The persuadable voter: Wedge issues in presidential campaigns*. Princeton, NJ: Princeton University Press.

59. Carmines, E. G., Ensley, M. J., & Wagner, M. W. (2012). Who fits the left-right divide? Partisan polarization in the American electorate. *American Behavioral Scientist*, 56(12), 1631–1653.

60. Franz, M., Ridout, T., & Goren, P. (2010). Political advertising and persuasion in the 2004 and 2008 presidential elections. *American Politics Research*, 38(2), 303–329.

61. Hill, S. J., Lo, J., Vavreck, L., & Zaller, J. (2013). How quickly we forget: The duration of persuasion effects from mass communication. *Political Communication*, 30(4), 521–547.

62. Bartels, L. M. (2014). Remembering to forget: A note on the duration of campaign advertising effects. *Political Communication*, 31(4), 532–544.

63. Kalla, J., & Broockman, D. (2018).

64. Gerber, A., Gimpel, J., Green, D., & Shaw, D. (2011). How Large and Long-lasting Are the Persuasive Effects of Televised Campaign Ads? Results from a Randomized Field Experiment. The American Political Science Review, 105(1), 135-150.

65. Brader, T. (2005).

66. Ridout, T. N., & Searles, K. (2011). It's my campaign I'll cry if I want to: How and when campaigns use emotional appeals. *Political Psychology*, 32, 439–458.

67. Lau, R., Sigelman, L., & Rovner, I. (2007). The effects of negative political campaigns: A meta-analytic reassessment. *Journal of Politics*, 69(4), 1176–1209.

68. Lau, Sigelman, & Rovner, 1183.

69. Weinberger, J., & Westen, D. (2008). RATS, we should have used Clinton: Subliminal priming in political campaigns. *Political Psychology*, 29, 631–651.

70. Helzer, E. G., & Pizarro, D. A. (2011). Dirty liberals!: Reminders of physical cleanliness influence moral and political attitudes. *Psychological Science*, 22(4), 517–522.

71. Inbar, Y., Pizarro, D. A., & Bloom, P. (2012). Disgusting smells cause decreased liking of gay men. *Emotion*, 12(1), 23–27.

72. Johnston, R., Hagen, M., & Jamieson, K. H. (2004). *The 2000 presidential election and the foundations of party politics*. New York, NY: Cambridge University Press.

73. Spenkuch, J., & Toniatti, D. (2018). Political advertising and election results. *The Quarterly Journal of Economics*, 133(4), 1981–2036.

74. Smets, K., & Van Ham, C. (2013). The embarrassment of riches? A meta-analysis of individual-level research on voter turnout. *Electoral Studies*, 32(2), 344–359.

75. Green, D., & Vavreck, L. (2008). Analysis of Cluster-Randomized Experiments: A Comparison of Alternative Estimation Approaches. *Political Analysis*, 16(2), 138–152.

76. Bond, R. M., Fariss, C. J., Jones, J. J., Kramer, A. D., Marlow, C., Settle,

J. E., & Fowler, J. H. (2012). A 61-million-person experiment in social influence and political mobilization. *Nature*, *489*(7415), 295–298.

77. Green, D. P., & Gerber, A. S. (2019). *Get out the vote: How to increase voter turnout.* Washington, DC: Brookings Institution Press.

78. Broockman, D., & Green, D. (2014). Do online advertisements increase political candidates' name recognition or favorability? Evidence from randomized field experiments. *Political Behavior, 36*(2), 263–289.

79. Fowler, E. F., & Ridout, T. N. (2009). Local television and newspaper coverage of political advertising. *Political Communication, 26*(2), 119–136.

80. Gruszczynski, M., & Wagner, M. W. (2017). Information flow in the 21st century: The dynamics of agenda-uptake. *Mass communication and society, 20*(3), 378–402.

81. https://www.youtube.com/watch?reload=9&v=Wo_Ejfc5hW8

82. Ridout, T., & Smith, G. (2008). Free advertising: How the media amplify campaign messages. *Political Research Quarterly, 61*(4), 598–608. Retrieved from http://www.jstor.org/stable/20299763

83. Fowler, E. F., & Ridout, T. N. (2009).

84. Cohen, Bernard C., The Press and Foreign Policy (1963). Princeton University Press. p. 13.

Chapter 9

1. Dahl, R. A. (1971). *Polyarchy: Participation and opposition.* New Haven, CT: Yale University Press.

2. Silver, N. (2011). On the maddeningly inexact relationship between unemployment and re-election, *FiveThirtyEight* (blog), *New York Times.* http://fivethirtyeight.blogs.nytimes.com/2011/06/02/on-the-maddeningly-inexact-relationship-between-unemployment-and-re-election/?_r=0

3. https://news.gallup.com/poll/259871/trump-approval-remains-low-40s.aspx

4. https://news.gallup.com/interactives/185273/presidential-job-approval-center.aspx?g_source=link_NEWSV9&g_medium=TOPIC&g_campaign=item_&g_content=Presidential%2520Job%2520Approval%2520Center

5. https://news.gallup.com/poll/243971/trump-job-approval-improves.aspx?g_source=link_NEWSV9&g_medium=TOPIC&g_campaign=item_&g_content=Trump%2520Job%2520Approval%2520Improves%2520to%252044%2525

6. Theiss-Morse, E. A., Wagner, M. W., Flanigan, W. H., & Zingale, N. H. (2018). *Political Behavior of the American Electorate*, 14th ed. CQ Press.

7. https://www.npr.org/2018/11/08/665197690/a-boatload-of-ballots-midterm-voter-turnout-hit-50-year-high

8. http://bostonreview.net/mcghee-nyhan-sides-midterm-postmortem

9. Prior, M. (2006). The incumbent in the living room: The rise of television and the incumbency advantage in US House elections. *The Journal of Politics, 68*(3), 657–673.

10. Graber, D. A. (1997). *Mass media and American politics*, 5th ed, Washington, DC: Congressional Quarterly Press.

11. https://www.journalism.org/2017/01/18/trump-clinton-voters-divided-in-their-main-source-for-election-news/

12. Graber, D. A., & Dunaway, J. (2017). *Mass media and American politics*, 10th ed., Washington, DC: CQ Press.

13. Graber and Dunaway, p. 403.

14. https://www.pewresearch.org/fact-tank/2018/06/05/almost-seven-in-ten-americans-have-news-fatigue-more-among-republicans/

15. https://www.politico.com/blogs/on-media/2016/02/les-moonves-trump-cbs-220001

16. https://shorensteincenter.org/pre-primary-news-coverage-2016-trump-clinton-sanders/;https://www.washingtonpost.com/news/politics/wp/2017/09/12/assessing-a-clinton-argument-that-the-media-helped-to-elect-trump/?utm_term=.aed936bef1ea

17. Dunaway, J., & Lawrence, R. G. (2015). What predicts the game frame? Media ownership, electoral context, and campaign news. *Political Communication*, 32(1), 43–60.

18. Jamieson, K. H., & Waldman, P. (2003). *The press effect: Politicians, journalists, and the stories that shape the political world*. New York, NY: Oxford University Press.

19. Graber, D. A., & Weaver, D. (1996). Presidential performance criteria: The missing element in election coverage. *Harvard International Journal of Press/Politics*, 1(1), 7–32.

20. Pease, A., & Brewer, P. R. (2008). The Oprah factor: The effects of a celebrity endorsement in a presidential primary campaign. *The International Journal of Press/Politics*, 13(4), 386–400.

21. Uscinski, J. E., & Goren, L. J. (2011). What's in a name? Coverage of Senator Hillary Clinton during the 2008 democratic primary. *Political Research Quarterly*, 64(4), 884–896.

22. Belt, T. L., Just, M. R., & Crigler, A. N. (2012). The 2008 media primary: Handicapping the candidates in newspapers, on TV, cable, and the internet. *The International Journal of Press/Politics*, 17(3), 341–369.

23. https://shorensteincenter.org/pre-primary-news-coverage-2016-trump-clinton-sanders/

24. Wells, C., Shah, D. V., Pevehouse, J. C., Yang, J., Pelled, A., Boehm, F., ... & Schmidt, J. L. (2016). How Trump drove coverage to the nomination: Hybrid media campaigning. *Political Communication*, 33(4), 669–676.

25. McGregor, S.C. (2019). Social media as public opinion: How journalists use social media to represent public opinion. *Journalism*.

26. https://www.cjr.org/analysis/tweets-russia-news.php

27. Harder, R. A., Sevenans, J., & Van Aelst, P. (2017). Intermedia agenda setting in the social media age: How traditional players dominate the news agenda in election times. *The International Journal of Press/Politics*, 22(3), 275–293.

28. Iyengar, S., Norpoth, H., & Hahn, K. S. (2004). Consumer demand for election news: The horserace sells. *The Journal of Politics*, 66(1), 157–175.

29. Toff, B. (2019). The "Nate Silver effect" on political journalism: Gatecrashers, gatekeepers, and changing newsroom practices around coverage of public opinion polls. *Journalism*, 20(7), 873–889.

30. https://shorensteincenter.org/news-coverage-2016-general-election/

31. De Vreese, C. H., Banducci, S. A., Semetko, H. A., & Boomgaarden, H.

G. (2006). The news coverage of the 2004 European Parliamentary election campaign in 25 countries. *European Union Politics*, 7(4), 477–504.

32. https://shorensteincenter.org/news -coverage-2016-general-election/

33. Hayes, D. (2008). Does the messenger matter? Candidate-media agenda convergence and its effects on voter issue salience. *Political Research Quarterly*, 61(1), 134–146

34. Hayes, D. (2008). Party reputations, journalistic expectations: How issue ownership influences election news. *Political Communication*, 25(4), 377–400.

35. Mondak, J. J. (1995). Media exposure and political discussion in US elections. *The Journal of Politics*, 57(1), 62–85.

36. Wells, C., Cramer, K. J., Wagner, M. W., Alvarez, G., Friedland, L. A., Shah, D. V., ... & Franklin, C. (2017). When we stop talking politics: The maintenance and closing of conversation in contentious times. *Journal of Communication*, 67(1), 131–157; Wagner, M. W., Wells, C., Friedland, L. A., Cramer, K. J., & Shah, D. V. (2014). Cultural worldviews and contentious politics: Evaluative asymmetry in high-information environments. *The Good Society*, 23(2), 126–144.

37. Settle, J. E., & Carlson, T. N. (2019). Opting out of political discussions. *Political Communication*, 36(3), 476–496.

38. Carmines, E. G., Gerrity, J. C., & Wagner, M. W. (2008). Did the media do it? The influence of news coverage on the 2006 Congressional elections. In *Fault Lines*, J. J. Mondak & D. G. Mitchell (Eds.), (pp. 22–41). New York, NY: Routledge Press.

39. https://www.independent.co.uk /news/world/americas/alex-jones-sa ndy-hook-school-shooting-conspi racy-false-flag-infowars-lawsuit -a8847016.html

40. Boydstun, A. E., Glazier, R. A., & Pietryka, M. T. (2013). Playing to the crowd: Agenda control in presidential debates. *Political Communication*, 30(2), 254–277.

41. Sigelman, L., & Sigelman, C. K. (1984). Judgments of the Carter-Reagan debate: The eyes of the beholders. *Public Opinion Quarterly*, 48(3), 624–628.

42. Benoit, W. L., & Hansen, G. J. (2004). Presidential debate watching, issue knowledge, character evaluation, and vote choice. *Human Communication Research*, 30(1), 121–144.

43. Holbert, R. L. (2005). Debate viewing as mediator and partisan reinforcement in the relationship between news use and vote choice. *Journal of Communication*, 55(1), 85–102.

44. Fridkin, K. L., Kenney, P. J., Gershon, S. A., & Serignese Woodall, G. (2008). Spinning debates: The impact of the news media's coverage of the final 2004 presidential debate. *The International Journal of Press/Politics*, 13(1), 29–51.

45. https://www.washingtonpost.com /news/fact-checker/wp/2016/09 /27/fact-checking-the-first-clinton -trump-presidential-debate/?utm _term=.cf223162a22b

46. Wintersieck, A. L. (2017). Debating the truth: The impact of fact-checking during electoral debates. *American Politics Research*, 45(2), 304–331.

47. Shah, D. V., Hanna, A., Bucy, E. P., Lassen, D. S., Van Thomme, J., Bialik, K., ... & Pevehouse, J. C. (2016). Dual screening during presidential debates: Political nonverbals and the volume and valence of

online expression. *American Behavioral Scientist, 60*(14), 1816–1843.

48. Schaffner, B. F. (2005). Priming gender: Campaigning on women's issues in US Senate elections. *American Journal of Political Science, 49*(4), 803–817.

49. Lawless, J. L., & Fox, R. L. (2012). *It still takes a candidate.* New York, NY: Cambridge University Press.

50. Dunaway, J., Lawrence, R. G., Rose, M., & Weber, C. R. (2013). Traits versus issues: How female candidates shape coverage of senate and gubernatorial races. *Political Research Quarterly, 66*(3), 715–726.

51. Hayes, D., & Lawless, J. L. (2015). A non-gendered lens? Media, voters, and female candidates in contemporary congressional elections. *Perspectives on Politics, 13*(1), 95–118.

52. Meeks, L., & Domke, D. (2016). When politics is a woman's game: Party and gender ownership in woman-versus-woman elections. *Communication Research, 43*(7), 895–921.

53. Kittilson, M. C., & Fridkin, K. (2008). Gender, candidate portrayals and election campaigns: A comparative perspective. *Politics & gender, 4*(3), 371–392.

54. Terkildsen, N., & Damore, D. F. (1999). The dynamics of racialized media coverage in congressional elections. *The Journal of Politics, 61*(3), 680–699.

55. Goldman, S. K. (2012). Effects of the 2008 Obama presidential campaign on White racial prejudice. *Public Opinion Quarterly, 76*(4), 663–687.

56. Dunaway, J. (2013). Media ownership and story tone in campaign news. *American Politics Research,* 41(1), 24–53; Kaplan, M., Goldstein, K., & Hale, M. (2005). Local news coverage of the 2004 campaigns. Los Angeles, CA: USC Annenberg School and University of Wisconsin.

57. Stromer-Galley, J. (2014). *Presidential campaigning in the internet age.* New York, NY: Oxford University Press; Kreiss, D. (2016). *Prototype politics: Technology -intensive campaigning and the data of democracy.* New York, NY: Oxford University Press.

58. Groshek, J., & Koc-Michalska, K. (2017). Helping populism win? Social media use, filter bubbles, and support for populist presidential candidates in the 2016 US election campaign. *Information, Communication & Society, 20*(9), 1389–1407.

59. Guess, A., Nyhan, B., & Reifler, J. (2018). Selective exposure to misinformation: Evidence from the consumption of fake news during the 2106 U.S. presidential campaign. http://www.ask-force.org/web/Fundamentalists/Guess-Selective-Exposure-to-Misinformation-Evidence-Presidential-Campaign-2018.pdf

60. Grinberg, N., Joseph, K., Friedland, L., Swire-Thompson, B., & Lazer, D. (2019). Fake news on Twitter during the 2016 U.S. presidential election. *Science* 363(6425), 374–378.

61. Hopmann, D. N., Vliegenthart, R., De Vreese, C., & Albæk, E. (2010). Effects of election news coverage: How visibility and tone influence party choice. *Political communication, 27*(4), 389–405.

62. Druckman, J. N., & Parkin, M. (2005). The impact of media bias: How editorial slant affects voters. *The Journal of Politics, 67*(4), 1030–1049.

63. Gerber, A. S., Karlan, D., & Bergan, D. (2009). Does the media matter? A

field experiment measuring the effect of newspapers on voting behavior and political opinions. *American Economic Journal: Applied Economics, 1*(2), 35–52.

64. DellaVigna, S., & Kaplan, E. (2007). The Fox News effect: Media bias and voting. *The Quarterly Journal of Economics, 122*(3), 1187–1234.

65. Oberholzer-Gee, F., & Waldfogel, J. (2009). Media markets and localism: Does local news en Espanol boost Hispanic voter turnout? *American Economic Review, 99*(5), 2120–2128.

66. Enos, R. D., & Fowler, A. (2018). Aggregate effects of large-scale campaigns on voter turnout. *Political Science Research and Methods, 6*(4), 733–751.

Chapter 10

1. Cook, T. (1998). *Governing with the news*. Chicago, IL: University of Chicago Press.

2. Mazzoleni, G. (1995). Towards a "videocracy"? Italian political communication at a turning point. *Eur. J. Commun. 10*, 291–319

3. Cook, T. E. (2006). The news media as a political institution: Looking backward and looking forward. *Political Communication, 23*(2), 159–171.

4. Page, B. I. (1996). *Who deliberates? Mass media in modern democracy*. Chicago, IL: University of Chicago Press.

5. Graber, D. A. (2003). *The power of communication: Managing information in public organizations*. Washington, DC: CQ Press.

6. Cook, T. E. (2006).

7. Herbst, S. (1998). Reading public opinion: How political actors view the democratic process. Chicago,

IL: University of Chicago Press; Edwards, G. C. (2003). *On deaf ears: The limits of the bully pulpit*. New Haven, CT: Yale University Press.

8. Wolfe, M., Jones, B. D., & Baumgartner, F. R. (2013). A failure to communicate: Agenda setting in media and policy studies. *Political Communication, 30*(2), 175–192.

9. Walker, J. L. (1977). Setting the agenda in the U.S. Senate: A theory of problem selection. *British Journal of Political Science, 7*, 423–445.

10. Wolfe, M., Jones, B. D., & Baumgartner, F. R. (2013).

11. Altheide, D. (1991). The impact of television news formats on social policy. *Journal of Broadcasting and Electronic Media, 35*(1): 3–21.

12. Protess, D. L., Cook, F. L., Curtin, T. R., Gordon, M. T., Leff, D. R., McCombs, M. E., & Miller, P. (1987). The impact of investigative reporting on public opinion and policymaking targeting toxic waste. *Public Opinion Quarterly, 51*(2), 166–185.

13. Cook, F. L., Tyler, T. R., Goetz, E. G., Gordon, M. T., Protess, D., Leff, D. R., & Molotch, H. L. (1983). Media and agenda setting: Effects on the public, interest group leaders, policy makers, and policy. *Public opinion quarterly, 47*(1), 16–35.

14. Baumgartner, F. R., & Jones, B. D. (1993). *Agendas and instability in American politics*. Chicago, IL: University of Chicago Press.

15. Kingdon, J. W. (1984). *Agenda, alternatives and public policies*. Boston, MA: Little, Brown.

16. Jones, B. D., & Wolfe, M. (2010). *Public policy and the mass media: An information processing approach*. In S.

Koch-Baumgarten & K. Voltmer (Eds.), Public policy and the media: The interplay of mass communication and political decision making (pp. 17–43). New York, NY: Routledge.

17. Yanovitzky, I. (2002). Effects of news coverage on policy attention and actions: A closer look into the media-policy connection. *Communication Research, 29*(4), 422–451.

18. Downs, A. (1972). Up and down with ecology: The issue attention cycle. *Public Interest, 28*, 28–50.

19. Wolfe, M., Jones, B. D., & Baumgartner, F. R. (2013).

20. Soroka, S. N. (2002). Issue attributes and agenda-setting by media, the public and policymakers in Canada. *International Journal of Public Opinion Research, 14*(3), 264–285.

21. Wolfe, M., Jones, B. D., & Baumgartner, F. R. (2013).

22. Edelman, M. J. (1985). *The symbolic uses of politics*. Urbana: University of Illinois Press.

23. Nelson, B. J. (1986). *Making an issue of child abuse: Political agenda setting for social problems*, Chicago, IL: University of Chicago Press. As cited in Wolfe, Jones and Baumgartner.

24. Riker, W. H. (1986). *The art of political manipulation*, New Haven, CT: Yale University Press.

25. Jones, B. D. (1994). *Reconceiving decision making in democratic politics: Attention, choice, and public policy*, Chicago, IL: University of Chicago Press.

26. https://www.nbcnews.com/politics/politics-news/wisconsin-legislature-send-abortion-bills-governor-who-plans-veto-them-n1014016

27. Lippman, W. (1922). *Public opinion*, New York, NY: Macmillan; Linsky,

M. (1986). *Impact: How the press affects federal policymaking*, New York, NY: Norton; Rochefort, D. A., & Cobb, R. W. (1993). Problem definition, agenda access and policy choice. *Policy Studies Journal, 21*, 56–72.

28. Gamson, W. A., & Modigliani, A. (1989). Media discourse and public opinion on nuclear power: A constructionist approach. *American Journal of Sociology, 95*, 1–37.

29. Jones, B. D., & Baumgartner, F. R. (2005). *The Politics of attention: How government prioritizes problems*, Chicago, IL: University of Chicago Press.

30. Kingdon, J. W. (1984). *Agendas, alternatives, and public policies*, Boston, MA: Little, Brown.

31. Baumgartner, F. R., Berry, J. M., Hojnacki, M., Kimball, D. C., & Leech, B. L. (2009). *Lobbying and policy change: Who wins, who loses, and why*, Chicago, IL: University of Chicago Press.

32. Carmines, E. G., Gerrity, J. C., & Wagner, M. W. (2010). How abortion became a partisan issue: Media coverage of the interest group-political party connection. *Politics & Policy, 38*(6), 1135–1158; Wagner, M. W. (2010). Great communicators? The influence of presidential issue framing on party Identification, 1975–2000. In *Winning with Words: The Origins and Impacts of Framing*, B. F. Schaffner, P. J. Sellers (Eds.), (pp. 136–159). New York, NY: Routledge Press; Carmines, E. G., Ensley, M. J., & Wagner, M. W. (2014). Why Americans can't get beyond the left-right divide. In J. C. Green, D. Coffey, & D. Cohen (Eds.), *The State of the Parties: The Changing Role of Contemporary Parties*, (pp. 55–72). Lanham, MD: Rowan and Littlefield.

33. Baumgartner, F. R., De Boef, S. L., & Boydstun, A. E. (2008). *The decline of the death penalty and the discovery of innocence*, New York, NY: Cambridge University Press.

34. Gruszczynski, M. W., & Michaels, S. (2012). The evolution of elite framing following enactment of legislation. *Policy Sciences*, 45(4), 359–384.

35. Gruszczynski, M., & Michaels, S. (2014). Localized concerns, scientific argumentation, framing, and federalism: the case of Devils Lake water diversion. *Journal of Natural Resources Policy Research*, 6(2–3), 173–193.

36. Green-Pedersen, C., & Stubager, R. (2010). The political conditionality of mass media influence: When do parties follow mass media attention? *British Journal of Political Science*, 40(3), 663–677.

37. Fawzi, N. (2018). Beyond policy agenda-setting: political actors' and journalists' perceptions of news media influence across all stages of the political process. *Information, Communication & Society*, 21(8), 1134–1150.

38. Baum, M. A., & Potter, P. B. (2019). Media, public opinion, and foreign policy in the age of social media. *The Journal of Politics*, 81(2), 747–756.

39. Gadarian, S. K. (2010). The politics of threat: How terrorism news shapes foreign policy attitudes. *The Journal of Politics*, 72(2), 469–483.

40. Graber, D. A., & Dunaway, J. (2017). *Mass media and American politics*, 10th ed. Washington, DC: CQ Press.

41. Crow, D. A., & Lawlor, A. (2016). Media in the policy process: Using framing and narratives to understand policy influences. *Review of Policy Research*, 33(5), 472–491.

Chapter 11

1. We stole this metaphor from *Lincoln*, Directed by Steven Spielberg and Written by Tony Kushner.

2. Gabielkov, M., Ramachandran, A., Chaintreau, A., & Legout, A. (2016). Social clicks: What and who gets read on Twitter? *Proceedings of the 2016 ACM SIGMETRICS International Conference on Measurement and Modeling of Computer Science*, 179–192.

3. Molla, R., & Wagner, K. (March, 2019). Facebook wants to share more local news, but it's having trouble finding it. *Vox*.

4. Ha, Anthony. (January, 2019). Facebook says it will invest $300M in local news. *Techcrunch*.

5. Su, L., Xenos, M., Rose, K., Wirz, C., Scheufele, D., & Brossard, D. (2018). Uncivil and personal? Comparing patterns of incivility in comments on the Facebook pages of news outlets. *New Media & Society*, 20(10), 3678–3699.

6. Tromble, R., & McGregor, S. C. (2019). You break it, you buy it: The naiveté of social engineering in tech- And how to fix it. *Political Communication*, 36(2), 324–332.

7. Pew Research Center. (2019). 10% of Americans don't use the internet. Who are they? https://www.pewresearch.org/fact-tank/2019/04/22/some-americans-dont-use-the-internet-who-are-they/

8. Roetters, J. (April, 2019). Cord cutting will accelerate in 2019, skinny bundles poised to fail (Report). *Variety*.

9. Shearer, E. (2018). Social media outpaces print newspapers in the US as a news source. *Pew Research Center*, 10. https://www.pewresearch.org/fact

-tank/2018/12/10/social-media
-outpaces-print-newspapers-in-the
-u-s-as-a-news-source/

10. Gottfried, J., Barthel, M., Shearer, E., & Mitchell, A. (2016). The 2016 presidential campaign—A news event that's hard to miss. *Pew Research Center*, 4.

11. Knight Foundation/Gallup. (2018). American views: Trust, media and democracy. https://knightfoundation .org/reports/american-views-trust -media-and-democracy/

12. Gottfried, J., & Barthel, M. (2018). Almost seven-in-ten Americans have news fatigue, more among Republicans. *Pew Research Center*.

13. Reuters Institute. (2017). Digital News Report 2017.

14. Palmer, R., & Toff, B. (2018). From news fatigue to news avoidance. *Nieman Lab*.

15. Fischer, S., & Vavra, S. (2017). The recent explosion of right-wing news sites. *Axios*. https://www.axios.com /the-partisan-explosion-of-digital -news-2279022772. html

16. Prior, M. (2013). Media and political polarization. *Annual Review of Political Science, 16*(1), 101–127.

17. Lelkes, Y., Sood, G., & Iyengar, S. (2017). The hostile audience: The effect of access to broadband internet on partisan affect. *American Journal of Political Science, 61*(1), 5–20.

18. Druckman, J., Levendusky, M., & McLain, A. (2018). No need to watch: How the effects of partisan media can spread via interpersonal discussions. *American Journal of Political Science, 62*(1), 99–112.

19. Mitchell, A., Gottfried, J., Fedeli, S., Stocking, G., & Walker, M. (2019). Many Americans say made-up news is a critical problem that needs to be fixed. *Pew Research Center. June, 5, 2019.*

20. Allcott, H., & Gentzkow, M. (2017). Social media and fake news in the 2016 election. *Journal of Economic Perspectives, 31*(2), 211–236.

21. Guess, A., Nyhan, B., & Reifler, J. (2018). Selective exposure to misinformation: Evidence from the consumption of fake news during the 2016 US presidential campaign. *European Research Council, 9.*

22. Gallup. (October, 2018). U.S. Media Trust Continues to Recover from 2016 Low. https://news.gallup.com /poll/243665/media-trust-continues -recover-2016-low.aspx

23. Gallup. (October, 2018).

24. Cunningham, B. (2003). Re-thinking objectivity. *Columbia Journalism Review, 42*(2), 24–32.

25. Ward, S. J. A., March, 2017. Engagement and pragmatic objectivity. *Center for Journalism Ethics*. https:// ethics.journalism.wisc.edu/2017 /03/27/engagement-and-pragmatic -objectivity/

26. Pew Research Center. (2019). State of the News Media 2018.

27. Bauder, D., & Lieb, D. A. (March, 2019). Decline in readers, ads leads hundreds of newspapers to fold. The Associated Press.

28. Abernathy, P. M. (2018). *The expanding news desert.* Center for Innovation and Sustainability in Local Media, School of Media and Journalism, University of North Carolina at Chapel Hill.

29. Abernathy, P. M. (2018).

30. Shafer, J., & Doherty, T. (June, 2017). The media bubble is worse than you

think. *Politico.* https://www.politico
.com/magazine/story/2017/04/25
/media-bubble-real-journalism-jobs
-east-coast-215048

31. Gerber, A., Karlan, D., & Bergan, D.
(2009). Does the media matter? A
field experiment measuring the effect
of newspapers on voting behavior and
political opinions. *American Economic
Journal: Applied Economics, 1*(2), 35–52.

32. Pew Research Center. (March,
2019). For local news, Americans
embrace digital but still want strong
community connection. https://
www.journalism.org/2019/03/26
/for-local-news-americans-embrace
-digital-but-still-want-strong-comm
unity-connection/

33. Gao, P., Lee, C., & Murphy, D.
(2020). Financing dies in darkness?
The impact of newspaper closures
on public finance. *Journal of Financial Economics, 135*(2), 445–467.

34. Weitzer, R., & Kubrin, C. E. (2004).
Breaking news: How local TV news
and real-world conditions affect fear of
crime. *Justice Quarterly, 21*(3), 497–520.

35. Ali, C., & Radcliffe, D. (2017). Small-
market newspapers in the digital age.
Tow Center for Digital Journalism.

36. Pew Research Center. (March, 2019).

37. Matsa, K. E. (2017). Buying spree
brings more local TV stations to
fewer big companies. *Pew Research
Center, 11.* https://www.pewresearch
.org/fact-tank/2017/05/11/buying
-spree-brings-more-local-tv-stations
-to-fewer-big-companies/

38. Abernathy, P. M. (2016). *The rise
of a new media baron and the emerg-
ing threat of news deserts.* Center for
Innovation and Sustainability in
Local Media, University of North
Carolina Chapel Hill.

39. Mitchell, A., Gottfried, J., Barthel,
M., & Shearer, E. (2016). The modern news consumer: News attitudes
and practices in the digital era. Pew
Research Center, 7 July. https://www
.journalism.org/2016/07/07/the
-modern-news-consumer/

40. Mitchell, A., Gottfried, J., Barthel,
M., & Shearer, E. (2016).

41. American Press Institute. (2014).
Social and demographic differences
in news habits and attitudes. https://
www.americanpressinstitute.org
/publications/reports/survey-rese
arch/social-demographic-differences
-news-habits-attitudes/

42. Gottfried, J., & Grieco, E. (2018).
Younger Americans are better than
older Americans at telling factual
news statements from opinions. *Pew
Research Center.* https://www.pewre
search.org/fact-tank/2018/10/23
/younger-americans-are-better-than
-older-americans-at-telling-factual
-news-statements-from-opinions/

43. Wineburg, S., McGrew, S.,
Breakstone, J., & Ortega, T. (2016).
Evaluating information: The corner-
stone of civic online reasoning. *Stanford Digital Repository, 8,* 2018.

44. Duncan, M. (2019). The effectiveness of credibility indicator interven-
tions in a partisan context. *Newspaper
Research Journal, 40*(4), 487–503.

45. Doherty, C., Kiley, J., & Jameson,
B. (2016). Partisanship and political animosity in 2016. *Pew Research
Center, 75.* https://www.pewresearch
.org/fact-tank/2016/06/22/key-facts
-partisanship/

46. Center, P. (2014). Political polarization in the American public.
https://www.people-press.org/2014
/06/12/political-polarization-in-the
-american-public/

47. Hare, C., Poole, K. T., & Rosenthal, H. (2014). Polarization in Congress has risen sharply. Where is it going next? *Washington Post*, *13*.

48. Barnidge, M., Gunther, A. C., Kim, J., Hong, Y., Perryman, M., Tay, S. K., & Knisely, S. (2017). Politically motivated selective exposure and perceived media bias. *Communication Research*, *1*, 22.

49. Perryman, M. R. (2020). Where the other side gets news: Audience perceptions of selective exposure in the 2016 election. *International Journal of Public Opinion Research*, *32*(1), 89–110.

50. Perryman, M. R. (2017). *Public perceptions of partisan selective exposure,* ProQuest Dissertations and Theses.

51. McCall, J. (July, 2018). Freak show coverage of Trump creates media chaos. *The Hill*.

52. Rosenstiel, T. (December, 2016). What the post-Trump debate over journalism gets wrong. *Brookings*, *20*.

53. Faris, R., Roberts, H., Etling, B., Bourassa, N., Zuckerman, E., & Benkler, Y. (2017). Partisanship, propaganda, and disinformation: Online media and the 2016 US presidential election. *Berkman Klein Center Research Publication*, *6*.

54. Patterson, T. 2016. News coverage of the 2016 election: How the press failed the voters. The Shorenstein Center. Retrieved from https://shorensteincenter.org/news-coverage-2016-general-election/#Trumps_Coverage.

55. Silver, N. (September, 2017). The media has a probability problem. *FiveThirtyEight*.

56. Larson, S. G. (2003). Misunderstanding margin of error: Network news coverage of polls during the 2000 general election. *Harvard International Journal of Press/Politics*, *8*(1), 66–80.

57. Glasser, S. B. (December, 2016). Covering politics in a 'post-truth' America. *Brookings*.

58. Kakutani, M. (July, 2018). The death of truth: how we gave up on facts and ended up with Trump. *The Guardian*, *14*.

59. Davis, W. (August, 2016). The age of post-truth politics. *The New York Times*.

60. Mantzarlis, A. (February, 2017). What does "the death of expertise" mean for fact-checkers? *Poynter*. https://www.poynter.org/fact-checking/2017/what-does-the-death-of-expertise-mean-for-fact-checkers/

61. Clifton, D. (October, 2017). Trump and Putin's strong connection: Lies. *Mother Jones*. https://www.motherjones.com/politics/2017/10/trump-and-putin-strong-connection-lies/

62. McIntyre, L. (November, 2018). Lies, damn lies and post-truth. *The Conversation*. http://theconversation.com/lies-damn-lies-and-post-truth-106049

63. Sullivan, A. (September, 2017). America wasn't built for humans. *The Intelligencer*.

64. Lewandowsky, S., Ecker, U. K., & Cook, J. (2017). Beyond misinformation: Understanding and coping with the "post-truth" era. *Journal of Applied Research in Memory and Cognition*, *6*(4), 353–369.

Index